Developing Apps with Python and Flet

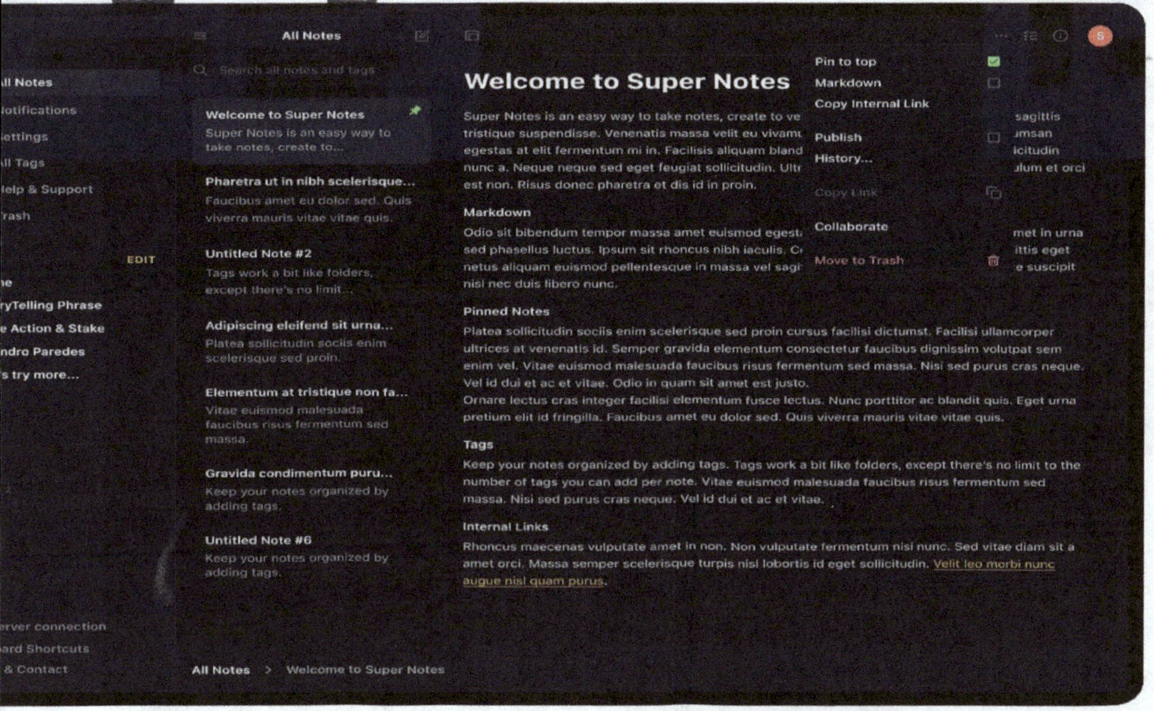

rom Novice
o Professional
eveloper in
ne Hour

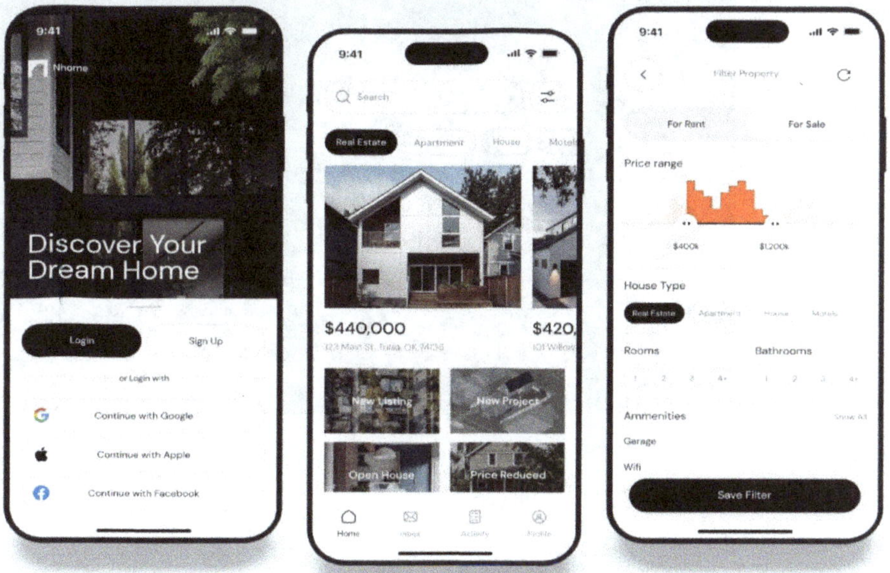

Williams Asiedu

Developing Apps with Python and Flet

From Novice to Professional Developer in One Hour

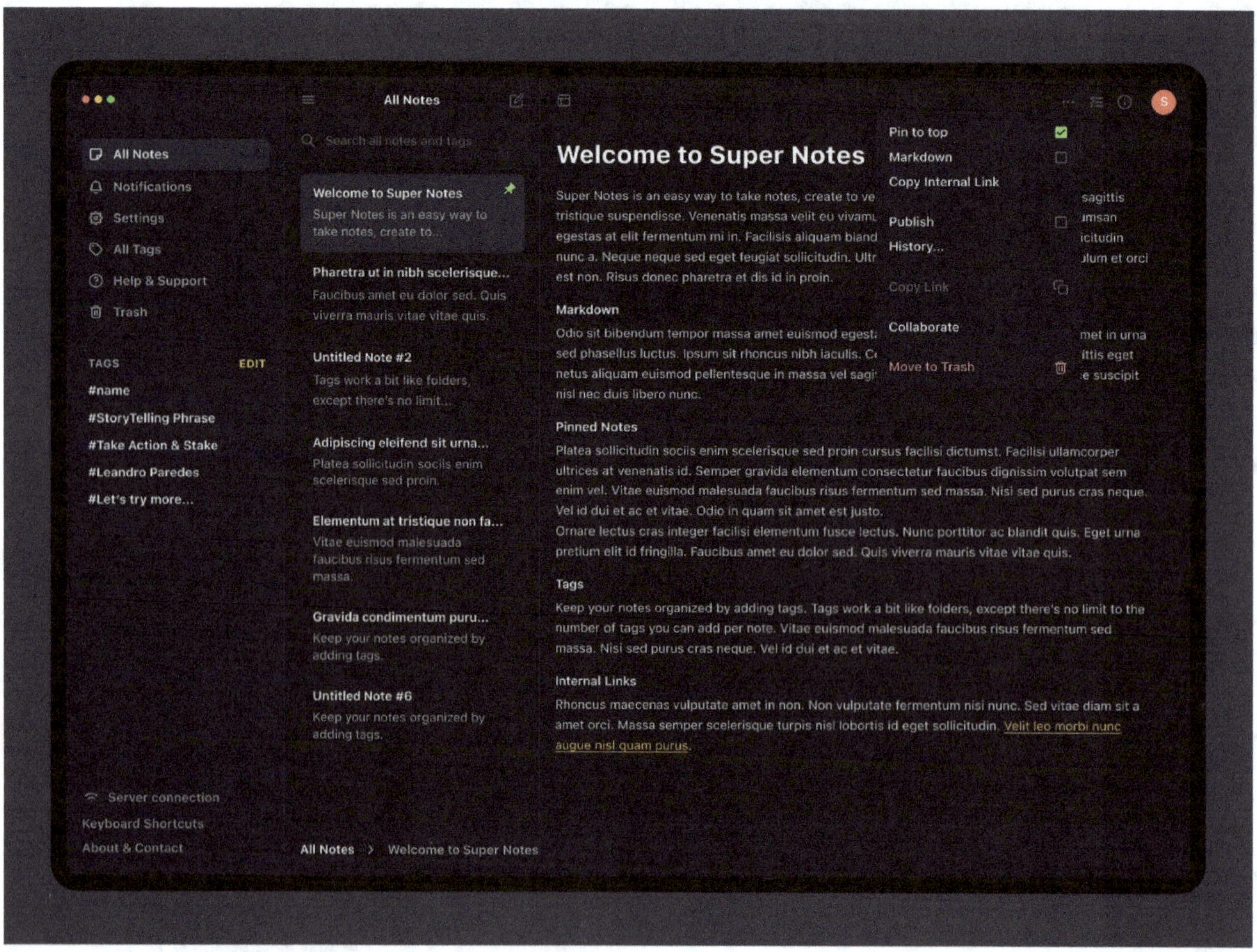

Developing Apps with Python and Flet

Ouereila Publishing House

Table of Contents

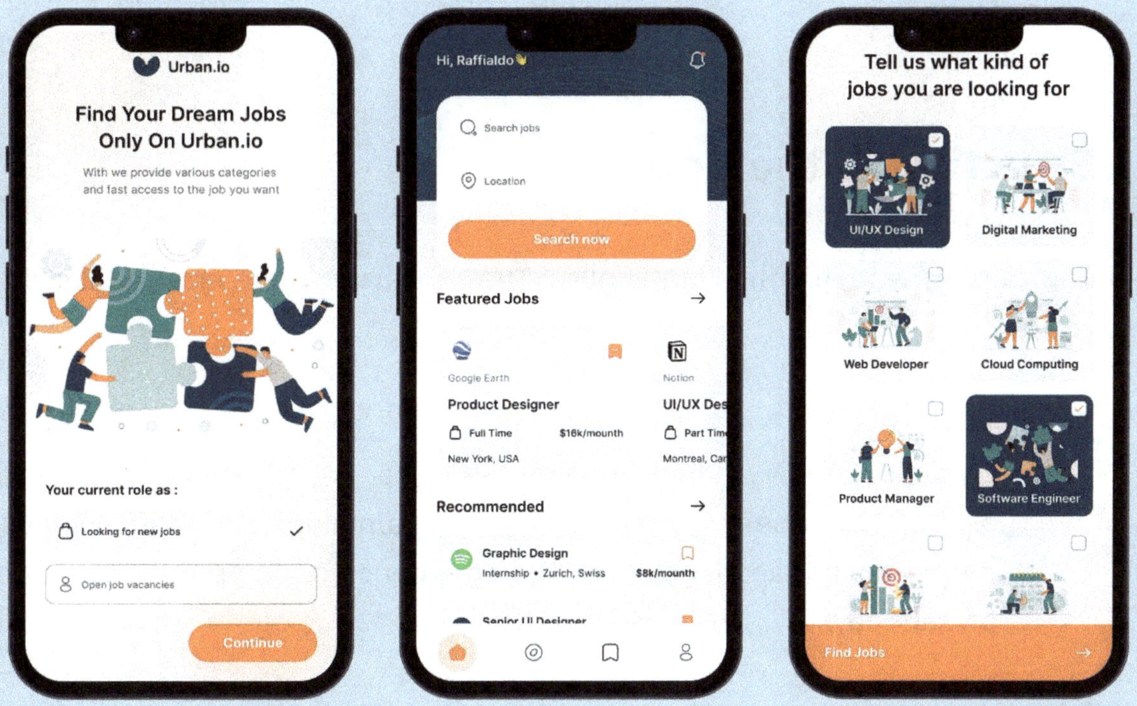
Urban.io
Find Your Dream Jobs Only On Urban.io
With we provide various categories and fast access to the job you want
Your current role as :
Looking for new jobs
Open job vacancies
Continue
Hi, Raffialdo
Search jobs
Location
Search now
Featured Jobs
Google Earth
Notion
Product Designer
Full Time
$16k/mounth
New York, USA
Recommended
Graphic Design
Internship • Zurich, Swiss
$8k/mounth
Tell us what kind of jobs you are looking for
UI/UX Design
Digital Marketing
Web Developer
Cloud Computing
Product Manager
Software Engineer
Find Jobs

Preface

Introduction

In today's world, software exerts immense control over our daily lives. Almost every task or duty we perform relies heavily on software. As a result, software applications play a crucial role in various fields, including education, healthcare, manufacturing, communication, transportation, entertainment, and many more.
For instance, calculators, e-book readers, and word processors are used in the education sector, demonstrating the wide-ranging impact of software in our lives.

Who This Book is For

This book is designed for anyone with no prior knowledge of programming who aspires to develop mobile, desktop, and web applications for personal use or commercial purposes. You don't need any programming skills to get started; you only need a basic understanding of English to follow the content of this book. People of all ages and educational backgrounds can use this book to embark on their journey into the world of software development.

Structure of the Book

Language

This book is written entirely in English. The explanations are clear, understandable, and concise.

Chapters

- **Chapter 1:** This chapter begins with the need for computer programming, highlighting the significance of programming and the various types of programming languages from the emergence of computer programming to the present day.

- **Chapter 2:** This chapter delves into the Python language, discussing its origin, why it is a preferred language, and how to get started with it.
- **Chapter 3:** Here, you will find a comprehensive tutorial on Python, complete with examples in each section to facilitate learning.
- **Chapter 4:** This chapter explains Graphical User Interfaces (GUIs) and the various programming languages associated with GUI development.
- **Chapter 5:** Focused on the Flet framework toolkit, this chapter covers the process involved in setting it up and creating final packages for distribution across different devices.
- **Chapter 6:** This chapter provides an in-depth tutorial on the Flet GUI framework components, featuring numerous examples and code snippets to illustrate the lessons.
- **Chapter 7:** The final chapter serves as the back matter of the book.

Code Snippets

Throughout the book, you will find code snippets presented in boxes that span almost the entire width of the page in black color. These snippets consist of sample code that has been tried and tested to enhance understanding and facilitate learning. This format allows you to follow along even without practicing on a device.

In Chapter 6, where Flet Controls are explained, most code snippets are very small in size. To see them clearly, you can zoom in on your device. Additionally, you can copy the code and run it on your setup to experiment further.

Images

The images included in the book are screenshots of executed code, provided for demonstration purposes.

Words with Hashtags

Words with hashtags link to other parts of the book that may have the same or similar meaning, helping you to navigate related topics efficiently.

Colors

Different colors are used in the book to facilitate easy differentiation, highlight important points, and emphasize keywords.

Note

Most pages contain a "Note" box to highlight important cases or statements that require special attention.

Light up

The "Light up" box provides additional important information and delves deeper into the tutorial content.

Summary

At the end of each chapter, you will find a summary that encapsulates the entire tutorial. This section includes keywords, review questions, related tutorials, and projects for you to try your hands on.

Wishing You a Happy Coding

Enjoy the journey of programming. Happy coding! 😘

Chapter 1

INTRODUCTION TO COMPUTER PROGRAMMING

After completing this chapter, you will be able to:

Define programming language

Understand the two types of programming languages

Know the various kinds of the programming languages.

Introduction

Understanding the underlying mechanisms of computers and modes of communication has underscored the necessity for efficient programming. Today, programming permeates our daily lives, accessible to all without the need for formal certification. It has become an integral aspect of digital market dynamics, with software proliferation driving industry growth.

Programming languages serve as the cornerstone of software development, representing the gateway to becoming a programmer or app developer. Over the years, these languages have evolved significantly, transitioning from complex structures to user-friendly interfaces. This century's programming languages are notably more intuitive, facilitating easier comprehension and application in development processes.

Credit is due to the inventors of modern programming languages for their tireless efforts and contributions to software development. Their innovations have not only democratized programming but also empowered individuals from diverse backgrounds to participate in the digital economy.

Programming Languages

Just as the name implies, language serves as a means of communication between two parties. Similarly, programming languages facilitate communication between users and computers through the use of symbols and objects, known as mnemonics. Since the inception of computers, programmers have continuously introduced new languages into the fold, each building upon or slightly altering the structure or syntax of its predecessors.

Programming languages are distinguished by their unique syntax, semantics, and intended applications. These languages range from low-level assembly languages, which directly interact with hardware, to high-level languages like Python and Java, which prioritize readability and ease of use. Despite their diversity, all programming languages share the common goal of enabling humans to instruct computers to perform specific tasks efficiently and accurately.

How the Programming Languages work

The fundamental language of computers is binary code, consisting of sequences of ones (1) and zeroes (0). For example, the binary code 101 is interpreted by the computer as the digit 5. Known as machine language, this binary code is the sole language that computers inherently understand. However, communicating with computers through binary code directly is arduous and impractical for users.

To bridge this gap, programming languages are utilized to facilitate communication between users and computers. These languages are designed to be more human-readable and intuitive, allowing users to express instructions in a familiar syntax. When a user writes code in a high-level programming language, a special software called a compiler or interpreter translates this code into machine language that the computer can execute.

In essence, programming languages act as an intermediary, enabling users to convey instructions to computers in a more accessible manner, while compilers and interpreters serve as translators, converting these instructions into the binary code that computers comprehend. This process streamlines the programming workflow, making it feasible for individuals to develop software and interact with computers effectively.

Types of Programming Languages

Low-Level Programming Languages:

Also known as machine language, low-level languages directly interact with hardware and consist of binary code represented by 0s and 1s. They are the most basic form of programming languages and are specific to the architecture of the computer's processor.

High-Level Programming Languages:

High-level languages are designed to be more user-friendly and abstracted from hardware specifics. They use natural language elements, symbols, and objects to make programming easier and more intuitive for humans. These languages are then compiled or interpreted into machine code.

Table 1: High-Level Programming Languages

Language	Year	Origin	Inventor
Fortran	1950	-	IBM
Cobol	1960	-	Grace Hopper
Lisp	1958	-	John McCarthy
Pascal	1970	-	Niklaus Wirth
C	1970	BCPL	Denis Ritchie
C++	1980	C	Bjarne Stroustrup
Perl	1987	C	Larry Wall
Python	1991	C, ABC	Guido Van Rossum
Java	1991	C	James Goslin (Oracle)
JavaScript	1995	ECMAScript	Netscape
C#	2000	Java, C++, Delphi	Anders Hejisberg
Kotlin	2011	Java	JetBrains
Dart	2011	C++	Google

Chapter Summary

Programming languages are formal languages comprised of instructions used to produce various kinds of output, primarily in computer programming. They enable humans to communicate with machines and develop software applications. Key elements of programming languages include syntax (rules for structure), semantics (meaning of the instructions), and paradigms (styles of programming such as procedural, object-oriented, and functional). Common examples include Python, Java, C++, and JavaScript, each with its own unique features and use cases.

Keywords

compiler
interpreter
mnemonics

Discussion

1. What are the primary purposes of programming languages?
2. What are the key elements that define a programming language?
3. Can you name some common programming paradigms and give an example of a language for each?
4. What are the differences between C, C++ and C#?

Chapter 2

STARTING PYTHON

After completing this chapter, you will be able to:

List some importance of the Python language

Install Python on Windows, Linux and MacOS

Understand editors or IDEs

Use the Python IDLE

Use Visual Studio Code to run Python

Run Python scripts

Understand Python Modules.

Python is a versatile and powerful programming language renowned for its readability, simplicity, and broad applicability across various domains. Developed by Guido Van Rossum in the late 1980s at the National Research Institute in the Netherlands, Python officially debuted in 1991. Since then, it has gained widespread adoption and popularity, becoming one of the most widely used programming languages globally.

Python's distinguishing features include being high-level, object-oriented, interactive, interpreted, and general-purpose. Its flexibility makes it suitable for a wide range of applications, including app development, data science, robotics, artificial intelligence, machine learning, web development, and game development.

One of Python's key strengths lies in its readability and simplicity. Python code is designed to resemble plain English, with keywords and syntax that are easy to understand and remember. This high-level scripting language allows developers to write concise and elegant code, facilitating rapid development and prototyping.

Moreover, Python boasts a vibrant and supportive community of developers and enthusiasts. This extensive community support ensures a wealth of resources, libraries, and frameworks readily available for developers to leverage in their projects, further enhancing Python's appeal and utility.

In essence, Python's combination of readability, versatility, and community support makes it an excellent choice for both beginners and experienced developers seeking to tackle a diverse range of programming challenges. Whether you're building web applications, analyzing data, or developing machine learning algorithms, Python offers the tools and resources necessary to bring your ideas to life effectively and efficiently.

Installing Python

Python is an open-source programming language, which means it is free to use and modify. It can be freely downloaded from the Python software Foundation's website at https://www.python.org

Note

Python 3.8 or higher is required for developing the Flet application

#Windows

Installing Python on Windows is indeed straightforward and hassle-free. Here's a concise guide:

1. **Download Python:** Visit the Python Software Foundation website (https://www.python.org/) and download the Python installer suitable for your Windows version.

2. **Run the Installer:** Once the download is complete, navigate to the location of the downloaded executable file (.exe) and double-click on it to launch the Python installer.

3. **Installation Wizard:** The installation wizard will guide you through the setup process. You can customize the installation by selecting optional features or changing the installation directory if desired.

4. **Configure Environment Variables:** During the installation process, ensure that you check the box labeled "Add Python to PATH." This option automatically configures the system environment variables to include the Python executable, making it accessible from any command prompt or PowerShell window.

5. **Complete Installation:** Follow the prompts in the installation wizard to complete the installation process. Once the installation is finished, you can verify that Python is correctly installed by opening a command prompt and typing python --version. You should see the installed Python version displayed.

That's it! Python is now installed on your Windows system, and you're ready to start coding. Enjoy exploring the world of Python programming!

#Linux

Indeed, Linux distributions often come with Python pre-installed. However, users may wish to install a different version or manage Python installations themselves. Here are the steps to install Python on Linux:

1. **Update Package Lists:** Open a terminal and update the package lists to ensure you have the latest information about available packages. Use the command:

```
sudo apt update
```

2. **Install Python:** Use the package manager to install Python. The package name might vary slightly depending on your distribution. For Python 3, you can use:

```
sudo apt install python3
```

3. **Verify Installation:** After the installation is complete, verify that Python is installed correctly by running:

```
Python3 --version
```

4. **Optional: Install pip (Python Package Manager):** Pip is a package manager for Python that allows you to install and manage additional libraries and packages. You can install pip using the following command:

```
sudo apt install python3-pip
```


That's it! You've successfully installed Python on your Linux system. You can now start using Python for development or other purposes.

#MacOS

1. **Check Python Version (Optional):** macOS usually comes with a pre-installed version of Python 2.x. You can check the version by opening the Terminal and running:

```
python --version
```

2. **Install Homebrew (Optional):** Homebrew is a package manager for macOS that simplifies the process of installing software. If you don't have Homebrew installed, you can do so by running the following command in Terminal:

```
/bin/bash -c "$(curl -fsSL
https://raw.githubusercontent.com/Homebrew/install/HEAD/install.sh)"
```

3. **Update Homebrew (Optional):** After installing Homebrew, it's a good idea to update it to ensure you have the latest version of available packages:

```
brew update
```

4. **Install Python with Homebrew:** Use Homebrew to install Python by running the following command in Terminal:

```
brew install python
```

5. **Verify Installation:** After the installation is complete, verify that Python is installed correctly by running:

```
python3 –version
```

6. **Optional: Install pip (Python Package Manager):** If pip is not installed automatically, you can install it using the following command:

```
sudo easy_install pip
```


Editors

Editors, or Integrated Development Environments (IDEs), are applications that enable users to write, edit, debug, and run programming code. They typically feature user-friendly interfaces with integrated tools, compilers, and debuggers tailored for specific languages. Some editors support multiple languages, while others are designed for a particular language.

Popular editors for Python development include:

- PyCharm
- Visual Studio Code
- Sublime Text
- Notepad++

Additionally, Python comes with its own integrated environment called IDLE. IDLE provides an interactive environment for writing and running Python code in real-time, making it particularly useful for practicing coding skills.

Using IDLE

Using IDLE for Python coding is straightforward. Here's how to get started:

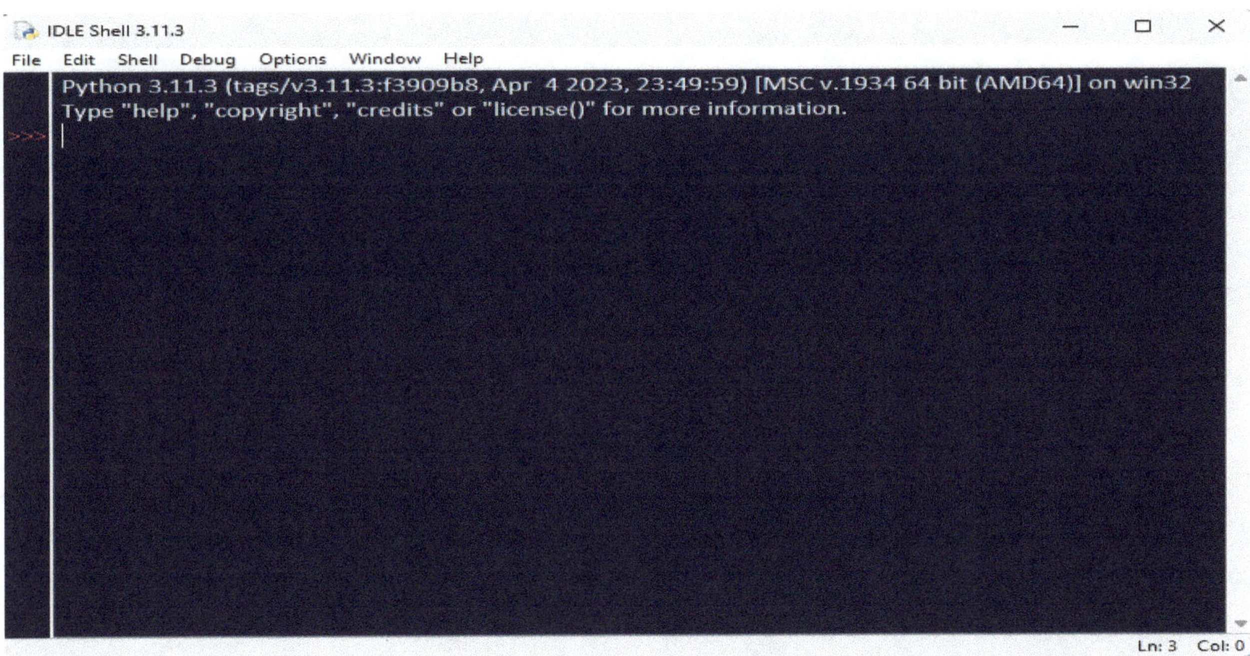

1. **Launch IDLE:**
   On Windows, open the Start menu and type "IDLE" to launch the IDLE editor.
   On Linux, open a terminal and type "idle" to launch IDLE.

2. **Create a New File:**
   Once IDLE is open, click on the "File" menu and select "New File," or simply press Ctrl + N. This will open a new window where you can start writing your Python code.

3. **Write Your Code:**
   Start writing your Python code in the new file window. You can use all the features of the IDLE editor, such as syntax highlighting and auto-indentation, to make coding easier.

4. **Run Your Code:**
   After writing your code, you can run it by clicking on the "Run" menu and selecting "Run Module," or by pressing F5.
   IDLE will execute your code and display the output in the interactive shell window.

Additionally, Python provides other interactive environments like IPython, which offers more advanced features and graphical capabilities for Python coding.

You can also use the native OS shell or command interface for simple Python coding tasks. This approach works the same way across all operating systems, including Windows, Linux, and macOS. Simply open a terminal or command prompt, type "python" to enter the Python interactive shell, and start coding directly in the shell environment.

Using the Python Interactive Shell

1. **Open the Command Line Interface (CLI):**

- On Windows, type "cmd" into the Windows search bar and press Enter to open the Command Prompt.
- On Linux or macOS, open a terminal window.

2. **Launch the Python Interactive Shell:**

- In the Command Prompt or terminal window, type "python" and press Enter.
- This command starts the Python interpreter and opens the interactive shell, allowing you to enter Python code and receive immediate feedback.


```
C:\Users\Asiedu>python
Python 3.11.3 (tags/v3.11.3:f3909b8, Apr  4 2023, 23:49:59) [MSC v.1934 64 bit (AMD64)] on win32
Type "help", "copyright", "credits" or "license" for more information.
>>>
```

That's it! You're now using the interactive Python shell, where you can experiment with Python code, test small snippets, and explore the language's features in real-time.

Running Python

Running Python code can be accomplished through various methods and integrated development environments (IDEs) like PyCharm, Visual Studio Code, and IDLE. Here's a specific example using Visual Studio Code:

Visual Sudio Code (VS Code)

VS Code is a versatile IDE developed by Microsoft, supporting numerous programming languages such as C, C++, Java, Python, C#, JavaScript, and HTML/CSS. It offers IntelliSense extensions to streamline programming tasks by providing suggestions for classes, functions, variables, and bug detection and correction. Additionally, VS Code is lightweight and features a user-friendly interface with buttons for running and debugging code.

#Windows

1. **Download VS Code:**
Visit the Visual Studio Code website or use the following link to download the VS Code executable file: Visual Studio Code Download.

2. **Run the Installer:**
   Once the download is complete, double-click on the downloaded executable file (usually named something like VSCodeSetup.exe) to run the installer.

3. **Follow Installation Instructions:**
   Follow the on-screen instructions provided by the installer to complete the installation process. You can choose installation options such as adding VS Code to the PATH and creating desktop shortcuts.

#Linux

1. **Download VS Code:**
   On Linux, you can install Visual Studio Code using your distribution's package manager. For example, on Ubuntu, you can use the following commands in the terminal:

```
sudo apt update
sudo apt install code
```

#MacOS

1. **Download VS Code:**
   Visit the Visual Studio Code website or use the following link to download the VS Code for macOS: Visual Studio Code Download.

2. **Install VS Code:**
   Once the download is complete, open the downloaded .dmg file.
   Drag the Visual Studio Code icon to the Applications folder to install VS Code on your macOS system.

After installing Visual Studio Code, you can launch it from the Start menu (Windows), applications menu (macOS), or by typing "code" in the terminal (Linux).

To run Python code in Visual Studio Code

Install Python Extension (if not already installed):

1. Open Visual Studio Code.

2. Go to the Extensions view by clicking on the square icon on the sidebar or pressing Ctrl + Shift + X.
3. Search for "Python" or "Pylance" in the Extensions view and install the Python extension provided by Microsoft.

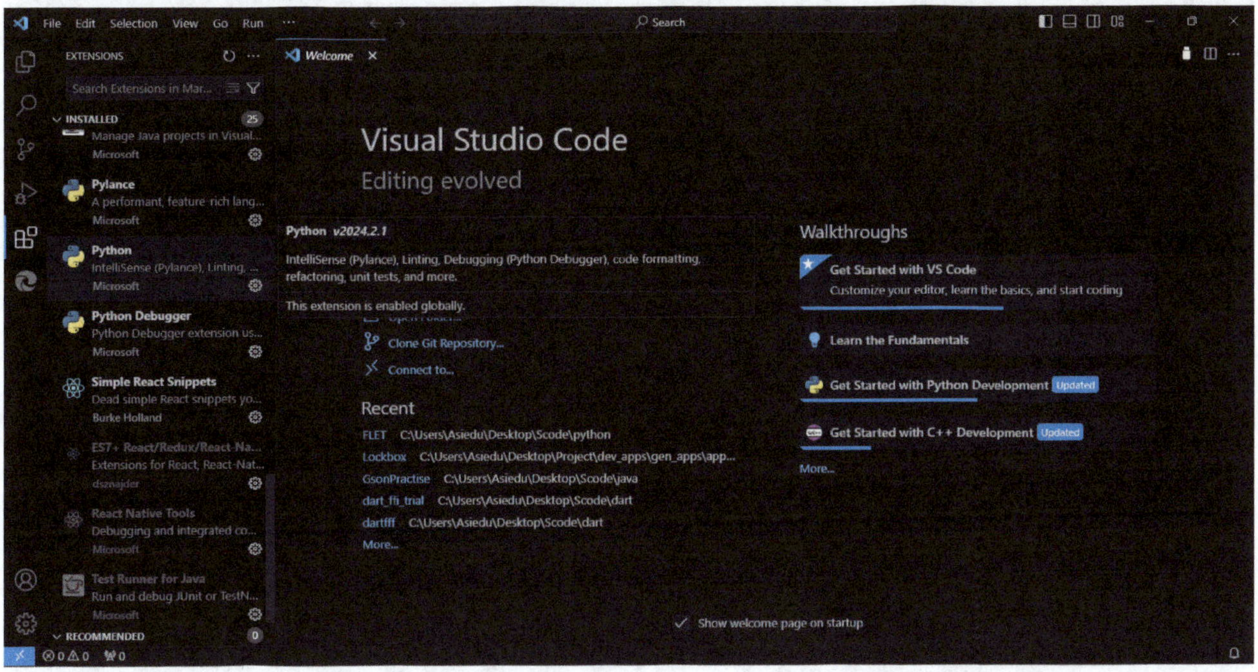

Create or Open Python File:

Create a new Python file or open an existing one in Visual Studio Code.

1. Click on the "File" menu at the top of the VS Code window.
2. Select "New File" to create a new file.

Name Your Python File:

Type the preferred name of your Python file (e.g., "my_python.py").

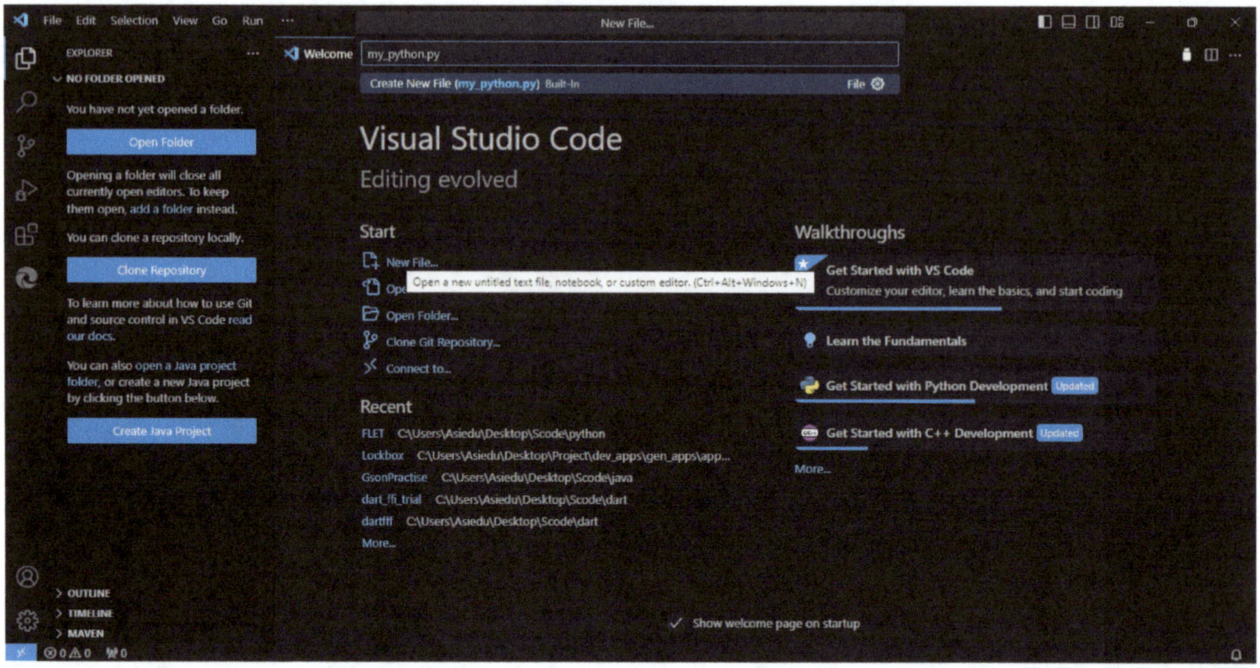

Write Python Code:

Write your Python code in the editor window. VS Code provides syntax highlighting and IntelliSense suggestions to assist you while coding.

Run Python Code:

1. To run your Python code, you can use the Run button located in the toolbar at the top of the editor window. Alternatively, you can use the keyboard shortcut Ctrl + F5.

2. VS Code will execute your Python code and display the output in the integrated terminal.

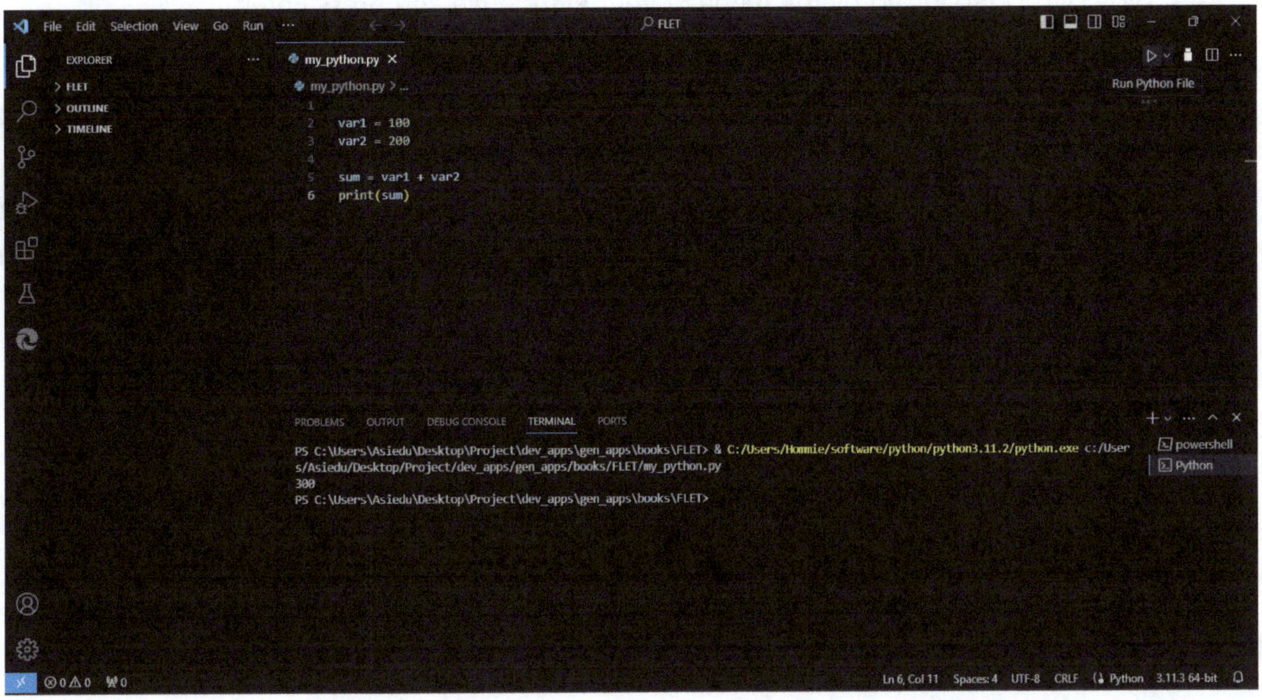

Executing Python from the Command Line

Running Python code from the command line or shell using the python command is a simple and universal approach that works across all operating systems, including Windows, Linux, and macOS.
Here's how you can run Python code from the command line:

Open the Command Line or Terminal:

1. On Windows, open the Command Prompt by searching for "cmd" in the Start menu.
2. On Linux or macOS, open the Terminal application.

Navigate to the Directory Containing Your Python File (Optional):

3. Use the cd command to navigate to the directory containing your Python file if it's not already there.

Run the Python File:

4. Type python followed by the name of your Python file and press Enter.
5. For example: python my_script.py

```
PS C:\Users\Asiedu\Desktop\Project\dev_apps> python my_python.py
300
PS C:\Users\Asiedu\Desktop\Project\dev_apps>
```

View Output (If Any):

If your Python script produces any output, such as printed messages or results, it will be displayed in the terminal after running the script.

This method provides a straightforward way to execute Python code directly from the command line or shell, making it convenient for quick tests or running scripts without the need for an integrated development environment (IDE) or text editor.

Light up

Python files are commonly recognized by their extensions: **.py** for regular Python scripts and **.pyw** for scripts that run without displaying a console window.

Modules or Libraries

Python modules are collections of code that provide additional functionality to Python programs. These modules are essentially Python files containing **classes**, **functions** and **objects** that can be imported and used in other Python scripts. They help simplify coding tasks by providing pre-defined solutions to common problems, thus saving developers time and effort.

While some modules are included in the Python standard library, many others are developed and maintained by the Python community. These external modules cover a wide range of domains and purposes, catering to diverse needs and preferences. For example, there are modules for web development, data analysis, machine learning, game development, and much more.

The beauty of Python modules lies in their versatility and flexibility. Developers can choose and install only the modules they need for their specific projects, allowing for a lightweight and efficient development process. For example, game developers may focus on installing modules essential for game development, while graphic designers may prefer using image processing libraries or modules to enhance their workflow.

Moreover, the open-source nature of Python encourages collaboration and contribution to module development, ensuring a rich ecosystem of tools and resources for Python programmers worldwide.

Installing Python Modules with Pip

Installing Python modules is straightforward using the **pip** command, which is included as part of the Python package. Here's how you can install a Python module using pip on the command line or shell of any operating system:

1. **Open the Command Line or Terminal:**
   Open the command line or terminal on your operating system.

2. **Use the pip Command:**
Type the following command and replace module_name with the name of the module you want to install:

```
pip install module_name
```

Press Enter to execute the command.

For example, to install the NumPy module, you would type:

```
pip install numpy
```

Once the installation is complete, you can start using the module in your Python code. Using the module in your Python code is as simple as using the import keyword followed by the name of the module. For example

```
import numpy
```

This statement imports the specified module into your Python script, allowing you to use its classes, functions, and variables within your code.

Note

import statement will be covered in more detail in later chapters.

Light up

Bugs, also known as errors, are issues in the code that prevent it from running correctly or producing the expected output. They can occur due to various reasons, such as: logic error, semantic error, syntax error and runtime error.

Page Summary

Python, created by Guido van Rossum and first released in 1991, emphasizes code readability and simplicity. It is an interpreted, high-level language that supports multiple programming paradigms, including object-oriented, procedural, and functional programming. Python uses indentation to define code blocks, features dynamic typing, and has a straightforward syntax with constructs like if, for, and while. This makes it a versatile and widely-used language in various fields, from web development to data science.

Keywords

open-source
object-oriented
debugging
compilers
ipython
intellisense
pylace
class
function
object

Discussion

1. Who created Python and when was it first released?
2. How does Python define code blocks, and what programming paradigms does it support?
3. What are some key features of Python's syntax that contribute to its readability and simplicity?

Chapter 3

OVERVIEW OF CORE PYTHON

After completing this chapter, you will be able to understand:

Variables and Comment

Various Reserved or Keywords

Operators

Data Types

Numbers (Integers and Float)

Strings and its methods

List and its various methods

Dictionary

Tuples

Set

Decision making statements

Loop or control statements

Functions (Built-In Functions and User-defined Functions)

Class and Object

Handling Errors or Exceptions

Variable

Variable, also known as an identifier, is a term used to describe a letter or word that stores a value. Variables represent data stored in the computer's memory and can consist of any combination of letters, alphabets, or alphanumeric characters.

Example:

Single value assignment

```
>>> var1 = 50
>>>
```

Multiple value assignment

```
>>> myvar1, myvar2 = 3, 5
>>> x = y = 'COMPUTER'
>>>
```

In the above example:

- **var1** is assigned to 50. Therefore, it holds a value of 50 in the computer memory.
- **myvar1** and **myvar2** are assigned to 3 and 5 respectively.
- **x** and **y** are assigned to the same value "COMPUTER".

Rules for naming Variables

1. Variables are case sensitive.
   example: **myvar** is not equal to **Myvar**.

2. Variables cannot begin with a number but can be followed by numbers.
   example: **myvar25**, **my63var.**

3. Variables can begin with underscores.
   example: **_myvar**

Comments

Comments in programming serve as a means to document code, offer explanations, or add notes for better understanding. In Python, comments are not executed; rather, Python identifies them and skips their execution. Comments in Python are denoted by the '#' symbol.

For example:

```
>>>
>>> x = 28 #A Number
>>> y = "programming" #A String
>>>
```

Discussion

Identify the valid variables

1. xyz = [2, 4],
2. xAm = 100,
3. 45x = "brown fox"
4. _var = 5
5. _8var = "machine"

Reserved Words

Python, like many programming languages, has a set of reserved keywords that serve specific purposes and functions within the language. These keywords are not available for use as variable names or for any other purpose in a Python program. Each reserved word carries a distinct and predefined functionality that is essential for the language's structure and operation.

Some Keywords used in Python programming

print	chr	hex	max	super	finally
len	else	range	raise	next	type
set	if	bin	sum	map	or
int	True	try	as	with	global
dict	False	eval	bool	while	local
list	and	not	str	for	catch
exec	del	dir	any	def	return
id	local	help	in	open	lambda

hex()

The hex keyword returns the hexadecimal of an integer or a number.

```
>>> hex(50)
'0x32'
>>>
```

bin()

The bin returns the binary of an integer or a number.

```
>>> bin(8)
'0b1000'
>>>
```


Operators

Operators are special symbols that appear between two operands (values or variables) and instruct the computer to perform specific operations. These operations can involve mathematical calculations, comparisons, assignments, and logical evaluations.

The various kinds of Python operators include:

- Arithmetic Operators
- Relational Operators
- Assignment Operators
- Logical Operators
- Identity Operators
- Membership Operators
- Bitwise Operators

Arithmetic Operators

Arithmetic operators are used to perform various mathematical functions on numeric data types in programming. They enable you to perform fundamental mathematical operations like addition, subtraction, multiplication, division, and more.

Addition(+)

```
x = 6
y = 14
sum = x + y
print(sum) #Output = 20
```

Multiplication(*)

```
var1 = 4
var2 = 2
product = var1 * var2
print(product) #Output = 8
```

Subtraction(-)

```
x = 5
y = 3
result = x - y
print(result) #Output = 2
```

Division(/)

```
x = 6
y = 24
result = y / x
print(result)  #Output = 4
```


Modulo(**%**)

```
first = 3
second = 17
result = first % second
print(result)  #Output = 2
```

Floor Division(**//**)

```
x = 9
y = 2
result = x // y
print(result)  #Output = 4
```

Exponentiation (******)

```
_xyx = 4
_mnp = 2
result = _xyz ** _mnp
print(result)  #Output = 16
```

Relational Operators

Relational operators, also known as comparison operators, are essential components of conditional statements in Python. They are used to compare two values or operands and determine the relationship between them. Relational operators return a Boolean value, either 'True' or 'False', based on the result of the comparison. Relational operators are crucial for making decisions in programs. They help answer questions like "Is this value equal to that one?" or "Is this value greater than that one?"

Equal to(**==**)

```
>>> 'wheat' == 'whate'
 False
```

Less than (**<**)

```
>>> 4 < 10
 True
```

Not equal to(!=)

```
>>> 'wheat' != 'whate'
 True
```

Greater than (>)

```
>>> 3 > 2
 True
```


Challenge

Write a program to utilize:
>= (greater than or equal to)
<= (less than or equal to)

Assignment Operators

Assignment operators serve the primary function of assigning a value on the right side to a variable on the left side. This assignment results in the variable holding the assigned value, thereby making it accessible for subsequent operations or references in your code. In Python, the most commonly used assignment operator is the equals sign (**=**), which assigns the value on the right side to the variable on the left side. For example:

```
>>> x = 5
>>> name, age = "Alice", 20
>>> z = y = 10
```

Additionally, Python supports compound assignment operators, which combine an arithmetic operation with assignment. These operators include **+=**, **-=**, ***=**, **/=**, **//=**, **%=**, and ****=**, where the operator before the equals sign performs the specified operation on the variable and the value on the right side, and assigns the result back to the variable on the left side.

Logical Operators

Logical operators are essential elements in Python used for making logical assumptions and decisions. They operate on Boolean values and return either 'True' or 'False' based on the logical conditions they evaluate. Logical operators are or, and, not. These operators are mostly used in decision making structures.

Identity Operators

Identity operators in Python are tools used to verify or check whether two variables or objects are stored at the same memory location. They allow you to determine if two variables or objects refer to the same entity in memory, rather than comparing their values. Identity operators are essential for understanding object identity and reference equality. The two identity operators are is and is not.

is

```
>>> x = 6
>>> y = 6
>>> z = 10
>>> x is y
 True
>>> x is z
 False
```

is not

```
>>> x = 6
>>> y = 6
>>> z = 10
>>> x is not y
 False
>>> x is not z
 True
```

Membership Operators

Membership operators in Python are tools used to check if a specific item is present in a collection of items. These operators are invaluable for determining whether an element belongs to a set, list, tuple, string, or any other iterable. They provide a straightforward way to search for the presence of an item within a container

in

```
>>> x = 'computer'
>>> 'com' in x
 True
```

not in

```
>>> var = [4, 8, 10]
>>> 3 not in var
 True
```


Data Types

Data encompasses raw values that can manifest in various forms, such as numbers, letters, special characters or a blend thereof. Data types serve to classify data based on their attributes and functionalities.

In Python, data types represent instances or objects of specific classes, each characterized by unique traits and behaviors. The Python programming language encompasses approximately eight fundamental data types. The various types of data types in Python include:

- Numbers (Integer and Float)
- String
- List
- Dictionary
- Tuple
- Set
- Boolean
- Bytes

 # Light up

To check the data type of an object, use the type() function.

```
>>> var = 100
>>> type(var)
 <class 'int'>
```

Numbers

Integer

The integer class encompasses all numbers, including negative numbers, without decimal points. The int() function is employed to convert from one type to the integer type.
Example: 2, 13, -5, 100, 2000 ......

Float

On the other hand, floats represent the class of all numbers with decimal points. To convert from one type to the float type, the float() function is utilized.
Example: -6.25, 8.5245, -5.3, 100.6 ......

Some methods used with number type

pow(x, y)

```
>>> x = 2
>>> y = 4
>>> pow(y, x) #y exponent x
 16
```

ceil(x)

```
>>>import math
>>> math.ceil(3.589)
 4
```

round(x, y)

```
>>> var = 20.58952
>>> y = 3
>>> round(var, y)
 20.59
```

cos(x)

```
>>>import math
>>> math.cos(45) #Cosine
 0.5253219888177297
```

sqrt(x)

```
>>> import math
>>> math.sqrt(49) #Square root
 7
```

sine(x)

```
>>>import math
>>> var = 15
>>> math.sin(var)  #Sine
 0.6502878401571168
```

 # Light up

The math is one of Python modules or libraries used to perform various mathematical functions. You can explore more methods of math with the dir() function.

```
>>> import math
>>> dir(math)
```


String

A string is a sequence of characters, including alphabets, numbers, or special characters, enclosed within quotes. String can be in a single or double quote.

Example:

```
var1 = "Hello World!"
var2 = 'brown fox'
```

 # Light up

Python provides a way to convert between different data types. To convert other types to strings, use the str() function.
eg. To convert integer to string
>>> var = 100
>>> mystr = str(var)
>>> print(mystr) #Output: "100"

String Indexing

Indexing refers to the position of each character in a string. The index of a string starts from zero and goes up to the length of the string minus one (0 to length-1). The first character or element of a string typically occupies index **0**, the next character takes index **1**, and so on.

For example

```
>>> var = "Computer"
>>> print(var[0])  #Output: C
>>> print(var[1])  #Output: o
>>> print(var[2])  #Output: m
>>> print(var[3])  #Output: p
```


Concatenating Strings

Concatenating strings involves adding two separate strings to form one complete string using the plus (+) operator.

For example

```
>>> var1 = "comp"
>>> var2 = "uter"
>>> var3 = var1 + var2
>>> print(var3)
 computer
```

Slicing Strings

String slicing allows you to extract substrings from a string. The syntax for string slicing is string[start : end], where **start** indicates where the slicing should begin and **end** indicates where it should end. Both start and end parameters can be omitted, in which case Python will set them to default values (0 for start and the last index of the string for end).

For example

```
>>> var = "Hello World"
>>> sub_str = var[6:11]
>>> print(sub_str)
 World
```

Some methods used with String type

len(str)

```
>>> var = 'computer'
>>> len(var) #length of the string
 8
```

index(str)

```
>>> var = 'python'
>>> var.index('t') #Index of 't'
 2
```


String[int]

```
>>> var = 'python'
>>> var[2]
 't'
```

upper( )

```
>>> var = 'python'
>>> var.upper()
 'PYTHON'
```

lower()

```
>>> var = 'Hello World'
>>> var.lower()
 'hello world'
```

isidentifier()

```
>>> var1 = '_xyz'
>>> var2 = '5xyz'
>>> var1.isidentifier()
 True
>>> Var2.isidentifier()
 False
```

count(str)

```
>>> mystr = 'programmer'
>>> mystr.count('m')
 2
```

endswith(str)

```
>>> mystr = 'python'
>>> mystr.endswith('n')
 True
```

isalpha( )

```
>>> var = 'computer'
>>> var.isalpha()
 True
```

replace(x, y)

```
>>> x = 'Hello'
>>> x.replace('e','a')
 'Hallo'
```

Light up

There are several methods to be used with string type. To find more methods, use the dir() function.

```
>>> myvar = "coding"
>>> dir(myvar)
```


List

A list is a collection of items of the same type or different types, enclosed in square brackets [ ]. Lists perform functions similar to arrays in C, C++, and Java. They can contain other lists, making them a preferred choice for storing large data of different types.

```
var1 = [1, 3, 5, 7]
var2 = ['cat', 'cow', 'dog']
var3 = [2, 4.5, 6, 'Python', 'Java']
```

The first element of a list occupies index 0, the next at index 1, and so on.

Slicing List

Lists can be divided to obtain sub-lists using slicing notation list[start : end]. The start parameter is optional and specifies where the division should begin. If start is not set, Python begins the division from the first element (index 0). Similarly, the end parameter is optional. If not specified, Python sets it to the last index of the list.
For example:

```
>>> var = [2, 4, 6, 8, 10]
>>> sublist = var[1:4]
>>> print(sublist)  #Output: [4, 6, 8]
```

Light up

The list() is the function for converting other types to list.
eg. converting from string to list:
>>> var = "Python"
>>> mylist = list(var)
>>> print(mylist)
['P', 'y', 't', 'h', 'o', 'n']

Some methods used with list

append(item)

```
>>> var = [2, 4]
>>> var.append(6)
>>> print(var)
 [2, 4, 6]
```

extend(list)

```
>>> mylis = [2, 4]
>>> var = [6, 8]
>>> mylis.extend(var)
>>> print(mylis)
 [2, 4, 6, 8]
```

insert(index, item)

```
>>> var = [2, 4]
>>> var.insert(0, 6)
>>> print(var)
 [6, 2, 4]
```

remove(item)

```
>>> mylis = ['cat', 'cow', 'fox']
>>> mylis.remove('cow')
>>> print(mylis)
 ['cat', 'fox']
```

reverse( )

```
>>> var = [2, 4, 6]
>>> var.reverse()
>>> print(var)
 [6, 4, 2]
```

pop( )

```
>>> mylis = [1, 2, 3, 4]
>>> mylis.pop()
 4
>>> print(mylis)
 [1, 2, 3]
```

sum(list)

```
>>> var = [2, 4, 6]
>>> result = sum(var)
>>> print(result)
 12
```

max(list)

```
>>> var = [20, 14, 30, 10]
>>> result = max(var)
>>> print(result)
 30
```

count(item)

```
>>> var = [2, 3, 4, 3]
>>> var.count(3)
 2
```

min(list)

```
>>> var = [20, 14, 30, 10]
>>> result = min(var)
>>> print(result)
 10
```


Tuple

Tuples are collections of elements of different data types enclosed in parentheses ( ) and separated by commas. The elements of tuples are immutable, meaning they cannot be changed once created, but they can still be accessed.

For example

```
var1 = (1, 3, 5)
var2 = ('Python', 'C++', 'C#')
var3 = (2, [1, 3], 'C#')
```

 # Light up

Converting from other types to tuples is easy with the tuple() function.
eg. a program to convert strings to tuples.
>>> var = "coding"
>>> var_tup = tuple(var)
>>> print(var_tup) #Output: ('c', 'o', 'd', 'i', 'n', 'g')

Some methods used with tuple

index(item)

```
>>> var = (1, 2, 3)
>>> var.index(2)
 1
```

count(item)

```
>>> var = (1, 3, 3, 5)
>>> var.count(3)
 2
```

max(tuple)

```
>>> var = (2, 3, 5)
>>> max(var)
 5
```

sum(tuple)

```
>>> var = (2, 3, 5)
>>> total = sum(var)
>>> print(total)
 10
```


Dictionary

A dictionary is a data structure that consists of a collection of key-value pair items, separated by commas, and enclosed within curly braces { }. Dictionaries can contain items of various data types. In a key-value pair, one item (the key) is associated with another item (the value), and they are linked by a colon (key : value).

For example

```
var1 = {"name":'Alice', "age": 25, "city":'New York'}
var2 = {"numbers":[2, 4], "languages":('Python', 'Java')}
```

Some methods used with dictionary

get(key), dictionary[key]

```
>>> mydict = {"name": 'Bob', "age": 30, "city": 'New York'}
>>> mydict.get('name')
 'Bob'
>>> mydict.get('age')
 30
>>> mydict['city']
 'New York'
```

pop(key)

```
>>> var = {'name':'John', 'id':456}
>>> var.pop('id')
 456
>>> print(var)
 {'name':'John'}
```

keys( )

```
>>> var = {'name':'John', 'id':456}
>>> var.keys()
 dict_keys(['name', 'id'])
```

values( )

```
>>> var = {'name':'John', 'id':456}
>>> var.values()
 dict_values(['John', 456])
```

update(dictionary)

```
>>> var1 = {'name':'John'}
>>> var2 = {'age':20}
>>> var = var1.update(var2)
>>> print(var)
 {'name':'John', 'age':20}
```


Set

A set is an unordered collection of unique elements. Sets enclose their members within curly braces { }. Sets can hold members of strings, integers, floats, and tuples, but not dictionaries, lists, or other sets. Sets are commonly used to perform mathematical operations such as intersection, union, or symmetric difference.

For example

```
myset1 = {2, 4, 6, 8}
myset2 = {1, 3, 'Python', 'Java'}
```

 # Light up

The set() function is used for converting other data types to set.
eg. converting a string to set.
>>> var = "coding"
>>> myset = set(var)
>>> print(myset) #Output: {'c', 'o', 'd', 'i', 'n', 'g' }

Some methods used with set

add(item)

```
>>> myset = {2, 4}
>>> myset.add(6)
>>> print(myset)
 {2, 4, 6}
```

discard(item)

```
>>> myset = {2, 4, 6}
>>> myset.discard(6)
>>> print(myset)
 {2, 4}
```

union(set)

```
>>> var1 = {2, 4}
>>> var2 = {1, 3}
>>> var = var1.union(var2)
>>> print(var)
 {1, 2, 3, 4}
```

intersection(set)

```
>>> set1 = {1, 3, 5}
>>> set2 = {2, 3, 6}
>>> set3 = set1.intersection(set2)
>>> print(set3)
 {3}
```


difference(set)

```
>>> set1 = {1, 2, 3, 4}
>>> set2 = {2, 4}
>>> set3 = set1.difference(set2)
>>> print(set3)
 {1, 3}
```

sum(set)

```
>>> myset = {2, 4, 6}
>>> total = sum(myset)
>>> print(total)
 12
```

max(set)

```
>>> myset = {2, 6, 4}
>>> maxi = max(myset)
>>> print(maxi)
 6
```

min(set)

```
>>> myset = {2, 6, 4}
>>> min = min(myset)
>>> print(min)
 2
```


Decision Making

Decision making is crucial in programming, especially when you want your program to execute only when a certain condition is true or false. These statements, known as conditional statements, are based on a Boolean value (True or False). There are three different kinds of conditional statements:

1. If Statement:

This is a simple conditional statement that executes a program or instructions if a condition is true or false.

```
if condition:
    #code
```

For example:

A program to print "Hello World", if a variable is equal to 5.

```
if var == 5:
    print("Hello World!")
```

2. If-Else Statement:

The if-else conditional statement provides two options for program execution. If the given condition is true, the program executes the statements in the if block; otherwise, if the condition is false, the statements within the else block execute.

```
if condition:
    #code
else:
    #code
```

For example:

A program to print "Great Python", if a variable is greater than 5, otherwise print "Good Python".

```
var = 4
if var > 5:
    print("Great Python")
else:
    print("Good Python")
```


3. If-Elif-Else Statement:

This conditional statement is necessary for multiple decision making.

```
if condition1:
   #code
elif condition2:
   #code
   ....
   ....
else:
   #code
```

For example:

A program to print "great python", if a variable is greater than 5. If it is less than 5, print "awesome python"; otherwise print 'good python'.

```
var = 3
if var > 5:
    print("Great Python")
elif var < 5:
    print("Awesome Python")
else:
    print("Good Python")
```


Loop

A loop is a control structure that enables the repetitive execution of a statement or a group of statements. Loops are built around conditions, steps, and statements. They keep executing as long as the condition is true. There are two kinds of loop structures in Python: for and while.

The **for** loop

The for loop is a control structure that allows the repetitive execution of statements in a top-to-bottom approach. It is used to iterate over elements of sequential data types such as lists, strings, or tuples.

Syntax

```
for item in iterable:
    #code
```

Note

Iterable is an object capable of returning its members one at a time. It can be traversed or looped over using a loop like a for loop. Examples include lists, tuples, strings, dictionaries, and sets.

Iterating through a string using **for** loop

```
>>> var = "code"
>>> for item in var:
...     print(item)
 c
 o
 d
 e
```

Iterating through a list using **for** loop

```
>>> var = [1, 2, 3, 4]
>>> for i in var:
...     print(i)
 1
 2
 3
 4
```


Range

Loop structures execute code based on user-given instructions, specifying where to begin, end, and the steps. These instructions can be easily implemented using the range() function.

The range() function is used to specify the range of values and steps a control structure must follow to execute the program. The **start** parameter is optional and denotes where to begin the loop. It is set to 0 by default. The **end** parameter must always be specified and denotes the integer to end the loop. The **step** is also an optional parameter that specifies the interval of execution. It is set to 1 by default.

For example:

end = 5

```
>>> for i in range(4):
...     print(i)
...
 0
 1
 2
 3
```

start = 2, end = 4

```
>>> for i in range(2,4):
...     print(i)
...
 2
 3
```

start =1, end = 6, step = 2

```
>>> for i in range(1, 6, 2):
...     print(i)
...
 1
 3
 5
```

start = 2, end = 10, step = 2

```
>>> for i in range(2, 10, 2):
...     print(i)
...
 2
 4
 6
 8
```


The while loop

The while loop is another control structure used to iterate or repeatedly execute a set of statements based on a true condition. The loop terminates when the condition is no longer true.

Syntax

```
while condition:
    #code
```

For example

```
>>> i = 0
>>> while i < 4:  #repeat iteration until i = 4 (condition becomes false)
        i = i + 1
        print(i)
...
 1
 2
 3
 4
```

The break statement

The break statement is a Python keyword used mostly in loop structures to halt or terminate execution prematurely once a given condition is true.

For example

```
for i in range(1, 5):
    if i == 3:      #terminate loop once i = 3
        break
    print(i)
...
 1
 2
 3
```


The **continue** statement

The continue statement is also a Python keyword implemented in loops to skip a step or iteration when a particular condition is true.

For example

```
for i in range(1, 6):
    if i == 3:       #skip step 3
       continue
    print(i)
...
1
2
4
5
```


Function

A function is a block of organized and related statements used to perform a specific task. It can contain variables, loops, decision-making statements, other functions, statements, and objects that can be used repeatedly in different parts of a program. Functions are also referred to as methods, procedures, subprograms, routines, or subroutines.

Importance of Functions:

1. **Enhanced Readability and Comprehensibility:** Functions improve the readability and comprehensibility of a program by breaking it down into smaller, logical units. Each function performs a specific task, making the code easier to understand.

2. **Efficiency through Minimization of Repetitions:** Functions help minimize repetitions in code by encapsulating repetitive tasks into reusable blocks. This reduces the amount of code duplication and makes the program more efficient to maintain.

3. **Breaking Complex Programs into Smaller Segments:** Functions allow complex programs to be broken down into smaller and more manageable segments. Each function focuses on a specific aspect of the program's functionality, making it easier to develop and debug.

4. **Improved Time Efficiency:** By organizing code into functions, developers can optimize performance and improve time efficiency. Functions enable code reuse, which reduces development time and effort, leading to faster and more efficient programming.

Types of Functions in Python:

There are two types of functions in the Python programming language: Built-in Functions and User-defined Functions.

Built-in Functions:

Built-in functions are provided by the Python language and are readily available to be used in programs. They serve various purposes and are commonly used for tasks such as mathematical operations, data conversion, string manipulation, and more.

Examples include: sum(), eval(), hex(), bin(), oct(), chr(), ord(), dir(), del(), max(), min(), len()

Example of using built-in functions

```
var = [2, 4, 6]
total = sum(var)
print(total) #Output: 12
```

User-defined Functions:

User-defined functions are functions created by the user according to Python syntax. These functions allow developers to encapsulate specific tasks or operations into reusable blocks of code, enhancing code modularity and reusability.

Syntax:

```
def function_name(parameters):
    #statements or code

    return #code
```

The def Keyword:

The def keyword is used to define a function in Python. It is the keyword used to create a function.

Function Name:

The function name is the identifier given to the function. It can start with either a capital or lowercase letter and can include underscores, but it cannot start with a number.

Parameters:

Parameters, also known as arguments, are optional and used to pass data or values to the function. They are specified within the parentheses following the function name.

Colon:
A colon (:) marks the end of the function header, indicating the start of the function block or body.

Statement(s):
Every function block or body contains at least one statement, which defines the actual logic or purpose of the function. These statements are executed when the function is called.

The return Statement:
The return keyword is optional and is used if the function is defined to return or produce a value. If the function is designed to return no value, there is no need to use the return statement.

Example1 : A function to print 'Hello World'

```
def hello():
    print('Hello World!')
```

Example 2: A function to accept two numbers and return their sum.

```
def total(x, y):
    result = x + y

    return result
```

Calling Functions:

Calling a function simply means executing the function. Function calls can be made through the Python prompt, within another function, or within a program.

Calling Functions through the Prompt:

```
>>> def greetings(name):
        print(f"hello {name}")
```

```
>>> greetings("Alice")
 hello Alice
```

Calling Functions within Another Program:

```
def greet(name):
    print(f'hello {name}')


def myfun():
    greet('John')  #Calling the greet function
```

Calling Functions through a Program:

```
def total(*args):
    results = sum(args)

    return results

sum1 = total(10, 20) # Calling the function
print(sum1)   #Output: 30

sum2 = total(2, 4, 9)
print(sum2)   #Output: 15
```


Anonymous Functions:

Python functions are normally defined with the def keyword, but there is another way to create functions without using the **def** keyword and a function name. This can be achieved using Python Lambda functions.

Syntax

```
variable = lambda arguments:expression
```

Variable: This is the variable that will store the lambda function.
Argument: These are the input values provided to the lambda function.
Expression: This is the logic that defines the function.

Example1: Lambda function to add two numbers

```
var = lambda x, y : x + y

print(var(2, 3)) #Output: 5
```

Example2 : Lambda function to square numbers.

```
var = lambda x : x**2

print(var(4)) #Output: 16
```

Example3 : Lambda function to check if a number is even.

```
var = lambda x : x%2 == 0

print(var(2)) #Output: True
print(var(3)) #Output: False
```


Class and Object

Python is a purely object-oriented programming (OOP) language where everything is an object. A **class** is a data type, similar to built-in types like list, string, dictionary, float, or integer.
An **object**, on the other hand, is an instance of a class and can be any named entity, such as functions, integers, strings, floats, classes, methods, and files.
Objects are created from classes, and each object is called an instance of a class. Classes can have functions or variables, where functions defined in a class are called methods and variables are called class attributes.

Creating a Class:

```
class class_name:

    #Class variables or attributes
    variable1 = value1
    variable2 = value2

    #Class Methods or functions
    def function_name(args):
        #Code
        pass
```

Example, creating a simple mathematics class

```
class Mathematics:

    pi = 3.14159
    sum = 50

    def total():
        print('Hello ')
```


Creating Object:
Creating an object of a class means making instances of the class.

```
object_name = ClassName()
```

Accessing Methods and Attributes of a Class

Methods and attributes of a class can be accessed using the object of the class.

Example, consider the mathematics class

```
#Creating class
class Mathematics:

    #attributes
    pi = 3.14159
    sum = 50

    #method
    def total(x, y):
        return x + y


#Creating Object
obj = Mathematics

print(obj.sum)    #Output: 50
print(obj.total(2, 4))    #Output: 6
```

The init Method:

The '__init__()' method is a class constructor used to initialize objects created from a class. It serves a role similar to the '*main()*' method in other programming languages like

C, C++, and Dart. The '__init__()' method is where class attributes are declared, and the actual program execution or code processing begins.
The '__init__()' method takes at least one argument, which is typically named '**self**'. The 'self' parameter refers to the instance of the class and is passed as the first parameter to the method. It allows class methods to access instance-specific attributes. Attributes declared within the '__init__()' method can be accessed and utilized by all functions or methods within the class that use the 'self' parameter.

Here's a basic example of using the '__init__()' method in a Python class:

```
class Mathematics:

    def __init__(self):
        self.pi = 3.14159
        self.total = 100

    def average(self,n):
        avg = self.total/n  #Using total, defined in init
        return avg

    def square(self):
        return self.pi ** 2


myobj = Mathematics()
print(myobj.average(10))   #Output: 10.0
print(myobj.square())   #Output: 9.869587728099999
```


Handling Errors or Exceptions

Coding sometimes leads to various forms of errors, and it's essential to manage them when they occur. In programming, exception handling is a crucial concept for managing errors or unexpected issues that can arise during code execution. Errors in Python can be broadly categorized into two types: syntax errors and runtime errors.

Syntax Error:

A syntax error occurs when the structure of a program does not adhere to the rules and syntax of the Python language. Common causes of syntax errors in Python include:

1. Incorrect indentation.
2. Missing colons.
3. Empty blocks without the pass keyword.

Runtime Error:

Runtime errors or exceptions occur during the execution of the program. These errors are not related to syntax but to issues that arise when code runs.

Some Runtime exceptions

ZeroDivisionError	It occurs when a number is divided by zero
KeyError	It occurs when a key is not found in a dictionary
NameError	This is when a variable is not found in the local or global scope
IndexError	This happens when an item's index is not in the range
IndentationError	It occurs due to wrong indentation in the program
FloatingPointError	Operations on floating point fail
ImportError	It happens, when an imported module is not found
AssertionError	It occurs when assertion statements fail
AttributeError	An attribute or reference assignment fails

UnicodeError	It happens when there is an encoding or decoding error
EOFerror	When the input() function reaches the end-of-file condition

Handling Exceptions

Python provides several mechanisms to catch and handle exceptions when they occur during program execution. Two fundamental constructs for exception handling are the try...except and try...finally statements.

try...except

The code that may raise an exception is placed in the try block. If an exception occurs, the code in the except block is executed. ErrorType is optional and is used to handle specific types of errors.

Syntax

```
try:
    # Code likely to raise an exception
except ErrorType:
    # Code to handle the exception
```

Example

```
try:
    var = 5
    result = var/0  #Zero division likely to raise exception
except ZeroDivisionError:
    print('error')
```


try...finally

In the try block, code likely to produce an error is placed. The finally block contains code that will be executed whether an exception is raised or not.

Syntax

```
try:
    # Code likely to produce an error
finally:
    # Code that will be executed whether an exception is raised or not
```

Example

```
try:
    var = 5
    result = var/0 #Code likely to raise exception
finally:
    print("Hello World!")
```


Page Summary

Data types

Python supports various data types such as integers, floats, strings, lists, tuples, dictionaries, and sets. These data types can be manipulated and combined to perform various operations.

1. What are the differences between mutable and immutable data types in Python? Provide examples of each.
2. How do you convert between different data types in Python? Give examples.
3. Explain the difference between lists and tuples in Python, and when you would choose one over the other.

Function

Functions in Python are blocks of reusable code that perform a specific task. They can accept inputs (parameters), process them, and return outputs.

1. What is the difference between parameters and arguments in Python functions?
2. How do you define a function in Python, and what are the components of a function definition?
3. Explain the concept of variable scope in Python functions. How does it affect the accessibility of variables within and outside of functions?

Classes and Objects

Python is an object-oriented programming language, allowing the creation and manipulation of classes and objects. Classes are blueprints for creating objects with attributes and methods.

1. What is a class, and how do you define one in Python?
2. Explain the difference between attributes and methods in Python classes, and how they are accessed.
3. How do you create an instance of a class (an object) in Python, and how can you access its attributes and methods?

Decision Making

Decision-making in Python involves using conditional statements such as **if**, **elif**, and else to execute code based on certain conditions.

1. What is the syntax for an if statement in Python, and how does it work?
2. How do you use the **elif** and else statements in Python to handle multiple conditions?
3. Explain the difference between the **==** and **is** operators in Python, and when you would use each.

Page Summary

Loops

Loops in Python are used to iterate over a sequence (such as lists, tuples, or dictionaries) or execute a block of code repeatedly.

1. What is the syntax for a for loop in Python, and how does it work?
2. How do you use the range() function in combination with a for loop to iterate over a sequence of numbers?
3. What is a while loop, and how does it differ from a for loop? Provide examples of when each would be used.

Keywords

lambda
range
continue
break
return
key-value
slicing
concatenating
iterable

Discussion

1. Think about Bytes as data type. How different is it from the other types?
2. Which data types are iterable?
3. Name some function keywords?
4. Discuss the differences between **for** and **while** loops?

Chapter 4

GRAPHICAL USER INTERFACE (GUI) FRAMEWORK

After completing this chapter, you will be able to understand:

GUI frameworks or ToolKits

Various programming language frameworks

Kinds of applications

Platforms specification

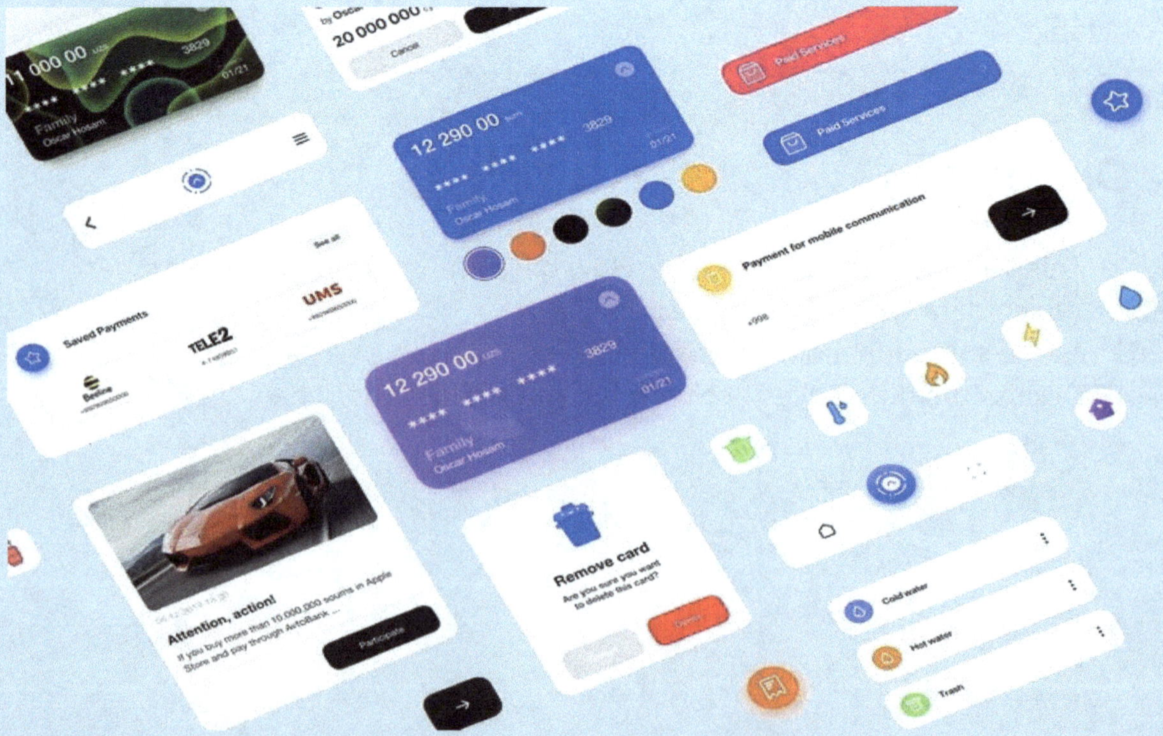

Graphical User Interface Framework

Being a programmer or familiarized with a particular programming language alone is insufficient to start developing mobile or desktop applications. The program is the most important part of the development since it contains all the logic for controlling the interface. Knowing how to code in a particular program is the first step followed by the knowledge in adding or integrating a specific Graphical User Interface (GUI) Framework.

The program acts as the backend while the Graphical User Interface acts as the frontend.
At this point, I assume you have a little idea about how to program in Python.
A Graphical User Interface (GUI) Framework provides developers with a set of tools, libraries, and components to create visually appealing and interactive user interfaces for their applications. These frameworks abstract away the complexities of low-level graphics programming, allowing developers to focus on designing intuitive and user-friendly interfaces.

There are several GUI frameworks available for Python, each with its own strengths and weaknesses. Some popular options include Tkinter, PyQt, Kivy, wxPython, and PyGTK. These frameworks offer a variety of features such as support for different platforms, rich widget libraries, and integration with other tools and technologies.

Choosing the right GUI framework depends on various factors such as the type of application being developed, target platform, performance requirements, and personal preference. It's essential to explore and evaluate different options to find the framework that best fits your needs and project requirements.

In the following sections, we'll explore some of the most popular GUI frameworks for Python, their features, and how to get started with them. Whether you're building a simple desktop application or a complex mobile app, there's a GUI framework out there to help you bring your ideas to life.

Understanding Graphical User Interface

In the realm of software development, creating applications extends beyond mere coding. It involves crafting interactive experiences that users engage with through Graphical User Interfaces (GUIs). Whether it's a mobile app on a smartphone or a desktop program on a computer, the GUI serves as the gateway to user interaction.

At the core of every GUI are widgets – the elemental components of user interface design. These widgets encompass a myriad of elements, ranging from buttons and text fields to menus, toolbars, and icons. Each widget fulfills a specific function, empowering users to perform actions such as clicking, scrolling, dragging, touching, and moving.

Buttons facilitate action triggers, toggles enable state-switching, text fields empower text input, and sliders allow for value adjustment. Moreover, widgets like animations, icons, menus, and dialog boxes enhance the user experience by providing visual appeal and additional functionality.

Collectively, these widgets form the Graphical User Interface (GUI) of an application, offering users an intuitive platform for interacting with the underlying software. GUI frameworks provide developers with toolsets and libraries to efficiently create and manage these interfaces.

Whether developing a mobile app, a desktop application, or even a web-based tool, understanding GUI frameworks is essential for designing engaging and user-friendly experiences. By leveraging the capabilities of GUI frameworks, developers can streamline the development process and deliver applications that meet the needs and expectations of their users.

Exploring GUI Frameworks Across Programming Languages

GUI frameworks, also known as toolkits, play a pivotal role in facilitating user interaction and enhancing the visual appeal of applications. These frameworks serve as the front-end interface, enabling seamless program execution and user engagement. It's worth noting that GUI frameworks are typically tailored to specific programming languages, ensuring compatibility and optimal performance. Here's a glimpse into some of the prominent GUI toolkits available across various programming languages:

Language	Framework
Python	Flet, PyQt, PySide, Kivy/KivyMD, TKinter
C++	Qt
JavaScript	React
Dart	Flutter
Object C	Swift
Java	Swing, JavaFx

Each of these GUI frameworks offers unique features and capabilities, catering to the diverse needs of developers across different programming languages. Whether you're building a desktop application, a mobile app, or a web-based tool, selecting the right GUI framework can significantly impact the user experience and the overall success of your project.

The popularity and widespread adoption of a GUI framework often hinge on two key factors: its support for both mobile and desktop applications, and its ease of implementation within programming projects. Let's delve deeper into these aspects:

Support for Mobile and Desktop Apps:

1. A GUI framework that caters to both mobile and desktop platforms offers versatility and flexibility to developers. This versatility allows developers to target a broader audience and deploy their applications across multiple devices seamlessly.
2. Mobile support ensures that developers can create engaging and user-friendly interfaces for smartphones and tablets, while desktop support enables the development of robust applications for PCs and laptops.
3. GUI frameworks that provide a consistent user experience across different platforms contribute to their popularity and adoption.

Ease of Implementation:

- Developers value GUI frameworks that are easy to understand, integrate, and utilize in their projects. A framework with clear documentation, intuitive APIs, and comprehensive tutorials accelerates the learning curve for developers, enabling them to quickly grasp its features and capabilities.
- Simplified syntax and straightforward implementation procedures streamline the development process, reducing development time and effort.
- Additionally, a supportive and active developer community often contributes to the popularity of a GUI framework. Communities provide valuable resources, forums for discussion, and opportunities for collaboration, fostering a conducive environment for learning and growth.

Kinds of Applications

Before embarking on the journey of application development, it's crucial to determine the specific purpose of the app. There are various kinds of applications that cater to different needs and preferences:

1. Educational Apps:
    - Designed to facilitate learning and knowledge acquisition.
    - Offer interactive lessons, quizzes, and educational games.
    - Target a wide range of subjects and age groups.

2. Entertainment Apps (e.g., media player):
    - Aim to provide users with diverse forms of entertainment.
    - Offer music, movies, and other multimedia content through players or streaming services.

3. Utility Apps (e.g., cleaner, antivirus):
    - Serve practical purposes such as system optimization, security, and maintenance.
    - Ensure the device functions efficiently and remains secure from threats.

4. Gaming Apps:
    - Offer a wide variety of games across different genres and styles.
    - Entertain users with diverse gameplay experiences.

5. Social Media Apps:
    - Connect individuals worldwide, facilitating interaction and content sharing.
    - Provide various social networking functionalities for engaging with others.

6. Reading and eBooks:
    - Provide digital access to books, articles, and other written content.
    - Allow users to conveniently read on their devices.

7. Photo and Video Editing Apps:
    - Enable users to edit and enhance visual content such as images and videos.
    - Offer tools for cropping, filters, effects, and more to enhance creativity and sharing capabilities.

Platform Specification

Once you've identified the type of application you intend to develop, it's essential to consider the platform on which the app will run. Most GUI frameworks support multiple platforms, including Android, iOS, Windows, macOS, and Linux. With these frameworks, you can write code once and deploy it across various platforms seamlessly.

Platform Extensions:

Example

Platform	Extension
Android	.apk (Android Application Package) / .aab (Android App Bundle)
iOS	.ipa (iOS App Store Package
Windows	.exe (Executable File)
macOS	.dmg (Disk Image)
Linux	.deb (Debian Package), rpm (Red Hat Package Manager)

Page Summary

GUI (Graphical User Interface) frameworks are libraries or toolkits that provide developers with pre-built components and functions for creating graphical interfaces in software applications. These frameworks streamline the process of designing and implementing user interfaces, allowing developers to focus on application logic rather than low-level graphics programming. Different programming languages have their own GUI frameworks tailored to their syntax and ecosystem. For example, Java has Swing and JavaFX, Python has Tkinter and PyQt, and JavaScript has React and Angular, each offering a range of features and capabilities to suit diverse application requirements.

Keywords

backend
frontend
widget
animation
toolkits

Discussion

1. What is the purpose of GUI frameworks in software development?
2. How do GUI frameworks help streamline the process of creating graphical interfaces?
3. Can you name some GUI frameworks and their respective programming languages, and explain how they are tailored to suit the syntax and ecosystem of each language?
4. What are some advantages of using GUI frameworks specific to the programming language you are familiar with?
5. How do GUI frameworks handle events and user interactions in software applications?
6. Can you describe a scenario where the choice of a specific GUI framework influenced the development process or the user experience of an application?

Chapter 5

SETTING UP FLET

After completing this chapter, you will be able to understand:

Flet

Development process

Flet installation

Setting up IDE

Creating Flet project

Platform testing

Designing the interface

Packaging and publishing app

Flet

Flet is a framework designed for crafting interactive multi-user web, desktop, and mobile applications using languages such as Python. Its widgets, known as controls, are built upon Flutter by Google. Flet's UI implementation is notably straightforward compared to other frameworks, making it accessible even to those without prior experience in frontend development.

Reasons to Choose Flet:

1. Flet eliminates the need for pre-existing knowledge or experience in application development.

2. It boasts a rich UI wrapped with Flutter widgets provided by Google.

3. Flet requires minimal dependencies and SDKs—only Python and Flet are necessary.

4. With Flet, developers can write code once and deploy their applications across multiple platforms, including Windows, macOS, Android, iOS, Linux, and the Web.

5. Its hot reload feature enables developers to swiftly visualize changes during the development process.

Development Process:

1. Install Flet
2. Configure the Integrated Development Environment (IDE).
3. Create a Flet Project.
4. Test the project across various platforms.
5. Design the user interface.
6. Package and publish the application.

① Flet Installation

To install Flet, you can use the Python pip package in the command line or shell.

#Windows and MacOS:

1. Press Ctrl + Shift + P to open PowerShell on Windows or Terminal on MacOS.
2. Use the following command:

```
pip install Flet
```

To upgrade the Flet module, you can run:

```
pip install flet --upgrade
```

The Flet package also provides a Command Line Interface. To check the version of Flet, use the command:

```
flet --version
```

#Linux:

Linux users need to ensure that GStreamer libraries are installed for Flet to run smoothly. Although most Linux distributions come with these libraries pre-installed, encountering an error like the one below indicates the need to install GStreamer.

Error while loading shared libraries: libstapp-1.0.so.0:cannot open shared object file: No such file or directory.

To resolve this, you can install GStreamer by running the following command.

```
sudo apt-get update
sudo apt-get install libgstreamer1.0-dev libgstreamer-plugins-base1.0-dev
libgstreamer-plugins-bad1.0-dev gstreamer1.0-plugins-base gstreamer1.0-plugins-
good gstreamer1.0-plugins-bad gstreamer1.0-plugins-ugly gstreamer1.0-libav
gstreamer1.0-doc gstreamer1.0-tools gstreamer1.0-x gstreamer1.0-alsa
gstreamer1.0-gl gstreamer1.0-gtk3 gstreamer1.0-qt5 gstreamer1.0-pulseaudio
```

② Setting up IDE

While coding in Python doesn't necessarily require a complex Integrated Development Environment (IDE), using one can greatly enhance productivity. For this project, Visual Studio Code is recommended as the preferred IDE.

It's important to choose an IDE that can automate tasks, facilitate debugging, and speed up coding processes. Visual Studio Code provides a user-friendly interface with robust features for Python development.

 # Note

Refer to the beginning of this chapter in the book for more information about IDEs and detailed steps on setting up Visual Studio Code.

③ Creating Flet Project

#Desktop Applications

Developing a Flet app for desktop is notably simpler and more straightforward than for mobile platforms. All you need to do is create a Python file using any IDE or even a simple text editor, and then execute the Python script. Below is an example of a basic Flet app.

```
#myfletapp.py

import flet

def main(page: flet.Page):
    pass

flet.app(target = main)
```

For desktop applications, you can simply run the project using the Python command or with the run buttons provided by various IDEs.

Example commands:

```
PS C:\ FLET> python myfletapp.py
```

or

```
PS C:\ FLET> flet run myfletapp.py
```

These commands will initiate the execution of your Flet project, allowing you to start developing your desktop application with ease.

#Mobile Applications

Developing mobile applications with Flet requires a slightly different approach compared to desktop applications, as additional dependencies may need to be added.

To create a Flet project for mobile applications, you can use the following command:

```
flet create your_project
```

This command will generate the project structure for your mobile application, including additional files such as assets, main.py, requirements.txt, and pyproject.toml.

```
/assets/
  Icon.png
main.py
requirements.txt
pyproject.toml
```

Here's a breakdown of the project structure:

assets/:
This directory contains application assets, including media files (such as images, sound, and videos) and other files required by the app. It also includes images used for package icons and splash screens. If only Icon.png is provided, it will be used as the source image to generate icons and splash screens for all platforms.

main.py:
This file serves as the entry point for the program and is where the execution begins. It is considered the heart of the application.

requirements.txt:
This file contains all the dependencies required for creating the Flet app. If this file is not provided, only the Flet dependency will be installed during packaging.

pyproject.toml:
This file is meant for reading dependencies, although it is not yet supported as of the time of writing this book.

④ Platform Testing

Testing your application across different platforms is a critical step in the development process as it allows you to observe how your app behaves on various devices, including computers, mobile devices, and the web. With each code implementation, you can quickly see the effects on the testing device, ensuring smooth functionality across platforms.

#Desktop Platforms

For desktop platforms like **Windows**, **macOS**, and **Linux**, testing is straightforward. After coding, simply run the app and observe it appear on the screen.

Alternatively, you can use the Flet command-line interface (CLI) to run the app on desktops. Here's how:

```
flet run myapp.py
```

Additionally, you can run the app from the command line using the Python command:

```
python myapp.py
```

or if the file is located in a specific path:

```
python /path/to/myapp.py
```

 # Note

There would be further explanation of the code in upcoming chapters of this book. Stay tuned for more insights.

#Mobile Platforms

Testing Flet App on Android

Testing your app on Android devices is a straightforward process that requires only your computer and mobile phone. Here's how to do it:

Create a Flet project with the command `flet create your_app`

1. Ensure that your Android device and computer are connected to the same Wi-Fi or local network. Additionally, an internet connection is required when creating a Flet app for the first time.

2. Install the Flet app on your Android mobile device from the Play Store. This app allows you to monitor how your app performs on a mobile device.

3. It is recommended to create a Python virtual environment and work within the workspace. However, you can still work directly from your device if needed.

4. Navigate to your working folder using the command `cd your_app`

5. Run the app using the command `flet run --android` This command starts the Flet development server.

6. A QR code containing the project URL will be displayed in the terminal.

7. Open the Camera app on your Android device or any QR code scanner app. Point the camera at the QR code and click on the URL to open it in the Flet app you installed.

8. Alternatively, you can manually start your app in Flet by clicking the "+" button and typing its URL into the Flet app.

Testing Flet App on iOS

To test your app on iOS devices, follow these steps:

Create a Flet project with the command `flet create your_app`

1. Ensure that your iOS device and computer are connected to the same Wi-Fi or local network. Additionally, an internet connection is required when creating a Flet app for the first time.

2. Install the Flet app on your iOS mobile device from the App Store. This app allows you to observe your app's behavior on the mobile device.

3. It is recommended to create a Python virtual environment and work within the workspace. However, you can still work directly from your device if needed.

4. Navigate to your working folder using the command `cd your_app`

5. Run the app using the command. `flet run --iOS` This command starts the Flet development server with your app.

6. A QR code containing the project URL will be displayed in the terminal.

7. Open the Camera app on your iOS device or any QR code scanner app. Point the camera at the QR code and click on the URL to open it in the Flet app you installed.

8. A dialog asking for permission to access your local network will appear. Click "Allow" to see your Flet app running on your iOS device.

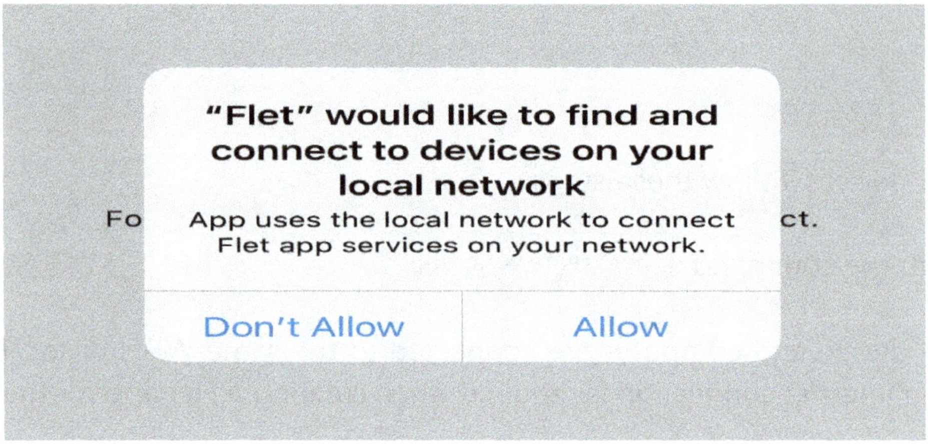

9. Alternatively, you can manually start your app in Flet by clicking the "+" button and typing its URL into the Flet app.

⑤ Designing the Interface

Building UI

In Flet, the user interface (UI) is composed of various widgets known as controls. These controls are structured in a hierarchy or tree-like fashion, with each control having a parent except for the page.

Controls facilitate smooth interaction between humans and computers, and they are implemented as regular Python classes. Each control comes with its unique set of methods or functions, referred to as properties, which can be used to customize its behavior and appearance. While some control properties are common across multiple controls, others are specific to certain controls. There exists a wide range of controls that can be employed to create a comprehensive application, and these controls are categorized into different domains based on their similar features or functions.

The Basic App Structure

In Flet applications, the basic structure follows a common pattern:

```
#myfletapp.py

import flet

def main(page: flet.Page):
    pass

flet.app(target = main)
```

This structure serves as the foundation for all Flet applications. The function `main()` acts as the central point of execution, serving as the entry point for the application. Within this function, the primary logic of the application is defined.

The `page` parameter represents the top-level control in the Flet application. It serves as the parent control for all other controls within the application. Controls are organized in a hierarchical manner, with the `Page` control serving as the root of this hierarchy.

Controls can be added, removed, or manipulated within the `page` using methods such as `add`, `insert`, and `remove`. Additionally, the `Page` control can contain other controls and even nested pages.

By default, the **Page** control applies a column layout, allowing controls to be arranged vertically from top to bottom. This layout simplifies the organization of controls within the application, enhancing the user interface design process.

Finally, the `flet.app()` function is used to initialize the application and ensure that the window or app remains active, listening for user interactions and sessions.

⑥ Packaging and Publishing Apps

Packaging and publishing apps is the final step after successful development. It involves bundling the app and all its dependencies into an executable file, allowing users, to run it on their computer or mobile devices without needing to install the Python interpreter or the modules.

For mobile platforms like Android and iOS, you will typically need to package your app according to the platform's requirements. For Android, you will generate an APK (Android Package) file which can be uploaded to the Google Play Sore.

For iOS, you will create an IPA (iOS App Store Package) file, which can be submitted to the Apple App Store.

Platforms and their package extensions.

Platform	Extension
Android	.apk (Android Application Package) / .aab (Android App Bundle)
iOS	.ipa (iOS App Store Package
Windows	.exe (Executable File)
macOS	.dmg (Disk Image)
Linux	.deb (Debian Package), rpm (Red Hat Package Manager)

Packaging Desktop Apps (Flet pack)

Once the Flet app is successfully created, tested, and behaves as intended, the next task is to package it into a specific app format tailored for the target platform.

When building Flet apps, packaging desktop applications is streamlined through Flet's integration with PyInstaller. PyInstaller is employed to convert Python files into executable formats compatible with Windows, macOS, and Linux systems. Flet enhances this process by encapsulating PyInstaller's functionality, allowing developers to package Flet apps and their dependencies into a single cohesive unit.

To begin, ensure PyInstaller is installed by executing the following command in the terminal.

```
pip install pyinstaller
```

Once installed, navigate to the directory containing your **.py** file and initiate the packaging process with the following command.

```
flet pack your_app.py
```

The resulting executable file will mirror the name of your program file. If desired, customize the executable's name using the `--name` parameter in the command.

```
flet pack your_app.py --name your_bundle_name
```

Following packaging, the bundled Flet app can be found within the **dist** folder. Verify its functionality by executing the appropriate command based on your operating system:

On **macOS**

```
open dist/your_app.app
```

On **Windows**

```
dist/your_app.exe
```


On **Linux**

```
dist/your_app
```

Customizing package icon

By default, the package icon is set to a diskette. To change this, include the `--icon` parameter with the `--flet pack` command. However, before this customization can be successful, Python pillow must be installed.

Execute the following command to install Python pillow:

```
pip install pillow
```

After installing Python pillow, you can add your icon using the following command.

```
flet pack --icon path_to_icon.png
```

Replace <path_to_icon.png> with the path to your desired icon file.

After crafting your executables, you can streamline distribution by zipping the **dist** folder and providing it to your users. They can effortlessly run the application by simply opening it, eliminating the need for Python and Flet installation.

Packaging Mobile, Desktop and Web Apps (Flet build)

Once your Flet app has been successfully developed and tested for compatibility on various devices, the next crucial step is packaging it into target platforms such as APK/AAB, IPA, macOS, Linux, and Windows for distribution.

This process is streamlined through the `--flet build` command, which supersedes both `--flet pack` (for desktop app packaging) and `--flet publish` (for static website packaging) commands. `--flet build` empowers you to convert your Flet app into Android or iOS bundles, desktop apps, and static websites seamlessly.

For desktop app packaging, `--flet build` diverges from the reliance on PyInstaller, as seen in **flet pack**. Instead, it leverages the Flutter SDK to produce fast, offline, fully customizable executables. These executables, tailored for Windows, Linux, and macOS, embed the Python runtime within, operating in-process. You can personalize these desktop apps with your own icons, about dialog, and metadata, ensuring a polished and tailored user experience.

Prerequisites and Requirements

Flutter SDK

Install Flutter SDK version 3.16 or higher and ensure the paths to both the Flutter and Dart commands are added to the PATH environment variable.

macOS: It's recommended to install Flutter SDK using the "Download and install" approach.

Linux: Preferably, install Flutter SDK via Method 2: Manual installation. Avoid installing Flutter with snap.

Pay attention to Flutter's specific requirements for each platform:

- **macOS**: Ensure Xcode and CocoaPods are installed.
- **Windows**: Visual Studio 2022 is recommended.
- **Linux**: Additional tools and libraries may be required, depending on the distribution.

Installing Flutter SDK

For Windows:

1. Visit the Flutter SDK download page: Flutter SDK Download.
2. Click on the Windows button to download the Flutter SDK.
3. Once the download is complete, unzip the package.
4. Move the extracted folder to a location where you want to keep the Flutter SDK, for example, C:\src\flutter.
5. Add Flutter's bin directory to your system's PATH environment variable. For detailed steps, refer to the Flutter installation guide for Windows.
6. Run `flutter doctor` in your command prompt to verify Flutter installation and to install any necessary dependencies.

For macOS:

1. Visit the Flutter SDK download page: Flutter SDK Download.
2. Click on the macOS button to download the Flutter SDK.
3. Once the download is complete, unzip the package.
4. Move the extracted folder to a location where you want to keep the Flutter SDK, for example, /usr/local/flutter.
5. Add Flutter's bin directory to your PATH environment variable by adding the following line to your shell configuration file (like ~/.bashrc, ~/.zshrc, or ~/.bash_profile):
   ```
   export PATH="$PATH:/usr/local/flutter/bin"
   ```
6. Run `flutter doctor` in your terminal to verify Flutter installation and to install any necessary dependencies.

For Linux:

1. Visit the Flutter SDK download page: Flutter SDK Download.
2. Click on the Linux button to download the Flutter SDK.
3. Once the download is complete, unzip the package.
4. Move the extracted folder to a location where you want to keep the Flutter SDK, for example, /usr/local/flutter.
5. Add Flutter's bin directory to your PATH environment variable by adding the following line to your shell configuration file (like ~/.bashrc, ~/.zshrc, or ~/.bash_profile):
   ```
   export PATH="$PATH:/usr/local/flutter/bin"
   ```
6. Run `flutter doctor` in your terminal to verify Flutter installation and to install any necessary dependencies.

Windows Requirements

When executing `flet build` on Windows, you may encounter the following error message:

```
Building with plugins requires symlink support.

Please enable Developer Mode in your system settings. Run
  start ms-settings:developers
to open settings.
```

To resolve this issue, follow these steps to enable Developer Mode:

1. Open the Run dialog by pressing Win + R.
2. Type start ms-settings:developers and press Enter.
3. This will open the Developers settings page in the Windows Settings app.
4. Toggle Developer Mode to on.

Linux Requirements

GStreamer
Building Flet apps on Linux requires GStreamer libraries installed.
To install minimal set of GStreamer libs on Ubuntu/Debian run the following commands:

```
apt install libgtk-3-dev libgstreamer1.0-dev libgstreamer-plugins-base1.0-dev
```


Building Platform Matrix

The following matrix shows which OS you should run `flet build` command on in order to build a package for specific platform:

Build on / Target platform	ipa	apk/aab	macos	linux	windows	web
macOS	✅	✅	✅			✅
Windows		✅		✅ (WSL)	✅	✅
Linux		✅		✅		✅

Building Android APK with Flet

Use `flet build apk` or `flet build apk path/to/app` to generate an Android APK file from your app. This command builds the release version, which doesn't support debugging and is suitable for deployment to app stores.
If you're planning to publish your app on the Google Play Store, consider using Android App Bundles (AAB) or splitting the APK to reduce its size. AAB is the recommended format for publishing to the Play Store as it optimizes the app size.

Building Android App Bundle (AAB) with Flet

Execute `flet build aab` or `flet build aab path/to/app` to create an Android App Bundle (AAB) file from your app. Similar to building an APK, this command generates the release version suitable for app store deployment.
App bundles are preferred for publishing to the Play Store as they improve app size optimization.

Note

Know the difference between the commands flet build apk and flet build aab /path/to/app. The former is utilized when operating within the same working folder.

Building iOS Archive and IPA with Flet

On a macOS host, you can use `flet build ipa` or `flet build ipa /path/to/app` to build an iOS archive bundle and IPA file for distribution. To generate the IPA successfully, ensure you provide correct values for the following arguments:

- **--org:** Organization name in reverse domain name notation (e.g., com.mycompany). It's combined with --project to form the iOS and Android bundle ID. Default is com.flet.
- **--project:** Project name in C-style identifier format (lowercase alphanumerics with underscores). Used to build bundle ID and as a name for bundle executable. By default, it's the name of the Flet app directory.
- **--team:** Team ID to locate the provisioning profile. If no team ID is provided, an unsigned iOS archive will be generated.

Building Desktop Applications with Flet

#Windows

To build a Windows desktop application.

```
flet build windows
```

#macOS

To generate a macOS desktop application.

```
flet build macos
```

#Linux

To create a Linux desktop application.

```
flet build linux
```


Icons Customization

You can customize app icons for all platforms (excluding Linux) using images in the assets directory of your Flet app. Here are the details for each platform:

- **iOS**: Use icon_ios.png (or any supported image format). Recommended minimum size is 1024 px. The image should not have transparency (alpha channel). Defaults to icon.png with alpha-channel automatically removed.
- **Android**: Utilize icon_android.png (or any supported image format). Recommended minimum size is 192 px. Defaults to icon.png.
- **Web**: Employ icon_web.png (or any supported image format). Recommended minimum size is 512 px. Defaults to icon.png.
- **Windows**: Use icon_windows.png (or any supported image format). An ICO file of 256 px size will be produced. Defaults to icon.png. If icon_windows.ico file is provided, it will be copied to windows/runner/resources/app_icon.ico unmodified.
- **macOS**: Utilize icon_macos.png (or any supported image format). Recommended minimum size is 1024 px. Defaults to icon.png.

By customizing icons for different platforms, you can enhance the visual appeal of your desktop applications built with Flet.

Note

In the upcoming chapter, we'll delve into Flet controls. While most demonstrations and practical examples will be showcased on Window platforms, it's important to note that the concepts can be applied similarly across other platforms like Android, iOS, Linux and macOS

Chapter Summary

Flet is an open-source UI toolkit developed by Google, designed for building cross-platform applications with a single codebase. It uses the Python programming language and offers a rich set of pre-built controls for creating beautiful and responsive user interfaces. Flet's hot reload feature allows developers to quickly iterate on their code, making the development process faster and more efficient. Its layered architecture provides flexibility and performance optimization, enabling developers to create high-quality apps for various platforms, including iOS, Android, web, and desktop.

Keywords

controls
properties
domain
executable
pyinstaller

Discussion

1. What is Flet, and what makes it a popular choice for cross-platform app development?
2. How does Flet's hot reload feature benefit developers during the development process?
3. Can you explain Flet's architecture and how it contributes to the performance and flexibility of applications built with Flet?

Chapter 6

FLET CONTROLS

After completing this chapter, you will be able to understand:

1. Page
2. AppBar
3. FloatingActionButton
4. NavigationBar
5. Text
6. Icon
7. Image
8. Column
9. Row
10. Stack
11. Container
12. Card
13. ListTile
14. CircleAvartar
15. NavgationDrawer
16. ListView
17. GridView
18. ElevatedButton
19. TextButton
20. IconButton
21. OutlinedButton
22. Radio
23. Checkbox
24. Switch
25. Tabs
26. BottomSheet
27. TextField
28. Page View
29. Dropdown
30. Snackbar
31. AlertDialog
32. MenuBar
33. ProgressBar
34. FilePicker
35. Audio
36. Video
37. GestureDetector

Page

Every Flet app starts with a page that adds other controls, serving as the root of the Flet app. A page is automatically generated at the onset of a new user session. Page can contain various controls and even other pages. Utilizing properties such as add, insert and remove.

In Flet, the Column layout is applied automatically to pages by default. This layout facilitates controls to be added vertically, following a top-to-down approach.

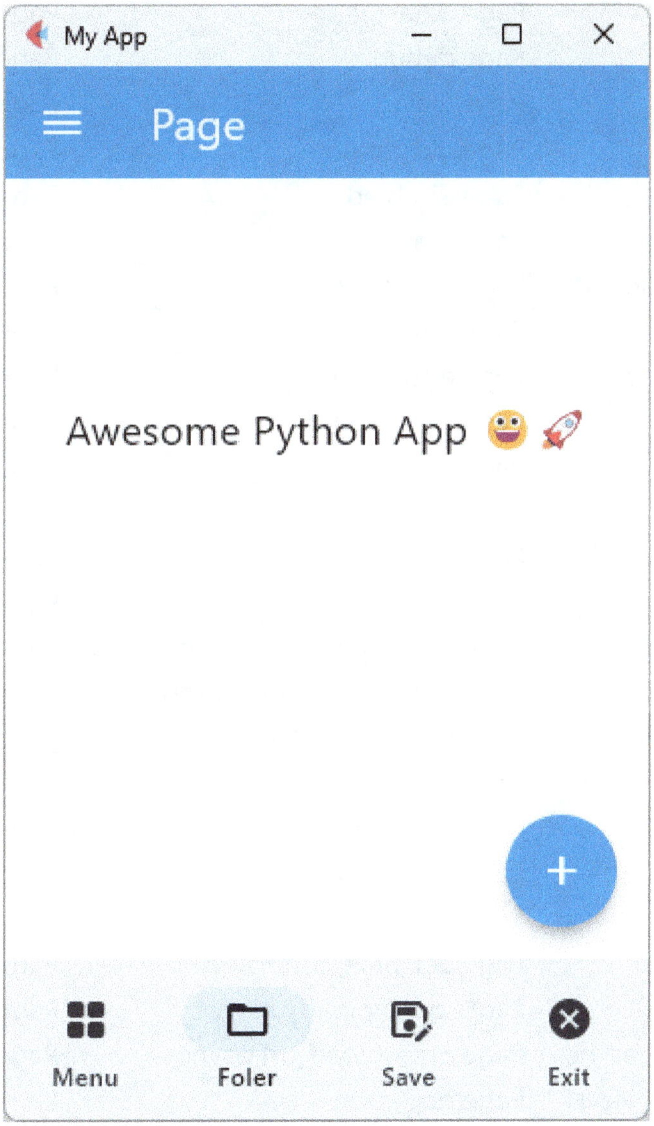

Available Methods

Method	Method	Method
Page.add	Page.close_in_app_web_view_async	Page.go_async
Page.add_async	Page.col	Page.height
Page.adaptive	Page.connection	Page.horizontal_alignment
Page.appbar	Page.controls	Page.index
Page.auth	Page.copy_attrs	Page.insert
Page.auto_scroll	Page.dark_theme	Page.insert_async
Page.banner	Page.data	Page.invoke_method
Page.before_update	Page.debug	Page.invoke_method_async
Page.bgcolor	Page.dialog	Page.is_isolated
Page.bottom_appbar	Page.did_mount	Page.launch_url
Page.bottom_sheet	Page.disabled	Page.launch_url_async
Page.build	Page.drawer	Page.login
Page.build_update_commands	Page.end_drawer	Page.login_async
Page.can_launch_url	Page.error	Page.logout
Page.can_launch_url_async	Page.error_async	Page.logout_async
Page.clean	Page.event_handlers	Page.loop
Page.clean_async	Page.executor	Page.media
Page.client_ip	Page.expand	Page.name
Page.client_storage	Page.expand_loose	Page.navigation_bar
Page.client_user_agent	Page.expires_at	Page.on_app_lifecycle_state
Page.close_banner	Page.fetch_page_details_async	Page.on_close
Page.close_banner_async	Page.floating_action_button	Page.on_connect
Page.close_bottom_sheet	Page.floating_action_button_location	Page.on_disconnect
Page.close_bottom_sheet_async	Page.fonts	Page.on_error
Page.close_dialog	Page.get_clipboard	Page.on_event_async
Page.close_dialog_async	Page.get_clipboard_async	Page.on_keyboard_event
Page.close_drawer	Page.get_control	Page.on_login
Page.close_drawer_async	Page.get_next_control_id	Page.on_logout
Page.close_end_drawer	Pagte.get_upload_url	Page.on_media_change
Page.close_end_drawer_async	Page.get_upload_url_async	Page.on_resize
Page.close_in_app_web_view	Page.go	Page.on_route_change

Method	Method	Method
Page.on_scroll	Page.show_bottom_sheet_async	Page.window_center_async
Page.on_scroll_interval	Page.show_dialog	Page.window_close
Page.on_view_pop	Page.show_dialog_async	Page.window_close_async
Page.on_window_event	Page.show_drawer	Page.window_destroy
Page.opacity	Page.show_drawer_async	Page.window_destroy_async
Page.overlay	Page.show_end_drawer	Page.window_focused
Page.padding	Page.show_end_drawer_async	Page.window_frameless
Page.page	Page.show_semantics_debugger	Page.window_full_screen
Page.platform	Page.show_snack_bar	Page.window_height
Page.platform_brightness	Page.show_snack_bar_async	Page.window_left
Page.pubsub	Page.snack_bar	Page.window_max_height
Page.pwa	Page.snapshot	Page.window_max_width
Page.query	Page.spacing	Page.window_maximizable
Page.remove	Page.splash	page.window_maximized
Page.remove_async	Page.theme	Page.window_min_height
Page.remove_at	Page.theme_mode	Page.window_min_width
Page.remove_at_async	Page.title	Page.window_minimizable
Page.route	Page.tooltip	Page.window_minimized
Page.rtl	Page.uid	Page.window_movable
Page.run_task	Page.update	Page.window_opacity
Page.run_thread	Page.update_async	Page.window_prevent_close
Page.scroll	Page.url	Page.window_progress_bar
Page.scroll_to	Page.vertical_alignment	Page.window_resizable
Page.scroll_to_async	Page.views	Page.window_skip_task_bar
Page.session	Page.visible	Page.window_title_bar_hidden
Page.session_id	Page.web	Page.window_to_front
Page.set_clipboard	Page.width	Page.window_to_front_async
Page.set_clipboard_async	Page.will_unmount	Page.window_top
Page.show_banner	Page.window_always_on_top	Page.window_visible
Page.show_banner_async	Page.window_bgcolor	Page.window_width
Page.show_bottom_sheet	Page.window_center	

Properties

title = text

The page.title sets the title or the name of your application, typically found at the top of the application.

```
page.title = "My App"
```

bgcolor = string

The **page.bgcolor** enables the user to set the background or page color. In Flet, colors can have values of hex or named color.

```
page.bgcolor = flet.colors.BLUE  #Color name
page.bgcolor = '#ff0000'  #Hex color
```

add(control)

The **page.add()** method is used to add controls to the page. The arrangement and priority of the controls depend on the developer.

```
text = flet.Text("Hello Pythonist")
page.add(text)
page.update()
```


add_async(control)

The **page.add_async()** method adds control or a set of controls asynchronously.

```
text = flet.Text("Hello World!")
page.add_async(text)
page.update()
```

#Note

- The page.update() simply updates changes made in adding controls.
- You may encounter other properties with the async suffix. These properties are used to perform asynchronous operations.

Python

```
#myfletapp.py

import flet

def main(page: flet.Page):
    page.title = "My App"
    page.bgcolor = flet.colors.WHITE

    text = flet.Text("my text")
    button = flet.ElevatedButton("click me")

    page.add(text)
    page.add(button)
    page.update()

flet.app(target = main)
```

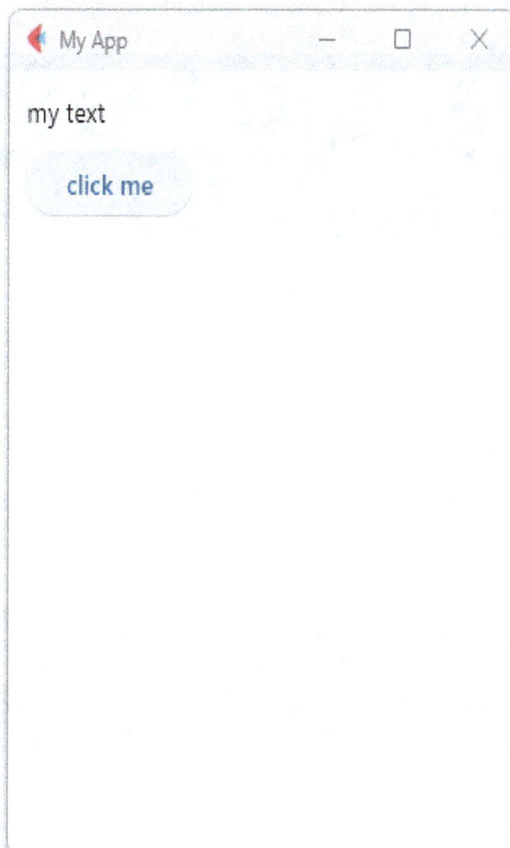

remove(control)

The **page.remove()** method removes a specified control from the list of controls.

```
text = flet.Text("my text")
page.add(text)
page.remove(text)
```

remove_at(index)

The **page.remove_at()** method removes a control at the specified index from the list of controls.

```
page.remove_at(2)
```

insert(index, control)

The **page.insert()** provides a way to add a control to the existing list of page controls at a particular position by specifying the index.

```
text = flet.Text("my text")
page.insert(3, text)
page.update()
```

clean()

The **page.clean()** method clears the entire list of controls from the page, returning a blank page.

```
page.clean()
page.update()
```


Controls

The **page.controls** property provides a way to manage a list of controls on the page by providing properties for adding, removing, inserting, copying, reversing, sorting, accessing, and counting controls.

controls.append(control)

The **page.controls.append()** serves as an alternative way to use the **page.add()** property for adding controls to the page.

```
but = flet.OutlinedButton('click me')
page.controls.append(but)
page.update()
```

```python
#myfletapp.py

import flet

def main(page: flet.Page):
    page.title = "My App"
    page.bgcolor = "#EEEEEE"

    but1 = flet.OutlinedButton('click 1')
    but2 = flet.OutlinedButton('click 2')
    but3 = flet.OutlinedButton('click 3')

    page.add(but1, but2, but3)

    text = flet.Text('awesome app')
    page.insert(1, text)
    page.update()

flet.app(target = main)
```

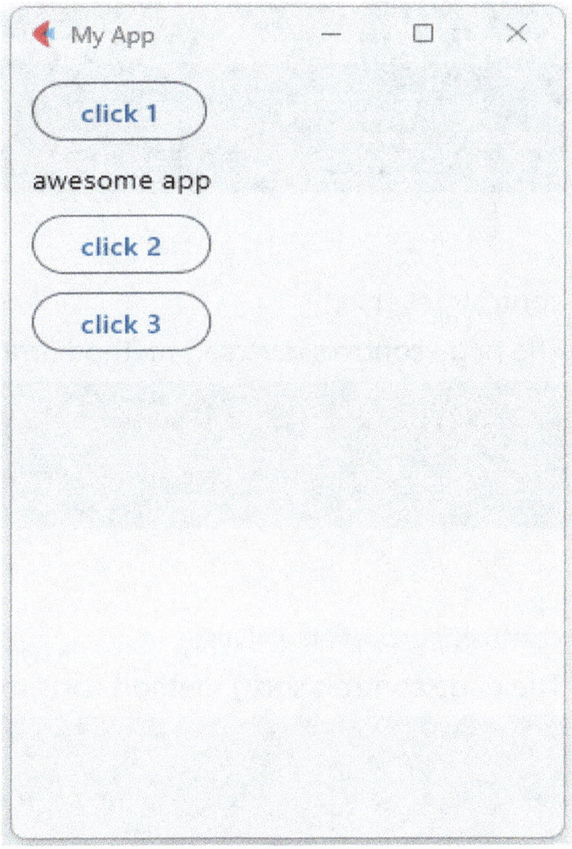

controls.remove(control)

The **page.controls.remove()** method is used for removing a specified control from the page.

```
but = flet.OutlinedButton('click me')
page.controls.remove(but)
page.update()
```

controls.pop()

The **page.controls.pop()** is used for removing the last control from the list of controls.

```
page.controls.pop()
page.update()
```

controls.insert(index, control)

The **page.controls.insert()** method inserts a particular control at a specific index on the page.

```
text = flet.Text('my text')
page.controls.pop(3, text)
page.update()
```

controls.reverse()

The **page.controls.reverse()** method arranges the list of controls in reverse order.

```
page.controls.reverse()
page.update()
```

controls.sort(reverse=False)

The **page.controls.sort()** method sorts the list of controls.

```
page.controls.sort()
page.update()
```


controls.index(control, start, stop)

The **page.controls.index()** method returns the index of a control from the list of controls within a given range.

```
text = flet.Text('my text')
page.controls.index(text, 0, 4)
```

controls.count(control)

The **page.controls.count()** method returns the number of occurrences of a particular control.

```
page.controls.count()
```

controls.copy()

The **page.controls.copy()** method returns a shallow copy of the list of controls on the page.

```
page.controls.copy()
```

Python

```
#myfletapp.py

import flet

def main(page: flet.Page):
    page.title = "My App"
    page.bgcolor = "#FFFFFF"

    text1 = flet.Text('Flet 1')
    text2 = flet.Text('Flet 2')
    text3 = flet.Text('Flet 3')

    page.controls.append(text1)
    page.controls.append(text2)
    page.controls.append(text3)

    page.controls.reverse()
    page.update()

flet.app(target = main)
```

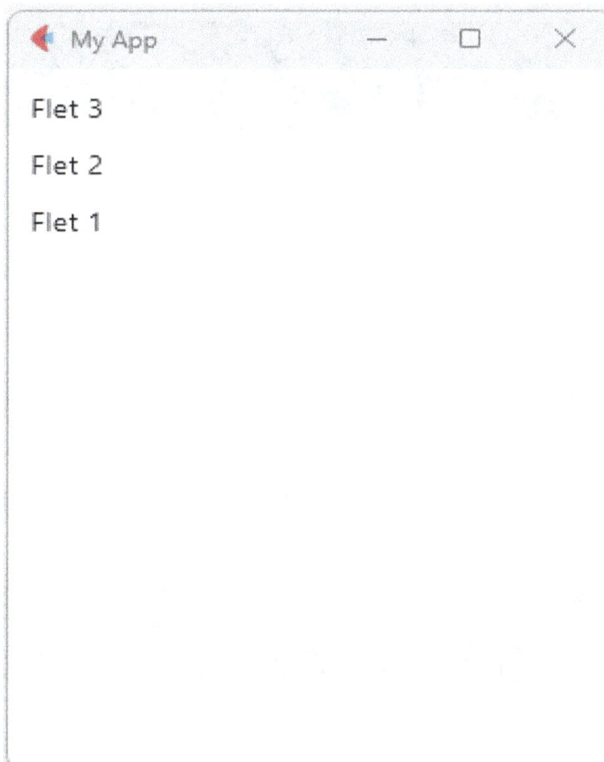

auto_scroll = True

The **page.auto_scroll** property is a Boolean method. When set to True, it automatically moves the scrollbar position to the end when children are updated.

```
page.auto_scroll = True
```

scroll = scrollMode

The **page.scroll** property allows for vertical scrolling to prevent page content (controls) from overflowing. There are five **ScrollMode** options available:

1. None (default): The row is non-scrollable, and its content could overflow.
2. AUTO: Scrolling is enabled, and the scrollbar is only shown when scrolling occurs.
3. ADAPTIVE: Scrolling is enabled, and the scrollbar is always shown when running the app as web or desktop.
4. ALWAYS: Scrolling is enabled, and the scrollbar is always shown.
5. HIDDEN: Scrolling is enabled, but the scrollbar is always hidden.

```
page.scroll = flet.ScrollMode.ALWAYS
```

padding = int

The **page.padding** property creates space between controls and their edges. The default value is 10 pixels from each side (top, bottom, right, left).

```
page.padding = 30
```


appbar = AppBar() #

The **page.appbar** adds an AppBar to the page. The AppBar is a control that bears the title, leading control, and action buttons.

```
page.appbar = flet.AppBar()
page.update()
```

banner = Banner() #

The **page.banner** adds the Banner control to the page.

```
page.banner = flet.Banner()
page.update()
```

drawer = NavigationDrawer() #

The **page.drawer** implements the drawer control. The drawer is a control bearing a list of menus that slides from the start edge of the page.

```
page.drawer = flet.NavigationDrawer()
page.update()
```

floating_action_button = FloatingActionButton() #

The **page.floating_action_button** returns a floating button control on top of the page content.

```
page.floating_action_button = flet.FloatingActionButton()
page.update()
```

Light up

AppBar, Banner, NavigationDrawer and FloatingActionsButton are controls that will be studied in upcoming chapters.

height and width

The **page.height** and **page.width** return the height and width of the page, respectively. These do not consider outside boundaries.

```
height = page.height
width = page.width
```

window_height and window_width

The **page.window_height** and **page.window_width** are similar to height and width, but these return the actual height and width of the application or windows.

```
height = page.window_height
width = page.window_width
```

platform

The **page.platform** returns the operating system on which the application is running. Values could be PagePlatform.WINDOWS, PagePlatform.LINUX, PagePlatform.ANDROID, PagePlatform.IOS

window_bgcolor = string (Desktop only)

The **page.window_bgcolor** sets the background color of the application window.

```
page.window_bgcolor = flet.colors.RED
```

window_left = int (Desktop only)

The **page.window_left** sets the horizontal position of the window application on the desktop screen .

window_top = int (Desktop only)

The **page.window_top** sets the vertical position of the window application on the desktop screen.

window_center() (Desktop only)
The **page.window_center()** position the application at the center of the screen.

window_close()
The **page.window_close()** method closes the window.

window_resizable = bool (Desktop only)
The **page.window_resizable** is set to True to make the window application resizable.

window_minimizable = bool (Desktop only)
The **page.window_minimizable** is set to True to allow the application to be minimized.

window_maximizable = bool (Desktop only)
The **page.window_maximizable** is set to True to allow the application to be maximized.

window_movable = bool (Desktop only)
The **page.window_movable** is set to False to prevent the application from changing its position.

window_visible = bool (Desktop only)
The **page.window_visible** is set to False to hide the application from view.

Events

on_resize = function
The **page.on_resize** fires when the application is resized.

```
def resized():
    print("size changed")

page.on_resize = resized()
page.update()
```


on_close = function

The **page.on_close** fires when the application is closed.

```
def closed():
    print("closed")

page.on_close = close()
page.update()
```

Other Methods

show_banner(banner = flet.Banner())

The **page.show_banner()** is used to display the banner at the top of the page.

```
page.show_banner(banner=flet.Banner())
```

show_bottom_sheet(bottom = flet.BottomSheet())

The **page.show_bottom_sheet()** method displays the bottom sheet.

```
page.show_bottom_sheet(bottom_sheet = flet.BottomSheet())
```

show_dialog(dialog = flet.AlertDialog() #)

The **page.show_dialog()** method displays dialog on the page.

```
page.show_dialog(dialog = flet.AlertDialog())
```


show_drawer(drawer = flet.NavigationDrawer() #)
The **page.show_drawer()** method displays the application drawer.

```
page.show_drawer(drawer = flet.NavigationDrawer())
```

show_snack_bar(snack_bar = flet.SnackBar()#)
The **page.show_snack_bar()** method displays the snackbar. The snackbar is a panel that displays a piece of message at the bottom of the application when an event occurs.

```
page.show_snack_bar(snack_bar = flet.SnackBar(content= flet.Text('Hello')))
```

close_bottom_sheet
The **page.close_bottom_sheet()** closes the active bottom sheet.

```
page.close_bottom_sheet()
```

close_banner
The **page.close_banner()** closes the active banner.

```
page.close_banner()
```

close_drawer
The **page.close_drawer()** closes the application drawer.

```
page.close_drawer()
```

get_clipboard
The **page.get_clipboard()** gets the last text value saved to the clipboard.

```
page.get_clipboard()
```


Page Summary

A page is the root of all controls that host other controls. It adds controls using a top-to-bottom approach. The default layout is the Column layout.

Keywords

Column
NavigationDrawer
FloatingActionButton
Banner
BottomSheet
NavigationBar
SnackBar

Discussion

1. Differentiate between page.add_sync() and page.add().
2. Find more about page.overlay().
3. What is the difference between clean and clean_async.
4. Learn more about page.go and page.go_async.
5. Find the difference between insert and insert_async.

Common Properties

Flet Controls offer various properties and methods for customization, some unique to specific controls while others are shared among all. Common methods are uniformly applied across controls. Here are some common methods and their application approach.

Property	Value	Property	Value
key	string	col	int
ref	Ref	opacity	float
height	float	scale	int
width	float	offset	Offset
top	float	aspect_ratio	int
bottom	float	data	Any
right	float	rtl	bool
left	Ref	tooltip	str
rotate	float	animate_opacity	AnimationValue
alignment	Alignment	animate_offset	AnimationValue
visible	bool	animate_size	AnimationValue
disabled	bool	animate_position	AnimationValue
expand	bool	animate_rotation	AnimationValue
expand_lose	bool	animate_scale	AnimationValue
adaptive	bool	on_animation_end	AnimationValue

key = string
In Flet, a key is an identifier for a Control, allowing Flet to uniquely identify and track them. Keys are used for control state management, efficient control updates, and handling rendering.

ref = flet.Ref
In Flet **ref** is reference to a specific control or element within the UI hierarchy.

height = float
The **height** property is utilized to set the vertical dimension of the control.

width = float
The **width** property sets the horizontal dimension of the control.

top = float
This property is used to set the distance of the control from the top of the Stack control.

bottom = float
The bottom sets the distance from the bottom edge of the control to the bottom of a Stack control.

right = float
The distance that the child's right edge is inset from the right of the edge. It works only in Stack controls.

left = float
The distance that the child's left edge is inset from the left of the stack. It is effective inside Stack only.

adaptive = true
It is the ability of a control to adjust its appearance or behavior based on the device's characteristics, such as screen size, orientation and platform.

rotate = float
The **rotate** property turns control around an axis. It requires float value.

disabled = bool
Every control has disabled property which is False by default. Disabled property is mostly used with data entry controls like TextField, Dropdown, Checkbox and buttons.

```
text = flet.Text(
        'Hello World!',
        height=100,
        width= 200,
        disabled= True,
        adaptive= True
    )
```


data = Any

Arbitrary data that can be attached to a control.

rtl = bool

The right to left (rtl) property applies right alignment or changes the direction of the text from right to left when set to true.

```
flet.Text(
  rtl= True
)
```

visible = bool

Setting visible to False completely prevents control (and all its children if any) from rendering on a page canvas. Thus, control is hidden. Every **control** has visible property set to True by default.

tooltip = string

A textual display that provides information about a control and its purpose.

expand = bool

This property determines whether the stack should expand to fill its parent. If set to true, the stack will grow to fill the available space.

opacity = float

The **opacity** defines the degree of visibility of a control

offset = flet.Offset(x, y)

The **offset** property sets the initial position of a control where the **x** determines the horizontal axis and **y** determines the vertical axis.

tooltip = string

The **tooltip** adds an extra information to a control which is only visible when that control gains focus.

AppBar

The **AppBar** is a control situated at the top of each page, typically bearing the page title and buttons that trigger various actions. It commonly incudes the drawer buttons, navigation buttons and action buttons.

Available Methods

Property	Value	Property	Value
leading	control	bgcolor	string
leading_width	float	automatically_imply_leading	bool
title	control	elevation	float
center_title	bool	action	List[control]
toolbar_height	float	color	string

leading = control

The **leading** is the control at the left side of the **AppBar**, often comprises buttons represented by icons.

```
page.appbar = flet.AppBar(
 leading = flet.IconButton(icon=flet.icons.MENU)
 )
```

title = control

The **title** property specifies the title of the page within the app.

```
page.appbar = flet.AppBar(
    title = flet.Text('AppBar'),
 )
```

leading_width = float

The **leading_width** sets the width or space between the leading control and the title.

```
page.appbar = flet.AppBar(
 leading_width = 100,
 )
```

center_title = bool

When the **center_title** is set to True, the AppBar's title is aligned or positioned at the center.

```
page.appbar = flet.AppBar(
 center_title =True,
 )
```

automatically_imply_leading = bool

The **AppBar** has a leading control by default. When **automatically_imply_leading** is set to False, Flet removes the leading control.

```
page.appbar = flet.AppBar(
automatically_imply_leading = False,
 )
```


elevation = int

The **elevation** property adds shadow effect to AppBar control.

```
page.appbar = flet.AppBar (
 elevation = 10
)
```

color = string

The **color** property applies color to the title, leading control and actions controls.

```
page.appbar = flet.AppBar(
    color = flet.colors.WHITE,
)
```

bgcolor = string

The **bgcolor** specifies the background color of the AppBar.

```
page.appbar = flet.AppBar(
    bgcolor = flet.colors.BLUE,
)
```

actions = List[controls]

The **actions** property is a list of controls, usually consisting of buttons intended for specific actions.

```
page.appbar = flet.AppBar(

    actions= [
        flet.IconButton(
            icon = flet.icons.NOTIFICATIONS,
            on_click = noti_fun  #A callback function
        ),
        flet.IconButton(
            icon = flet.icons.ACCOUNT_CIRCLE_OUTLINED,
            on_click = account_fun #A callback function
        )
    ]
)
```


Python *Code 1.00*

```python
import flet

def main(page: flet.Page):
    page.title = "My App"
    page.bgcolor = "#DDDDDD"
    page.padding = flet.padding.only(left=50, top=50)

    def fun1():
        pass
    def fun2():
        pass
    def fun3():
        pass

    page.appbar = flet.AppBar(
       leading= flet.IconButton(
           icon= flet.icons.ARROW_BACK,
           on_click = fun1()
           ),
       title = flet.Text('AppBar'),
       color = flet.colors.WHITE,
       bgcolor = flet.colors.TEAL,

       actions = [
            flet.IconButton(
               icon = flet.icons.ALARM_ON_OUTLINED,
               on_click= fun2()
           ),
            flet.IconButton(
               icon = flet.icons.IMAGE_OUTLINED,
               on_click= fun3()
           )
       ]
    )
    page.update()

flet.app(target = main)
```

Lighten

When implementing flet.NavigationDrawer, the AppBar's leading icon is automatically set to the drawer icon (usually represented as menu icon).

Page Summary

The AppBar control provides a consistent navigation and title area at the top of the screen in Flet applications.

- The AppBar is the horizontal control typically found on top of the page.
- The AppBar bears the title of the app.
- It has a leading control by default.

Keywords

elevation
leading
actions
IconButton

Discussion

1. Create an AppBar with a red background.
2. Differenciate between AppBar and BottomAppBar?
3. Where do you think BottomAppBar would be positioned?
4. What is the main role of the AppBar?
5. Why is the AppBar always positioned on top of the page?
6. How can the AppBar control be customized to include additional actions or controls, such as search bars or dropdown menus?
7. What strategies can be used to handle dynamic content in the AppBar, such as changing titles or icons based on user interactions?

FloatingActionButton

In Flet, a **FloatingActionButton**, as the name implies, is a floating button positioned above the page content, usually remaining fixed in place and not scrolling with the page content. This button is consistently available for immediate use.

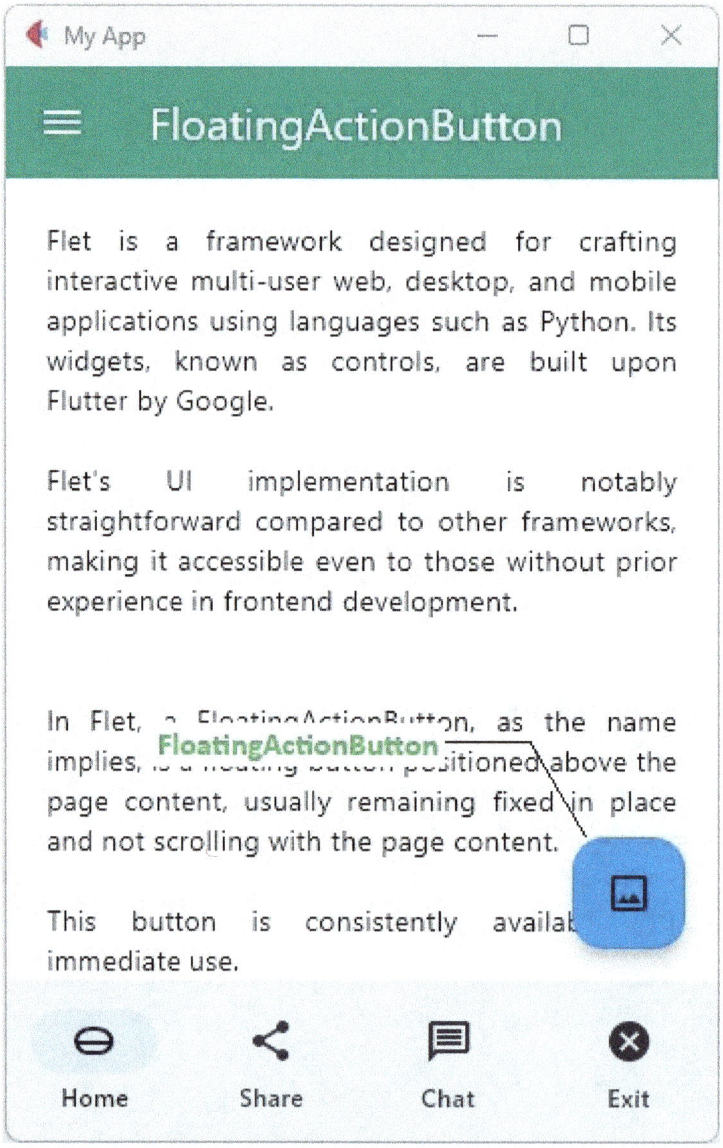

Available Methods

Property	Value	Property	Value
text	string	shape	OutlineShape
icon	string	autofocus	bool
bgcolor	string	mini	bool
control	Control	url	string
on_click	function	url_target	string

text = string

The **text** property adds text to the **FloatingActionButton**.

```
page.floating_action_button = flet.FloatingActionButton(
  text= "Add Image"
  )
```

icon = string

This property specifies the icon of the **FloatingActionButton**.

```
page.floating_action_button = flet.FloatingActionButton(
icon= flet.icons.IMAGE_OUTLINED,
  )
```

bgcolor = string

The **bgcolor** sets the background color to a desired color.

```
page.floating_action_button = flet.FloatingActionButton(
bgcolor=flet.colors.BLUE,
  )
```

content = Control

The **content** property replaces the FloatingActionButton's icon and text with a control.

```
page.floating_action_button = flet.FloatingActionButton(
  content= flet.Icon(
           name= flet.icons.ACCOUNT_CIRCLE_OUTLINED)
  )
```


on_click = function

The **on_click** property defines the purpose of the button by assigning it to a function which trigger an action.

```
def floating_fun(e):
    print('floating clicked')

page.floating_action_button = flet.FloatingActionButton(
    on_click= floating_fun,
)
```

shape= flet.OutlinedShape

The **shape** defines the appearance of the **FloatingActionButton** by specifying the shape. The available shapes include:

- flet.RoundedRectangleBorder(type: str, radius: int)
- flet.StadiumBorder(type: str)
- flet.CircleBorder(type: str)
- flet.BeveledRectangleBorder(type: str, radius: int)
- flet.OutlinedBorder(type: str)
- flet.ContinousRectangleBorder(type: str, radius: int)

```
page.floating_action_button = flet.FloatingActionButton(
  shape= flet.CircleBorder()

)
```

autofocus = bool

Setting the **autofocus** property to True ensures that the button remains active or focused at all times.

```
page.floating_action_button = flet.FloatingActionButton(
autofocus= True
)
```


url = string

The **url** property assigns a web URL to the button, enabling it to open a web page when clicked.

```
    page.floating_action_button = flet.FloatingActionButton(
    url="https://www.google.com"
    )
```

mini = bool

Setting the **mini** property to True keeps the button small in size.

```
    page.floating_action_button = flet.FloatingActionButton(
    mini = True
    )
```

Python *Code 1.1.0*

```
import flet

def main(page: flet.Page):
    page.title = "My App"
    page.bgcolor = 'white'
    page.padding = flet.padding.all(10)

    page.appbar = flet.AppBar(
      color= flet.colors.WHITE,
      title= flet.Text("Learning Hub"),
      bgcolor= "teal"
    )
    page.drawer = flet.NavigationDrawer()

    page.floating_action_button = flet.FloatingActionButton(
         bgcolor=flet.colors.BLUE,
         icon= flet.icons.SEARCH_OUTLINED,
         text= "Search",
         autofocus= True,
         shape = flet.RoundedRectangleBorder(radius=20),
         on_click = lambda _: print("searching"),
    )
    Image = flet.Image(src="C:\\image16.jpg", height= 350,
                       width = page.width, fit = flet.ImageFit.FILL)


    col = flet.Column( width= page.width,height= page.height,
        alignment= flet.MainAxisAlignment.START,
        horizontal_alignment= flet.CrossAxisAlignment.CENTER,
        controls=[image]
    )

    page.add(col)
    page.update()

flet.app(target = main)
```

My App
Learning Hub
Search

Page Summary

The FloatingActionButton control is a round button typically used for primary or high-importance actions in a Flet app, such as adding a new item or starting a new task.

- The FloatingActionButton does not scroll with the page.
- The FloatingActionButton is necessary for a situation where the same action or function is common in every page.

Keywords

Image
ImageFit
Column

Discussion

1. In what scenarios would you use a FloatingActionButton versus a regular raised button or an IconButton?
2. How can you customize the appearance of the FloatingActionButton, such as changing its background color or shape?
3. What are some best practices for positioning the FloatingActionButton within a Flet layout, especially when dealing with different screen sizes or orientations?
4. Discuss about the function of **FloatingActionButtonLocation**.

NavigationBar

The Flet **NavigationBar** serves as a convenient panel located at the bottom of the application, housing a series of buttons (NavigationDestination), each designated to execute specific functions for user ease. These buttons are visually represented by icons accompanied by descriptive labels, ensuring intuitive navigation. Users can readily identify active or focused buttons through indicators such as border, change in background color, icon appearance, label color or size adjustments.

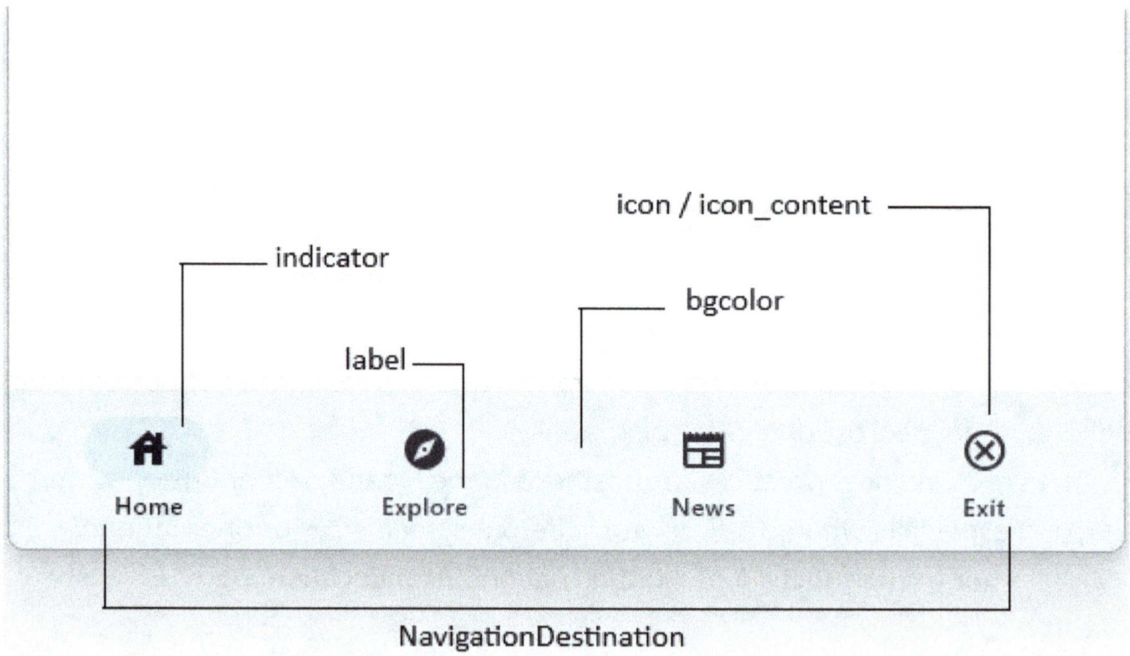

Available Methods

Property	Value	Property	Value
destinations	List[NavigationDestination]	indicator_color	string
selected_index	int	indicator_shape	OutlinedBorder
bgcolor	string	surface_tint_color	string
label_behavior	NavigationBarLabelBehavior	border	Border
elevation	int	on_change	function
shadow_color	string		

destinations = [flet.NavigationDestination]

The **destinations** defines the list of button items within the navigation bar.

```
    page.navigation_bar = flet.NavigationBar(
        destinations= [
            flet.NavigationDestination(
                icon=flet.icons.HOUSE_SHARP,
                label='Home'
            ),
        ])
```

NavigationDestination

The Flet NavigationDestination component facilitates the creation of button items, allowing for the specification of icons and their corresponding labels, along with changes upon selection. The available options include:

- label
- icon
- icon_content
- selected_icon
- selected_icon_content
- tooltip
- ref

label = string

The **label** assigns meaning to the icon, typically positioned beneath it, aiding in user comprehension.

```
 flet.NavigationDestination(
                label='Exit',
 )
```

icon = string

The **icon** method specifies the icon serving as button.

```
flet.NavigationDestination(
          icon=flet.icons.CANCEL_OUTLINED,
    )
```

icon_content = flet.Icon

Alternatively, **icon_content** offers a different method for utilizing icons through the **flet.Icon().**

```
    flet.NavigationDestination(
                icon_content= flet.Icon(
                     name= flet.icons.MENU
          ))
```

selected_icon = string

The **selected_icon** method specifies the icon to display when the item is selected or clicked.

```
    flet.NavigationDestination(
                label='Favorite',
                icon=flet.icons.FAVORITE_OUTLINE,
                selected_icon=flet.icons.FAVORITE,
           ),
```

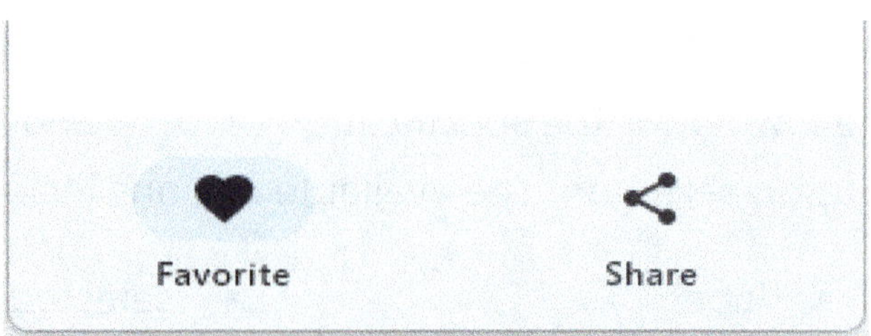

selected_index = int

This is the index of the currently selected button item in the NavigationDestination List. The **selected_index** is None if no destination is selected.

```
page.navigation_bar = flet.NavigationBar(
    selected_index= 2,
)
```

bgcolor = string

The **bgcolor** property specifies the background color of the navigation bar.

```
page.navigation_bar = flet.NavigationBar(
     bgcolor = flet.colors.GREY
)
```

label_behavior = flet.NavigationBarLabelBehavior

The **label_behavior** specifies how the label should behave within the navigation bar. Labels can always be shown, hidden or shown only when it's selected. The available methods include:

- ALWAYS_SHOW
- ALWAYS_HIDE
- ONLY_SHOW_SELECTED

```
page.navigation_bar = flet.NavigationBar(
     label_behavior= flet.NavigationBarLabelBehavior.ALWAYS_SHOW
)
```

elevation = int

The **elevation** property sets the navigation bar's background shadow effect.

```
page.navigation_bar = flet.NavigationBar(
     elevation = 5
)
```

shadow_color = string

The **shadow_color** specifies the navigation bar's shadow color.

```
page.navigation_bar = flet.NavigationBar(
     shadow_color= flet.colors.BLACK
)
```


indicator_color = string

The **indicator_color** specifies the color of the indicator, highlighting the active navigation button.

```
page.navigation_bar = flet.NavigationBar(
    indicator_color = flet.colors.BLACK
)
```

surface_tint_color = string

The **surface_tint_color** applies faded color to the navigation bar.

```
page.navigation_bar = flet.NavigationBar(
    surface_tint_color= flet.colors.BLACK
)
```

Python Code 1.2.0

```python
import flet

def main(page: flet.Page):
    page.title = "My App"
    page.bgcolor = "#FFFFFF"
    page.padding = flet.padding.only(left=70, top=50)

    page.navigation_bar = flet.NavigationBar(
        elevation= 30,
        shadow_color=flet.colors.GREY,
        surface_tint_color= flet.colors.BLUE,
        indicator_color= flet.colors.GREEN,
        destinations= [
            flet.NavigationDestination(
                label='Dashboard',
                icon=flet.icons.DASHBOARD,
            ),
            flet.NavigationDestination(
                label='Web',
                icon=flet.icons.WEB,
            ),
            flet.NavigationDestination(
                label='News',
                icon=flet.icons.NEWSPAPER,
            )],)

    page.update()
flet.app(target = main)
```

on_change = function

The **on_change** assigns a function which is called on button item selection.

```
page.navigation_bar = flet.NavigationBar(
        on_change = buttonSelected()
)
```

indicator_shape= flet.OutlinedShape

The **indicator_shape** defines the appearance of the indicator by specifying the shape. The available shapes include

- flet.RoundedRectangleBorder(type: str, radius: int)
- flet.StadiumBorder(type: str)
- flet.CircleBorder(type: str)
- flet.BeveledRectangleBorder(type: str, radius: int)
- flet.OutlinedBorder(type: str)
- flet.ContinousRectangleBorder(type: str, radius: int)

```
page.navigation_bar = flet.NavigationBar(
    indicator_shape= flet.CircleBorder()
)
```

border = flet.border.all, flet.border.only

The **border** sets boundary edges of the navigation bar.

```
page.navigation_bar = flet.NavigationBar(
    border= flet.border.all(
        width= 3,
        color= flet.colors.RED
      ))
```


Python *Code 1.2.1*

```python
import flet

def main(page: flet.Page):
    page.title = "My App"
    page.bgcolor = "#FFFFFF"
    page.padding = flet.padding.all(value=100)

    def buttonSelected(e):
        page.controls.clear()
        index = e.control.selected_index

        if index == 0:
            page.add(flet.Text('Dashboard'))

        if index == 1:
            page.add(flet.Text('Web'))

        if index == 2:
            page.add(flet.Text('News'))

    page.navigation_bar = flet.NavigationBar(
       surface_tint_color= flet.colors.BLUE,
       indicator_color= flet.colors.GREEN,
       on_change = buttonSelected,
       destinations= [
            flet.NavigationDestination(
               label='Dashboard',
               icon=flet.icons.DASHBOARD,
           ),
             flet.NavigationDestination(
               label='Web',
               icon=flet.icons.WEB,
           ),
             flet.NavigationDestination(
               label='News',
               icon=flet.icons.NEWSPAPER,
           )
       ],)

    page.update()

flet.app(target = main)
```

My App
Dashboard
Dashboard
Web
News

My App
News
Dashboard
Web
News

Page Summary

The NavigationBar control allows for easy navigation between different screens or pages within a Flet app, typically displayed at the bottom of the screen.

Keywords

surface_tint_color
labels
indicator

Discussion

1. How can you implement a bottom navigation bar with multiple tabs using the NavigationBar control, and how does it handle navigation state management?
2. What are some common patterns for handling navigation transitions or animations between screens in a Flet app with a NavigationBar?
3. Can you discuss the trade-offs between using a bottom navigation bar versus other navigation patterns, such as tabs or drawer menus, in terms of user experience and app design?
4. Discuss about the **CupertinoNavigationBar**.

Text

The text control is utilized to display textual information within a Flet application. It presents text content in the form of a string, allowing developers to convey information, messages, or instructions to users effectively.

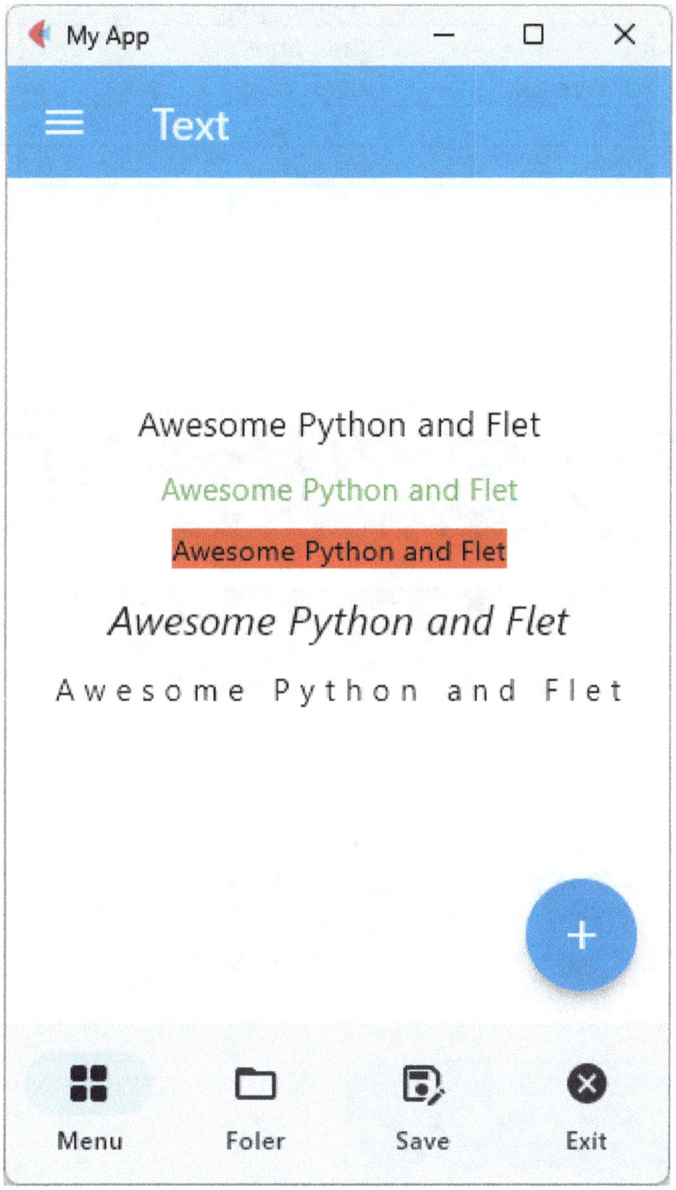

Available Methods

Property	Value	Property	Value
value	strings	bgcolor	string
spans	ListTextSpan	semantics_label	string
text_align	string	style	TextStyle
font_family	string	theme_style	TextThemeStyle
size	int	max_lines	int
weight	FontWeight	overflow	TextOverflow
italic	bool	selectable	bool
color	string	no_wrap	bool

value = string

The **value** property represents the actual content of the text control.

```
flet.Text(
    value = "Awesome Flet"
)
```

Or

```
flet.Text(
    "Awesome Flet"
)
```

color = string

This property is used to set the color of the text.

```
text = flet.Text("Awesome Python", color="green")
page.add(text)
```

bgcolor = string
The **bgcolor** property is used to give the text a background color.

```
text = flet.Text(
  value = "Awesome Python",
  bgcolor= "teal"
 )
```

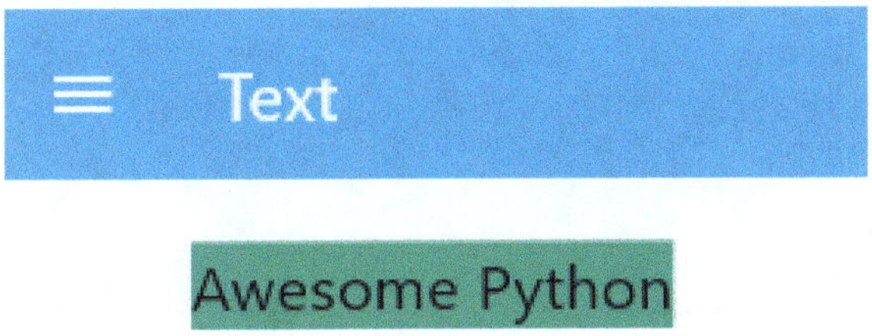

size = int
This property sets the size of the text. It requires an integer value.

```
flet.Text(
  value = "Hello World!",
  size = 20
)
```

weight = flet.FontWeight
This applies boldness or thickness to text. The values include BOLD and NORMAL.

```
text = flet.Text(
  value = "Awesome Python",
  weight= flet.FontWeight.BOLD
)
```

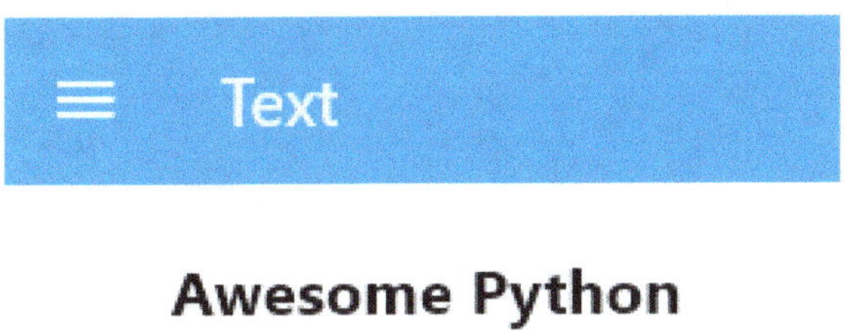

italic = bool

This property is used to give text an italic or slant style. It requires Boolean value.

```
flet.Text(
  value = "Hello World!",
  italic= True
)
```

max_lines = int

The **max_lines** restricts text to a number of lines it can occupy. It requires integer value.

```
flet.Text(
  max_lines = 2
)
```

rotate = float

The **rotate** property turns text around an axis. It requires float value

```
flet.Text(
  "Hello World!"
  rotate = 0.60
)
```

opacity = float
The **opacity** sets the level or degree of text visibility.

```
flet.Text(
  value = "Awesome Flet",
  opacity= 0.5
)
```

rtl = bool
The right to left (**rtl**) property applies right alignment or changes the direction of the text from left-to-right to right-to-left when set to True.

```
flet.Text(
  rtl= True
)
```

text_align = flet.TextAlign
The **text_align** is utilize to apply alignment to text, offering options such as LEFT, RIGHT, CENTER, END, JUSTIFY, START and NONE.

```
flet.Text(
  text_align = flet.TextAlign.JUSTIFY
)
```

overflow = flet.TextOverFlow
This property is utilized to handle text when it exceeds the space available for it to be displayed. The available options include FADE, VISIBLE, CLIP, ELLIPSIS and NONE.

```
flet.Text(
  overflow = flet.TextOverflow.VISIBLE
)
```

font_family = string
The **font_family** property sets font for styling the text.

```
flet.Text(
  font_family ="consolas"
)
```


flet.TextStyle()

style = flet.TextStyle
This property provides a very simple and alternative ways to format or style text. There are several methods available for styling text which include:

- size
- height
- italic
- weight
- decoration
- decoration_color
- decoration_tickness
- decoration_style
- font_family
- bgcolor
- color
- shadow
- letter_spacing
- foreground

decoration = flet.TextDecoration
This property decorates text with lines. Decoration values include UNDERLINE, OVERLINE, LINE_THROUGH and NONE.

```
text = flet.Text("Awesome Python",
    style = flet.TextStyle(decoration= flet.TextDecoration.OVERLINE)
  )
```

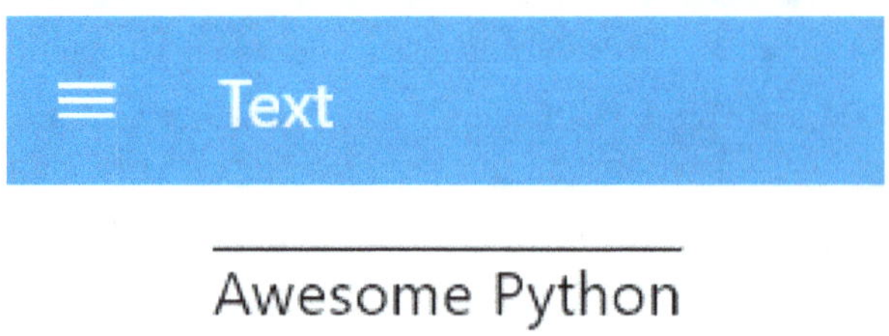

decoration_style = flet.TextDecorationStyle
After applying decoration to text, **decoration_style** let you choose line styles to apply to the text. This includes WAVY, DASHED, DOTTED, DOUBLE and SOLID.

```
text = flet.Text(
    "Awesome Python",
     style = flet.TextStyle(
             decoration= flet.TextDecoration.UNDERLINE,
             decoration_style= flet.TextDecorationStyle.WAVY)
            )
```


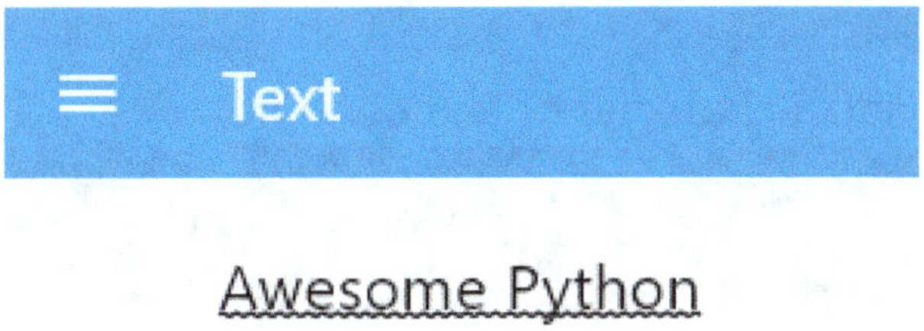

decoration_thickness = int

This property is utilized to add boldness or thickness to decorated lines.

```
flet.Text(
    style = flet.TextStyle(decoration_thickness = 5)
)
```

shadow = flet.BoxShadow

The **shadow** property adds shadow effects to text enhancing its visual appeal. It offers various methods which include

- color
- offset
- blur_radius
- spread_radius
- blur_style

```
text = flet.Text(
     value = "Happy Coding",
     style= flet.TextStyle( size= 20,
            shadow= flet.BoxShadow(
                color=flet.colors.GREY,
                spread_radius= 20,
                blur_radius= 4,
                offset= flet.Offset(3, 5),
                blur_style= flet.ShadowBlurStyle.SOLID)
     ),
 )
```

letter_spacing

This property sets the spaces between the individual character of text content.

```
text = flet.Text("Awesome Python",
                 style=flet.TextStyle(letter_spacing= 8)
    )
```

flet.TextSpan()

spans =[*flet.TextSpan]

The **spans** method offers a means to enrich text content by applying textual effects to individual segments within the text.

```
text = flet.Text(
  value = "Python",
  spans = [
    flet.TextSpan( text="\tJava", style= flet.TextStyle(color= "Orange")),
    flet.TextSpan( text="\tPython", style= flet.TextStyle(color= "Green")),
    flet.TextSpan( text="\tC++", style= flet.TextStyle(color= "Red")),
    flet.TextSpan( text="\tDart", style= flet.TextStyle(color="Blue")),
    ]
  )
```

Page Summary

The Text control displays a string of text with customizable styling options such as font size, color, and alignment.

Keywords

BoxShadow
TextSpan
TextStyle

Discussion

1. How do you handle text overflow or text wrapping in the Text control when dealing with long strings of text?
2. What are some advanced text styling options available in Flet, such as custom fonts, text shadows, or text decorations?

Icon

In Flet **Icons** are small images or graphics utilized to convey meaning within messages or information. Flet offers a variety of icons organized into different categories such as navigation, files, communication, media, social, action device, alert, miscellaneous and more, facilitating intuitive visual communication within applications.

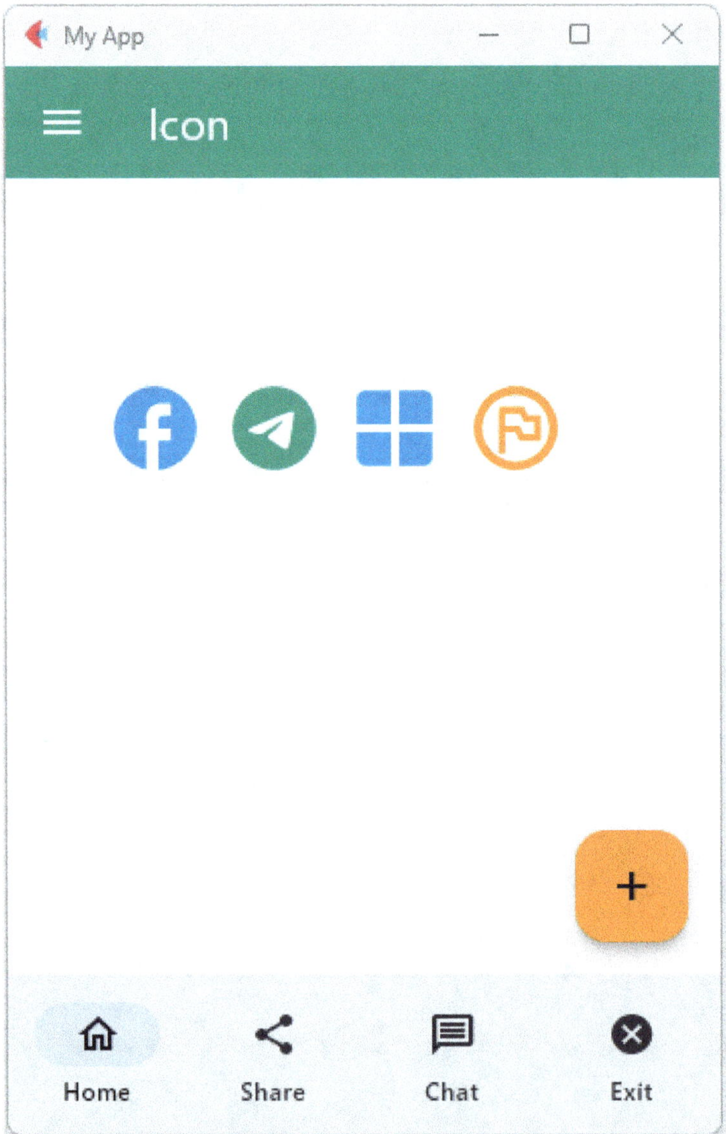

Available Methods

Property	Value	Property	Value
name	string	color	string
semantic_label	string	size	float

name = string
The **name** property specifies the icon name.

```
flet.Icon(
    name= flet.icons.FACEBOOK_OUTLINED,
  ),
```

color = string
The **color** property adds color to the icon.

```
flet.Icon(
    name= flet.icons.FACEBOOK_OUTLINED,
    color=flet.colors.BLUE,
  ),
```

size = int
This property sets the size of the text. It requires an integer value.

```
flet.Icon(
    name= flet.icons.FACEBOOK_OUTLINED,
    size=50
  ),
```

semantic_lable = string
This property adds a descriptive identifier to the Icon control.

```
flet.Icon(
    name= flet.icons.FACEBOOK_OUTLINED,
    semantics_label= flet.Text('facebook')
  ),
```


Python Code 1.3.0

```python
import flet

def main(page: flet.Page):
    page.title = "My App"
    page.bgcolor = 'white'
    page.padding = flet.padding.all(20)

    page.appbar = flet.AppBar(
      color= flet.colors.WHITE,
      title= flet.Text("Icon"),
      bgcolor= "cyan"
    )
    page.drawer = flet.NavigationDrawer()


    nav = flet.NavigationBar(
        destinations= [
            flet.NavigationDestination(
                 label="Menu",
                 icon=flet.icons.GRID_VIEW_ROUNDED
            ),
            flet.NavigationDestination(
                label="Foler",
                icon=flet.icons.FOLDER_OPEN_OUTLINED
             ),
             flet.NavigationDestination(
                label="Save",
                icon=flet.icons.SAVE_AS_OUTLINED
             ),
            flet.NavigationDestination(
                label="Exit",
                icon=flet.icons.CANCEL
            )
    ])

    page.navigation_bar = nav
    page.floating_action_button = flet.FloatingActionButton(
             content=flet.Icon(name= flet.icons.ADD, color="white"),
             bgcolor= "BLUE", shape=flet.CircleBorder())


    page.add(flet.Icon(name= flet.icons.FACEBOOK_ROUNDED, color= "Green"),)
    page.add(flet.Icon(name= flet.icons.ALARM, color= "Blue"),)
    page.add(flet.Icon(name= flet.icons.SETTINGS, color= "teal"),)
    page.add(flet.Icon(name= flet.icons.WIDGETS, color= "teal"))
    page.add(flet.Icon(name= flet.icons.WIFI, color= "Red"))

    #page.add(col)
    page.vertical_alignment = flet.MainAxisAlignment.CENTER
    page.update()

flet.app(target = main)
```


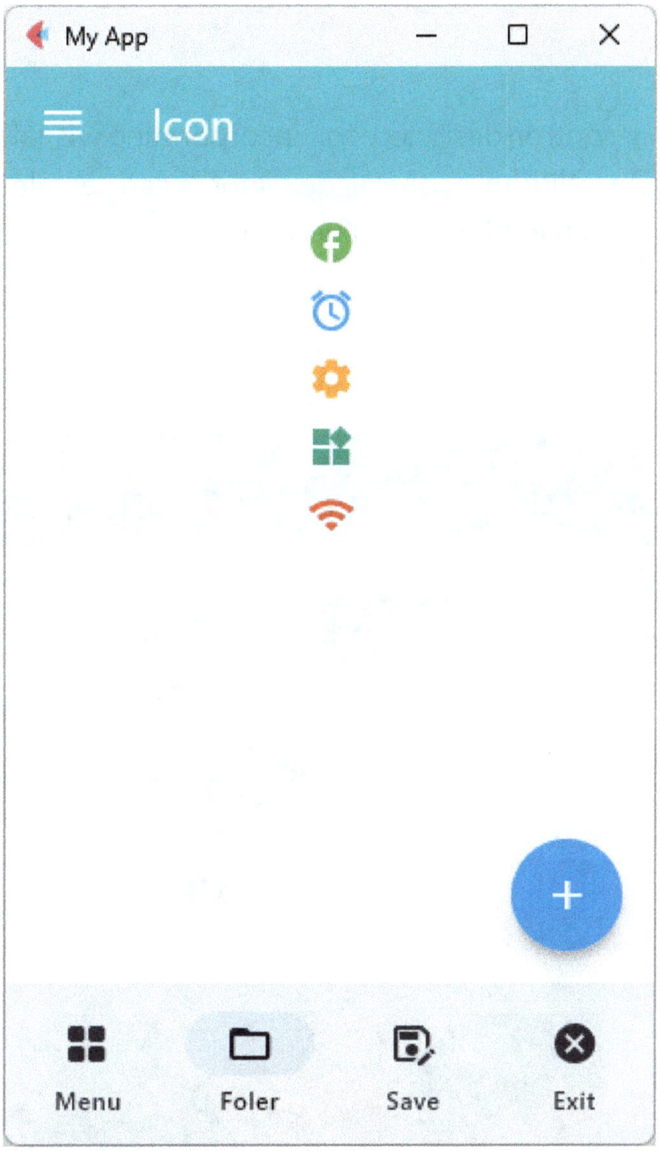
My App
Icon
Menu
Foler
Save
Exit

Image

Flet **Image** serves as a control designed for incorporating visual content, specifically pictures, into applications. With this control, developers can seamlessly integrate images to enhance the visual appeal and functionality of their user interfaces.

Available Methods

Property	Value	Property	Value
src	string	border_radius	BorderRadiusValue
src_base64	string	color	string
error_content	Control	color_blend_mode	BlendMode
repeat	ImageRepeat	semantic_label	string
fit	ImageFit	gapless_playback	bool

src = string

The **src** property specifies the path to the image file.

```
    flet.Image(
        src= "C:\\Users\\mypic.jpg",
    )
```

error_content = Control

The **error_content** adds control to replace the image if an error occurs whiles loading the image.

```
image = flet.Image(
  src= "C:\\Users\\mypic.jpg",
  error_content= flet.Text("Loading Failed"),
)
```

repeat = flet.ImageRepeat

The **repeat** property defines how the image should repeat both horizontally and vertically. The available options incude

- REPEAT,
- REPEAT_X,
- REPEAT_Y
- NO_REPEAT

```
image = flet.Image(
  src= "C:\\Users\\mypic.jpg",
  repeat= flet.ImageRepeat.REPEAT_X
)
```


REPEAT_Y

REPEAT_X

fit = flet.ImageFit

The **image_fit** specifies how an image behaves within its layout, offering options such as CONTAIN, COVER, FILL, FIT_HEIGHT, FIT_WIDTH, NONE and SCALE_DOWN.

```
image = flet.Image(
  src= "C:\\Users\\mypic.jpg",
  fit= flet.ImageFit.CONTAIN,
)
```

border_radius

The **border_radius** property defines the curvature at the meeting point of two adjacent edges of the image.

border_radius = flet.border_radius.all

```
image = flet.Image(
  src= "C:\\Users\\mypic.jpg",
  border_radius= flet.border_radius.all(20)

)
```


border_radius = flet.border_radius.only

```
    image = flet.Image(
      src= "C:\\Users\\child.jpg",
      border_radius= flet.border_radius.only(
            top_left= 5,
            top_right= 3,
            bottom_left= 2,
            bottom_right=5
        ))
```

Python **Code 1.4.0**

```python
import flet

def main(page: flet.Page):
    page.title = "My App"
    page.bgcolor = "#FFFFFF"
    page.padding = flet.padding.only(left=80, top=50)

    image1 = flet.Image(
      src= "C:\\Users\\child.png",
      fit= flet.ImageFit.CONTAIN,
      height= 200,
      width= 200,
      border_radius= flet.border_radius.all(50)
    )

    image2 = flet.Image(
      src= src= "C:\\Users\\design.jpg",
      fit= flet.ImageFit.CONTAIN,
      height= 200,
      width= 200,
      border_radius= flet.border_radius.only(
            top_left= 50,
            top_right= 0,
            bottom_left= 0,
            bottom_right=50
        ))
    page.add(image1, image2)
    page.update()

flet.app(target = main)
```

color = string

The **color** property is used to set color of the image. It is mostly used with the **color_blend_mode** property to add effects to the image.

```
image = flet.Image(
    src= "C:\\Users\\mypic.jpg",
    color=flet.colors.RED,
)
```

color_blend_mode = flet.BlendMode

The **color_blend_mode** property specifies how the color of one layer interacts with the colors of underlying layers. The available methods of the BlendMode include,

DARKEN	DIFFERENCE	DST_OVER	LUMINOSITY	PLUS	SRC_A_TOP
CLEAR	DST	EXCLUSION	MODULATE	SATURATION	SRC_IN
COLOR	DST_A_TOP	HARD_LIGHT	MULTIPLY	SCREEN	SRC_OUT
COLOR_BURN	DST_IN	HUE	NONE	SOFT_LIGHT	SRC_OVER
COLOR_DODGE	DST_OUT	LIGHTEN	OVERLAY	SRC	XOR

```
image = flet.Image(
  color=flet.colors.RED,
  color_blend_mode = flet.BlendMode.HUE
)
```

Python **Code 1.4.1**

```python
import flet

def main(page: flet.Page):
    page.title = "My App"
    page.bgcolor = "#FFFFFF"
    page.padding = flet.padding.only(left=70, top=50)

    image1 = flet.Image(
      src= "C:\\Users\\child.jpg",
      fit= flet.ImageFit.CONTAIN,
      height= 150,
      width= 150,
      color=flet.colors.RED,
      color_blend_mode=flet.BlendMode.HUE
    )
    image2 = flet.Image(
      src= "C:\\Users\\child.jpg",
      fit= flet.ImageFit.CONTAIN,
      height= 150,
      width= 150,
      color=flet.colors.BLUE,
      color_blend_mode=flet.BlendMode.DARKEN
    )
    page.add(image1,image2)
    page.update()

flet.app(target = main)
```

My App

Page Summary

The Image control displays an image from various sources such as the network, assets, or the device's file system, with options for resizing, cropping, and caching.

Keywords

ImageFit
hue
border_radius

Discussion

1. How can you efficiently load and display images from the network in a Flet app while ensuring a smooth user experience?
2. What are some techniques for optimizing image loading and caching to reduce network bandwidth and improve app performance?
3. Can you explain the difference between the fit and alignment properties in the Image control, and how they affect image layout and display?

Column

The **Column** control organizes or arranges its children in a vertical orientation, arranging them one below the other. The children are list of controls including other column controls.

Available Methods

Property	Value	Property	Value
controls	List[Controls]	expand	bool
alignment	MainAxisAlignment	expand_lose	bool
horizontal_alignmnet	CrossAxisAlignment	col	int
spacing	int	offset	Offset
tight	bool	aspect_ratio	int
wrap	bool	auto_scroll	bool
run_spacing	int	key	string

controls = [*Controls]
The **controls** method represents a list of children or controls.

```
controls =[
    flet.Text('Text1'),
    flet.Text('Text2'),
]
```

wrap = bool
When **wrap** is True, the column will distribute child controls into additional columns(runs) if they exceed the available space of a single column.

```
flet.Column(
    wrap=True
)
```

spacing = int
This method sets the horizonal space or gap between the children.

```
flet.Column(
    spacing= 50,
)
```


alignment = MainAxisAlignment

The **alignment** method controls the alignment of child Controls along the main axis of a layout. There are several options available:

START	CENTER	SPACE_BETWEEN
END	SPACE_AROUND	SPACE_EVENLY
NONE		

```
flet.Column(
    alignment= flet.MainAxisAlignment.CENTER,
)
```

START

END

CENTER

SPACE_AROUND

SPACE_BETWEEN

SPACE_EVENLY

horizontal_alignment = CrossAxisAlignment

The **horizontal_alignment** method controls the alignment of child controls along the cross axis of a layout. There are several options available:

START
END
CENTER
BASELINE
STRETCH
NONE

```
flet.Column(
    horizontal_alignment=flet.CrossAxisAlignment.START,
)
```

START

END

CENTER

STRETCH

run_spacing = int

The **run_spacing** creates spaces between the runs(columns) when wrap is True. By default, it has a value of 10.

```
flet.Column(
    wrap=True,
    run_spacing= 50,
)
```


tight = bool

This property defines the vertical space allocation. By default, it's set to False, meaning all available space is allocated to the children.

```
flet.Column(
    tight = True
)
```

scrollbar = bool

The **scrollbar** is set to true if it should automatically move its position to the end when children are updated.

```
flet.Column(
    scrollbar = True
)
```

scroll = flet.ScrollMode

The **scroll** method enables vertical scrolling for the Column to prevent its content from overflowing the available space. The default value is None. The available options include.

None(default): the column is non-scrollable and its content could overflow.

AUTO: scrolling is enabled and scroll bar is only shown when scrolling occurs.

ADAPTIVE: scrolling is enabled and scrollbar is always shown when running app as web or desktop.

ALWAYS: scrolling is enabled and scroll bar is always shown.

HIDDEN: scrolling is enabled, but scroll bar is always hidden.

```
flet.Column(
    scroll= flet.ScrollMode.ALWAYS
)
```


Events

The Column receives an instance of the **flet.OnScrollEvent** class with the following properties:

event_type: Describes the type of scroll event (start, update, end, user, over).

- start – control has started scrolling.
- update – control has changed its scroll position.
- end – control has stopped scrolling.
- user – user has changed the direction in which they are scrolling.
- over – control has not changed its scroll position because the change would have caused its scroll position to go outside its scroll bounds.

pixels: Current scroll position in logical pixels.
min_scroll_extent: Minimum in-range value for pixels.
max_scroll_extent: Maximum in-range value for pixels.
viewport_dimension: Extent of the viewport.
scroll_delta: Distance scrolled by the scrollable, set for update events.
direction: Direction of user scrolling (idle, forward, reverse), set for user events.
overscroll: Number of logical pixels the scrollable avoided scrolling, set for over events.
velocity: Velocity at which the **ScrollPosition** was changing when overscroll happened, set for over events.

```
    flet.Column(
        on_scroll = flet.OnScrollEvent(
            t=5,
            p=2,
            minse=10,
            maxse= 10,
            vd=10,
            sd=5,
            dir=1,
            os=6,
            v=20,
        )
)
```


Expanding Children

When a child Control is placed into a Column, it can be "expanded" to fill available space. Each Control has an expand property, which can be a Boolean (True for full space) or an integer specifying the "expand factor" to divide free space with other expanded child controls. Example:

```
column = flet.Column( width= page.width,height= 150,
  alignment= flet.MainAxisAlignment.START,
  horizontal_alignment= flet.CrossAxisAlignment.CENTER,

  controls=[
      flet.Container(height= 50, width=50, bgcolor= "blue"),
      flet.Container(expand=True, bgcolor= "orange"), #Expanded set to True
          ]
   )
```

Numeric expand factors distribute space accordingly, e.g., [1, 3, 1] for 20%, 60%, and 20% respectively:

```
flet.Column([
flet.Container(expand=1, content=flet.Text("Header")),
flet.Container(expand=3, content=flet.Text("Body")),
flet.Container(expand=1, content=flet.Text("Footer"))
])
```

Height calculation: child_height = (expand / sum(all_expands)) * 100%. If expand_loose is True, the child Control can vertically expand without requiring to fill all available space.

Python **Code 1.5.0**

```
import flet

def main(page: flet.Page):
    page.title = "My App"
    page.bgcolor = 'white'
    page.padding = flet.padding.all(10)


    page.appbar = flet.AppBar(
      color= flet.colors.WHITE,
      title= flet.Text("Column"),
      bgcolor= "#14171A"
    )
    page.drawer = flet.NavigationDrawer()


    nav = flet.NavigationBar(
        destinations= [
            flet.NavigationDestination(
                 label="Food",
                 icon=flet.icons.RICE_BOWL_OUTLINED
            ),
            flet.NavigationDestination(
                label="Cake",
                icon=flet.icons.CAKE_OUTLINED
             ),
             flet.NavigationDestination(
                label="Pizza",
                icon=flet.icons.LOCAL_PIZZA_OUTLINED
             ),
            flet.NavigationDestination(
                label="Exit",
                icon=flet.icons.CANCEL
            )
    ])

    page.navigation_bar = nav

    column = flet.Column( width= page.width,height= 150,
        alignment= flet.MainAxisAlignment.START,
        horizontal_alignment= flet.CrossAxisAlignment.CENTER,

        controls=[
          flet.Image(src="C:\\pizza.png", width= page.width, height=150),
          flet.Text("Ouch Pizza looks great", size= 20, font_family="Georgia"),
          flet.Image("C:\\Cupcakes.jpg", width= page.width, height=150),
          flet.Text("Cake for two", size= 20, font_family="Georgia"),
            ]
    )

    page.add(column)
    page.update()

flet.app(target = main)
```

My App
Column
Ouch Pizza looks great
Cake for two
Food
Cake
Pizza
Exit

Page Summary

The Column control arranges its children in a vertical array, allowing for easy organization of controls from top to bottom within a Flet layout.

Keywords

Container
border
pixels
expanded
horizontal_alignment

Discussion

1. How do you handle spacing and alignment between controls in a Column layout, especially when dealing with different screen sizes or orientations?
2. What are some strategies for creating responsive layouts with dynamic content in Column control?
3. Can you discuss the performance implications of nesting multiple Columns within each other versus using other layout control like Row or Flex?

Row

The **Row** control organizes or arranges its children in a horizontal orientation. The children are list of controls including row controls.

#Note

The method and properties available for the Column control are identical to those of the Row control.

Available Methods

Property	Value	Property	Value
controls	List[Controls]	bottom	int
alignment	MainAxisAlignment	expand	bool
vertical_alignmnet	CrossAxisAlignment	expand_lose	bool
spacing	int	col	int
tight	bool	offset	Offset
wrap	bool	aspect_ratio	int
run_spacing	int	auto_scroll	bool
ref	Ref	key	str

controls = [*Controls]

The **controls** method represents a list of children or controls.

```
        controls =[
            flet.Text('Text1'),
            flet.Text('Text2'),
        ]
```

wrap = bool

When **wrap** is True, the row will distribute child controls into additional row(runs) if they exceed the available space of a single row.

```
    flet.Row(
        wrap=True
    )
```

spacing = int

This method sets the horizontal space or gap between the children.

```
    flet.Row(
        spacing= 50,
    )
```


alignment = MainAxisAlignment

The **alignment** method controls the horizontal alignment of child controls along the main axis of a Row layout. There are several options available:

START
CENTER
SPACE_BETWEEN
END
SPACE_AROUND
SPACE_EVENLY
NONE

```
flet.Row(
    alignment= flet.MainAxisAlignment.CENTER,
)
```

START

END

CENTER

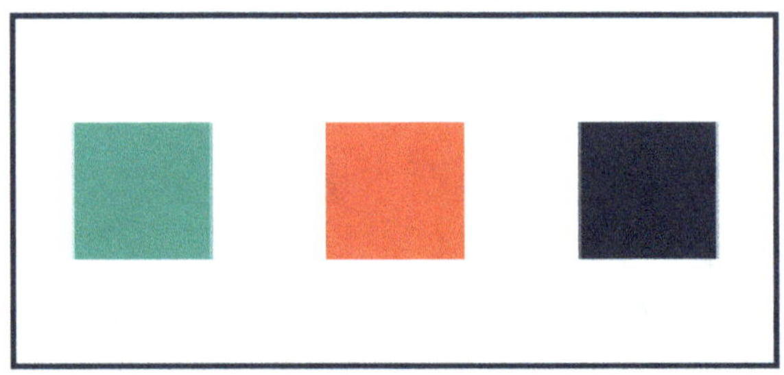

SPACE_AROUND

SPACE_BETWEEN

SPACE_EVENLY

vertical_alignment = CrossAxisAlignment

The **vertical_alignment** method controls the vertical alignment of child Controls within the row layout. There are several options available:

START	CENTER	STRETCH
END	BASELINE	NONE

```
flet.Row(
    vertical_alignment = flet.CrossAxisAlignment.START,
)
```

START

END

CENTER

STRETCH

run_spacing = int

The **run_spacing** creates spaces between the runs(rows) when wrap is True. By default, it has a value of 10.

```
flet.Row(
    wrap=True
    run_spacing= 50,
)
```


tight = bool

This property defines the vertical space allocation. By default, it's set to False, meaning all available space is allocated to the children.

```
flet.Row(
    tight = True
)
```

scrollbar = bool

The **scrollbar** is set to true if it should automatically move its position to the end when children are updated.

```
flet.Row(
    scrollbar = True
)
```

scroll = flet.ScrollMode

The **scroll** method enables horizontal scrolling for the Row to prevent its content from overflowing the available space. The default value is None. The available options include.

None(default): the row is non-scrollable and its content could overflow.

AUTO: scrolling is enabled and scroll bar is only shown when scrolling occurs.

ADAPTIVE: scrolling is enabled and scrollbar is always shown when running app as web or desktop.

ALWAYS: scrolling is enabled and scroll bar is always shown.

HIDDEN: scrolling is enabled, but scroll bar is always hidden.

```
flet.Row(
    scroll= flet.ScrollMode.ALWAYS
)
```


Events

The **on_scroll** event fires when the scroll position is altered by a user. The event handler receives an instance of the **flet.OnScrollEvent** class with the following properties:

event_type: Describes the type of scroll event (start, update, end, user, over).

- start – control has started scrolling.
- update – control has changed its scroll position.
- end – control has stopped scrolling.
- user – user has changed the direction in which they are scrolling.
- over – control has not changed its scroll position because the change would have caused its scroll position to go outside its scroll bounds.

pixels: Current scroll position in logical pixels.
min_scroll_extent: Minimum in-range value for pixels.
max_scroll_extent: Maximum in-range value for pixels.
viewport_dimension: Extent of the viewport.
scroll_delta: Distance scrolled by the scrollable, set for update events.
direction: Direction of user scrolling (idle, forward, reverse), set for user events.
overscroll: Number of logical pixels the scrollable avoided scrolling, set for over events.
velocity: Velocity at which the ScrollPosition was changing when overscroll happened, set for over events.

```
    flet.Row(
        on_scroll = flet.OnScrollEvent(
            t=5,
            p=2,
            minse=10,
            maxse= 10,
            vd=10,
            sd=5,
            dir=1,
            os=6,
            v=20,
        )
)
```


Expanding Children

When a child Control is placed into a Row, it can be "expanded" to fill available space. Each Control has an expand property, which can be a Boolean (True for full space) or an integer specifying the "expand factor" to divide free space with other expanded child controls. Example:

```
column = flet.Row( width= page.width,height= 150,
    alignment= flet.MainAxisAlignment.CENTER,
    vertical_alignment= flet.CrossAxisAlignment.CENTER,
    spacing=1,
    controls=[
        flet.Container(width=50, height=50, bgcolor="teal"),
        flet.Container(width=50, height=50, bgcolor="red", expand=True),
        flet.Container(width=50, height=50, bgcolor="#00334c"),
      ]
)
```

Numeric expand factors distribute space accordingly, e.g., [1, 3, 1] for 20%, 60%, and 20% respectively:

```
flet.Row([
flet.Container(expand=1, content=flet.Text("Header")),
flet.Container(expand=3, content=flet.Text("Body")),
flet.Container(expand=1, content=flet.Text("Footer"))
])
```

Width calculation: child_width = (expand / sum(all_expands)) * 100%. If expand_loose is True, the child Control can horizontally expand without requiring to fill all available space.

Python Code 1.5.0

```python
import flet

def main(page: flet.Page):
    page.title = "My App"
    page.bgcolor = 'white'
    page.padding = flet.padding.all(10)


    page.appbar = flet.AppBar(
      color= flet.colors.WHITE,
      title= flet.Text("Row"),
      bgcolor= "#14171A"
    )
    page.drawer = flet.NavigationDrawer()


    nav = flet.NavigationBar(
        destinations= [
            flet.NavigationDestination(
                 label="Food",
                 icon=flet.icons.RICE_BOWL_OUTLINED
            ),
            flet.NavigationDestination(
                label="Cake",
                icon=flet.icons.CAKE_OUTLINED
             ),
             flet.NavigationDestination(
                label="Pizza",
                icon=flet.icons.LOCAL_PIZZA_OUTLINED
             ),
            flet.NavigationDestination(
                label="Exit",
                icon=flet.icons.CANCEL
            )
    ])

    page.navigation_bar = nav


    row = flet.Row( width= page.width,height= 300,
        alignment= flet.MainAxisAlignment.CENTER,
        vertical_alignment= flet.CrossAxisAlignment.CENTER,
        scroll= flet.ScrollMode.ALWAYS,
        spacing=10,
        controls=[
          flet.Image(src="C:\\pizza.png", width= 150, height=150, fit=flet.ImageFit.FILL),
          flet.Image("C:\\Cupcakes.jpg", width= 150, height=150, fit=flet.ImageFit.FILL),

            ]
    )

    page.add(row)
    page.update()

flet.app(target = main)
```

My App
Row
Food
Cake
Pizza
Exit

Page Summary

The Row control arranges its children in a horizontal array, enabling the placement of controls from left to right within a Flet layout.

Keywords

Container
border
pixels
vertical_alignment
Expanded

Discussion

1. What strategies can you use to ensure that controls within a Row layout are responsive and adjust their size dynamically based on available screen space?
2. How do you handle alignment and spacing between controls in a Row layout, especially when dealing with different screen sizes or orientations?
3. Can you explain the difference between the **MainAxisAlignment** and **CrossAxisAlignment** properties in the Row control, and when each would be used?

Stack

The **Stack** is layout control that adds controls by placing one control over another. The Stack control allows it contents to use the **left**, **right**, **top** and **bottom** properties to position items.

Available Methods

Property	Value	Property	Value
controls	List[Controls]	top	float
clip_behavior	ClipBehavior	bottom	float
width	float	left	float
height	float	right	float
ref	Ref	expand	bool

controls = List[*Control]

A list of controls to be added to the stack. The controls are placed on top of each other according to their index in the list.

```
stack = flet.Stack(
    controls=[
      flet.Image(src="path\to\image"),
      flet.Text('Stack')
    ])
```

width = float

The **width** defines the horizontal dimension of the stack layout.

```
stack = flet.Stack(
    width= page.width,
    controls=[
      flet.Image(src="path\to\image"),
      flet.Text('Stack')
    ])
```

height = float

This property specifies the vertical dimension of the stack layout.

```
stack = flet.Stack(
    height= page.height,
    controls=[
      flet.Image(src="path\to\image"),
      flet.Text('Stack')
    ])
```


top = float

The **top** defines the distance from the top edge of the stack layout for a given control.

```
stack = flet.Stack(
    controls=[
      flet.Image(src="C:\\Users\\background.jpg"),
      flet.Image(
          src = "C:\\google.png", height=80, width=80,
          top = 120,
    )
    ])
```

bottom = float

The **bottom** defines the distance from the bottom edge of the stack layout for a given control

```
stack = flet.Stack(
    controls=[
      flet.Image(src="C:\\Users\\background.jpg"),
      flet.Image(
          src = "C:\\google.png", height=80, width=80,
          bottom = 100,
    )
    ])
```

left = float

The **left** defines the distance from the left edge of the stack layout for a given control.

```
stack = flet.Stack(
    controls=[
      flet.Image(src="C:\\Users\\background.jpg"),
      flet.Image(
          src = "C:\\google.png", height=80, width=80,
          left = 50,
    )
    ])
```

right = float

This defines the distance from the right edge of the stack layout for a given control.

```
stack = flet.Stack(
    controls=[
      flet.Image(src="C:\\Users\\background.jpg"),
      flet.Image(src = "C:\\google.png", height=80, width=80,
          right = 50,
    )
    ])
```

Python ●●● *Code 1.6.0*

```python
import flet

def main(page: flet.Page):
    page.title = "My App"
    page.bgcolor = 'white'
    page.padding = flet.padding.all(0)

    page.drawer = flet.NavigationDrawer()

    stack = flet.Stack(
        width=page.width,
        height=page.height,
        controls=[

          flet.Image(
              src="C:\\background.jpg",
              height=page.height-150,
              width=page.width,
              fit=flet.ImageFit.FILL
              ),

          flet.ListTile(
              leading= flet.Icon(name= flet.icons.GRID_VIEW_ROUNDED),
              title=flet.Text('Flet-Python'),
              trailing=  flet.Icon(name= flet.icons.NOTIFICATIONS_OUTLINED)
          ),
          flet.Text(
              "follow us",
               italic= True,
               top=160,
               left=150,
            ),

          flet.Row(
              top = 200,
              left = 100,
              controls=[
                  flet.Image(src="C:\\whatsapp.png", height= 30, width=30),
                  flet.Image(src="C:\\facebook.png", height= 30, width=30),
                  flet.Image(src="C:\\instagram.png", height= 30, width=30),
                  flet.Image(src="C:\\telegram.png", height= 30, width=30),
              ]
          )
        ])

    page.add(stack)
    page.update()

flet.app(target = main)
```

My App
Flet-Python
follow us

Page Summary

The Stack control allows for layering multiple controls on top of each other, facilitating complex layouts and designs in Flet apps.

Keywords

top
bottom
left
right

Discussion

1. How can you use the Stack control to create overlapping elements, such as overlays or floating action buttons?
2. What are some best practices for managing the order and positioning of controls within a Stack layout?
3. Can you discuss the performance implications of using the Stack control, especially when layering multiple controls with complex layouts?

Container

The **Container** component enables the decoration of a control with features such as background color and borders, while also providing options for positioning using **padding, margin**, and **alignment** properties.

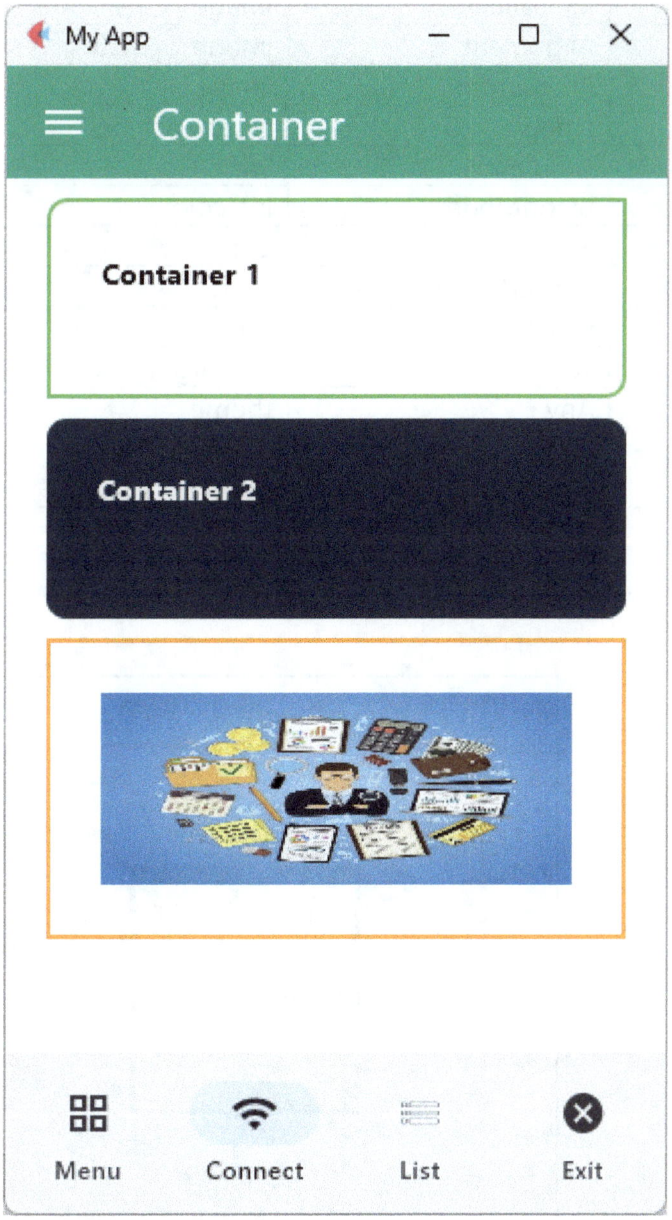

Available Methods

Property	Value	Property	Value
content	Control	image_repeat	ImageRepeat
padding	int, padding	image_fit	ImageFit
alignmnet	Alignment	image_opacity	float
margin	int, margin	shape	BoxShape
bgcolor	string	clip_behavior	ClipBehavior
gradient	Gradient	ink	bool
blend_mode	BlendMode	int_color	string
border	Border	blur	float
border_radius	BorderRadiusValue	shadow	BoxShadow
image_src	string	url	string
image_src_base64	string	url_target	string
on_long_press	Any	theme	Theme
on_hover	Any	theme_mode	ThemeMode
key	string	on_click	Any

Container

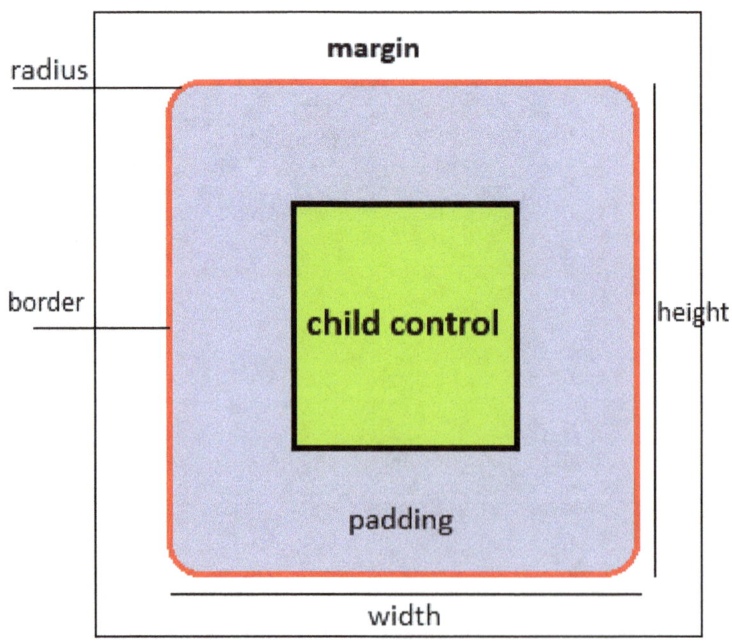

content = control

The **content** property adds a child control to the container.

```
container = flet.Container(
    content= flet.Icon(
        name=flet.icons.BOOK
    ),
)
```

padding = flet.padding

The **padding** method creates a space (top, right, bottom, left) between the child and the edges of the Container. Padding can be set with

- flet.padding.all(value=float)
- flet.padding.symmetric(vertical, horizontal)
- flet.padding.only(left=float, top=float, right=float, bottom=float)

```
container = flet.Container(
    content= flet.Text('Container'),
    padding= flet.padding.only(left=10, right=20)
)
```

margin = flet.margin

The **margin** method creates a space (top, right, bottom, left) between the Container and other controls within the page. Margin can be set with

- flet.margin.all(value=float)
- flet.margin.symmetric(vertical, horizontal)
- flet.margin.only(left=float, top=float, right=float, bottom=float)

```
container = flet.Container(
    content= flet.Text('Container'),
    margin= flet.margin.all(10)
)
```

bgcolor = string

The **bgcolor** property sets the background color of the container.

```
container = flet.Container(
    content= flet.Text('Container'),
    bgcolor= flet.colors.PURPLE
)
```


alignment = flet.alignment

The **alignment** method aligns the child control within the container. The alignment offers several options which include

center	bottom_center	bottom_left	bottom_right
center_left	center_right	top_center	top_right
top_left			

```
container = flet.Container(
    content= flet.Text('Container'),
    alignment= flet.alignment.center
)
```

shadow = flet.BoxShadow

The **shadow** property is used to add shadow effect to the container with preferred shadow color and degree.

```
container = flet.Container(
    shadow =  flet.BoxShadow(
        spread_radius=5,
        blur_radius= 6,
        color= flet.colors.GREY,
        offset= flet.Offset(2, 3)
    ),
    bgcolor= "blue",
    height= 100,
    width= page.width
)
```

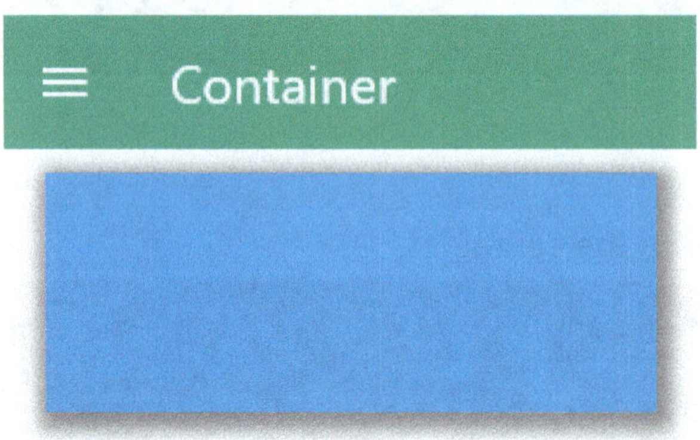

Gradient

The **gradient** property provides away to apply gradient background to containers. These gradients are composed of a series of colors. Flet supports three distinct types of gradients.

- LinearGradient:

  Linear gradients blend colors in a straight line, either horizontally, vertically or at an angle between two defined points.

- RadialGradient:

  This gradient type radiates outward from a central point, smoothly blending colors in a circular or elliptical pattern.

- SweepGradient:

  Sweep gradients blend colors in a circular pattern around center point, akin to radial gradient but without the transition to transparency in the center.

LinearGradient

Property	value	Property	value
colors	List[colors]	rotation	float
begin	alignment	type	string
tile_mode	GradientTileMode	stops	List[float]
end	alignment		

```
container = flet.Container(

    content= flet.Text('Container'),
    alignment= flet.alignment.center,
    height=100,
    width=page.width,
    gradient= flet.LinearGradient(
        colors= ["red", flet.colors.YELLOW, "green"],
        begin= flet.alignment.top_left,
        end=flet.alignment.bottom_left,
        tile_mode=flet.GradientTileMode.CLAMP
    ))
```

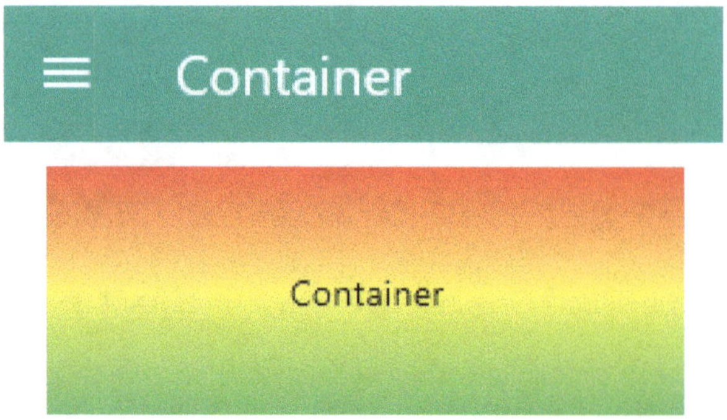

RadialGradient

Property	value	Property	value
colors	List[colors]	rotation	float
center	alignment	type	string
tile_mode	GradientTileMode	focal_radius	int
focal	alignment	stops	List[float]

```
container = flet.Container(
    content= flet.Text('Container'),
    alignment= flet.alignment.center,
    height=100,
    width=page.width,
    gradient= flet.RadialGradient(
        colors= [flet.colors.RED, flet.colors.YELLOW, flet.colors.GREEN],
        center= flet.alignment.center,
        focal= flet.alignment.bottom_right,
        radius= 3,
        tile_mode= flet.GradientTileMode.MIRROR
    )
)
```

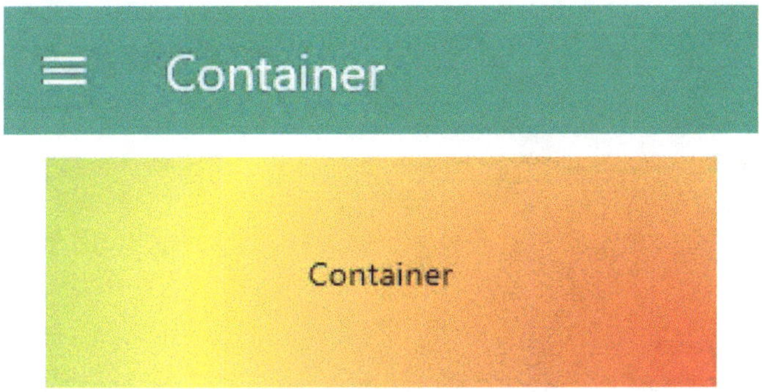

SweepGradient

Property	value	Property	value
colors	List[colors]	rotation	float
center	alignment	type	string
tile_mode	GradientTileMode	stop_angle	float
start_angle	float		

```
container = flet.Container(
    content= flet.Text('Container'),
    alignment= flet.alignment.center,
    height=100,
    width=page.width,
    gradient=  flet.SweepGradient(
       colors= ["red", "yellow", "green" ],
       center= flet.alignment.top_left,
       tile_mode= flet.GradientTileMode.CLAMP,
       start_angle= 0,
       end_angle= 0.58
    )
)
```

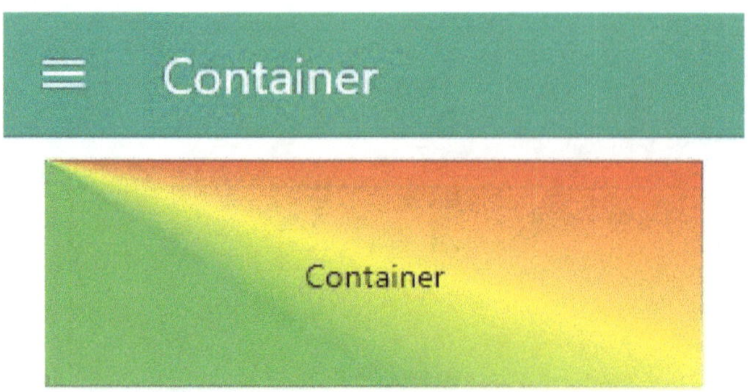

Border

In Flet, the Border feature allows customization of a container's outer edges. This customization can be achieved in two main ways: applying uniform border properties to all edges using **border.all**, or individually tailoring each edge by specifying BorderSide property.

border = flet.border

```
        border= flet.border.all(
            width= 3,
            color=flet.colors.BLUE
        )
```

or

```
        border= flet.border.only(
            left= flet.BorderSide(),
            right= flet.BorderSide(),
            bottom=flet.BorderSide(),
            top=flet.BorderSide(),
        )
```

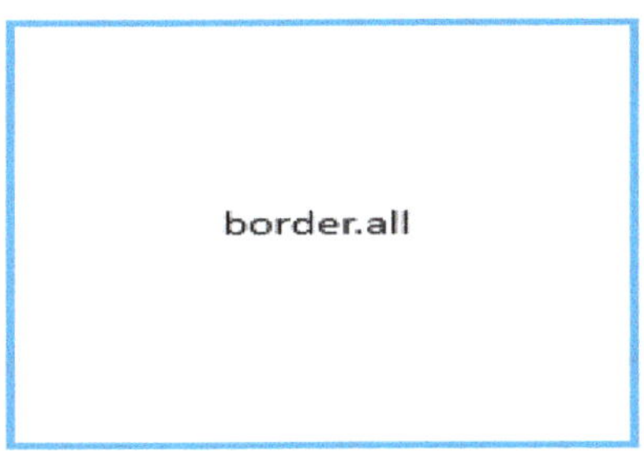

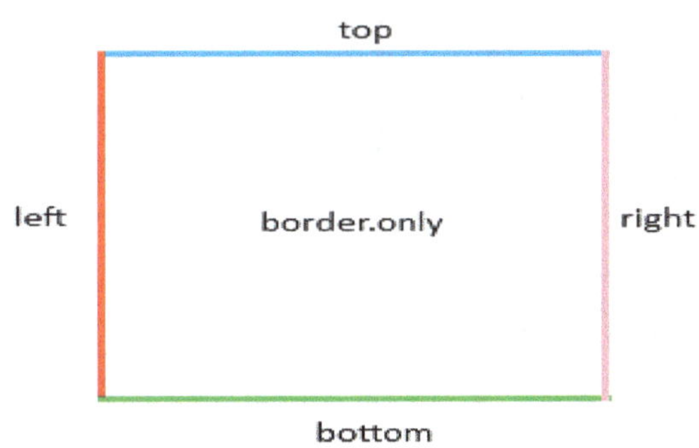

border = flet.Border

```
 border= flet.Border(
            left= flet.BorderSide(
                width= 2,
                color= flet.colors.GREEN
            ),
            right= flet.BorderSide(
                width=3,
                color=flet.colors.RED
            ))
```


border_radius

The **border_radius** property defines the curvature at the meeting point of two adjacent edges. It is only visible when the border property is implemented.

border_radius = flet.border_radius

```
border_radius= flet.border_radius.all(
        value= 5
    )
```

or

```
border_radius= flet.border_radius.only(
        top_left= 5,
        top_right= 10,
        bottom_left= 6,
        bottom_right=3
    )
```

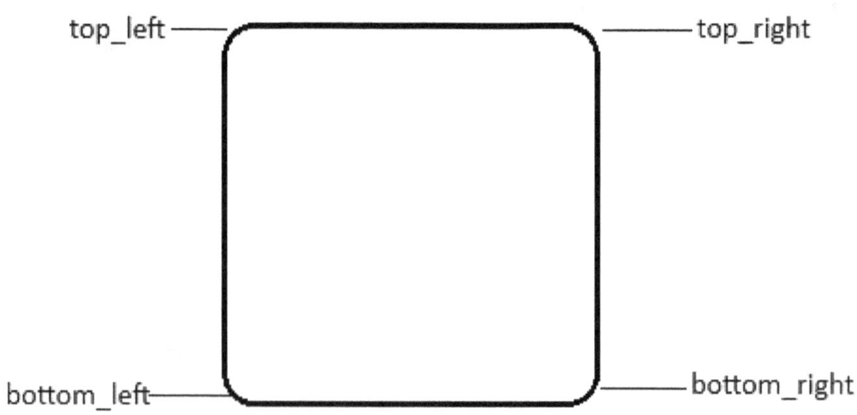

border_radius = flet.BorderRadius

```
    border_radius= flet.BorderRadius(
        top_left=5,
        top_right=10,
        bottom_left=4,
        bottom_right=2
    )
```


Python Code 1.7.0

```python
import flet

def main(page: flet.Page):
    page.title = "My App"
    page.bgcolor = flet.colors.WHITE
    page.padding = flet.padding.only(left=100, top=20)

    cont1 = flet.Container(
        content= flet.Text('Container 1'),
        alignment= flet.alignment.center,
        margin = flet.margin.all(10),
        height=150,
        width=150,
        border= flet.border.all(width=2, color=flet.colors.RED),
        border_radius= flet.border_radius.all(value= 40)

    )
    cont2 = flet.Container(
        content= flet.Text('Container 2'),
        alignment= flet.alignment.center,
        margin = flet.margin.all(10),
        height=150,
        width=150,
        border= flet.border.all(width=2, color=flet.colors.RED),
        border_radius= flet.BorderRadius(
          top_left= 30,
          top_right=0,
          bottom_left=0,
          bottom_right=30
        )
    )
    page.add(cont1, cont2)
    page.update()

flet.app(target = main)
```


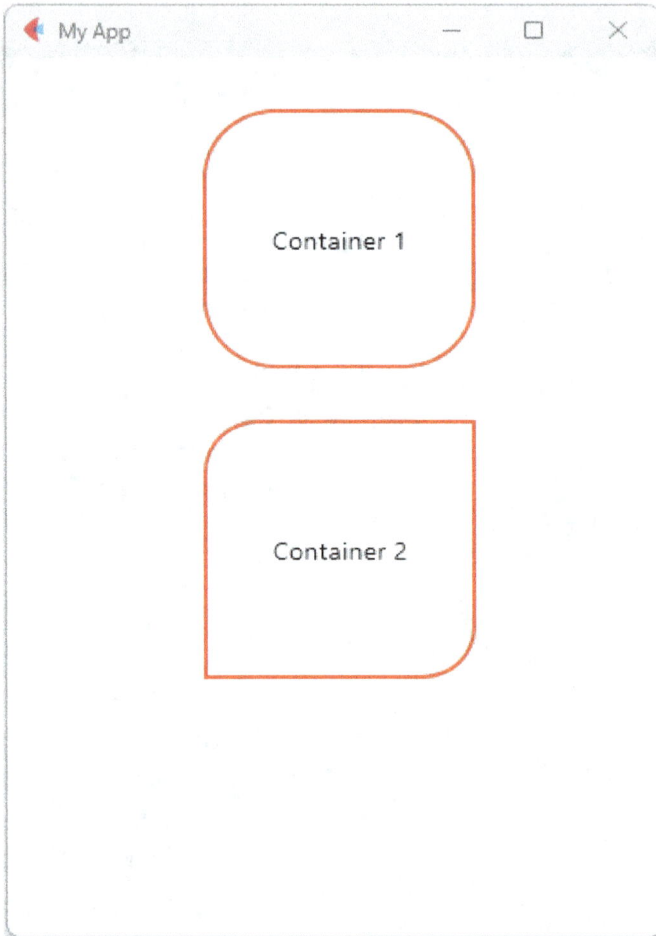

shape = flet.BoxShape

The **shape** property is used to define the shape of the container. There are two shapes available: CIRCLE and RECTANGLE.

```
shape = flet.BoxShape.CIRCLE
```

image_src = path\to\image

This property adds image to the container.

```
image_src= "path\\to\\image.jpg" #Windows path style
```


image_fit = flet.ImageFit

The **image_fit** specifies how an image behaves within a container, offering options such as CONTAIN, COVER, FILL, FIT_HEIGHT, FIT_WIDTH, NONE and SCALE_DOWN.

```
container = flet.Container(

    image_fit= flet.ImageFit.FILL,
    image_src= "C:\\Users\\Asiedu\\Desktop\\image.jpg",
)
```

image_opacity = float

The **image_opacity** determines the visibility degree of the image within the container, requiring a float value.

```
container = flet.Container(
    image_opacity=0.6,
    image_src= "C:\\Users\\Asiedu\\Desktop\\image.jpg",
    image_fit= flet.ImageFit.FILL,

    content= flet.Text('Container', weight= flet.FontWeight.BOLD, size=20),
    alignment= flet.alignment.center,
    height=100,
    width=page.width,
)
```

on_click = function

The **on_click** property assigns a callback function that is triggered whenever any area within the container is clicked.

```
container = flet.Container(
    on_click= lambda _: print("Container is clicked"),

    content= flet.Text('Container', weight= flet.FontWeight.BOLD, size=20),
    alignment= flet.alignment.center,
    height=100,
    width=page.width,
)
```

on_hover = function (Desktop only)

The **on_hover** assigns a callback function that fires when the mouse passes over the container's area. It's important to note that the **on_hover** property is exclusively available for desktop applications.

```
container = flet.Container(
    on_hover = lambda _: print("Container has been hovered"),

    content= flet.Text('Container'),
    alignment= flet.alignment.center,
    height=100,
    width=page.width,
)
```

on_long_press

This method assigns a callback function which trigger actions whenever the container is clicked for an extended period.

```
container = flet.Container(
    on_long_press = lambda _: print("Container has been pressed"),

    content= flet.Text('Container'),
    alignment= flet.alignment.center,
    height=100,
    width=page.width,
)
```


Python **Code 1.7.1**

```python
import flet

def main(page: flet.Page):
    page.title = "My App"
    page.bgcolor = 'white'
    page.padding = flet.padding.all(10)

    page.appbar = flet.AppBar(
      color= flet.colors.WHITE,
      title= flet.Text("Container"),
      bgcolor= "teal"
    )
    page.drawer = flet.NavigationDrawer()


    nav = flet.NavigationBar(
        destinations= [
            flet.NavigationDestination(
                 label="Menu",
                 icon=flet.icons.GRID_VIEW_OUTLINED
            ),
            flet.NavigationDestination(
                label="Connect",
                icon=flet.icons.WIFI
             ),
             flet.NavigationDestination(
                label="List",
                icon=flet.icons.LIST
             ),
            flet.NavigationDestination(
                label="Exit",
                icon=flet.icons.CANCEL
            )
    ])

    page.navigation_bar = nav

    text1 = flet.Text(
        spans= [
            flet.TextSpan(text="Hello,🖐",style= flet.TextStyle(size=25, weight=flet.FontWeight.BOLD)),
            flet.TextSpan(text="\nHave you heard about Flet Container?",style= flet.TextStyle(size=20, color="orange")),
            flet.TextSpan(text="\nWell, Flet Container function as a box to contain other controls.",style= flet.TextStyle(size=18)),
        ]
    )
    container1 = flet.Container(
        content= text1,
        padding= 20,
        border= flet.border.all(width=2, color="red"),
        alignment= flet.alignment.center,
        height=200,
        width=page.width,
    )

    text2 = flet.Text(
        text_align= flet.TextAlign.JUSTIFY,
        spans= [
            flet.TextSpan(text="Do You Know!,🤔",style= flet.TextStyle(size=25, weight=flet.FontWeight.BOLD)),
            flet.TextSpan(text="\nContainer can contain almost every control?",style= flet.TextStyle(size=20, color="Red")),
            flet.TextSpan(text='''\nContainers are indeed the mother of all controls.
                           Their ability to apply padding and margin on its content is awesome and unique.'''
                          ,style= flet.TextStyle(size=18)),
        ]
    )
    container2 = flet.Container(
        image_src= "C:\\Users\\asd7.jfif",
        image_fit= flet.ImageFit.FILL,
        image_opacity= 0.1,
        content= text2,
        padding= 8,
        border= flet.border.all(width=2, color="green"),
        border_radius= flet.border_radius.all(20),
        alignment= flet.alignment.center,
        height=200,
        width=page.width,
    )

    column = flet.Column( width= page.width,height= page.height,
        alignment= flet.MainAxisAlignment.START,
        horizontal_alignment= flet.CrossAxisAlignment.CENTER,
        scroll= flet.ScrollMode.ALWAYS,
        spacing=10,
        controls=[container1,container2]
    )


    page.add(column)
    page.update()

flet.app(target = main)
```


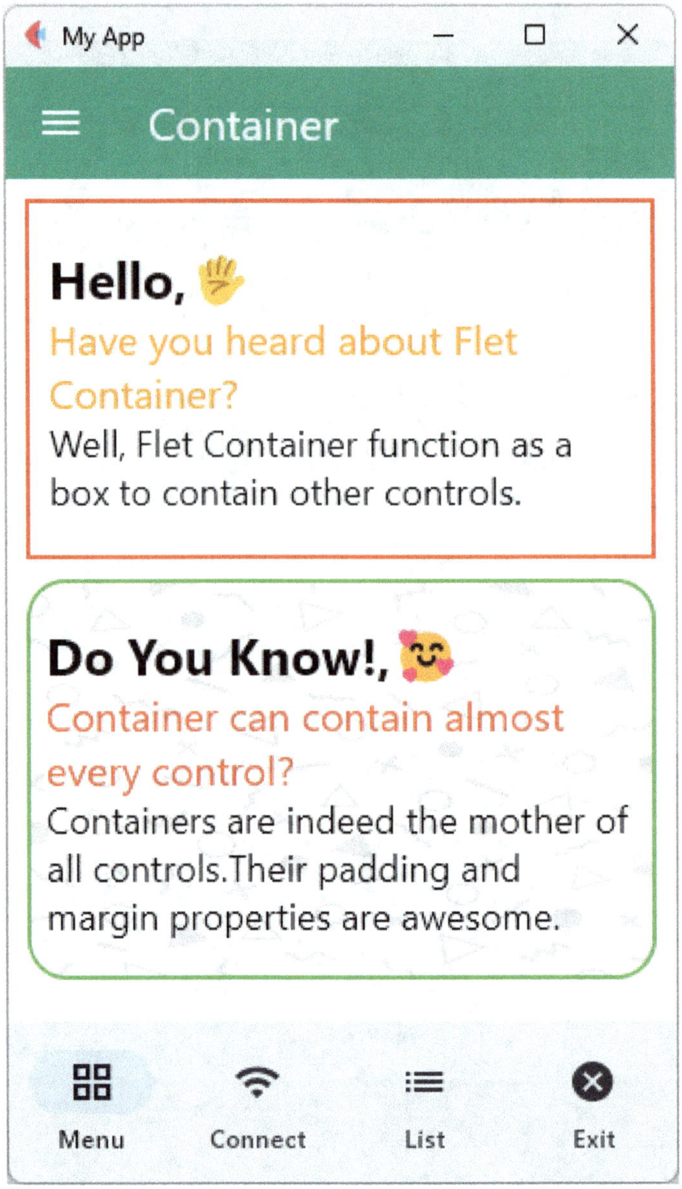
My App
Container
Hello,
Have you heard about Flet Container?
Well, Flet Container function as a box to contain other controls.
Do You Know!,
Container can contain almost every control?
Containers are indeed the mother of all controls.Their padding and margin properties are awesome.
Menu
Connect
List
Exit

Page Summary

The Container control is a versatile control that can contain other controls and provides options for styling, padding, margin, alignment, and more.

Keywords

padding
margin
image_opacity
gradiednt
image_src
BoxShape
border

Discussion

1. What are some best practices for using the Container control to create custom UI elements with specific shapes, borders, or backgrounds?
2. How do you handle padding and margin within a Container control to create spacing between child controls?
3. Can you explain the difference between the decoration and transform properties in the Container control, and when each would be used?

Card

A Card control typically represents a visually distinct and self-contained component used to display related content or information. It often resembles a physical card with rounded corners, providing a container for content such as text, images, or other controls.

Cards are commonly used in layout to organize and present data in an appealing and structured manner, offering a clean and intuitive user experience. They can include features like shadows, elevation and interactive elements.

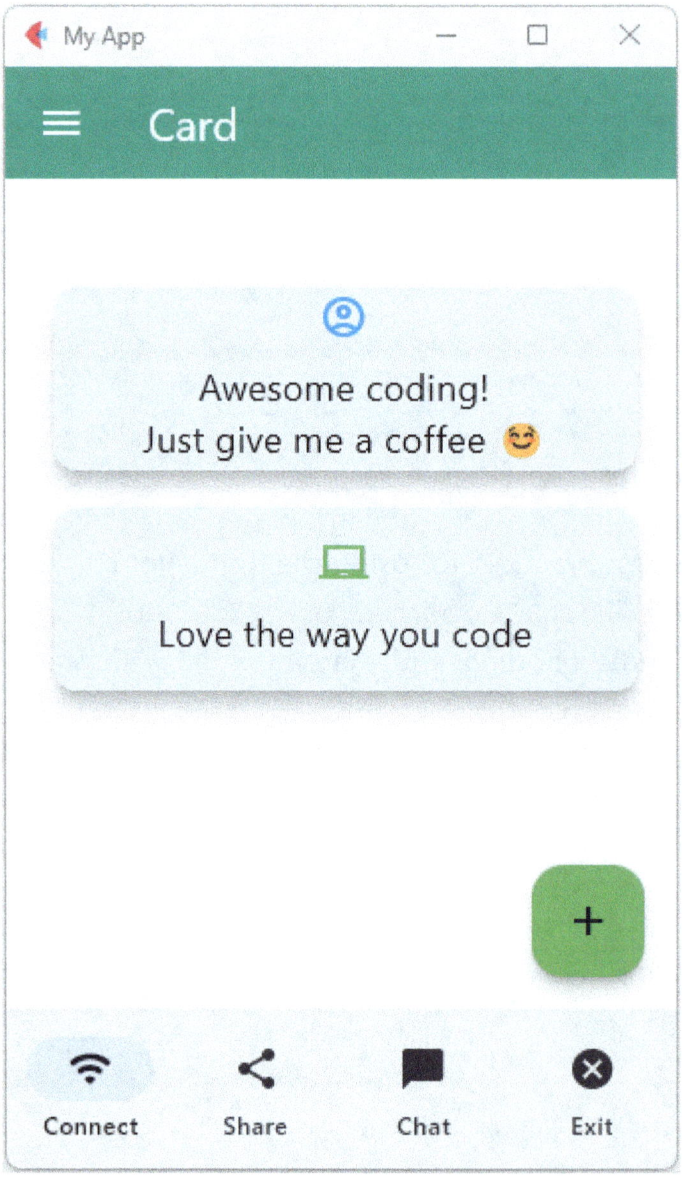

Available Methods

Property	Value	Property	Value
content	Control	surface_tint_color	string
elevation	int	shape	OutlinedBorder
shadow_color	string	color	string
margin	int, margin		

content = control

The **content** property adds a child control to the Card.

```
card = flet.Card(
  content= flet.Text('Hello World!')
)
```

elevation = int

The **elevation** property adds shadow effect to the Card control.

```
card = flet.Card(
  elevation= 10
)
```

shadow_color = string

The **shadow_color** specifies the Card's shadow color.

```
card = flet.Card(
  shadow_color= flet.colors.GREY
)
```

surface_tint_color = string

This property adds a faded color to the background of the Card controls.

```
surface_tint_color= flet.colors.RED,
```

 |

margin = float

The **margin** method creates a space (top, right, bottom, left) between the Card and other controls within the page. Margin can be set with

- flet.margin.all(value=float)
- flet.margin.symmetric(vertical, horizontal)
- flet.margin.only(left=float, top=float, right=float, bottom=float)

```
card = flet.Card(
    content= flet.Text('Card'),
    margin= flet.margin.all(10)
)
```

shape = borders

The **shape** property is used to define the shape of the Card. The available shapes are:
flet.RoundedRectangleBorder(type: str, radius: int)
flet.StadiumBorder(type: str)
flet.CircleBorder(type: str)
flet.BeveledRectangleBorder(type: str, radius: int)
flet.OutlinedBorder(type: str)
flet.ContinousRectangleBorder(type: str, radius: int)

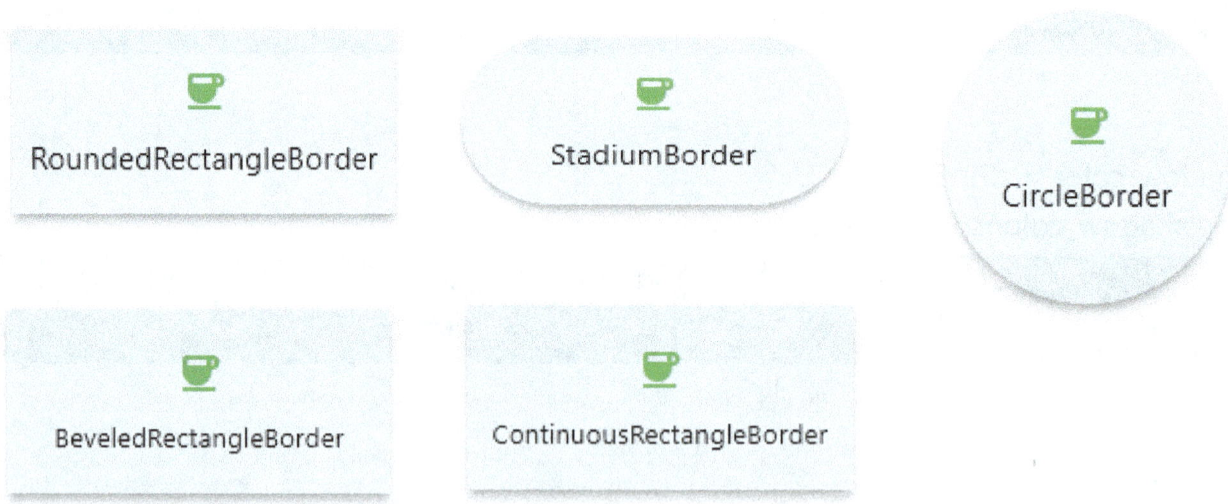


```
shape= flet.RoundedRectangleBorder(
        type= "roundedRectangle",
        radius= 0)
```


Python Code 1.8.0

```
import flet

def main(page: flet.Page):
    page.title = "My App"
    page.bgcolor = flet.colors.WHITE
    page.padding = flet.padding.only(left=50, top=50)

    column = flet.Column(
        alignment= flet.MainAxisAlignment.CENTER,
        horizontal_alignment= flet.CrossAxisAlignment.CENTER,
        tight= True,
        controls=[

        flet.Icon(
            name= flet.icons.FACEBOOK_OUTLINED,
            color=flet.colors.BLUE
        ),

        flet.Text(
            "Hey, this is Card!",
            size=18,
            text_align=flet.TextAlign.CENTER
        ),
        ]
    )
    card = flet.Card(
     content= column,
     elevation=5,
     height=100,
     width=200,
     surface_tint_color= flet.colors.GREEN,
     shape= flet.RoundedRectangleBorder(
         type= "roundedRectangle",
         radius= 2
     )
    )
    page.add(card)
    page.update()

flet.app(target = main)
```


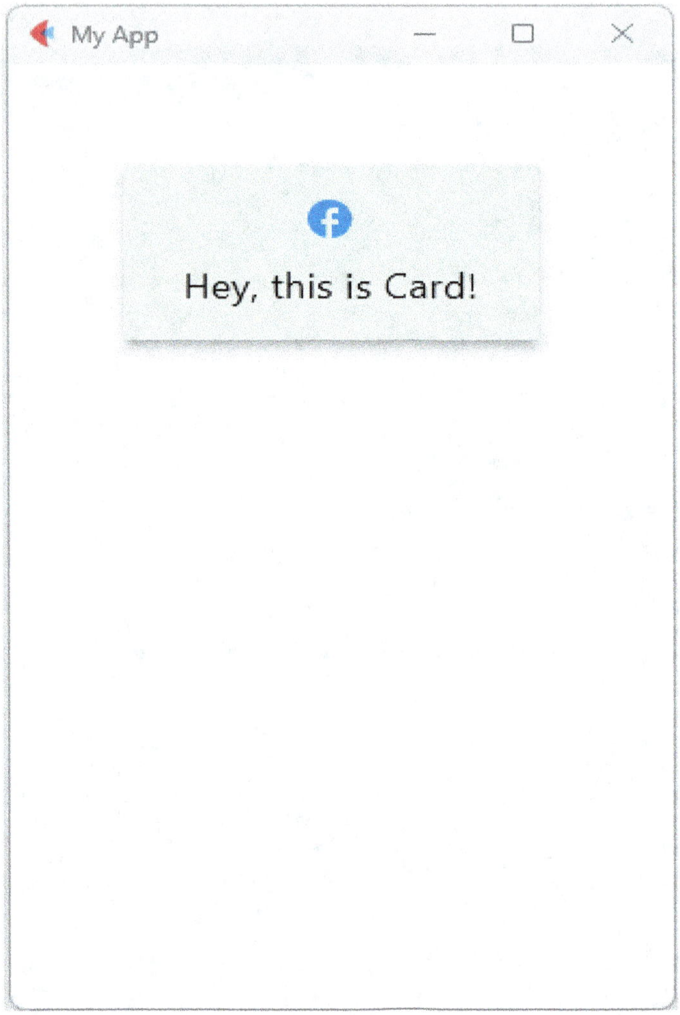
My App
Hey, this is Card!

Page Summary

The Card control is a material design card that provides a visually appealing way to display content, typically used for grouping related information in a Flet app.

Keywords

padding
margin
elevation
shape

Discussion

1. How can you customize the appearance of a Card control, such as adding shadows, elevation, or rounded corners?
2. What are some strategies for incorporating interactive elements, such as buttons or checkboxes, within a Card control?
3. Can you discuss the performance implications of using the Card control, especially when displaying large lists or grids of cards?

ListTile

ListTile is a streamlined row control featuring three essential elements: the **leading**, **title** (or subtitles) and **trailing** components. This versatile control is ideal for crafting interactive lists, enabling the inclusion of clickable labels accompanied by icons or additional controls. Its flexibility allows for the placement of elements before, after or both, enhancing both the presentation and functionality of the list.

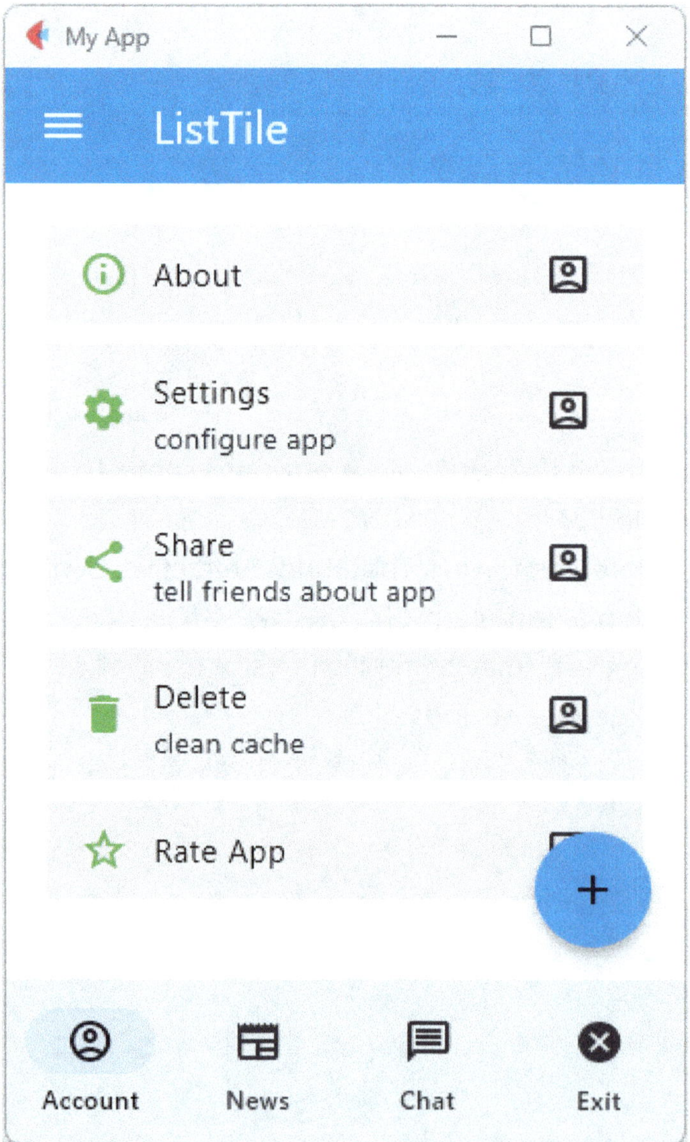

Available Methods

Property	Value	Property	Value
content_padding	PaddingValue	on_long_press	function
bgcolor	string	is_three_line	bool
bgcolor_activated	string	selected	bool
hover_color	string	dense	bool
leading	Control	autofocus	bool
title	Control	toggle_inputs	bool
subtitle	Control	url	string
trailing	Control	url_target	string
on_click	function		

leading = Control

This property adds a control at the left of the ListTile.

```
        flet.ListTile(
              leading= flet.Icon(
                  name= flet.icons.MESSAGE,
                  color=flet.colors.BLUE
              ),)
```

title = Control

This property sets the title of the list tile. The **title** shows the purpose of the list tile.

```
        flet.ListTile(
             title=flet.Text('Message', size=15)
        )
```

trailing = Control

This property appends a control to the rightmost position of the ListTile.

```
trailing = flet.Image(
                src = "C:\\Users\\python.jpg",
                height=30,
                border_radius = flet.border_radius.all(15)
            ),)
```

subtitle = Control

This property is utilized to provide additional or supplementary context.

```
flet.ListTile(
        subtitle= flet.Text('contact us, your feedback matters')
    )
```

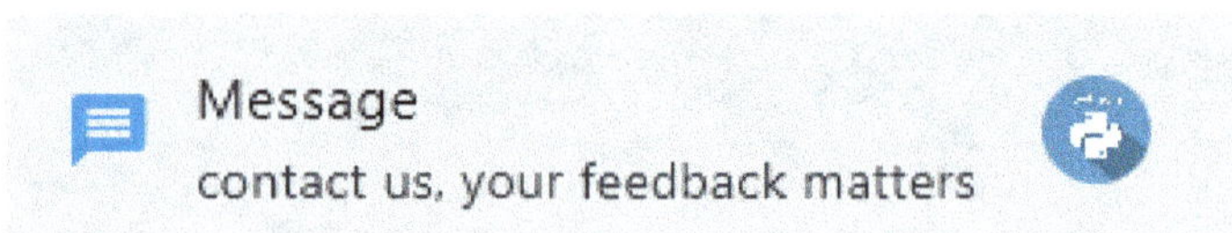

content_padding = float, flet.padding.all, flet.padding.only

This property is used to customize the spacing between the ListTile and its content.

```
flet.ListTile(
        content_padding= flet.padding.only(left = 100)
    )
```

bgcolor = string

The **bgcolor** specifies the background color of the ListTile.

```
listTile = flet.ListTile(
            bgcolor= "#B1BED2"
        )
```


bgcolor_activated = string

The **bgcolor_activated** specifies the background color when list tile is clicked.

```
listTile = flet.ListTile(
            bgcolor_activated = flet.colors.GREEN,
  )
```

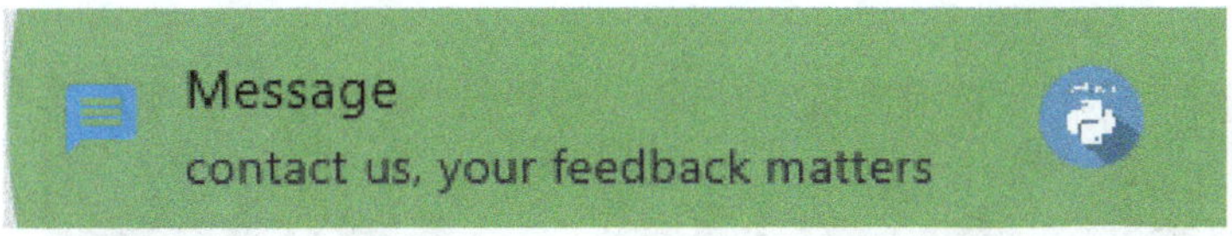

hover_color = string

The **hover_color** property specifies a temporary background color when the mouse cursor passes over the ListTile.

```
listTile = flet.ListTile(
            hover_color= flet.colors.GREY
  )
```

on_click = function

The **on_click** property assigns a function that executes when the ListTile is clicked.

```
listTile = flet.ListTile(
            on_click = myfunc()
  )
```

on_long_press = function

This method assigns a function which trigger actions whenever the ListTile is clicked for an extended period.

```
listTile = flet.ListTile(
            on_long_press = myfunc()
  )
```

is_three_line = bool

The **is_three_line** property modifies the appearance of the list tile to accommodate three lines of content instead of the default two.

```
listTile = flet.ListTile(
            is_three_line= True
  )
```

 |

autofocus = bool

When the **autofocus** is set to True, the list tile gains focus automatically.

```
listTile = flet.ListTile(
            autofocus = True
  )
```

Python Code 1.9.0

```python
import flet

def main(page: flet.Page):
    page.title = "My App"
    page.bgcolor = "#FFFFFF"
    page.padding = flet.padding.all(20)

    col2 = flet.Column(
        alignment= flet.MainAxisAlignment.CENTER,
        horizontal_alignment= flet.CrossAxisAlignment.CENTER,
        controls=[
           flet.ListTile(
              bgcolor="#EEEEEE",
              leading= flet.Icon(
                   name= flet.icons.MESSAGE,
                   color=flet.colors.BLUE
               ),
               title=flet.Text('Message', size=15),
               subtitle= flet.Text('contact us, your feedback matters'),
               trailing= flet.Icon(
                   name= flet.icons.ARROW_CIRCLE_RIGHT_OUTLINED,
                   color=flet.colors.GREY
               ),
           ),
            flet.ListTile(
              bgcolor="#EEEEEE",
              leading= flet.Icon(
                   name= flet.icons.SHARE,
                   color=flet.colors.BLUE
               ),
               title=flet.Text('Share', size=15),
               trailing= flet.Icon(
                   name= flet.icons.ARROW_CIRCLE_RIGHT_OUTLINED,
                   color=flet.colors.GREY
               ),
           ),
            flet.ListTile(
              bgcolor="#EEEEEE",
              leading= flet.Icon(
                   name= flet.icons.FAVORITE,
                   color=flet.colors.RED
               ),
               title=flet.Text('Donate', size=15),
               trailing= flet.Icon(
                   name= flet.icons.ARROW_CIRCLE_RIGHT_OUTLINED,
                   color=flet.colors.GREY
               ),
               subtitle= flet.Text('your generosity keeps us going'),
           )
        ],)
    page.add(col2)
    page.update()

flet.app(target = main)
```


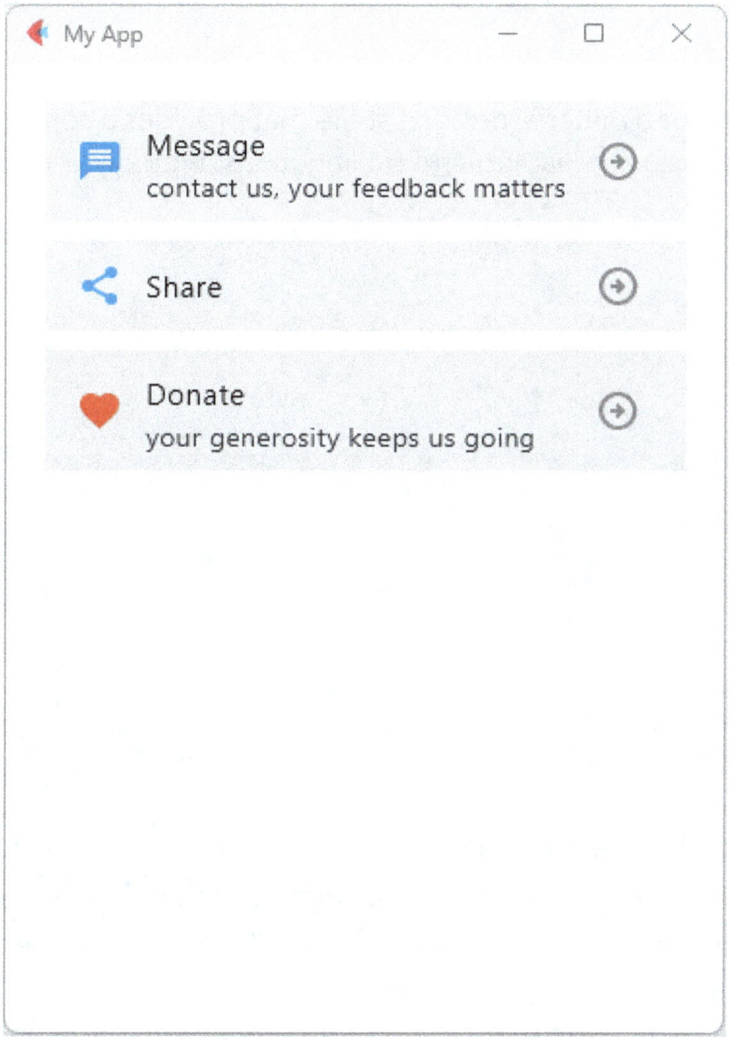

url = string

The **url** property assigns a web URL to the list tile, enabling it to open a web page when clicked.

```
    listTile = flet.ListTile(
                url="https://www.google.com"
      )
```


Page Summary

The ListTile control is a material design list tile that provides a convenient way to display a row of information with leading and trailing icons, typically used in lists or menus.

Keywords

leading
trailing
subtitle
title

Discussion

1. How can you handle user interactions, such as tapping or long-pressing, on a ListTile control to trigger actions or navigate to other screens?
2. What are some common use cases for ListTile controls in Flet app development, such as displaying lists of items or settings?
3. Can you explain the difference between the leading and trailing properties in the ListTile control, and when each would be used?

CircleAvatar

CircleAvatar is a circular control that can contain embedded content, with its size defined by radius.

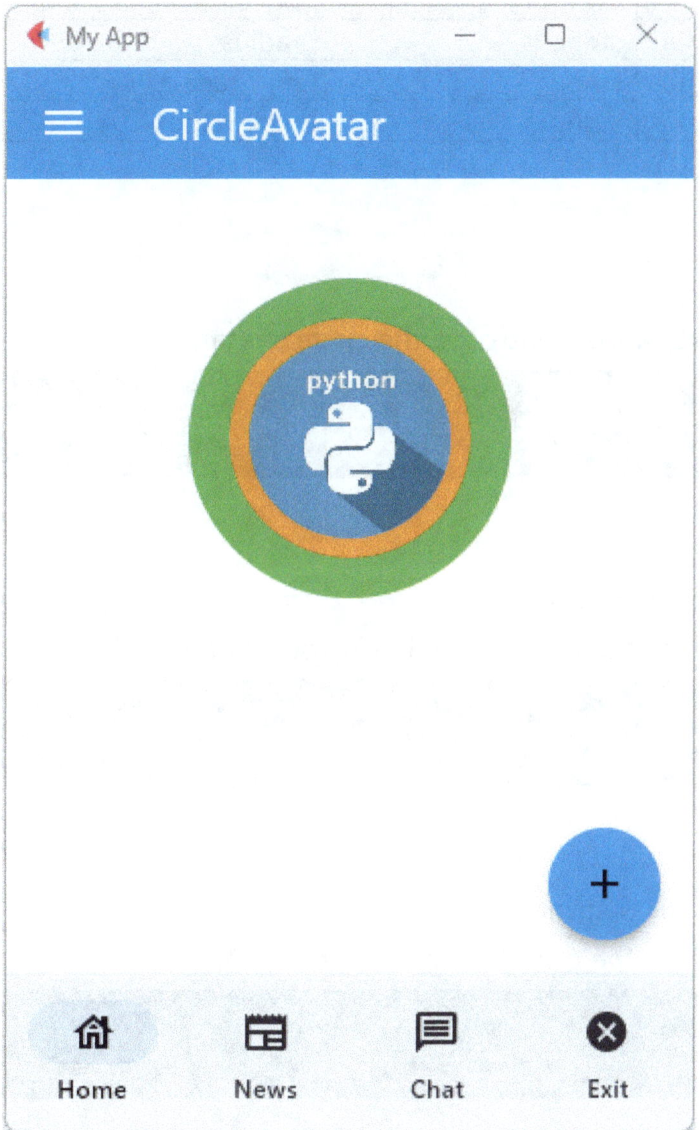

Available Methods

Property	Value	Property	Value
content	Control	bgcolor	string
background_image_url	string	radius	float
foreground_image_url	string	min_radius	float
color	string	max_radius	float

content = Control

The **content** property adds Control to the circle avatar.

```
flet.CircleAvatar(
            content= flet.Text('This is avatar')
        )
```

background_image_url = string

This property specifies the path to the background image file.

```
flet.CircleAvatar(
            background_image_url= 'car.jpg'
        )
```

foreground_image_url = string

This property specifies the path to the front image file.

```
flet.CircleAvatar(
            foreground_image_url= 'smallgirl.jpg'
        )
```

radius = float

The radius sets the radius of the **CircleAvatar**, determining its overall size.

```
circleAvatar = flet.CircleAvatar(
                radius= 35
    )
```


min_radius = float
This property sets the minimum radius for the **CirlceAvatar**, ensuring it does not shrink below a certain size.

```
    circleAvatar = flet.CircleAvatar(
                   min_radius= 37.5
    )
```

max_radius = float
This property sets the maximum radius for the CirlceAvatar, preventing it from growing beyond a defined size limit.

```
    circleAvatar = flet.CircleAvatar(
                   max_radius= 60.5
    )
```

Python *Code 2.0.0*

```python
import flet

def main(page: flet.Page):
    page.title = "My App"
    page.bgcolor = "#FFFFFF"
    page.padding = flet.padding.only(left=90, top=50)

    circle = flet.CircleAvatar(
        radius= 60,
        bgcolor= flet.colors.RED,
        content= flet.CircleAvatar(
            radius= 50,
            bgcolor= flet.colors.ORANGE,
            content= flet.CircleAvatar(
                radius=40,
                bgcolor=flet.colors.GREEN,
                content=flet.Image(
                    src="C:\\Users\\win.png"
                )
            )
        )
    )
    page.add(circle)
    page.update()

flet.app(target = main)
```

My App

Page Summary

CircleAvatar control displays a circular image or icon in a Flet application, commonly used for user profile pictures or icons.

Keywords

max_radius
min_radius
background_image_url
foreground_image_url

Discussion

1. How can you customize the appearance of a CircleAvatar, such as changing its size, background color, or border?
2. What are some strategies for efficiently loading and caching images in a CircleAvatar from different sources like the network or assets?
3. Can you discuss the accessibility considerations when using CircleAvatar, such as ensuring sufficient contrast for users with visual impairments?

NavigationDrawer

The **NavigationDrawer** is a sliding panel containing a list of controls that typically slides from one side of the page to the other, most commonly from left to right. It is closed by default and opens when the menu icon in the AppBar# is tapped. The NavigationDrawer# closes automatically when the user interacts with any part of the page outside of its area. Depending on user customization, the **NavigationDrawer** can cover either half or the entire page.

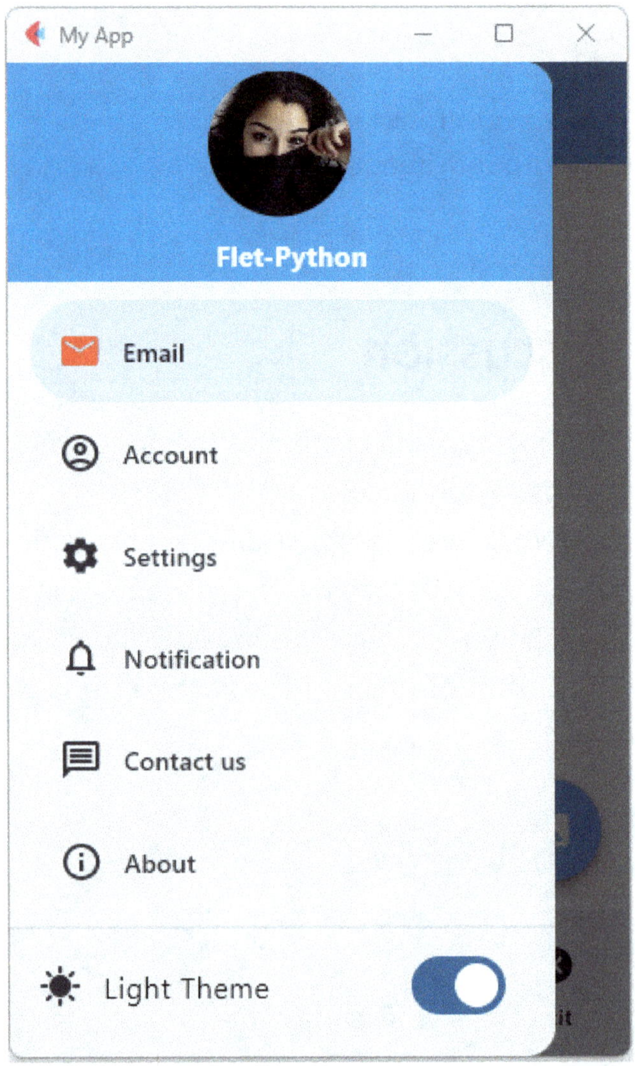

Available Methods

Property	Value	Property	Value
controls	List[Control]	shadow_color	string
open	bool	surface_tint_color	string
selected_index	int	tile_padding	PaddingValue
bgcolor	string	on_change	function
elevation	float	on_dismiss	function
indicator_color	string	indicator_shape	OutlinedShape

controls = List[*Controls]

The **controls** property is utilized to add control or content to the NavigationDrawer.

```
    page.drawer = flet.NavigationDrawer(
        controls=[
                flet.NavigationDrawerDestination(),
                flet.NavigationDrawerDestination(),
        ]),
```

NavigationDrawerDestination

The Flet NavigationDrawerDestination component facilitates the creation of button items, allowing for the specification of icons and their corresponding labels, along with changes upon selection. The available options include:

- label
- icon
- selected_icon
- selected_icon_content
- ref
- icon_content

label = string

The **label** assigns meaning to the icon, typically positioned beside it, aiding in user comprehension.

```
page.drawer = flet.NavigationDrawer(
    controls=[
        flet.NavigationDrawerDestination(
            label="Email",
        ),
 ],)
```

icon = string

The **icon** method specifies the icon used along with labels.

```
page.drawer = flet.NavigationDrawer(
    controls=[
        flet.NavigationDrawerDestination(
            label="Email",
            icon = flet.icons.EMAIL,
        ),
 ],)
```

icon_content = flet.Icon()

Alternatively, **icon_content** offers a different method for utilizing icons through the **flet.Icon().**


```
    page.drawer = flet.NavigationDrawer(
        controls=[
            flet.NavigationDrawerDestination(
                label="Email",
                icon_content= flet.Icon(
                    name= flet.icons.EMAIL,
                    color= flet.colors.RED
                )
            ),
     ],)
```

selected_icon = flet.icons

The **selected_icon** method specifies the icon to display when the item is selected or clicked.

```
    page.drawer = flet.NavigationDrawer(
        controls=[
            flet.NavigationDrawerDestination(
                label="Email",
                icon = flet.icons.EMAIL_OUTLINED,
                selected_icon=flet.icons.EMAIL
            ),
     ],)
```

open = bool

The **open** property keeps the drawer open all the times. By default, it is set to False.

```
    page.drawer = flet.NavigationDrawer(
        open= True,
),
```


selected_index = int

This is the index of the currently selected drawer item in the control list.

```
    page.drawer = flet.NavigationDrawer(
        selected_index=2,
),
```

elevation = int

The **elevation** property adds shadow effect to the **NavigationDrawer** control.

```
    page.drawer = flet.NavigationDrawer(
        elevation= 14,
    ),
```

shadow_color = string

This property defines the color of the drawer's shadow.

```
    page.drawer = flet.NavigationDrawer(
        shadow_color= flet.colors.with_opacity(10, 'GREY'),
    ),
```

surface_tint_color = string

The **surface_tint_color** provides a faded background color to the NavigationDrawer

```
    page.drawer = flet.NavigationDrawer(
        surface_tint_color= flet.colors.RED,
),
```

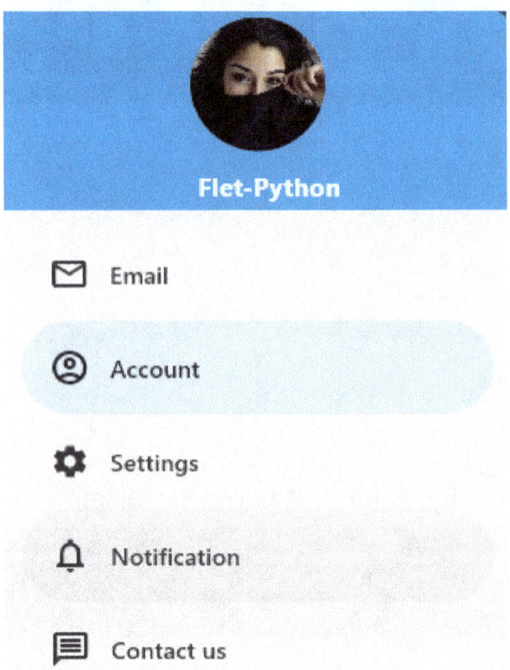

indicator_color = string

The **indicator_color** property specifies the color of the selection indicator, highlighting the active item within the drawer.

```
    page.drawer = flet.NavigationDrawer(
        indicator_color= flet.colors.with_opacity(0.5, "green"),
),
```

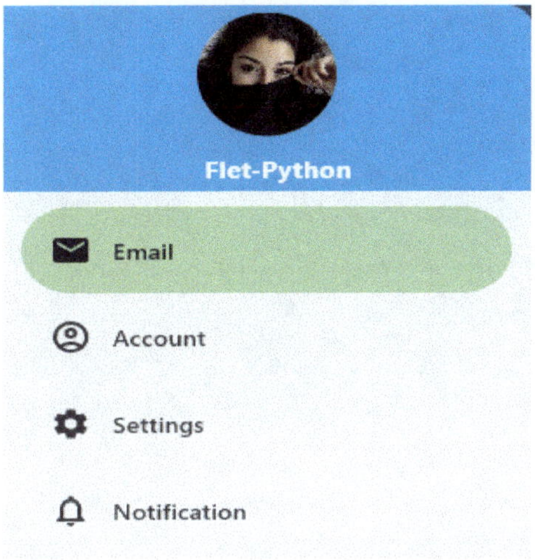

indicator_shape = OutlinedShape

The **indicator_shape** property specifies the shape of the selection indicator.

```
    page.drawer = flet.NavigationDrawer(
        indicator_shape= flet.RoundedRectangleBorder(radius=0),
),
```

Available Shapes

- flet.RoundedRectangleBorder(type: str, radius: int)
- flet.StadiumBorder(type: str)
- flet.CircleBorder(type: str)
- flet.BeveledRectangleBorder(type: str, radius: int)
- flet.OutlinedBorder(type: str)
- flet.ContinousRectangleBorder(type: str, radius: int)

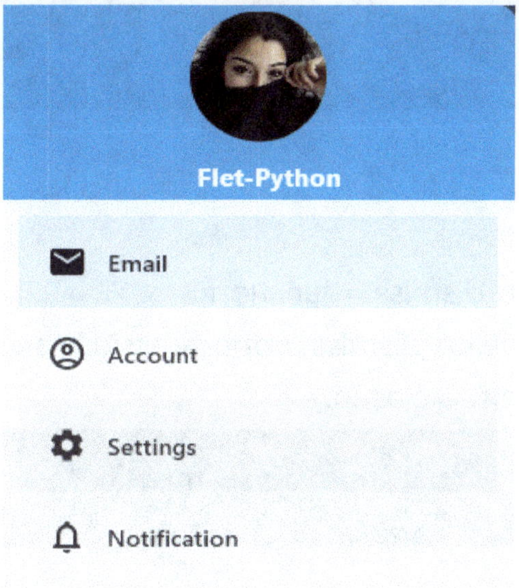

tile_padding = float, flet.padding.all, flet.padding.only

The **tile_padding** adds space between drawer items or content and the edges of the drawer.

```
    page.drawer = flet.NavigationDrawer(
        tile_padding= flet.padding.only(left=50),
),
```

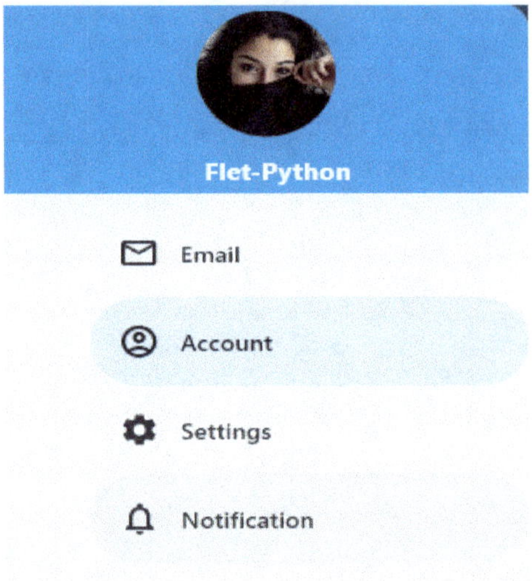

on_change = function

The **on_change** property assigns a function that triggers actions when a drawer item is selected.

```
    page.drawer = flet.NavigationDrawer(
        on_change=  myfunc,
),
```

on_dismiss = function

The **on_dismiss** property assigns a callback function that triggers actions when the drawer item is closed.

```
    page.drawer = flet.NavigationDrawer(
        on_dismiss =  closefunc,
),
```


Python *Code 2.1.0*

```
import flet

def main(page: flet.Page):
    page.title = "My App"
    page.bgcolor = flet.colors.WHITE

    def selectedFunc(e):
        index = e.control.selected_index,
        if index.__contains__(2):
            print('item two selected')
        if index.__contains__(3):
            print('item three selected')

    page.drawer = flet.NavigationDrawer(
        on_change = selectedFunc,
        indicator_shape= flet.RoundedRectangleBorder(radius=0),
        controls=[
            flet.Container(
                bgcolor= flet.colors.BLUE,
                height=120,
                content= flet.Column(
                    alignment = flet.MainAxisAlignment.CENTER,
                    horizontal_alignment=flet.CrossAxisAlignment.CENTER,
                    controls=[
                        flet.Image(
                            src="C:\\Users\\image.jpg",
                            border_radius=flet.border_radius.all(40),
                            height=80,
                            width=80
                        ),
                        flet.Text('\t\t\tFlet-Python', size=15, color=flet.colors.WHITE)
                    ]
                )
            ),
            flet.Container(
               height=10
            ),

            flet.NavigationDrawerDestination(
                label="Call",
                icon = flet.icons.CALL,
            ),
             flet.NavigationDrawerDestination(
                label="Account",
                icon= flet.icons.ACCOUNT_CIRCLE_OUTLINED
            ),
            flet.NavigationDrawerDestination(
                label="Settings",
                icon= flet.icons.SETTINGS
            ),

            flet.NavigationDrawerDestination(
                label="Notification",
                icon= flet.icons.NOTIFICATIONS_OUTLINED,
            ),
```



```
            flet.NavigationDrawerDestination(
               label="Contact us",
               icon= flet.icons.MESSAGE_OUTLINED,
           ),
             flet.NavigationDrawerDestination(
               label="About",
               icon= flet.icons.INFO_OUTLINE,
           ),
           flet.Divider(),

             flet.ListTile(
               leading=flet.Icon(
               name = flet.icons.SUNNY,
               ),
               title=flet.Text('Light Theme'),
               trailing= flet.Switch(
                   value= True,
                   height=20,
               )
           )
       ],
   )
   page.update()

flet.app(target = main)
```

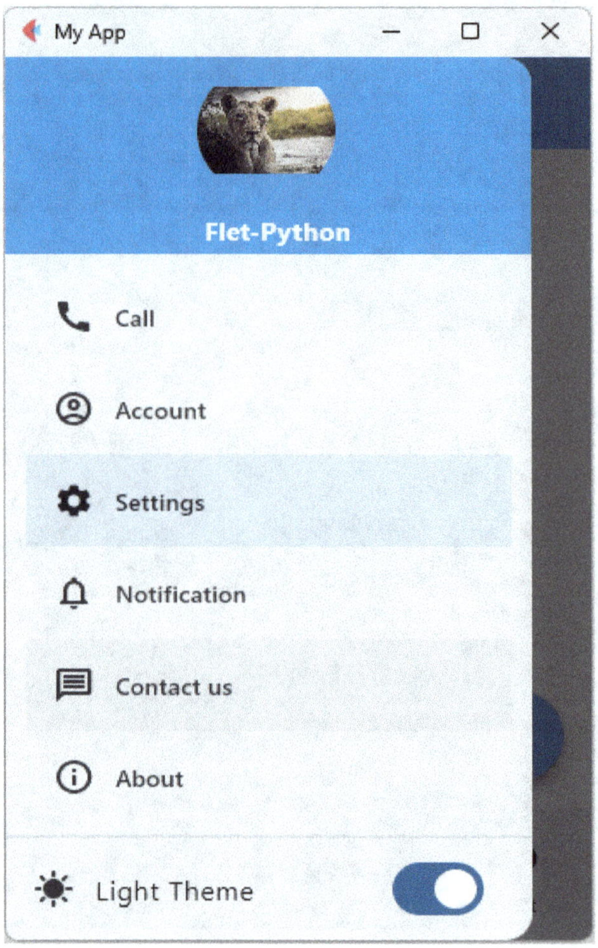

Page Summary

NavigationDrawer control provides a side panel for navigation in a Flet app, typically accessed via a hamburger icon.

Keywords

tile_padding
indicator_shape
indicator_color
on_dismiss

Discussion

1. How do you implement a NavigationDrawer with multiple navigation items and handle navigation state management?
2. What are some best practices for organizing and grouping navigation items within a NavigationDrawer?
3. Can you discuss the user experience implications of using a NavigationDrawer versus other navigation patterns like bottom navigation bars or tabs?

ListView

A **ListView** is a scrollable list of controls arranged linearly. It is highly efficient for displaying large lists, as it loads items on demand, ensuring smooth scrolling performance.

- **Orientation**: Displays its children one after another in the specified scroll direction (vertical or horizontal).
- **Cross Axis Requirement**: Children are required to fill the cross axis (eg. fill the width for a vertical ListView).

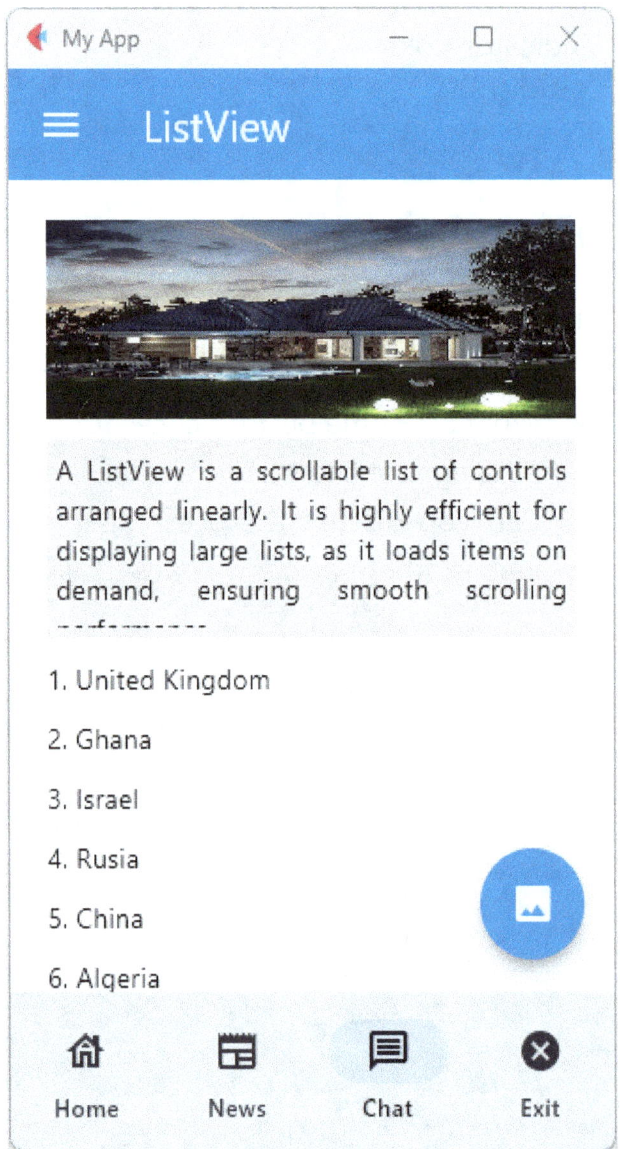

 |

Available Methods

Property	Value	Property	Value
controls	List[Control]	auto_scroll	bool
horizontal	bool	reverse	bool
spacing	float	on_scroll_interval	int
item_extent	int	on_scroll	function
divider_thickness	float	first_item_prototype	bool
padding	PaddingValue		

controls = List[*Control]

A list of controls to display inside the ListView.

```
list = flet.ListView(
  controls=[
      flet.Text('1. United Kingdom'),
      flet.Text('2. Ghana'),
      flet.Text('3. Israel'),
  ]
)
```

horizontal = bool

By default, **ListView** items are vertically oriented. If the **horizontal** property is set to True, items are laid out horizontally.

```
list = flet.ListView(
    horizontal= True,
)
```

spacing = float

This property sets the horizontal or vertical gap or space between items in the **ListView**.

```
list = flet.ListView(
    spacing=5,
)
```

item_extent = int

This property sets a fixed height or width (horizontal ListView) of an item to optimize rendering.

```
list = flet.ListView(
    item_extent= 5,
)
```

divider_thickness = float

ListView alternatively creates spaces between items by implementing the divider. The divider has a default value of zero(0).

```
list = flet.ListView(
    divider_thickness= 6,
)
```

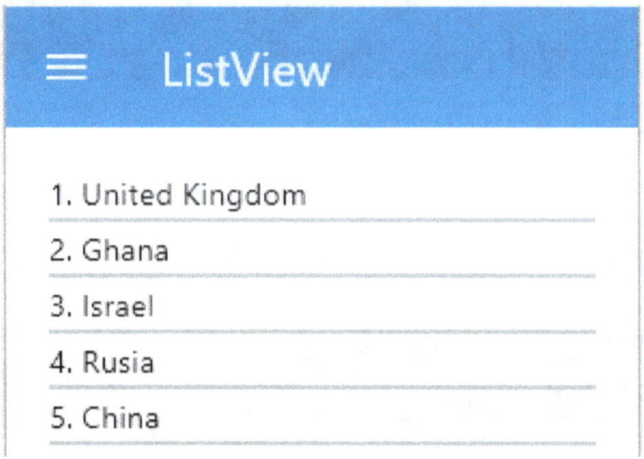

padding = float, flet.padding.all, flet.padding.only

The **padding** adds space or gap between the ListView items or content and the edges of the ListView control.

```
list = flet.ListView(
    padding = flet.padding.all(5),
)
```


auto_scroll = bool

If **auto_scroll** is set to True, it automatically moves the scrollbar to the end of the list when children are updated. Note, it must be False for **scroll_to()** method to work.

```
list = flet.ListView(
    auto_scroll = True,
)
```

reverse = bool

This property determines
whether the ListView items are to be arranged in the opposite way. It is False by default.

```
list = flet.ListView(
    reverse = True,
)
```

first_item_prototype = bool

If this property is True, the dimensions of the first item should be used as a prototype for all other items. i.e. their height or width will be the same as the first item.

```
list = flet.ListView(
    first_item_prototype = True,
)
```

on_scroll = function

The **on_scroll** property assigns a callback function which triggers action when the ListView is scrolled.

```
list = flet.ListView(
    first_item_prototype = True,
)
```


Python **Code 2.2.0**

```python
import flet

def main(page: flet.Page):
    page.title = "My App"
    page.bgcolor = "#FFFFFF"
    page.padding = flet.padding.all(10)

    list = flet.ListView(
        padding= flet.padding.only(bottom=10),
        spacing= 10,
        divider_thickness=1,
        controls=[
            flet.Text('1. Georgia'),
            flet.Text('2. Ohio'),
            flet.Text('3. Texas'),
            flet.Text('4. North Carolina'),
            flet.Text('5. South Carolina'),
            flet.Text('6. Massachusetts'),
            flet.Text('7. California'),
            flet.Text('8. Dagota'),
            flet.Text('9. Illinois'),
        ]
    )
    page.add(list)
    page.update()

flet.app(target = main)
```

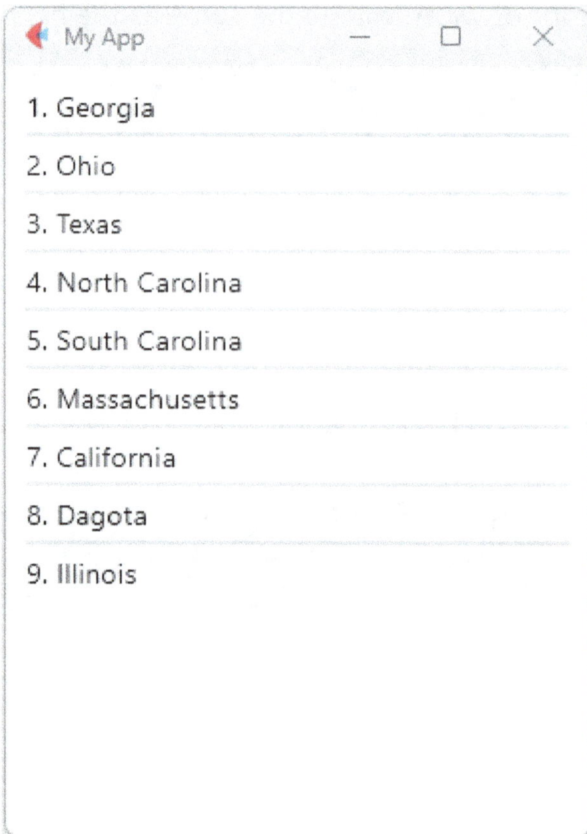

Page Summary

ListView control displays a scrollable list of items in a Flet app, allowing users to scroll through a large dataset.

Keywords

horizontal
item_extent
divider_thickness
first_time_prototype
reverse

Discussion

1. How do you optimize performance when working with large datasets in a ListView, such as lazy loading or item recycling?
2. What are some strategies for customizing the appearance of list items in a ListView, such as adding separators or customizing item layouts?
3. Discuss about the **CupertinoListTile**

GridView

The **GridView** control is a scrollable, two-dimensional array of controls arranged in rows and columns. It is highly versatile and can display a large number of items efficiently, making it suitable for layouts where items are presented in a grid format.

Orientation: Displays items in a grid, allowing both vertical and horizontal scrolling.

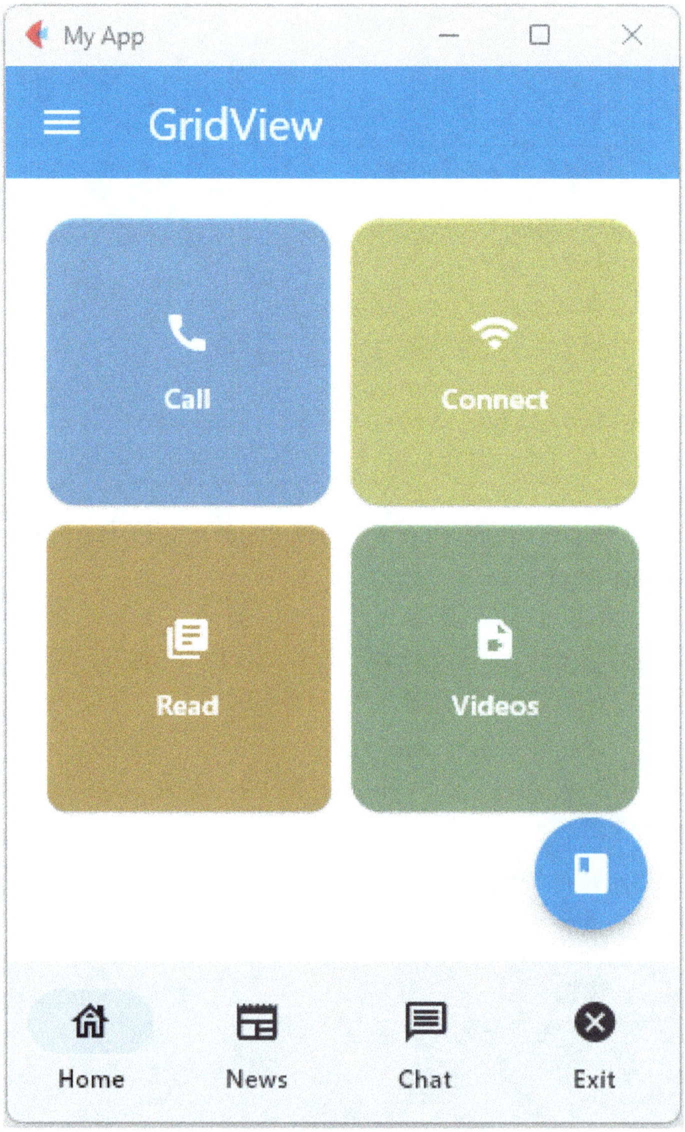

Available Methods

Property	Value	Property	Value
controls	List[Control]	run_spacing	bool
horizontal	bool	child_aspect_ratio	float
spacing	float	padding	PaddingValue
max_extent	int	runs_count	float

controls = List[Control]
A list of controls to display inside the GridView.

```
gridView = flet.GridView(
  controls=[
      flet.Text('Grid 1'),
      flet.Text('Grid 2'),
      flet.Text('Grid 3'),
  ]
)
```

max_extent = int
This property sets the maximum height or width of the grid item.

```
list = flet.GridView(
    max_extent = 500,
)
```

horizontal = bool
By default, GridView items are vertically oriented. If the **horizontal** property is set to True, items are laid out horizontally.

```
gridView = flet.GridView(
    horizontal= True,
)
```

padding = float, flet.padding.all, flet.padding.only
The **padding** adds space between the GridView items or content and the edges of the GridView control.

```
list = flet.GridView(
    padding = flet.padding.all(5),
)
```


runs_count

The **runs_count** defines the number of children or items in the cross axis.

```
list = flet.GridView(
    runs_count=3,
)
```

runs_count = 3

runs_count = 2

spacing = float

The **spacing** property defines the number of logical pixels between each child along the main axis.

```
list = flet.GridView(
    spacing = 30,
)
```

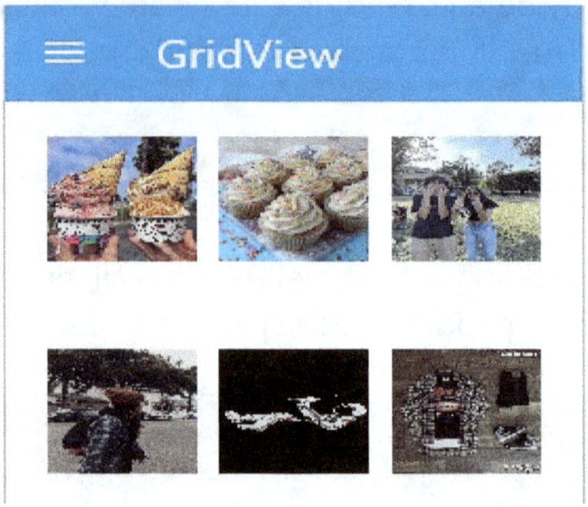

run_spacing = float

The **run_spacing** property defines the number of logical pixels between each child along the cross axis.

```
list = flet.GridView(
    run_spacing = 30,
)
```

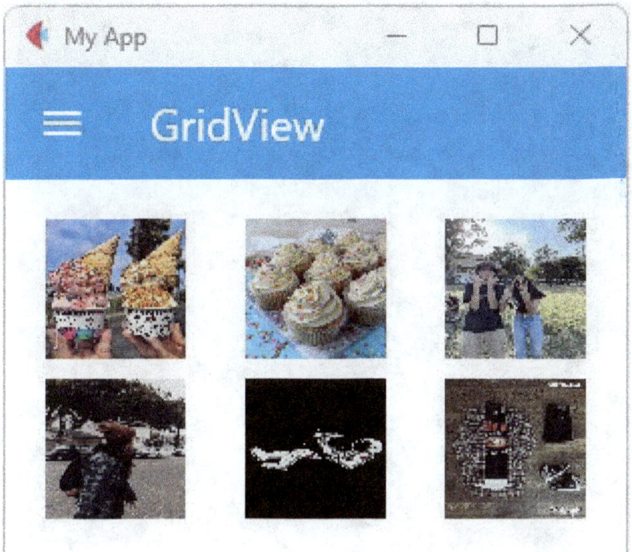

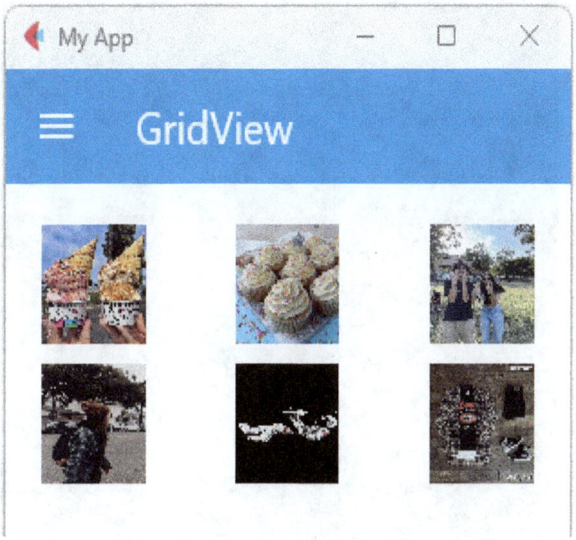

auto_scroll = bool

If **auto_scroll** is set to True, it automatically moves the scrollbar to the end of the list when children are updated. Note, it must be False for **scroll_to()** method to work.

```
list = flet.GridView(
    auto_scroll = True,
)
```

child_aspect_ratio = int

The **child_aspect_ratio** is the cross-axis to the main-axis extent of each child.

```
list = flet.GridView(
    child_aspect_ratio= 3,
)
```


Python **Code 2.3.0**

```python
import flet

def main(page: flet.Page):
    page.title = "My App"
    page.bgcolor = "#FFFFFF"
    page.padding = flet.padding.all(10)

    grid = flet.GridView(
        runs_count=2,
        controls=[
            flet.Image(
            src="C:\\Users\\image1.jpg",
            height=100,
            fit= flet.ImageFit.FILL
             ),
            flet.Image(
            src="C:\\Users\\Cupcakes.jpg",
            height=100,
            fit= flet.ImageFit.FILL
             ),
            flet.Image(
            src="C:\\Users\\vi amo.jpg",
            height=100,
            fit= flet.ImageFit.FILL
             ),

            flet.Image(
            src="C:\\Users\\Asiedu\\imag3.jpg",
            height=100,
            fit= flet.ImageFit.FILL
             ),

            flet.Image(
            src="C:\\Users\\label.jpg",
            height=100,
            fit= flet.ImageFit.FILL
             ),
            flet.Image(
            src="C:\\Users\\Brand.jpg",
            height=100,
            fit= flet.ImageFit.FILL
             ),
        ]
    )

    page.add(grid)
    page.update()

flet.app(target = main)
```

My App

Page Summary

GridView control displays a scrollable grid of items in a Flet app, allowing users to scroll horizontally or vertically through a collection of items.

Keywords

runs_count
max_extent
run_spacing
child_aspect_ratio
horizontal

Discussion

1. How do you configure the number of columns or rows in a GridView, and what are the considerations for choosing an appropriate grid layout?
2. What are some techniques for optimizing performance when working with large datasets in a GridView, such as lazy loading or caching?

ElevatedButton

The **ElevatedButton** is a material design button that has a shadow effect, giving it a raised or "elevated" appearance. It is commonly used for important actions and can be customized with various properties to match the desired look and functionality.

Available Methods

Property	Value	Property	Value
content	Control	style	ButtonStyle
text	string	autofocus	bool
icon	string	adaptive	bool
icon_color	string	url	string
color	string	url_target	string
bgcolor	string	on_hover	function
elevation	float	on_focus	function
on_click	function	on_blur	function
on_long_press	function		

text = string

The **text** property defines the text or label of the elevated button.

```
        flet.ElevatedButton(
                text= "click me",
            )
```

icon = string

This specifies the icon of the elevated button

```
        flet.ElevatedButton(
                text= "click me",
                icon= flet.icons.WIFI
            )
```

Note

For ElevatedButtons, the **icon** property cannot be used alone but it must be used together with the **text** property.

color = string

The **color** method defines the color for both icon and text.

```
flet.ElevatedButton(
    text= "click me",
    icon= flet.icons.WIFI,
    color= 'green'
)
```

icon_color = string

This property specifies the color of the button's icon.

```
flet.ElevatedButton(
    text= "click me",
    icon= flet.icons.WIFI,
    icon_color= 'orange'
)
```

bgcolor = string

The **bgcolor** specifies the background color of the button.

```
flet.ElevatedButton(
    text= "click me",
    icon= flet.icons.WIFI,
    color = flet.colors.WHITE,
    bgcolor = '#14171A'
)
```

elevation = float

The **elevation** specifies the degree of the shadow effect.

```
flet.ElevatedButton(
    text= "click me",
    icon= flet.icons.WIFI,
    color = "white",
    bgcolor = "#1DA1F2",
    elevation= 20,
)
```

on_click = function

The **on_click** defines a function which get fired when the button is clicked.

```
def clickmeFun(e):
    print('click me')

button = flet.ElevatedButton(
    on_click= clickmeFun,
)
```

on_long_press = function

This method defines a function to fire when the button is long-pressed.

```
def longPressFun(e):
    print('longPress')

button = flet.ElevatedButton(
    on_long_press= longPressFun,
)
```

on_hover = function (Desktop Only)

It assigns a function, which is fired when the mouse passes over the button.

```
def onHoverFun(e):
    print('hover')

button = flet.ElevatedButton(
    on_hover= onHoverFun,
)
```


adaptive = bool

When this property is True, it allows platform-specific design for the elevated button.

```
            flet.ElevatedButton(
                adaptive= True
            )
```

autofocus = bool

When the **autofocus** is set to True, the **ElevatedButton** gains focus automatically.

```
            flet.ElevatedButton(
                autofocus= True
            )
```

url = string

This property connects to the web when the button is clicked by assigning a web address.

```
            flet.ElevatedButton(
                url= "https://www.google.com"
            )
```

content = control

The **content** property is used in place of **text** and **icon** property to add more complex controls to the button, such as images and other controls.

```
        flet.ElevatedButton(
              height = 100,
              width = 200,
              content= flet.Column(
                  controls=[
                      flet.Image(src="C:\\notes.png",height=50,width=50),
                      flet.Text('Click to add note')
                  ]
              )
        )
```

ButtonStyle

The **ButtonStyle** offers more options to use material deign to customize the button.

- color
- bgcolor
- overlay_color
- shadow_color
- surface_tint_color
- elevation
- animation_duration
- padding
- shape
- side

color = string
The **color** method defines the color for both icon and text.

```
flet.ElevatedButton(
    text = "start",
    style= flet.ButtonStyle(
        color= 'black'
    )
)
```

bgcolor = string
The **bgcolor** specifies the background color of the button.

```
flet.ElevatedButton(
    text = "start",
    style= flet.ButtonStyle(
        bgcolor = flet.colors.with_opacity(0.5, 'green')
    )
)
```

overlay_color = string
This defines the background color when the button is focused or active.

```
flet.ElevatedButton(
    text = "start",
    style= flet.ButtonStyle(
        overlay_color = flet.colors.with_opacity(0.7, 'red')
    )
)
```

surface_tint_color = string

This property provides a faded background color to the button.

```
            flet.ElevatedButton(
                text = "start",
                style= flet.ButtonStyle(
                    surface_tint_color = 'yellow'
                )
            )
```

elevation = float

The **elevation** specifies the degree of the shadow effect.

```
            flet.ElevatedButton(
                text = "start",
                style= flet.ButtonStyle(
                    color = 'black',
                    elevation= 10
                ))
```

padding = float, flet.padding.all, flet.padding.only

The **padding** creates space between the content and edges of the button.

```
            flet.ElevatedButton(
                text = "start",
                style= flet.ButtonStyle(
                    padding= flet.padding.only(left= 20)
                )
            )
```

shape = flet.OutlinedBorder

The **shape** property defines the shape of the border. The available shapes include:

- flet.RoundedRectangleBorder(type: str, radius: int)
- flet.StadiumBorder(type: str)
- flet.CircleBorder(type: str)
- flet.BeveledRectangleBorder(type: str, radius: int)
- flet.OutlinedBorder(type: str)
- flet.ContinousRectangleBorder(type: str, radius: int)

```
flet.ElevatedButton(
    text = "start",
    style= flet.ButtonStyle(
        shape= flet.RoundedRectangleBorder(radius=0)
    )
)
```

side = flet.BorderSide

The **side** property allows customization of the button edges or the border by specifying the width and color.

```
flet.ElevatedButton(
    text = "start",
    style= flet.ButtonStyle(
        side= flet.BorderSide(
            width= 5,
            color= "red"
        )
    ))
```

animation_duration = int

This property specifies the duration of the click effect in seconds.

```
style= flet.ButtonStyle(
  animation_duration= 5
)
```


Python *Code 2.4.0*

```python
import flet

def main(page: flet.Page):
    page.title = "My App"
    page.bgcolor = flet.colors.WHITE
    page.padding = flet.padding.all(20)

    page.appbar = flet.AppBar(
      color= flet.colors.WHITE,
      title= flet.Text("ElevatedButton"),
      bgcolor=flet.colors.GREEN,
    )

    page.drawer = flet.NavigationDrawer()

    page.navigation_bar = flet.NavigationBar(
        destinations= [
           flet.NavigationDestination(
                 label="Home",
                 icon=flet.icons.HOUSE_OUTLINED
            ),
            flet.NavigationDestination(
                label="News",
                icon=flet.icons.NEWSPAPER_OUTLINED
             ),
              flet.NavigationDestination(
                label="Chat",
                icon=flet.icons.MESSAGE_OUTLINED
             ),
            flet.NavigationDestination(
                label="Exit",
                icon=flet.icons.CANCEL
            )
      ])
    def clickmeFun():
        print('click me')

    col = flet.Column(
        alignment= flet.MainAxisAlignment.START,
        horizontal_alignment=flet.CrossAxisAlignment.CENTER,
        height= page.height,
        width= page.width,
        controls=[

          flet.Text('Hello,', size= 50, font_family= "Georgia"),
          flet.Text('Welcome to my Flet App. Love what you code and what you create. Coding is Life☺'),
          flet.Container(height=20),

           flet.ElevatedButton(
                text = "start",
                height = 40,
                width= 150,
                color = 'white',
                bgcolor= "#14171a",
                elevation= 15,
                on_click = clickmeFun(),

            )
      ] )
    page.add(col)
    page.update()

flet.app(target = main)
```

My App
ElevatedButton
Hello,
Welcome to my Flet App. Love what you code and what you create. Coding is Life 😊
start
Home
News
Chat
Exit

Page Summary

ElevatedButton control creates a raised button in a Flet app, typically used for primary or high-importance actions.

Keywords

url
elevation
icon_color
ButtonStyle

Discussion

1. How can you customize the appearance of an ElevatedButton, such as changing its color, shape, or elevation?
2. What are some best practices for handling user interactions with an ElevatedButton, such as providing feedback on tap or handling long-press events?
3. Can you discuss the accessibility considerations when using ElevatedButton, such as ensuring adequate contrast for users with visual impairments?
4. Discuss about **CupertinoButton**.

TextButton

The **TextButton** is a material design button that does not have any elevation or shadow, making it appear flat against the interface. It is commonly used for less prominent actions in an application, such as navigation or secondary options.
TextButton is flat and typically consists of text without a background or shadow color.

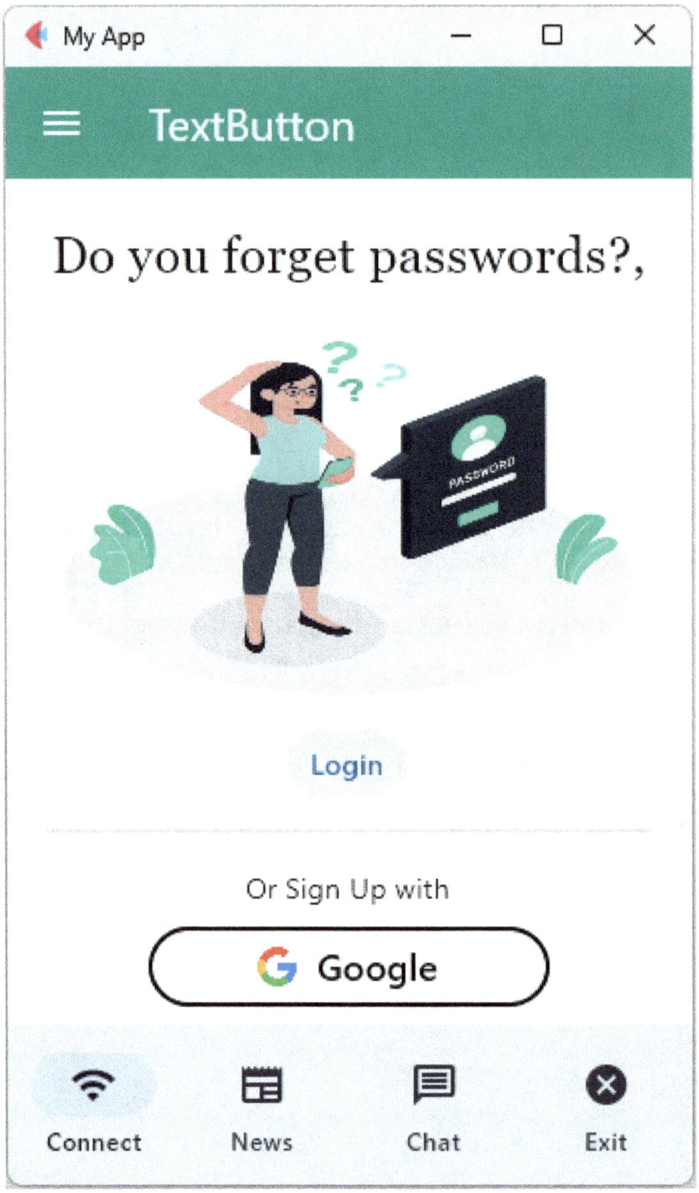

Available Methods

Property	Value	Property	Value
content	Control	adaptive	bool
text	string	autofocus	bool
icon	string	url	string
icon_color	string	url_target	string
on_click	function	on_hover	function
on_long_press	function	on_focus	function
style	ButtonStyle	on_blur	function

text = string

The **text** property defines the text or label of the text button.

```
flet.TextButton(
        text= "login",
    )
```

icon = string

This specifies the icon of the text button

```
flet.TextButton(
        text= "login",
        icon= flet.icons.LAPTOP
    )
```

 # Note

For TextButtons, the **icon** property can be used alone, unlike **ElevatedButtons** where **icons** must be used with **text** property.

icon_color = string
This property specifies the color of the icon.

```
            flet.TextButton(
                text= "login",
                icon= flet.icons.LAPTOP,
                icon_color= 'orange'
            )
```

on_click = function
The **on_click** defines a function which get fired whenever the button is clicked.

```
    def loginFun(e):
        print('login')

    button = flet.TextButton(
        on_click= loginFun,
    )
```

on_long_press = function
This method defines a callback function to fire when the button is long-pressed.

```
    def longPressFun(e):
        print('longPress')

    button = flet.TextButton(
        on_long_press= longPressFun,
    )
```

on_hover = function (Desktop Only)
It assigns a callback function, which is fired when the mouse passes over the button.

```
    def onHoverFun(e):
        print('hover')

    button = flet.TextButton(
        on_hover= onHoverFun,
    )
```


adaptive = bool

When this property is True, it allows platform-specific design for the text button.

```
flet.TextButton(
    adaptive= True
)
```

autofocus = bool

When the **autofocus** is set to True, the **TextButton** gains focus automatically.

```
flet.TextButton(
    autofocus= True
)
```

url = string

This property connects to the web when the button is clicked by assigning a web address.

```
flet.TextButton(
    url= "https://www.google.com"
)
```

content = control

The **content** property is used in place of **text** and **icon** property to add more complex controls to the button, such as images and other controls.

```
flet.TextButton(
    content= flet.Row(
        controls=[
          flet.Text('Sign Up'),
          flet.Image(src="C:\\Users\\google.png",height=20,width=20)
        ]
    )
)
```

ButtonStyle

The **ButtonStyle** offers more options to use material deign to customize the button.

- color
- bgcolor
- overlay_color
- shadow_color
- surface_tint_color
- elevation
- animation_duration
- padding
- shape
- side

color = string
The **color** method defines the color for both icon and text.

```
        flet.TextButton(
            content= flet.Row(
                controls=[
                    flet.Text('Sign Up'),
                    flet.Image(src = "C:\\googlr.png",height=20,width=20,)
                    ]
                ),
             style= flet.ButtonStyle(
                color= "black"
             )
            )
```

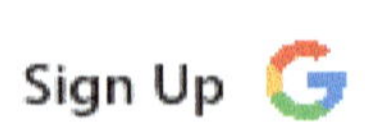

bgcolor = string
The **bgcolor** specifies the background color of the button.

```
        flet.TextButton(
            content= flet.Row(
                controls=[
                    flet.Text('Sign Up'),
                    flet.Image(src = "C:\\google.png",height=20,width=20,)
                    ]
                ),
            style= flet.ButtonStyle(
                color= "white",
                bgcolor= "black"
            )
            )
```

overlay_color = string
This defines the background color when the button is focused or active.

```
        flet.TextButton(
            text = "login",
            style= flet.ButtonStyle(
                overlay_color="green"
            )
            )
```

padding = float, flet.padding.all, flet.padding.only
The **padding** creates space between the content and edges of the button.

```
        flet.TextButton(
            text = "login",
            style= flet.ButtonStyle(
                padding= flet.padding.all(20)
            )
            )
```

shape = flet.OutlinedBorder

The shape property defines the shape of the border. The available shapes include:

- flet.RoundedRectangleBorder(type: str, radius: int)
- flet.StadiumBorder(type: str)
- flet.CircleBorder(type: str)
- flet.BeveledRectangleBorder(type: str, radius: int)
- flet.OutlinedBorder(type: str)
- flet.ContinousRectangleBorder(type: str, radius: int)

```
        flet.TextButton(
            text = "login",
            style= flet.ButtonStyle(
                shape= flet.RoundedRectangleBorder(radius=0)
            )
            )
```

side = flet.BorderSide

The side property allows customization of the button edges or the border by specifying the width and color.

```
        flet.TextButton(
            content= flet.Row(
                controls=[
                    flet.Text('Sign Up'),
                    flet.Image(src = "C:\\search.png",height=20,width=20,)
                    ]
                ),
            style= flet.ButtonStyle(
                side= flet.BorderSide(width=2, color='black')
          ))
```

animation_duration = int

This property specifies the duration of the click effect in seconds.

```
                style= flet.ButtonStyle(
                  animation_duration= 5
                )
```

Python **Code 2.5.0**

```python
import flet

def main(page: flet.Page):
    page.title = "My App"
    page.bgcolor = flet.colors.WHITE
    page.padding = flet.padding.all(20)

    page.appbar = flet.AppBar(
      color= flet.colors.WHITE,
      title= flet.Text("TextButton"),
      bgcolor=flet.colors.TEAL,
    )
    page.drawer = flet.NavigationDrawer()

    page.navigation_bar = flet.NavigationBar(
        destinations= [
           flet.NavigationDestination(
                 label="Connect",
                 icon=flet.icons.WIFI
            ),

            flet.NavigationDestination(
                label="News",
                icon=flet.icons.NEWSPAPER_OUTLINED
             ),

             flet.NavigationDestination(
                label="Chat",
                icon=flet.icons.MESSAGE_OUTLINED
             ),

            flet.NavigationDestination(
                label="Exit",
                icon=flet.icons.CANCEL
            )
        ]
    )

    def previousFun():
        print('previous')

    def nextFun():
        print('next')


    col = flet.Column(
        alignment= flet.MainAxisAlignment.START,
        horizontal_alignment=flet.CrossAxisAlignment.CENTER,
        height= page.height,
        width= page.width,
```



```
    controls=[
        flet.Text('Do you know\U0001F680, ', size= 35, font_family= "Georgia"),

        flet.Text('''
            Python has a large community. Its is widely used in data science,
            artificial intelligence, cybersecurity, and app development.
            What do you like about Python?\n\nFor me, I love app development
            with Python and Flet .\n\nTell me more about Flet \U0001F525.''',
            text_align= flet.TextAlign.JUSTIFY),
            flet.Container(height=20),

        flet.Row(
        alignment=flet.MainAxisAlignment.SPACE_BETWEEN,
        controls=[

        flet.TextButton(
            on_click = previousFun(),
            content= flet.Row(
                controls=[
                    flet.Icon(name = flet.icons.ARROW_CIRCLE_LEFT_OUTLINED),
                    flet.Text('previous'),
                    ]
                ),
            style= flet.ButtonStyle(
                side= flet.BorderSide(width=2, color='black'),
                color= 'orange'
            )
            ),

        flet.TextButton(
            on_click = nextFun(),
            content= flet.Row(
                controls=[
                    flet.Text('next'),
                    flet.Icon(name = flet.icons.ARROW_CIRCLE_RIGHT_OUTLINED),
                    ]
                ),
            style= flet.ButtonStyle(
                side= flet.BorderSide(width=2, color='black'),
                color= 'orange'
            ),
            ),

         ])
        ]
    )

    page.add(col)
    page.update()


flet.app(target = main)
```


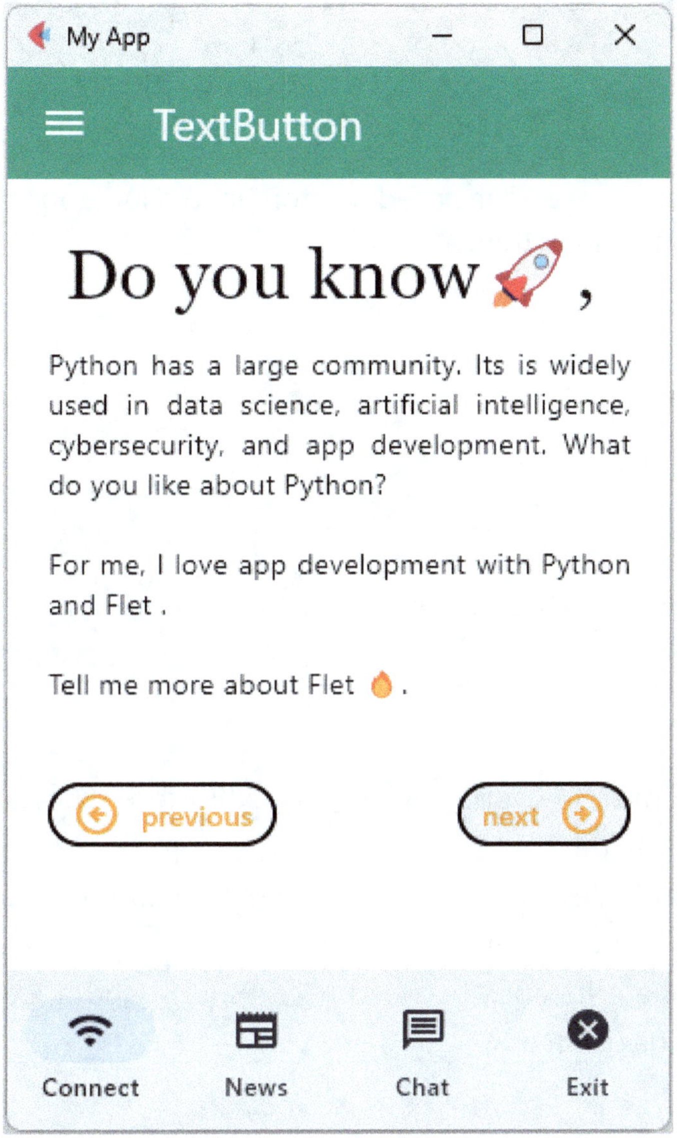
My App
TextButton
Do you know 🚀 ,
Python has a large community. Its is widely used in data science, artificial intelligence, cybersecurity, and app development. What do you like about Python?
For me, I love app development with Python and Flet .
Tell me more about Flet 🔥 .
previous
next
Connect
News
Chat
Exit

Page Summary

TextButton control creates a text-based button in a Flet app, typically used for secondary or less prominent actions.

Keywords

url
ButtonStyle
icon_color

Discussion

1. How do you customize the appearance of a TextButton, such as changing its text color, font size, or padding?
2. What are some strategies for visually indicating the state of a TextButton, such as highlighting it when pressed or disabled?
3. Can you discuss the difference between a TextButton and a ElevatedButton, and when each would be used?

IconButton

The **IconButton** is a material design button that displays an icon without a label. It is typically used for actions that are represented by icons, such as navigation, settings or other interactive elements.

IconButton consists solely of an icon and can include a background color or be transparent.

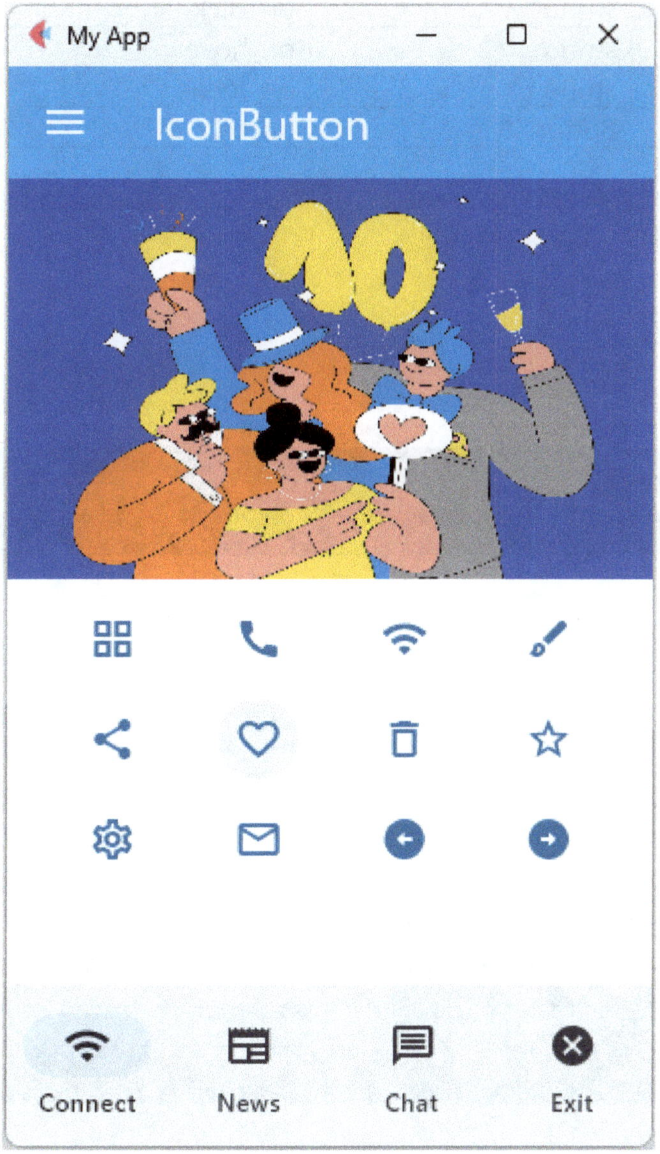

Available Methods

Property	Value	Property	Value
content	Control	adaptive	bool
icon	string	autofocus	bool
icon_color	string	url	string
icon_size	float	url_target	string
selected_icon	string	on_long_press	function
selected_icon_color	string	on_click	function
highlight_color	string	on_hover	function
bgcolor	string	on_focus	function
style	ButtonStyle	on_blur	function

icon = string

This specifies the icon of the IconButton.

```
flet.IconButton(
    icon = flet.icons.MENU
)
```

icon_color = string

The **icon_color** method defines the color of the button.

```
flet.IconButton(
    icon = flet.icons.MENU,
    icon_color= "orange"
)
```

icon_size = int

The **icon_size** property defines the size of the icon for the button.

```
flet.IconButton(
    icon = flet.icons.MENU,
    icon_color= "orange",
    icon_size= 50,
)
```

selected_icon = string

The **selected_icon** method specifies the icon to display when the button is in the selected state.

```
flet.IconButton(
    icon = flet.icons.EMAIL,
    selected_icon= flet.icons.EMAIL_OUTLINED,
)
```

selected_icon_color = string

This defines the temporary color of the icon when the button is in a selected state.

```
flet.IconButton(
    icon = flet.icons.EMAIL,
    selected_icon_color= 'red',
)
```

highlight_color = string

This defines the indicator color or temporary background color when the button is pressed or clicked.

```
flet.IconButton(
    icon = flet.icons.MENU,
    highlight_color= 'green'
)
```

bgcolor = string

This property specifies the background color of the button.

```
flet.IconButton(
    icon = flet.icons.MENU,
    bgcolor= 'blue'
)
```

on_click = function

The **on_click** defines a callback function which get fired when the button is clicked.

```
def menuFun(e):
    print('menu')

button = flet.IconButton(
    on_click= menuFun,
  )
```

on_long_press = function

This method fires a callback function when the button is long-pressed.

```
def longPressFun(e):
    print('longPress')

button = flet.IconButton(
    on_long_press= longPressFun,
  )
```

on_hover = function (Desktop Only)

It assigns a function, which is fired when the mouse passes over the button.

```
def onHoverFun(e):
    print('hover')

button = flet.IconButton(
    on_hover= onHoverFun,
  )
```


adaptive = bool

When this property is True, it allows platform-specific design for the icon button.

```
flet.IconButton(
    adaptive= True
)
```

autofocus = bool

When the **autofocus** is set to True, the IconButton gains focus automatically.

```
flet.IconButton(
    autofocus= True
)
```

url = string

This property connects to the web when the button is clicked by assigning a web address.

```
flet.IconButton(
    url= "https://www.google.com"
)
```

content = control

The **content** property is used in place of **icon** property to add more complex controls to the button, such as images and other controls. This property lets the **IconButton** behave like other buttons.

```
flet.IconButton(
    height=80,
    width=80,
    content= flet.Image(src="C:\\Users\\calendar.png")
)
```

ButtonStyle

- color
- bgcolor
- overlay_color
- shadow_color
- surface_tint_color
- elevation
- animation_duration
- padding
- shape
- side

color = string
The **color** method defines the color for the icon.

```
flet.IconButton(
    icon= flet.icons.LOCK_OUTLINE,
    style= flet.ButtonStyle(
        color= "orange"
    )
)
```

bgcolor = string
The **bgcolor** specifies the background color of the button.

```
flet.IconButton(
    icon= flet.icons.LOCK_OUTLINE,
    style= flet.ButtonStyle(
        color = "white",
        bgcolor = "#14171A"
    )
)
```

overlay_color = string
This defines the background color when the button is focused or active.

```
            flet.IconButton(
                icon= flet.icons.LOCK_OUTLINE,
                style= flet.ButtonStyle(
                    overlay_color= flet.colors.with_opacity(0.5, 'orange')
                )
            )
```

padding = float, flet.padding.all, flet.padding.only
The **padding** creates space between the content and edges of the button.

```
            flet.IconButton(
                icon= flet.icons.LOCK_OUTLINE,
                style= flet.ButtonStyle(
                    padding= 20
                )
            )
```

shape = flet.OutlinedBorder
The shape property defines the shape of the border. The available shapes include:

- flet.RoundedRectangleBorder(type: str, radius: int)
- flet.StadiumBorder(type: str)
- flet.CircleBorder(type: str)
- flet.BeveledRectangleBorder(type: str, radius: int)
- flet.OutlinedBorder(type: str)
- flet.ContinousRectangleBorder(type: str, radius: int)


```
            flet.IconButton(
                icon= flet.icons.LOCK_OUTLINE,
                style= flet.ButtonStyle(
                    shape= flet.RoundedRectangleBorder(radius=0)
                )
            )
```

side = flet.BorderSide

The side property allows customization of the button edges or the border by specifying the width and color.

```
            flet.IconButton(
                icon= flet.icons.LOCK_OUTLINE,
                style= flet.ButtonStyle(
                    side= flet.BorderSide(width=2, color= "blue")
                )
            )
```

animation_duration = int

This property specifies the duration of the click effect in seconds.

```
                style= flet.ButtonStyle(
                  animation_duration= 5
                )
```


Python **Code 2.6.0**

```python
import flet

def main(page: flet.Page):
    page.title = "My App"
    page.bgcolor = 'white'
    page.padding = flet.padding.all(10)

    page.appbar = flet.AppBar(
      color= flet.colors.WHITE,
      title= flet.Text("IconButton"),
      bgcolor=flet.colors.BLUE,
    )

    page.drawer = flet.NavigationDrawer()

    page.navigation_bar = flet.NavigationBar(
        destinations= [
           flet.NavigationDestination(
                 label="Connect",
                 icon=flet.icons.WIFI
            ),

            flet.NavigationDestination(
                label="News",
                icon=flet.icons.NEWSPAPER_OUTLINED
             ),

              flet.NavigationDestination(
                label="Chat",
                icon=flet.icons.MESSAGE_OUTLINED
             ),
            flet.NavigationDestination(
                label="Exit",
                icon=flet.icons.CANCEL
            )
        ]
    )
    col = flet.Column(
        alignment= flet.MainAxisAlignment.START,
         horizontal_alignment=flet.CrossAxisAlignment.CENTER,
        height= page.height,
        width= page.width,
        controls=[
          flet.Card(
              color = flet.colors.WHITE,
              elevation=0,
              height=100,
              content= flet.Row(
                  controls=[
                      flet.Image(src="C:\\Users\\em6.png"),
                      flet.Text("'Hello',\nDo you love your code. Alright,just sit down, sip a coffee and code in your style!\u2615"
                            , text_align=flet.TextAlign.JUSTIFY, expand=True),
                      flet.Container(width=5)
                  ]
              )),
          flet.Card(
              color = ('white'),
              height=100,
              elevation= 2,
              content= flet.Column(
                  controls=[
                     flet.Row(
                         alignment= flet.MainAxisAlignment.SPACE_EVENLY,
                         controls=[
                             flet.IconButton(icon=flet.icons.MENU, icon_color='black'),
                             flet.IconButton(icon=flet.icons.LOCK_OUTLINE, icon_color='black'),
                             flet.IconButton(icon=flet.icons.LOCK_OPEN_OUTLINED, icon_color='black'),
                         ]
                     ),
                     flet.Row(
                          alignment= flet.MainAxisAlignment.SPACE_EVENLY,
                         controls=[
                             flet.IconButton(icon=flet.icons.SETTINGS_OUTLINED, icon_color='black'),
                             flet.IconButton(icon=flet.icons.CALENDAR_MONTH_OUTLINED, icon_color='black'),
                             flet.IconButton(icon=flet.icons.SHOPPING_BAG_OUTLINED, icon_color='black'),
                         ]
                     )
                  ]
              )
          ),
        flet.Row(
            alignment= flet.MainAxisAlignment.SPACE_EVENLY,
                controls=[
                    flet.IconButton(height=60, width=60, content=flet.Image(src="C:\\notes.png")),
                    flet.IconButton(height=60, width=60, content=flet.Image(src="C:\\settings.png")),
                    flet.IconButton(height=60, width=60, content=flet.Image(src="C:\\Userspaper.png")),
                ]
            ),
        flet.Row(
            alignment= flet.MainAxisAlignment.SPACE_EVENLY,
                controls=[
                    flet.IconButton(height=60, width=60, content=flet.Image(src="C:\\mik1.png")),
                    flet.IconButton(height=60, width=60, content=flet.Image(src="C:\\calendar.png")),
                    flet.IconButton(height=60, width=60, content=flet.Image(src="C:\\feedback.png")),
                ]
            ),
        ])
    page.add(col)
    page.update()

flet.app(target = main)
```


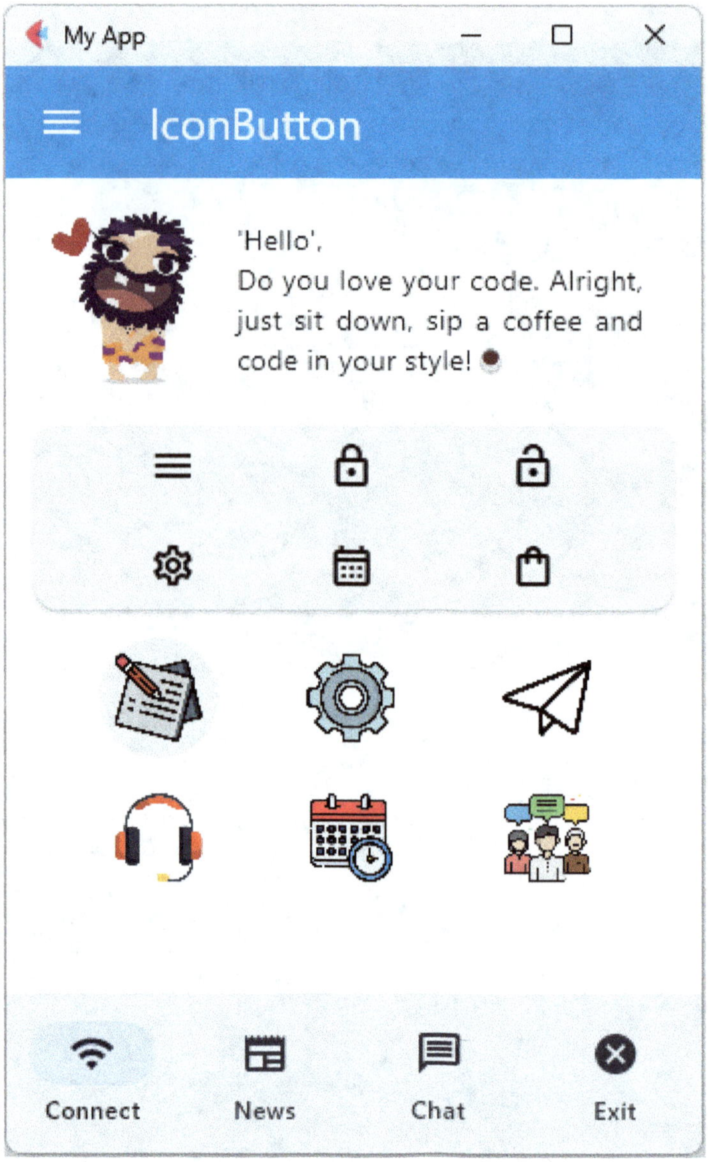
My App
IconButton
'Hello',
Do you love your code. Alright, just sit down, sip a coffee and code in your style!
Connect
News
Chat
Exit

Page Summary

IconButton control creates an icon-based button in a Flet app, allowing users to perform actions with a single tap.

Keywords

url
highlight_color
selected_icon
selected_icon_color

Discussion

1. How can you customize the appearance of an IconButton, such as changing its icon size, color, or padding?
2. What are some techniques for providing additional context or tooltips for IconButton actions to improve usability?
3. Can you discuss the performance implications of using IconButton control, especially when rendering a large number of icons on the screen?

OutlinedButton

The **OutlinedButton** is a material design button that displays a border outlined around its content. It is typically used for less prominent actions compared to **ElevatedButton**, but it provides more emphasis than **TextButton** due to its outlined border.

Available Methods

Property	Value	Property	Value
content	Control	url	string
text	string	url_target	string
icon	string	on_long_press	function
icon_color	string	on_click	function
style	ButtonStyle	on_hover	function
adaptive	bool	on_focus	function
autofocus	bool	on_blur	function

text = string

The **text** property defines the text or label of the outlined button.

```
flet.OutlinedButton(
        text= "project",
    )
```

icon = string

This specifies the icon of the outlined button

```
flet.OutlinedButton(
        text= "project",
        icon= flet.icons.ROCKET_LAUNCH_OUTLINED

    )
```

icon_color = string

This property specifies the color of the button's icon.

```
flet.OutlinedButton(
    text= "Project",
    icon= flet.icons.ROCKET_LAUNCH_OUTLINED,
    icon_color = 'red'
)
```

content = control

The **content** property is used in place of **text** and **icon** property to add more complex controls to the button, such as images and other controls.

```
flet.OutlinedButton(
    height= 40,
    content= flet.Row(
        alignment = flet.MainAxisAlignment.CENTER,
        controls=[
            flet.Text('Send', size=25),
            flet.Image(src="C:\\Users\\send.png")
        ]
    ) )
```

adaptive = bool

When this property is True, it allows platform-specific design for the outlined button.

```
flet.OutlinedButton(
    adaptive= True
)
```

autofocus = bool

When the **autofocus** is set to True, the OutlinedButton gains focus automatically.

```
flet.OutlinedButton(
    autofocus= True
)
```


url = string
This property connects to the web when the button is clicked by assigning a web address.

```
flet.OutlinedButton(
    url= "https://www.google.com"
)
```

ButtonStyle

- color
- bgcolor
- overlay_color
- shadow_color
- surface_tint_color
- elevation
- animation_duration
- padding
- shape
- side

color = string
The **color** method defines the color for the icon.

```
flet.OutlinedButton(
    text= "Facebook",
    icon=flet.icons.FACEBOOK_OUTLINED,
    style= flet.ButtonStyle(
        color= "blue"
    )
)
```

bgcolor = string

The **bgcolor** specifies the background color of the button.

```
flet.OutlinedButton(
    text= "Facebook",
    icon=flet.icons.FACEBOOK_OUTLINED,
    style= flet.ButtonStyle(
        color = "white",
        bgcolor= "#14171A"
    )
)
```

overlay_color = string

This defines the background color when the button is focused or active.

```
flet.OutlinedButton(
    icon= flet.icons.LOCK_OUTLINE,
    style= flet.ButtonStyle(
        overlay_color= flet.colors.with_opacity(0.5, 'teal')
    )
)
```

padding = float, flet.padding.all, flet.padding.only

The **padding** creates space between the content and edges of the button.

```
flet.OutlinedButton(
    text= "Facebook",
    icon=flet.icons.FACEBOOK_OUTLINED,
    style= flet.ButtonStyle(
        padding = 25
    )
)
```

shape = flet.OutlinedBorder
The shape property defines the shape of the border. The available shapes include:

- flet.RoundedRectangleBorder(type: str, radius: int)
- flet.StadiumBorder(type: str)
- flet.CircleBorder(type: str)
- flet.BeveledRectangleBorder(type: str, radius: int)
- flet.OutlinedBorder(type: str)
- flet.ContinousRectangleBorder(type: str, radius: int)

```
flet.OutlinedButton(
    text= "Facebook",
    icon=flet.icons.FACEBOOK_OUTLINED,
    style= flet.ButtonStyle(
        shape= flet.RoundedRectangleBorder(radius=5)
    )
)
```

side = flet.BorderSide
The side property allows customization of the button edges or the border by specifying the width and color.

```
flet.OutlinedButton(
    text= "Facebook",
    icon=flet.icons.FACEBOOK_OUTLINED,
    style= flet.ButtonStyle(
        side= flet.BorderSide(width=2, color= "red")
    )
)
```

animation_duration = int
This property specifies the duration of the click effect in seconds.

```
style= flet.ButtonStyle(
  animation_duration= 5
)
```


Python **Code 2.7.0**

```
#myfletapp.py
import flet

def main(page: flet.Page):
    page.title = "My App"
    page.bgcolor = "#FFFFFF"
    page.padding = flet.padding.all(0)

    stack = flet.Stack(
     height= page.height,
     width= page.width,
     controls=[
         flet.Image(src="C:\\background.jpg"),
         flet.Text('Good morning,',
                   size=35,
                   color='white',
                   top= 50,
                   left=50
                   ),
         flet.OutlinedButton(
             bottom = 230,
             left = 100,
             text = "Login",
             style= flet.ButtonStyle(
                 color= "green",
                 padding= flet.padding.only(left=50, right=50),
                 shape= flet.RoundedRectangleBorder(radius=5),
                 side= flet.BorderSide(width=1, color="white")
             )
         ),

        flet.OutlinedButton(
             bottom = 180,
             left = 20,
             text = "Facebook",
             icon= flet.icons.FACEBOOK_OUTLINED,
             icon_color = "blue",
             style= flet.ButtonStyle(
                 color= "white",
                 side= flet.BorderSide(width=1, color="white")
             )
         ),

        flet.OutlinedButton(
             bottom = 180,
             left = 180,
             style= flet.ButtonStyle(
                 color= "white",
                 side= flet.BorderSide(width=1, color="white"),
                 padding= flet.padding.only(left=20, right=20),
             ),
            content=flet.Row(
                controls=[
                    flet.Image(
                        "C:\\Users\\search.png",
                        height=20,
                        width=20,
                        fit =flet.ImageFit.FILL),
                    flet.Text("Google")
                ]
            )
         )
      ]
    )

    page.add(stack)
    page.update()

flet.app(target = main)
```

My App
Good morning,
I NEED
MORE
SPACE
Login
Facebook
Google

Page Summary

OutlinedButton control creates a button with an outlined border in a Flet app, providing a visually distinct alternative to raised or text-based buttons.

Keywords

url
icon_color
ButtonStyle

Discussion

1. How do you customize the appearance of an OutlinedButton, such as changing its border color, width, or radius?
2. What are some best practices for styling OutlinedButton to ensure consistency with the app's design language and theme?
3. Can you discuss the difference between an OutlinedButton and a TextButton, and when each would be used?

Radio

The **RadioButton** is a selection control that allows users to choose one option from a set of mutually exclusive options. It is typically used in forms and dialogs where a user must select a single option from a list.
RadioButton is best used when there are multiple options, but only one can be selected at a time.

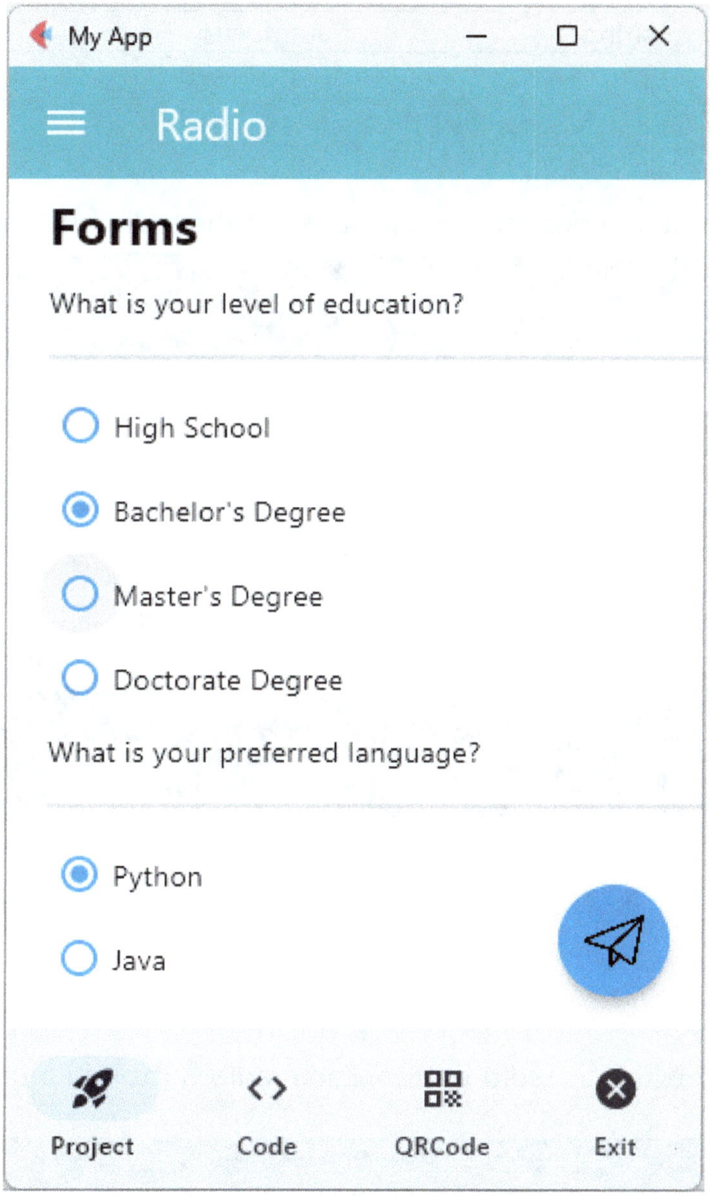

Available Methods

Property	Value	Property	Value
label	string	style	ButtonStyle
label_position	LabelPosition	on_hover	function
label_style	TextStyle	on_focus	function
value	string	on_blur	function
fill_color	string	adaptive	bool
active_color	string	autofocus	bool

label = string

The **label** is the text that defines the main purpose of the radio button.

```
        flet.Radio(
            label="computer",
            ),
```

label_position

By default, labels are positioned on the right side of the radio icon. This property allows changing the position of the label. The available options are LEFT, RIGHT, and NONE.

```
        flet.Radio(
            label="Computer",
            label_position= flet.LabelPosition.LEFT
        ),
```

value = string

The **value** associated with this radio button. Each radio button in a group should have a unique value.

```
        flet.Radio(
            label="Computer",
            value="computerValue"
        ),
```


fill_color = string

The color that fills the radio button when selected.

```
        flet.Radio(
            label="Computer",
            fill_color= "red"
        ),
```

active_color = string

The color of the radio button's outline when it is selected.

```
        flet.Radio(
            label="Computer",
            active_color= "green"
        ),
```

TextStyle

Labels can be styled in different formats using the **TextStyle**.

label_style = flet.TextStyle

- size
- height
- italic
- weight
- decoration
- decoration_color
- decoration_tickness
- decoration_style
- font_family
- bgcolor
- color
- shadow
- letter_spacing
- foreground

size = int

This property sets the size of the label. It requires an integer value.

```
    flet.Radio(
        label="Computer",
        label_style = flet.TextStyle(
        size=20
    )),
```

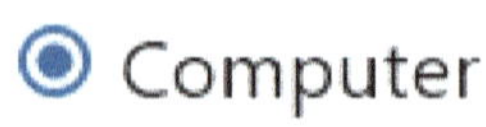

color = string

The **color** property sets the label color.

```
    flet.Radio(
        label="Computer",
        label_style = flet.TextStyle(
        color = "green"
    )),
```

bgcolor = string

The **bgcolor** defines the background color for the label.

```
    flet.Radio(
        label="Computer",
        label_style = flet.TextStyle(
        bgcolor = "blue"
    )),
```

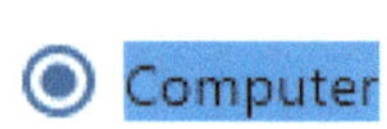

letter_spacing = int

The **letter_spacing** defines the spaces between the characters in the label.

```
    flet.Radio(
        label="Computer",
        label_style = flet.TextStyle(
        letter_spacing = 5
    )),
```


decoration = flet.TextDecoration

This property decorates label with lines. Decoration values include UNDERLINE, OVERLINE, LINE_THROUGH and NONE.

```
        flet.Radio(
            label="Computer",
            label_style = flet.TextStyle(
            decoration= flet.TextDecoration.UNDERLINE
        )),
```

decoration_style = flet.TextDecorationStyle

After applying decoration to the label, **decoration_style** let you choose line styles to apply to the text. This includes WAVY, DASHED, DOTTED, DOUBLE and SOLID.

```
        flet.Radio(
            label="Computer",
            label_style = flet.TextStyle(
            decoration= flet.TextDecoration.OVERLINE,
            decoration_style= flet.TextDecorationStyle.DOTTED
        )),
```

decoration_thickness = int

This property is utilized to add boldness or thickness to text with decorated lines.

```
        flet.Radio(
            label="Computer",
            label_style = flet.TextStyle(
            decoration= flet.TextDecoration.UNDERLINE,
            decoration_thickness=5,
            decoration_color='red'
        )
        ),
```

RadioGroup

RadioGroup is the control that adds and manages groups of radio buttons, ensuring that only one radio button in the group can be selected at any time.

- content
- value
- change

content = control

The content property adds a child control to the **RadioGroup** typically a layout control such as **Column**, **Row**, **ListView**, or **GridView** which in turn contains the radio buttons.

```
flet.RadioGroup(
       content= flet.Column(
           controls =[
             flet.Radio(label="Male", value="male", fill_color='blue'),
             flet.Radio(label="Female", value="female", fill_color='blue'),
             ]
         )
     ),
```

value = string

The value represents the currently selected Radio value within the **RadioGroup**. This property is used to identify which radio button is selected and be used to set the initial selected value or retrieve the selected value for processing.

```
flet.RadioGroup(
      value = "male",
      content= flet.Column(
           controls =[
              flet.Radio(label="Male", value="male", fill_color='blue'),
              flet.Radio(label="Female", value="female", fill_color='blue'),
              ]
          )
      ),
```


on_change = function

This is a callback function that is triggered when the selected value in the **RadioGroup** changes.

```
def changeFun(e):
    value = e.control.value
    if value == "male":
        print("Male selected!")

    if value == "female":
        print("female selected!")

radio = flet.RadioGroup(
          on_change = changeFun,
          value = "male",
          content= flet.Column(
              controls =[
              flet.Radio(label="Male", value="male", fill_color='blue'),
              flet.Radio(label="Female", value="female", fill_color='blue'),
             ]
          )
      ),
```


Python **Code 2.8.0**

```
import flet

def main(page: flet.Page):
    page.title = "My App"
    page.bgcolor = 'white'
    page.padding = flet.padding.only(left=20, top= 5, right=20)


    def myTheme(e):
        value = e.control.value
        print(value)

    def myNotification(e):
        value = e.control.value
        print(value)

    def myBackup(e):
        value = e.control.value
        print(value)

    col = flet.Column(
        height= page.height,
        width= page.width,
        alignment= flet.MainAxisAlignment.START,
        horizontal_alignment= flet.CrossAxisAlignment.START,
        controls=[
        flet.Text('Settings', size=25),
        flet.Divider(),
        flet.Text('Theme',color='orange'),

        flet.RadioGroup(
              on_change = myTheme,
              value = "light",
              content= flet.Row(
                  controls =[
                  flet.Radio(label="Light", value="light", fill_color='green'),
                  flet.Radio(label="Dark", value="dark", fill_color='green'),
                  ]
              )
           ),
        flet.Divider(),
        flet.Text('Notification',color='orange'),

        flet.RadioGroup(
              on_change = myNotification,
              value = "with_sound",
              content= flet.Column(
                  controls =[
                  flet.Radio(label="Off", value="off", fill_color='green'),
                  flet.Radio(label="With sound", value="with_sound", fill_color='green'),
                  flet.Radio(label="Silent", value="silent", fill_color='green'),
                  ]
              )
           ),
        flet.Divider(),
        flet.Text('Backup', color='orange'),

        flet.RadioGroup(
              on_change = myBackup,
              value = "monthly",
              content= flet.Column(
                  controls =[
                  flet.Radio(label="None", value="none", fill_color='green'),
                  flet.Radio(label="Daily", value="daily", fill_color='green'),
                  flet.Radio(label="Weekly", value="weekly", fill_color='green'),
                  flet.Radio(label="Monthly", value="monthly", fill_color='green'),
                  ]
              )
           ),

        ]
    )

    page.add(col)
    page.update()

flet.app(target = main)
```


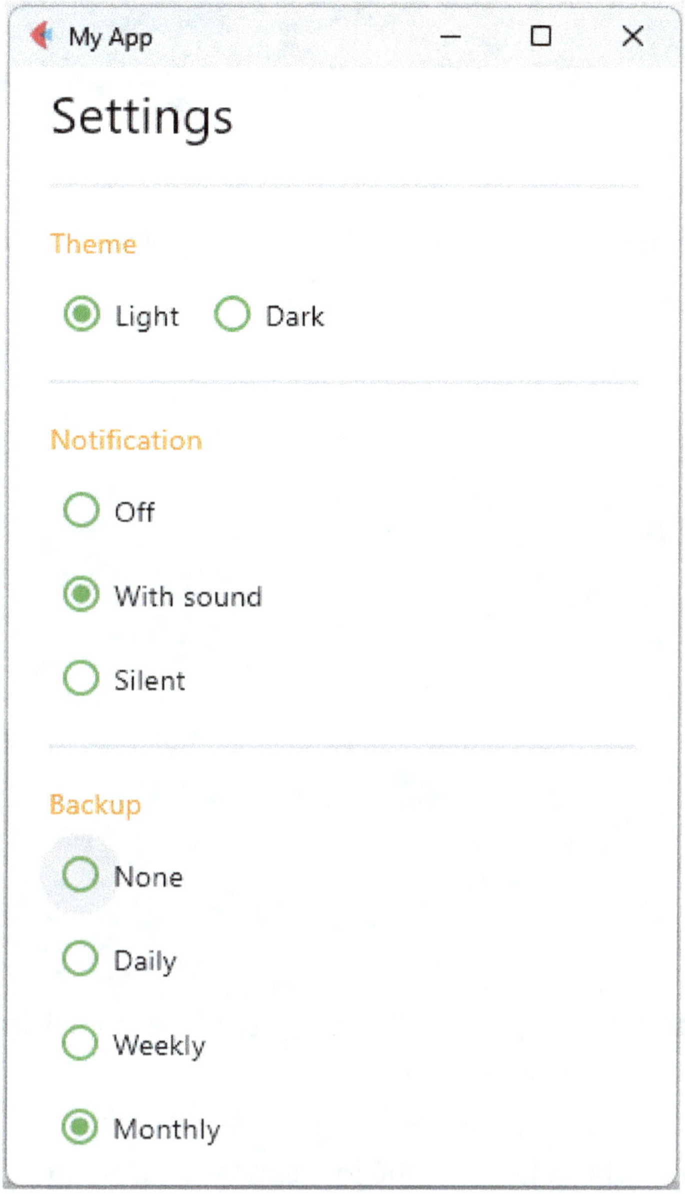
My App
Settings
Theme
Light
Dark
Notification
Off
With sound
Silent
Backup
None
Daily
Weekly
Monthly

Page Summary

Radio control creates a radio button in a Flet app, allowing users to select a single option from a list of mutually exclusive choices.

Keywords

value
active_color
label_position
label_style
fill_color
RadioGroup

Discussion

1. How do you group multiple Radio controls together to ensure that they behave as a single group with exclusive selection?
2. What are some strategies for handling the state management of Radio buttons, such as updating the selected value in response to user input?
3. Can you discuss the accessibility considerations when using Radio buttons, such as providing clear labels and descriptions for each option?
4. What is **CupertinoRadio?**

Checkbox

The **Checkbox** is a selection control that allows users to make binary choices, typically to select or deselect an option. It is often used in forms, settings, and dialogs where multiple selections are required or optional.

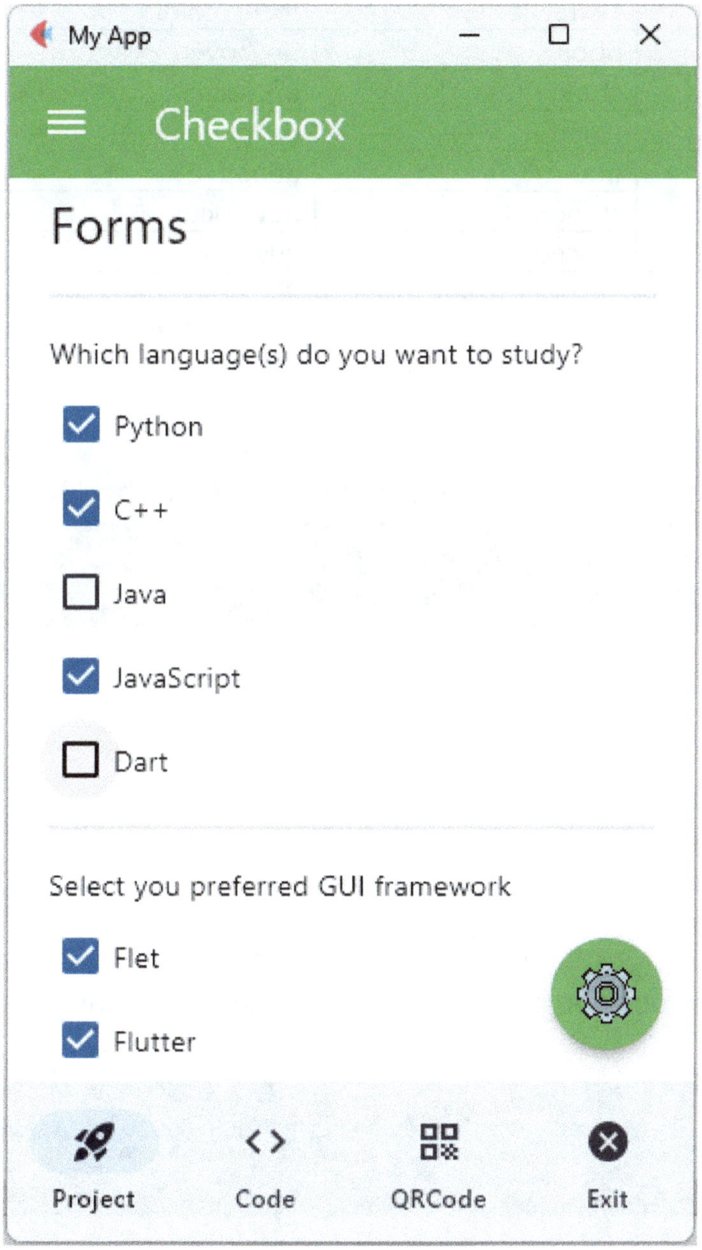

Available Methods

Property	Value	Property	Value
label	string	check_color	string
label_position	LabelPosition	hover_color	string
label_style	TextStyle	focus_color	string
value	bool	on_hover	function
fill_color	string	on_focus	function
active_color	string	on_blur	function
tristate	bool	adaptive	bool
overlay_color	string	autofocus	bool
on_change	function	key	string

label = string

The **label** is the text that defines the main purpose of the checkbox

```
flet.Checkbox(
    label= "Python"
),
```

label_position

By default, labels are positioned on the right side of the checkbox icon. This property allows changing the position of the label. The available options are LEFT, RIGHT and NONE.

```
flet.Checkbox(
    label= "Python",
    label_position= flet.LabelPosition.LEFT
),
```

value = bool
The value indicates whether the checkbox is currently selected (True) or not (False).

```
flet.Checkbox(
    label= "Python",
    value= False
),
```

fill_color = string
The color that fills the checkbox when selected.

```
flet.Checkbox(
    label="Python",
    fill_color= "red"
),
```

active_color = string
The color to use when the checkbox is selected.

```
flet.Radio(
    label="Computer",
    active_color= "green"
),
```

check_color = string
This property defines the color of the checkmark when the checkbox is selected.

```
flet.Checkbox(
    label= "Python",
    check_color="orange"
),
```

overlay_color = string
The **overlay_color** defines the indicator color of the checkbox.

```
        flet.Checkbox(
            label= "Python",
            overlay_color= "green"
        ),
```

hover_color = string (Desktop Only)
This property defines the color when the mouse passes over the Checkbox control.

```
        flet.Checkbox(
            label= "Python",
            hover_color = "orange"
        ),
```

on_change = function'
It registers a callback function that is triggered when the state of the checkbox changes.

```
def checkFunc(e):
        value = e.control.value
        pass

check = flet.Checkbox(
            label= "Python",
            on_change= checkFunc
        ),
```

tristate = bool
If this property is set to True, the checkbox can have three states: True, False and Null. The Null state is represented by a dash.

```
        flet.Checkbox(
            label= "Python",
            tristate= True
        ),
```


TextStyle

Labels can be styled in different formats using the **TextStyle.**

label_style = flet.TextStyle

- size
- height
- italic
- weight
- decoration
- decoration_color
- decoration_tickness
- decoration_style
- font_family
- bgcolor
- color
- shadow
- letter_spacing
- foreground

size = int
This property sets the size of the label. It requires an integer value.

```
flet.Checkbox(
    label= "Python",
    label_style = flet.TextStyle(
        size=20
    )
),
```

color = string
The **color** property sets the label color.

```
flet.Checkbox(
    label= "Python",
    label_style = flet.TextStyle(
        color = "orange"
    )
),
```

bgcolor = string

The **bgcolor** defines a background color for the label.

```
            flet.Checkbox(
                label= "Python",
                label_style = flet.TextStyle(
                    bgcolor = "grey"
                )
            ),
```

letter_spacing = int

The **letter_spacing** defines the spaces between the characters in the label.

```
            flet.Checkbox(
                label= "Python",
                label_style = flet.TextStyle(
                    letter_spacing= 5
                )
            ),
```

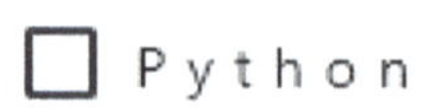

decoration = flet.TextDecoration

This property decorates label with lines. Decoration values include UNDERLINE, OVERLINE, LINE_THROUGH and NONE.

```
            flet.Checkbox(
                label= "Python",
                label_style = flet.TextStyle(
                    decoration= flet.TextDecoration.LINE_THROUGH
                )
            ),
```

decoration_style = flet.TextDecorationStyle
After applying decoration to text, **decoration_style** let you choose line styles to apply to the text. This includes WAVY, DASHED, DOTTED, DOUBLE and SOLID.

```
        flet.Checkbox(
            label= "Python",
            label_style = flet.TextStyle(
                    decoration= flet.TextDecoration.OVERLINE,
                    decoration_style= flet.TextDecorationStyle.DOTTED
            )
        ),
```

decoration_thickness = int
This property is utilized to add boldness or thickness to text with decorated lines.

```
        flet.Checkbox(
            label= "Python",
            label_style = flet.TextStyle(
                    decoration= flet.TextDecoration.UNDERLINE,
                    decoration_thickness=3,
                    decoration_color='red'
            )
        ),
```

Python *Code 2.9.0*

```python
import flet

def main(page: flet.Page):
    page.title = "My App"
    page.bgcolor = 'white'
    page.padding = flet.padding.only(left=20, top= 5, right=20)

    page.appbar = flet.AppBar(
      color= flet.colors.WHITE,
      title= flet.Text("Checkbox"),
      bgcolor=flet.colors.GREEN,
    )

    page.drawer = flet.NavigationDrawer()

    page.floating_action_button = flet.FloatingActionButton(
    bgcolor=flet.colors.GREEN,
    shape= flet.CircleBorder(),
    content= flet.Image(
        src= "C:\\Users\\Asiedu\\Desktop\\Scode\\python\\Chatbox\\appico\\settings.png", width=30, height=30, fit= flet.ImageFit.FILL
    )
    )
    page.navigation_bar = flet.NavigationBar(
        destinations= [
           flet.NavigationDestination(
                 label="Project",
                 icon=flet.icons.ROCKET_LAUNCH
             ),

            flet.NavigationDestination(
                label="Code",
                icon=flet.icons.CODE
             ),

             flet.NavigationDestination(
                label="QRCode",
                icon=flet.icons.QR_CODE_OUTLINED
             ),

            flet.NavigationDestination(
                label="Exit",
                icon=flet.icons.CANCEL
            )
        ]
    )

    def termsFunc(e):
        value = e.control.value
        if value == True:
            print('terms accepted')

    def privacyFunc(e):
        value = e.control.value
        if value == True:
            print('privacy accepted')


    col = flet.Column(
        height= page.height,
        width= page.width,
        alignment= flet.MainAxisAlignment.START,
        horizontal_alignment= flet.CrossAxisAlignment.START,
        controls=[
           flet.Text('Terms and Conditions', size = 25),
           flet.Divider(),
           flet.Text('''1. Acceptance of Terms:\nBy accessing and using our service,you accept and agree to be bond by the terms and provision of
                       this agreement.''',
                    text_align= flet.TextAlign.JUSTIFY),

           flet.Text('''2. Privacy Policy:\nYour use of the service is also subject to our Privacy Policy.
                    Please review Privay Policy to understand our practices.''',
                    text_align= flet.TextAlign.JUSTIFY),

           flet.Container(height=20),
           flet.Checkbox(
               label= "I agree to the Terms and Conditions.",
               fill_color="blue",
               on_change= termsFunc,
               ),

           flet.Checkbox(
               label= "I agree to Privacy Policy.",
               fill_color="blue",
               on_change= privacyFunc,
               ),
         ]
    )
    page.add(col)
    page.update()

flet.app(target = main)
```


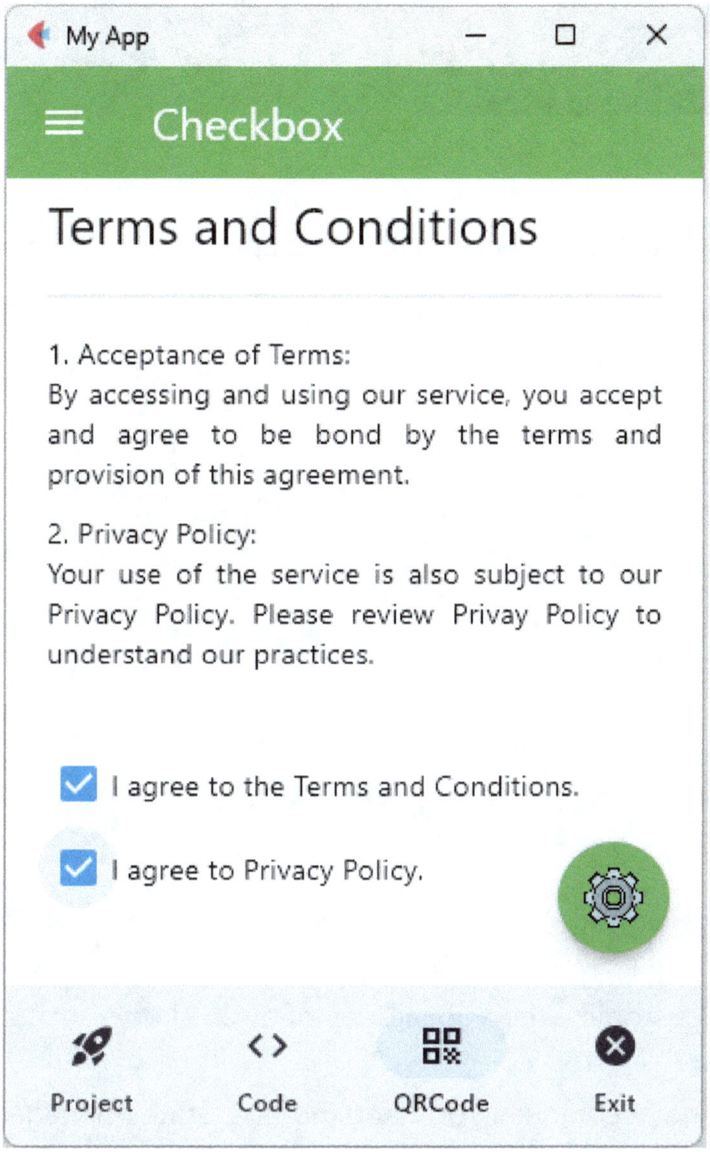
My App
Checkbox
Terms and Conditions
1. Acceptance of Terms:
By accessing and using our service, you accept and agree to be bond by the terms and provision of this agreement.
2. Privacy Policy:
Your use of the service is also subject to our Privacy Policy. Please review Privay Policy to understand our practices.
I agree to the Terms and Conditions.
I agree to Privacy Policy.
Project
Code
QRCode
Exit

Page Summary

Checkbox control creates a checkbox in a Flet app, allowing users to toggle a binary state on or off.

Keywords

value
active_color
label_position
label_style
fill_color
overlay_color
tristate

Discussion

1. How can you customize the appearance of a Checkbox, such as changing its size, color, or shape?
2. What are some techniques for handling the state management of Checkbox controls, such as updating the selected value in response to user input?
3. Can you discuss the difference between controlled and uncontrolled Checkbox control, and when each would be used?
4. Fine more about the **CupertinoCheckbox** and discuss about it.

Switch

The **Switch** control is useful for scenarios where a user needs to toggle a setting or feature on and off.

Available Methods

Property	Value	Property	Value
label	string	thumb_icon	string
label_position	LabelPosition	focus_color	string
label_style	TextStyle	on_change	function
value	bool	on_focus	function
active_color	string	on_blur	function
active_track_color	string	adaptive	bool
thumb_color	string	autofocus	bool
inactive_track_color	string		

label = string

The **label** defines the description or primary purpose of the switch.

```
flet.Switch(
    label= "notification"
)
```

label_position = flet.LabelPosition

This property specifies where the label should be positioned in relation to the switch icon. By default, the label is positioned at the right side. The available options are RIGHT, NONE and LEFT.

```
flet.Switch(
    label= "notification",
    label_position= flet.LabelPosition.LEFT
)
```

active_color = string
The color to display when the switch is toggled on.

```
        flet.Switch(
            label= "notification",
            active_color= "green"
        )
```

active_track_color = string
The **active_track_color** property defines the color of the track when the switch is in the "on" position.

```
        flet.Switch(
            label= "notification",
            active_track_color= "orange"
        )
```

inactive_track_color = string
The **inactive_track_color** property defines the color of the track when the switch is in the "off" position.

```
        flet.Switch(
            label= "notification",
            inactive_track_color= "red"
        )
```

value = bool
The **value** indicates whether the Switch is currently toggled (True) or not (False).

```
        flet.Switch(
            label= "notification",
            value = True
        )
```


active_thumb_color = string
This property defines the color of the thumb (the circular indicator) when the switch is in either "on" or "off" position.

```
        flet.Switch(
            label= "notification",
            thumb_color= "teal"
        )
```

thumb_icon = string
The **thumb_icon** specifies the icon to be displayed on the thumb of the switch.

```
        flet.Switch(
            label= "notification",
            thumb_icon= flet.icons.ARROW_CIRCLE_RIGHT_OUTLINED
        )
```

on_change = function'
The **on_change** registers a callback function that is triggered when the state of the switch changes.

```
    def switchFunc(e):
        value = e.control.value
        print(value)

    switch = flet.Switch(
                label= "notification",
                on_change= switchFunc
        )
```

 |

TextStyle

Labels can be styled in different formats using the **TextStyle**.

label_style = flet.TextStyle

- size
- height
- italic
- weight
- decoration
- decoration_color
- decoration_tickness
- decoration_style
- font_family
- bgcolor
- color
- shadow
- letter_spacing
- foreground

size = int
This property sets the size of the label. It requires an integer value.

```
flet.Switch(
    label= "notification",
    label_style = flet.TextStyle(
        size=25
    )
)
```

color = string

The **color** property sets the label color.

```
flet.Checkbox(
    label= "notification",
    label_style = flet.TextStyle(
        color = "green"

    )
),
```

bgcolor = string

The **bgcolor** defines a background color of the label.

```
            flet.Switch(
                label= "notification",
                label_style = flet.TextStyle(
                   bgcolor = "grey"
               )
            )
```

letter_spacing = int

The **letter_spacing** defines the spaces between the characters in the label.

```
            flet.Switch(
                label= "notification",
                label_style = flet.TextStyle(
                   letter_spacing= 5
               )
            )
```

decoration = flet.TextDecoration

This property decorates label with lines. Decoration values include UNDERLINE, OVERLINE, LINE_THROUGH and NONE.

```
            flet.Switch(
                label= "notification",
                label_style = flet.TextStyle(
                   decoration= flet.TextDecoration.LINE_THROUGH
               )
            )
```

decoration_style = flet.TextDecorationStyle
After applying decoration to text, **decoration_style** let you choose line styles to apply to the text. This includes WAVY, DASHED, DOTTED, DOUBLE and SOLID.

```
            flet.Switch(
                label= "notification",
                label_style = flet.TextStyle(
                    decoration= flet.TextDecoration.OVERLINE,
                    decoration_style= flet.TextDecorationStyle.DOTTED
                )
            )
```

decoration_thickness = int
This property is utilized to add boldness or thickness to the label with decorated lines.

```
            flet.Switch(
                label= "notification",
                label_style = flet.TextStyle(
                    decoration= flet.TextDecoration.UNDERLINE,
                    decoration_thickness=3,
                    decoration_color='red'
                )
            )
```

Page Summary

Switch control creates an on/off switch in a Flet app, allowing users to toggle a binary state between two options.

Keywords

value
active_color
label_position
label_style
fill_color
thumb_icon
thumb_color
active_track_color

Discussion

1. How do you customize the appearance of a Switch, such as changing its color, size, or thumb icon?
2. What are some strategies for handling the state management of Switch controls, such as updating the selected value in response to user input?
3. Can you discuss the accessibility considerations when using Switch controls, such as providing clear labels and descriptions for each state?
4. Discuss about the **CupertinoSwitch**

Tabs

The **Tabs** are user interface control that allows the organization of content into separate, navigation sections within the same space. Each tab represents a different view or section and users can switch between these sections by clicking or tapping on the corresponding tab.

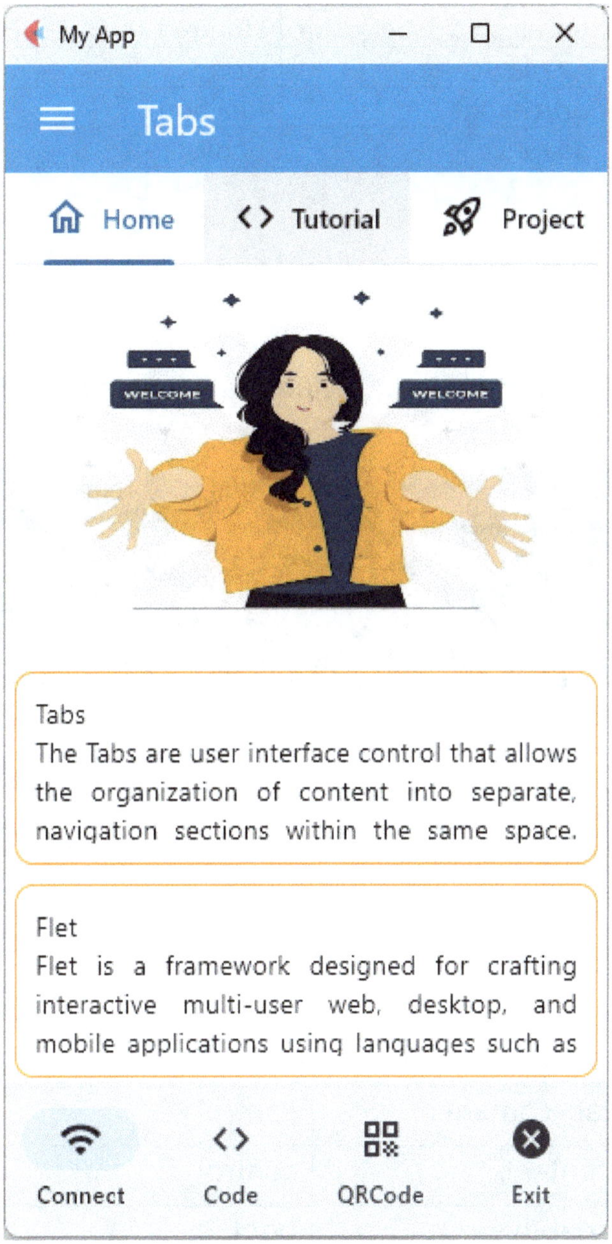

Available Methods

Property	Value	Property	Value
tabs	List[tabs]	indicator_border_side	BorderSide
selected_index	int	indicator_padding	PaddingValue
scrollable	bool	indicator_tab_size	bool
tab_alignment	TabAlignment	label_color	string
animation_duration	int	unselected_label_color	string
divider_color	string	overlay_color	string
indicator_color	string	on_change	function
indicator_border_radius	BorderRadius	adaptive	bool

tabs = List[tabs]

This defines the list of tabs to display. Each Tab object typically includes a label (text) and icon.

```
tabs = flet.Tabs(
            tabs=[
              flet.Tab(),
              flet.Tab()
            ]
        )
```

Tab

A Tab is a control that represents a page or view within a set of Tabs.

text	string	tab_content	control
icon	string	content	control
visible	bool	adaptive	bool

text = string

This property defines the label of the Tab or page. It can be used without an icon.

```
tabs = flet.Tabs(
        tabs=[
          flet.Tab(text = "Home"),
          flet.Tab(text = "Tutorial"),
          flet.Tab(text = "Project"),
        ]
    )
```

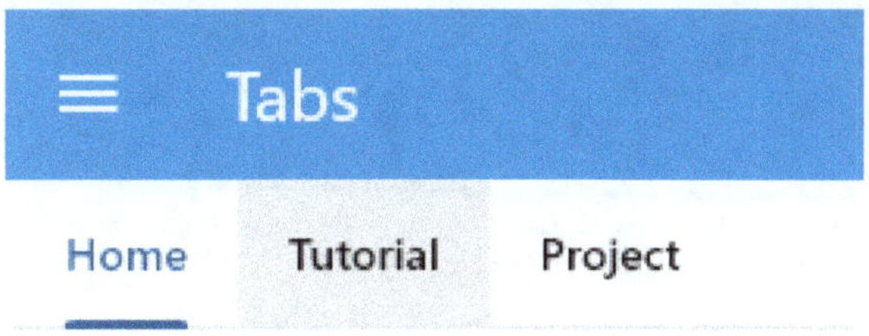

icon = string

The **icon** property provides a visual representation for the Tab. It can be used alone or alongside the **text** property.

```
tabs = flet.Tabs(
       tabs=[
         flet.Tab(text = "Home", icon = flet.icons.HOUSE_OUTLINED),
         flet.Tab(text = "Tutorial", icon = flet.icons.CODE),
         flet.Tab(text = "Project", icon = flet.icons.ROCKET_LAUNCH_OUTLINE),
       ]
   )
```

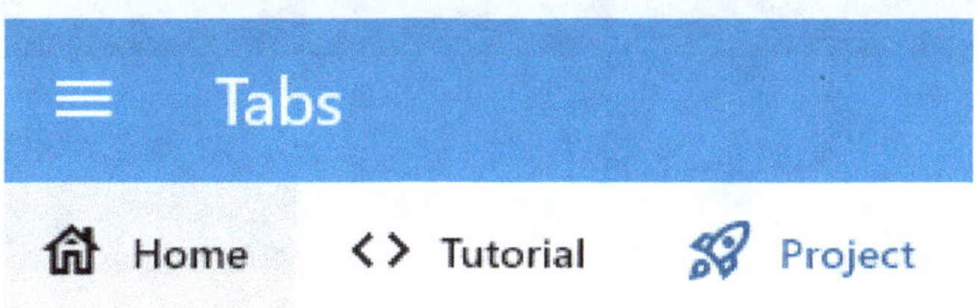

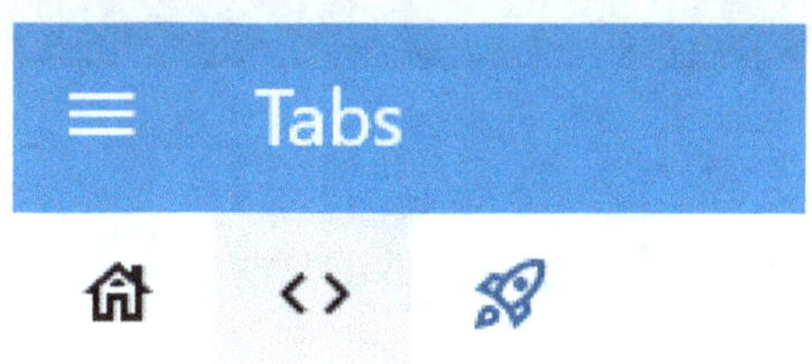

 |

tab_content = control

The **tab_content** can replace both icon and text properties, allowing for more complex controls and customization.

```
tabs = flet.Tabs(
        tabs=[
          flet.Tab(tab_content=flet.Image(src="C:\\image1.png")),
          flet.Tab(tab_content=flet.Image(src="C:\\rocket.png")),
        ]
    )
```

content = control

This defines the content of the page associated with the tab

```
tabs = flet.Tabs(
        tabs=[
          flet.Tab(
              text= "Home",
              icon= flet.icons.HOME_OUTLINED,
              content= flet.Text("Hello\nThis is HomePage",size= 20)
          ),
          flet.Tab(
              text= "Tutorial",
              icon= flet.icons.CODE,
              content= flet.Text("Hello\nThis is Tutorial Page",size= 20)
          ),
          flet.Tab(
              text= "Project",
              icon= flet.icons.ROCKET_LAUNCH_OUTLINED,
              content= flet.Text("Hello\nThis is Project Page",size= 20)
          )
        ]
    )
```

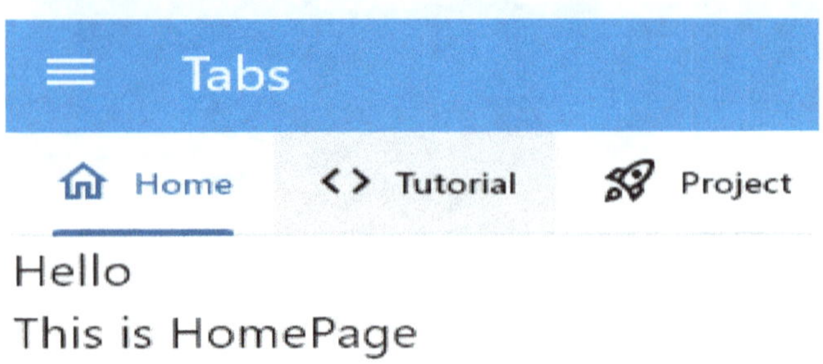

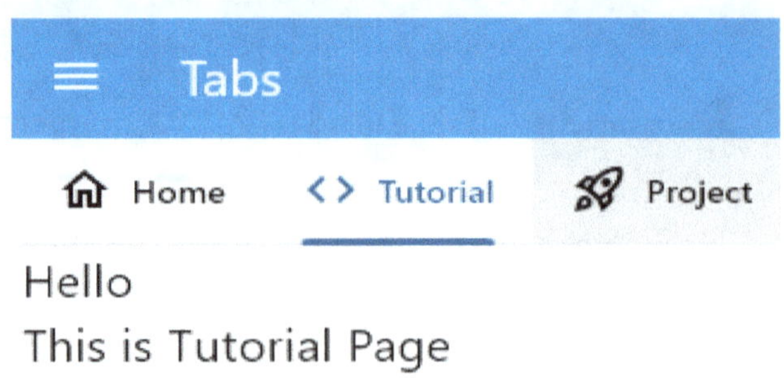

tab_alignment = flet.TabAlignment

This property specifies the arrangement of the Tab labels. The available options are CENTER, FILL, START and START_OFFSET.

```
    tabs = flet.Tabs(
            tab_alignment= flet.TabAlignment.CENTER,
            tabs=[
              flet.Tab(text= "Home", icon= flet.icons.HOME_OUTLINED,),
              flet.Tab(text= "Tutorial" ,icon= flet.icons.CODE,),
              flet.Tab(text= "Project" ,icon= flet.icons.ROCKET_LAUNCH_OUTLINED,)
              ]
        )
```

lable_color = string

This specifies the color of the active tab labels.

```
    tabs = flet.Tabs(
             label_color= "orange",
        )
```

current_index = int

This is the index of the currently selected tab. Changing this value will switch the active tab.

```
  tabs = flet.Tabs(
             selected_index=2,
        )
```

 |

indicator_color = string

The color of the indicator that shows which tab is currently selected.

```
    tabs = flet.Tabs(
            indicator_color="green",
            tabs=[
               flet.Tab(text= "Home", icon= flet.icons.HOME_OUTLINED,),
               flet.Tab(text= "Tutorial" ,icon= flet.icons.CODE,),
               flet.Tab(text= "Project" ,icon=flet.icons.ROCKET_LAUNCH_OUTLINED)
             ]
        )
```

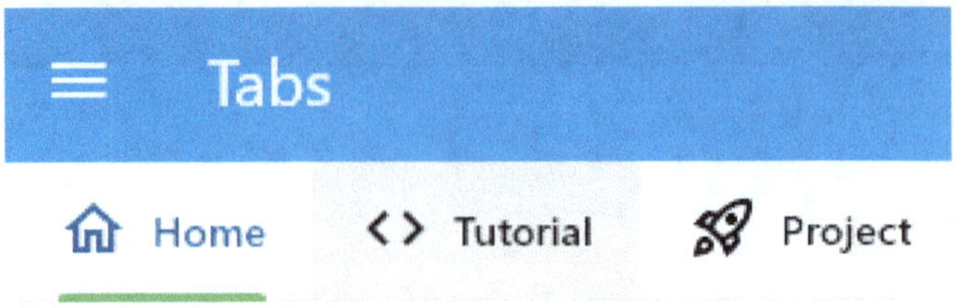

divider_color = string

This specifies the color of the line beneath the tabs.

```
    tabs = flet.Tabs(
            divider_color ="red",
        )
```

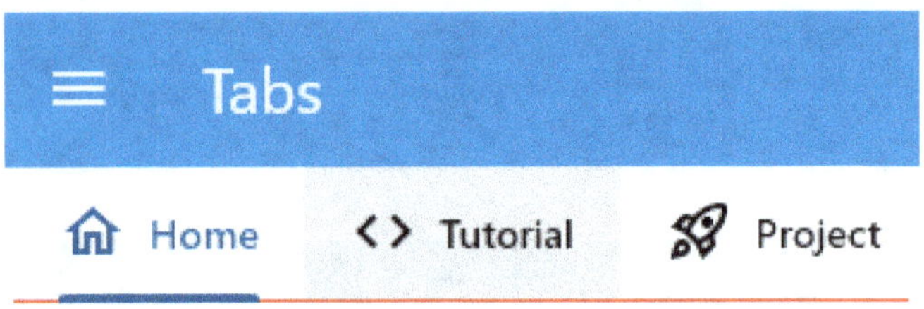

unselected_color = string

The color of the label when the tab is in an unselected state.

```
    tabs = flet.Tabs(
            unselected_label_color ="teal",
        )
```

overlay_color = string

The color to display when the Tab is clicked or hovered.

```
    tabs = flet.Tabs(
            overlay_color = 'cyan',
        )
```

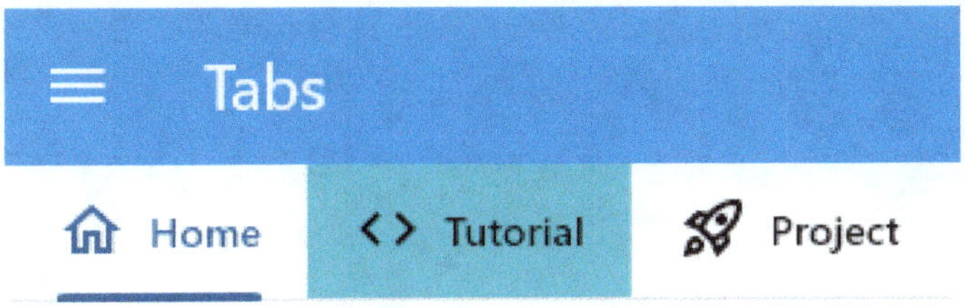

animation_duration = float

This defines the time in seconds for a tap to produce a splash effect.

```
    tabs = flet.Tabs(
            animation_duration= 5,
        )
```

scrollable = bool

When this property is set to False, it prevents each Tab or page from scrolling.

```
  tabs = flet.Tabs(
            scrollable = False,
        )
```

indicator_border_side

This property allows the customization of the border edges of the indicator, including its color and width.

```
    tabs = flet.Tabs(
            indicator_border_side= flet.BorderSide(width=10, color= "green"),
        )
```

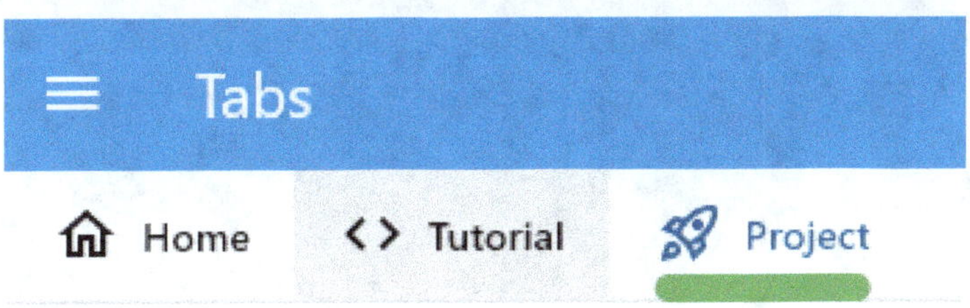

indicator_border_radius = float, flet.border_radius.all, flet.border_radius.only

This defines the degree of curvature of the indicator.

```
    tabs = flet.Tabs(
            indicator_border_side= flet.BorderSide(width=10, color= "green"),
            indicator_border_radius= flet.border_radius.only(top_left=5, bottom_right= 5),
        )
```

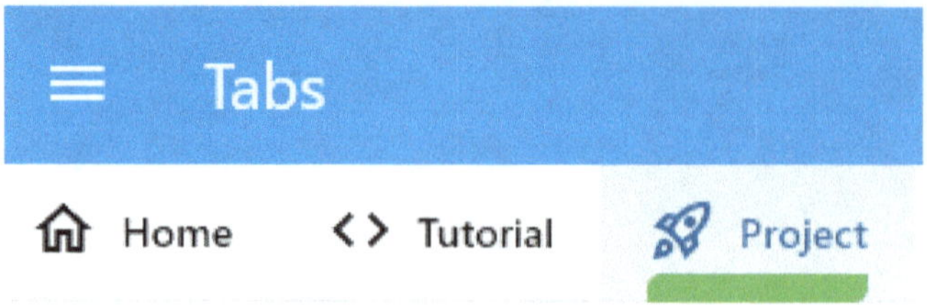

adaptive = bool

When this property is True, it allows platform-specific design for the elevated button.

```
    tabs = flet.Tabs(
            adaptive= True,
        )
```

indicator_tab_size = float

It defines the size of the indicator relative to the tab.

```
    tabs = flet.Tabs(
            indicator_tab_size = 15,
        )
```

on_change = function

This property registers a callback function that is triggered when the user switches tabs. It receives new index of the selected tab as a parameter.

```
def tabFunc(e):
    index = e.control.selected_index
    print(f"page {index} is opened")

tabs = flet.Tabs(
         on_change= tabFunc,
         tabs=[
            flet.Tab(text= "Home", icon= flet.icons.HOME_OUTLINED),
            flet.Tab(text= "Tutorial" ,icon= flet.icons.CODE),
            flet.Tab(text= "Project" ,icon= flet.icons.ROCKET_LAUNCH_OUTLINED)
            ]
    )
```


Python Code 3.0.0

```python
import flet

def main(page: flet.Page):
    page.title = "My App"
    page.bgcolor = 'white'
    page.padding = flet.padding.only(left=5, top= 0, right=5)

    page.appbar = flet.AppBar(
      color= flet.colors.WHITE,
      title= flet.Text("Tabs"),
      bgcolor=flet.colors.BLUE,
    )

    page.drawer = flet.NavigationDrawer()

    page.navigation_bar = flet.NavigationBar(
        destinations= [
           flet.NavigationDestination(
                 label="Connect",
                 icon=flet.icons.WIFI
            ),

            flet.NavigationDestination(
                label="Code",
                icon=flet.icons.CODE
             ),

             flet.NavigationDestination(
                label="QRCode",
                icon=flet.icons.QR_CODE_OUTLINED
             ),

            flet.NavigationDestination(
                label="Exit",
                icon=flet.icons.CANCEL
            )
        ]
    )

    def tabFunc(e):
        index = e.control.selected_index
        print(f"page {index} is opened")


    tabs = flet.Tabs(
            on_change= tabFunc,
            tab_alignment= flet.TabAlignment.CENTER,
            tabs=[
               flet.Tab(text= "Books", icon= flet.icons.BOOK_OUTLINED,
                   content=flet.Column(
                       controls=[
                           flet.Container(
                               margin= flet.margin.only(top=20, bottom=20),
                               border_radius= flet.border_radius.all(10),
                               border= flet.border.all(width=1, color='green'),
                               padding=10,
                               height = 80,
                               width = page.width,
                               content=flet.Text('Hello\nHow well and often do you read your books?')
                           ),
                           flet.Image(src="C:\\books.jpg", height=200, width=page.width, fit=flet.ImageFit.FILL)
                       ]
                   )
                ),
               ######
               flet.Tab(text= "Social" ,icon= flet.icons.FAMILY_RESTROOM_OUTLINED,
                    content=flet.Column(
                       controls=[
                           flet.Container(
                               margin= flet.margin.only(top=20, bottom=20),
                               border_radius= flet.border_radius.all(10),
                               border= flet.border.all(width=1, color='green'),
                               padding=10,
                               height = 80,
                               width = page.width,
                               content=flet.Text('Hi\nHow do you relate with friends and family?')
                           ),
                           flet.Image(src="C:\\family.jpeg", height=200, width=page.width, fit=flet.ImageFit.FILL)
                       ]
                   )
                 ),
             ]
        )


    page.add(tabs)
    page.update()

flet.app(target = main)
```

My App
Tabs
Books
Social
Hello
How well and often do you read your books?
Connect
Code
QRCode
Exit

My App
Tabs
Books
Social
Hi
How do you relate with friends and family?
Connect
Code
QRCode
Exit

Page Summary

Tabs control creates a tab bar with multiple tabs in a Flet app, allowing users to switch between different content views.

Keywords

divider_color
tabs
selected_index
scrollable
tab_alignment

Discussion

1. How do you implement a Tabs control with custom tab indicators or styles to match the app's design language and theme?
2. What are some techniques for managing state and content synchronization between different tab views in a Tabs control?
3. Can you discuss the performance implications of using Tabs control, especially when rendering a large number of tabs or complex content within each tab?

BottomSheet

The **BottomSheet** is a user interface control that slides up from the bottom of the screen to display additional content or options. It can be used to prevent a variety of content such as menus, forms or actions without navigating away from the current screen.

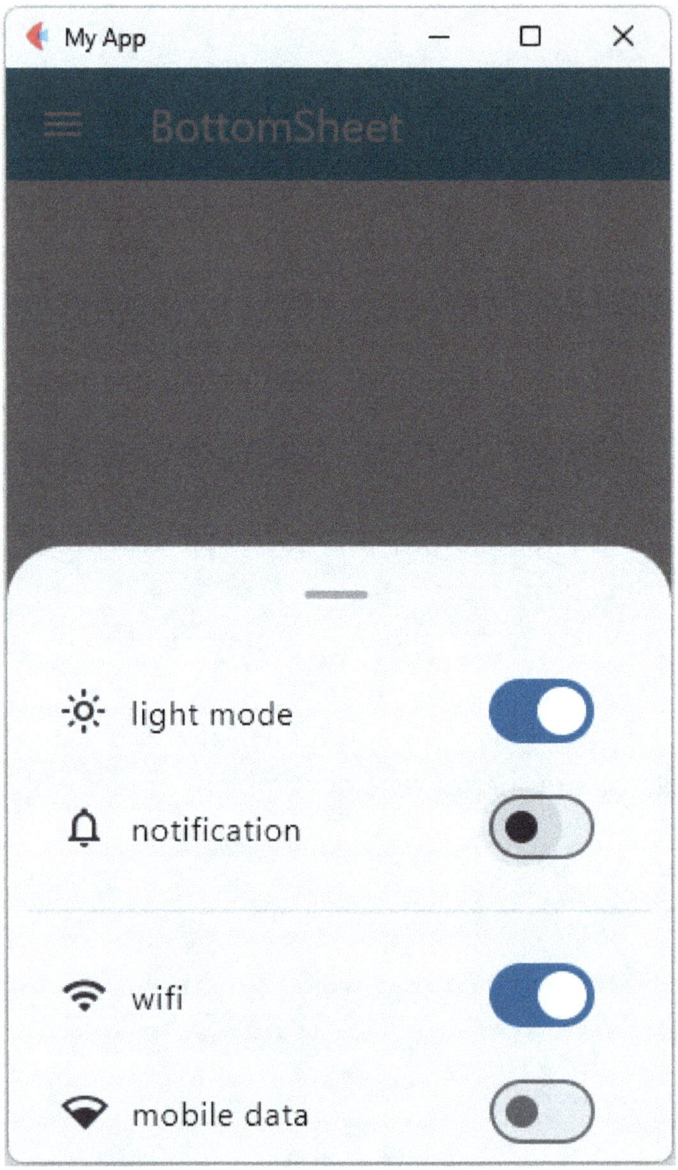

Available Methods

Property	Value	Property	Value
content	control	dismissible	bool
open	bool	enable_drag	bool
elevation	float	show_drag_handle	bool
bgcolor	string	use_safe_area	bool
maintain_bottom_view_insects_padding	bool	is_scroll_controlled	bool
on_dismiss	function	ref	Ref

content = control

The **content** defines the primary content of the bottom sheet, which can be any type of control or layout.

```
    bottomsheet = flet.BottomSheet(
        content= flet.Column(
                controls=[
                   flet.Text('light mode'),
                   flet.Text('notification'),
                ]
            )
        )

    page.overlay.append(bottomsheet)
    page.update()

flet.app(target = main)
```

Note

When using a **BottomSheet**, it is crucial to use **page.overlay.append**. This is because bottom sheets are modal and cannot be added directly to the main page content.

open = bool

This property is False by default but when it is set to True, the bottom sheet is displayed.

```
    bottomsheet = flet.BottomSheet(
        open= True,
    )
```

elevation = float

The **elevation** of the bottom sheet, which affects its shadow.

```
    bottomsheet = flet.BottomSheet(
        elevation= 10,
    )
```

background = string

This property specifies the background color of the bottom sheet.

```
    bottomsheet = flet.BottomSheet(
        open= True,
        bgcolor= flet.colors.with_opacity(0.5, 'blue'),
    )
```

on_dismiss = function

This property registers a callback function that is triggered when the bottom sheet is dismissed.

```
def dismissFunc(e):
    print('BottomSheet is closed')

bottomsheet = flet.BottomSheet(
    on_dismiss= dismissFunc,
    content= flet.Container(
              padding= 10,
              content = flet.Column(
                  controls=[
                     flet.Text('light mode'),
                     flet.Text('notification'),
              ]
          )
      ))
```

enable_drag = bool

The **enable_drag** property specifies whether the bottom sheet can be dragged up and down and dismissed by swiping downwards.

```
bottomsheet = flet.BottomSheet(
        enable_drag= True,
    )
```

show_drag_handle = bool

This property specifies whether to display drag handle at the top of the bottom sheet or not.

```
bottomsheet = flet.BottomSheet(
    open= True,
    show_drag_handle= True,
    content= flet.Container(
              padding= 10,
              width= 350,
              content=flet.Column(
                controls=[
                  flet.Text('light mode'),
                  flet.Text('notification'),
              ]
          )
    ))
```

Python **Code 3.1.0**

```python
import flet

def main(page: flet.Page):
    page.title = "My App"
    page.bgcolor = 'white'
    page.padding = flet.padding.all(0)

    page.appbar = flet.AppBar(
      color= flet.colors.WHITE,
      title= flet.Text("BottomSheet"),
      bgcolor=flet.colors.CYAN,
    )

    page.drawer = flet.NavigationDrawer()

    page.navigation_bar = flet.NavigationBar(
        destinations= [
           flet.NavigationDestination(
                 label="Connect",
                 icon=flet.icons.WIFI
            ),

            flet.NavigationDestination(
                label="Code",
                icon=flet.icons.CODE
             ),

             flet.NavigationDestination(
                label="QRCode",
                icon=flet.icons.QR_CODE_OUTLINED
             ),

            flet.NavigationDestination(
                label="Exit",
                icon=flet.icons.CANCEL
            )
        ]
    )

    def openSheet(e):
        bottomsheet.open = True
        page.update()


    bottomsheet = flet.BottomSheet(
        #open=True,
        show_drag_handle= True,
        content= flet.Container(
                 padding= flet.padding.only(left=10, right=10),
                 width= 350,
                 content=flet.Column(
                   controls=[
                        flet.ListTile(
                         leading= flet.Icon(name=flet.icons.IMAGE_OUTLINED),
                         title= flet.Text('Save Image')
                     ),
                         flet.ListTile(
                         leading= flet.Icon(name=flet.icons.UPLOAD_FILE_OUTLINED),
                         title= flet.Text('Upload File')
                     ),
                        flet.ListTile(
                         leading= flet.Icon(name=flet.icons.DELETE_OUTLINE),
                         title= flet.Text('Delete')
                     ),
                        flet.ListTile(
                         leading= flet.Icon(name=flet.icons.COPY_OUTLINED),
                         title= flet.Text('Copy')
                     ),
                        flet.ListTile(
                         leading= flet.Icon(name=flet.icons.PRINT_OUTLINED),
                         title= flet.Text('Print')
                     ),
                 ]
             )
        ))

    button = flet.OutlinedButton(
        text= 'open sheet',
        width= 200,
        height= 40,
        on_click= openSheet
    )

    col = flet.Column(
        width= page.width,
        height= page.height,
        alignment= flet.MainAxisAlignment.CENTER,
        horizontal_alignment= flet.CrossAxisAlignment.CENTER,
        controls= [
           button
        ]
    )

    page.add(col)
    page.overlay.append(bottomsheet)
    page.update()

flet.app(target = main)
```

 |

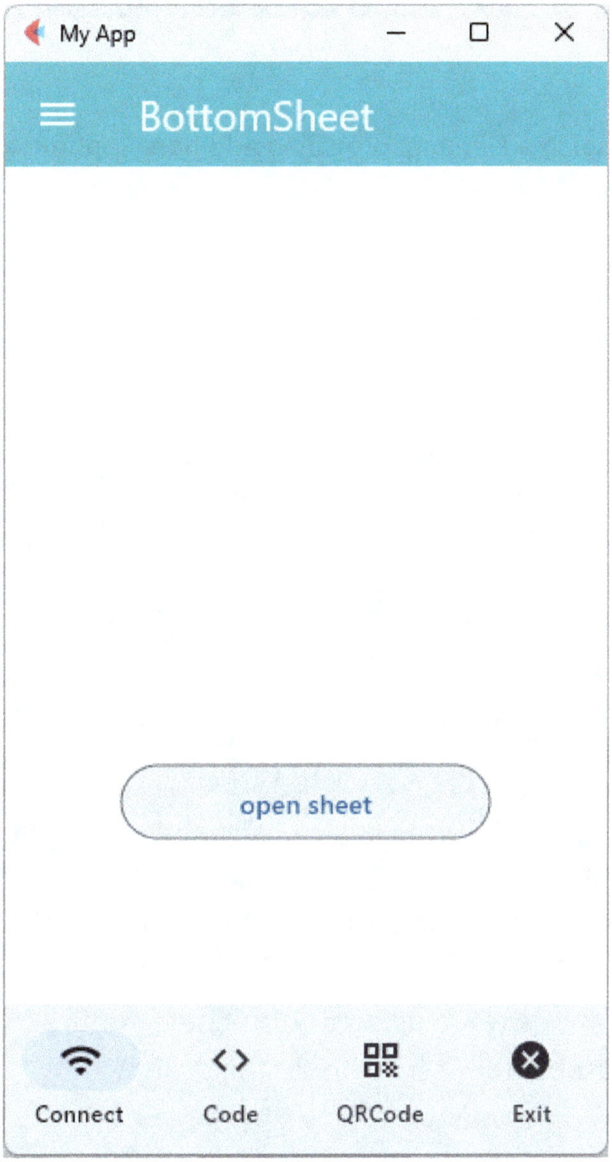
My App
BottomSheet
open sheet
Connect
Code
QRCode
Exit

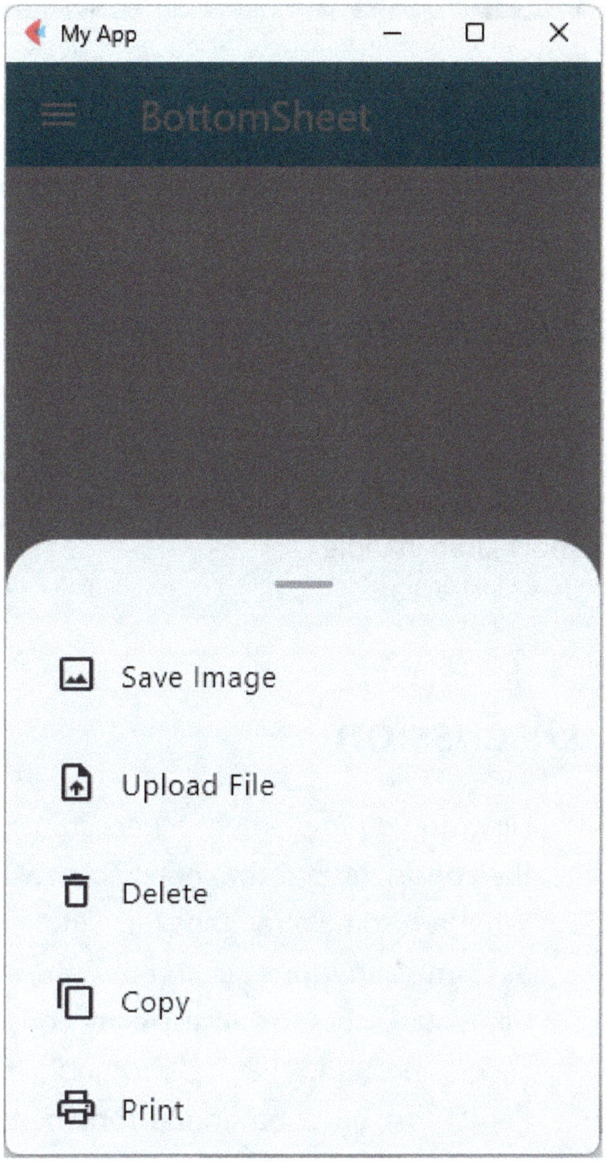
My App
BottomSheet
Save Image
Upload File
Delete
Copy
Print

Page Summary

BottomSheet control creates a bottom sheet modal in a Flet app, providing additional options or actions without obstructing the main content.

Keywords

dismissible
on_dismiss
enable_drag
show_drag_handle
use_safe_area

Discussion

1. How do you implement a persistent or modal BottomSheet control, and what are the considerations for choosing between the two?
2. What are some strategies for handling user interactions with a BottomSheet, such as dismissing it or selecting options within it?
3. Can you discuss the accessibility considerations when using BottomSheet controls, such as ensuring that it is navigable and usable for users with disabilities?
4. Read more on **CupertinoBottomSheet** and **SafeArea**

Snackbar

A **Snackbar** is a floating panel that displays a message typically from the bottom of the application for a specified duration. It is often used to communicate various types of messages about the application's operations, such as successful actions, warnings, alerts, and more. Additionally, a Snackbar can handle user interactions through buttons.

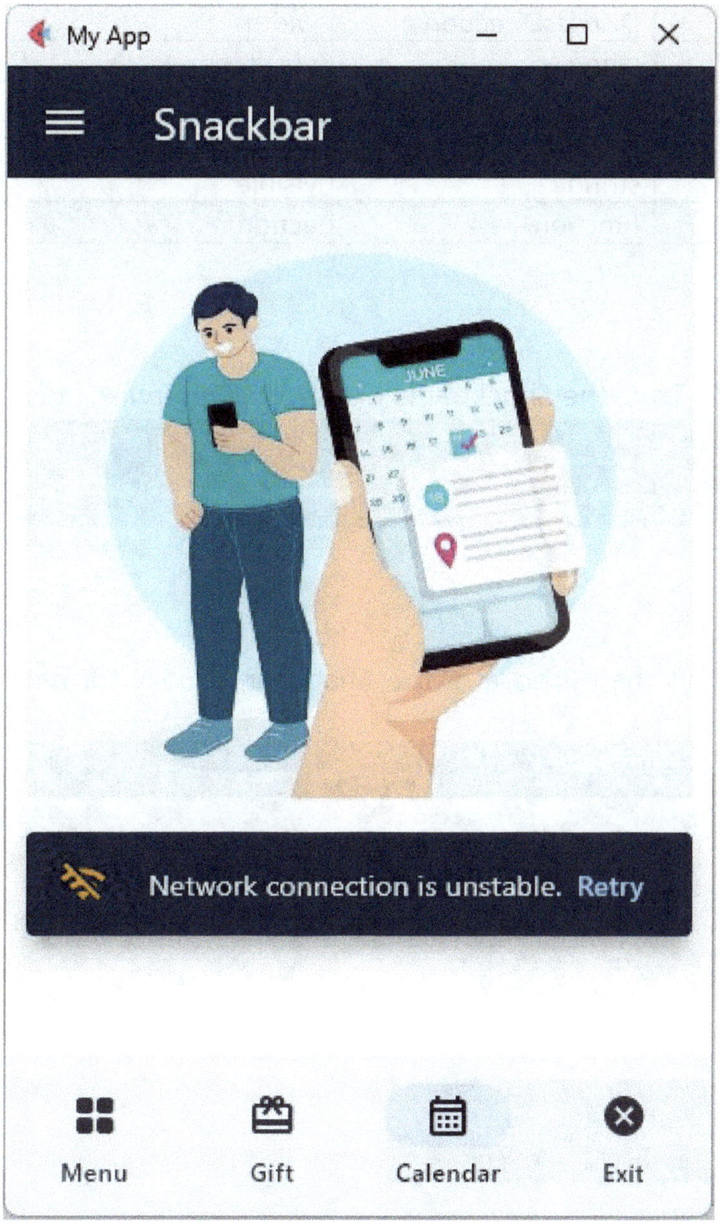

Available Methods

Property	Value	Property	Value
content	control	duration	int
open	bool	margin	MarginValue
behavior	SnackbarBehavior	padding	PaddingValue
dismiss_direction	DismissDirection	width	float
show_close_icon	string	elevation	float
action_color	string	ref	Ref
close_icon_color	string	disabled	bool
bgcolor	string	visible	bool
on_action	function	action	string

open = bool

When **open** is set to True, the Snackbar is displayed. Otherwise, it is closed.

```
snackbar = flet.SnackBar(
  open = True,
)
```

content = control

This property displays the purpose of the **Snackbar**, usually formatted as a string within controls.

```
snackbar = flet.SnackBar(
  open = True,
  content= flet.Row(
      controls=[
          flet.Icon(name=flet.icons.WIFI_OFF_OUTLINED,color="orange"),
          flet.Text("Network connection is unstable.")]
  ),
)
```

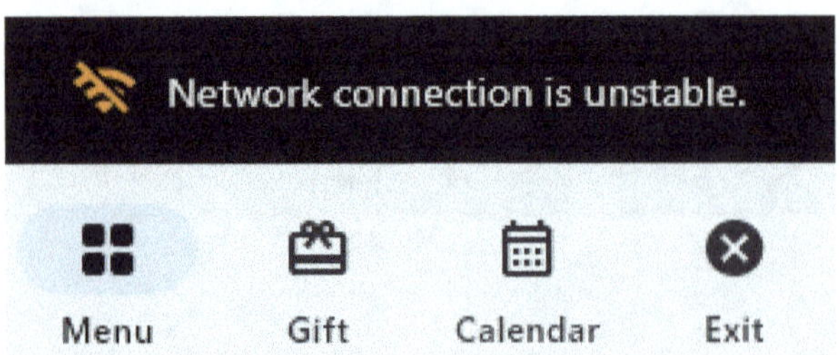

behavior = flet.SnackbarBehavior
This defines the overall behavior of the **Snackbar**, whether it should be fixed or floated. The available options are FIXED and FLOATING.

```
snackbar = flet.SnackBar(
  behavior= flet.SnackBarBehavior.FLOATING,
  open = True,
)
```

Floating

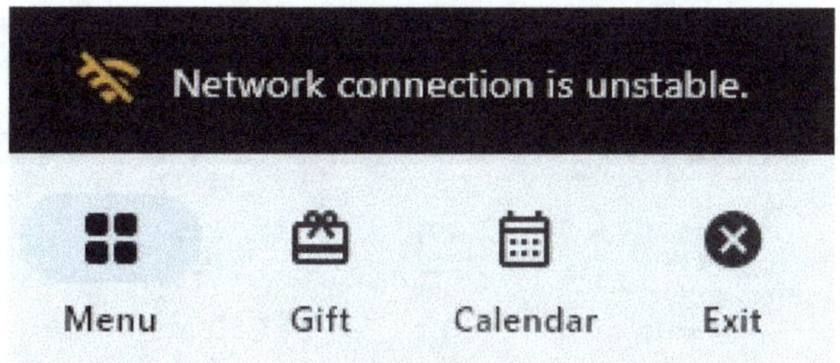

Fixed

dismiss_direction = DismissDirection
This indicates the direction in which the **Snackbar** exits the screen. Common directions include DOWN, UP, HORIZONTAL, VERTICAL, START_TO_END, END_TO_START and None.

```
snackbar = flet.SnackBar(
  open = True,
  dismiss_direction= flet.DismissDirection.UP,
)
```

show_close_icon = bool
When this property is set to True, the **Snackbar** includes a close button that allows users to manually dismiss it.

```
snackbar = flet.SnackBar(
  open = True,
  show_close_icon= True,
  close_icon_color= "green",
)
```

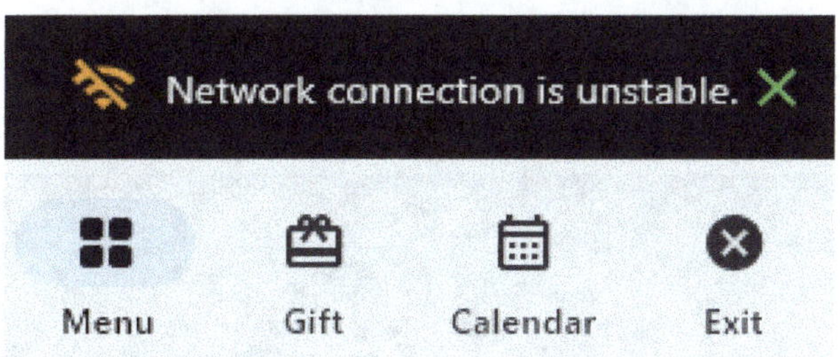

action = string

This represents the text button or set of buttons included in the **Snackbar**. These buttons allow users to perform specific actions directly from the **Snackbar**.

```
snackbar = flet.SnackBar(
  action= "Retry",
  action_color= "teal",
)
```

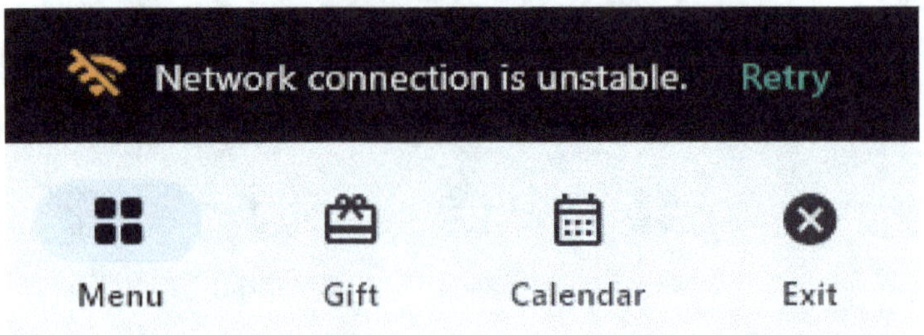

bgcolor = string

The **bgcolor** property specifies the color for the background.

```
snackbar = flet.SnackBar(
  open = True,
  bgcolor="#00334c"
)
```

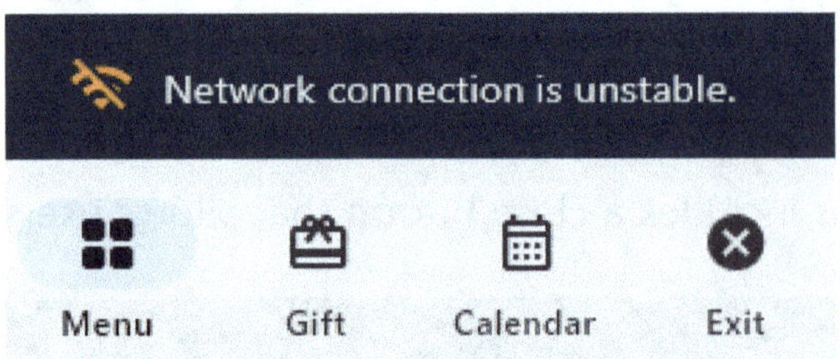

duration = int

Specifies the time period for which the Snackbar remains visible before automatically dismissing. This is often set in milliseconds.

```
snackbar = flet.SnackBar(
    open = True,
    duration=3000, #(3 seconds)
  )
```


margin = float, flet.margin.all, flet.margin.only

The **margin** defines the space around the Snackbar, affecting its placement relative to other UI elements.

```
snackbar = flet.SnackBar(
  margin= flet.margin.all(20),
  behavior= flet.SnackBarBehavior.FLOATING,
)
```

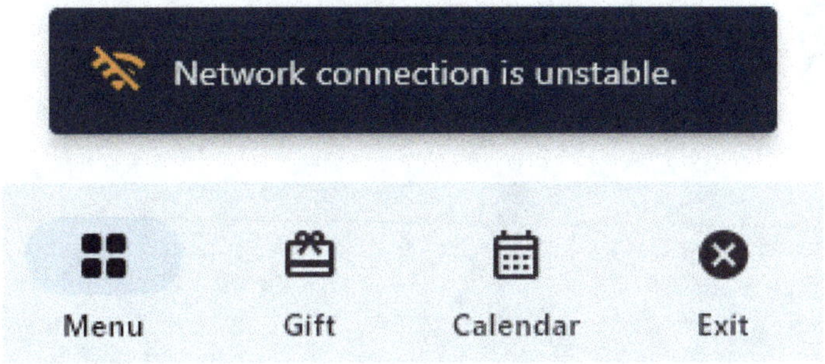

elevation = float

The **elevation** defines the degree of shadow effect of the **Snackbar**.

```
snackbar = flet.SnackBar(
  elevation= 20,
  behavior= flet.SnackBarBehavior.FLOATING,
)
```

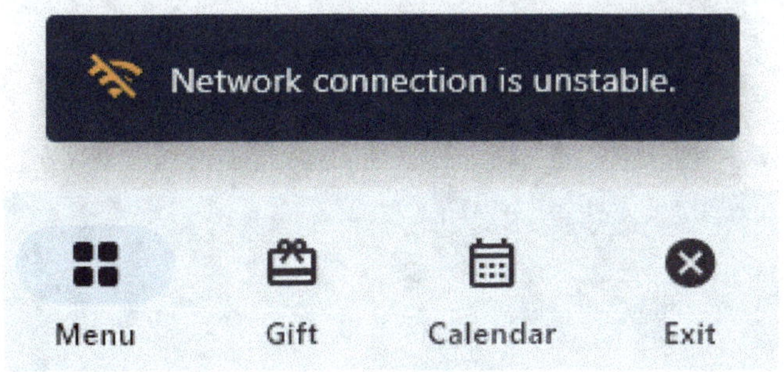

Note

The Snackbar **behavior** property must be set to FLOATING before both **margin** and **elevation** can work.

padding = float, flet.padding.all, flet.padding.only
This sets the space between the **Snackbar**'s content and its edges.

```
snackbar = flet.SnackBar(
  padding= flet.padding.all(30),
)
```

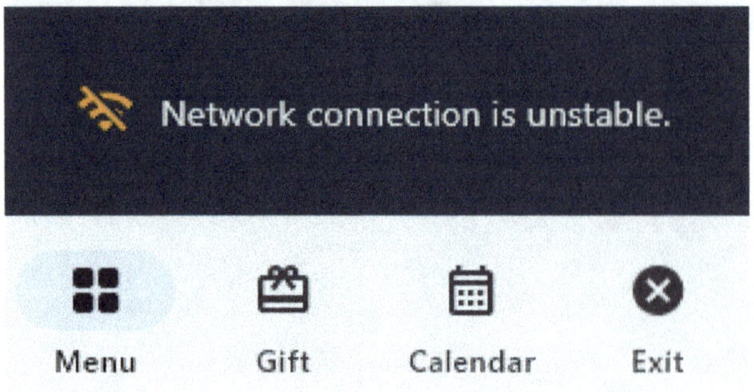

on_action = function
An event that fires when an action button within the Snackbar is clicked or pressed. This allows the application to respond to user interactions with the Snackbar.

```
def onUpdate(e):
    print("Updating")

snackbar = flet.SnackBar(
  on_action= onUpdate,
  action= "Update Now",
  content= flet.Row(
      controls=[
          flet.Icon(name=flet.icons.DOWNLOAD_OUTLINED,color="green"),
          flet.Text("New update available.")]
  ),
)
```

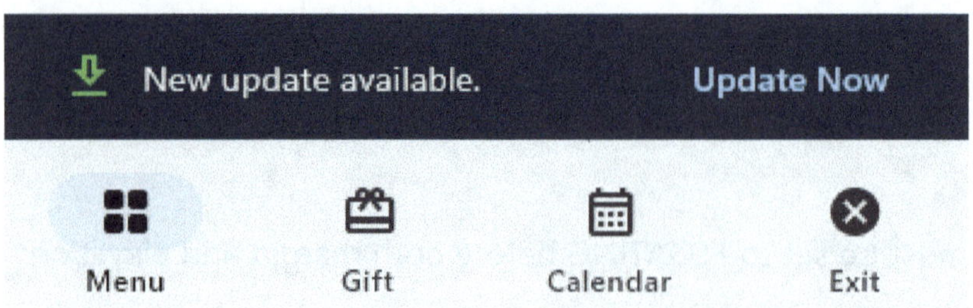

Python *Code 3.2.0*

```
import flet

def main(page: flet.Page):
    page.title = "My App"
    page.bgcolor = 'white'
    page.padding = flet.padding.all(20)

    page.appbar = flet.AppBar(
      color= flet.colors.WHITE,
      title= flet.Text("Snackbar"),
      bgcolor="#00334c",
    )
    page.drawer = flet.NavigationDrawer()

    nav = flet.NavigationBar(
        destinations= [
           flet.NavigationDestination(
                 label="Menu",
                 icon=flet.icons.GRID_VIEW_ROUNDED
            ),

            flet.NavigationDestination(
                label="Gift",
                icon=flet.icons.WALLET_GIFTCARD_OUTLINED
             ),

             flet.NavigationDestination(
                label="Calendar",
                icon=flet.icons.CALENDAR_MONTH_OUTLINED
             ),

            flet.NavigationDestination(
                label="Exit",
                icon=flet.icons.CANCEL
            )
        ]
    )
    page.navigation_bar = nav

    def savePage(e):
        snackbar.open = True
        page.update()

    def closeSnack(e):
        snackbar.open = False
        page.update()

    button = flet.OutlinedButton(
        text= "Save Page",
        on_click= savePage,
        width=150,
    )

    snackbar = flet.SnackBar(
      elevation=10,
      duration= 60000,
      action= "close",
      on_action= closeSnack,
      behavior= flet.SnackBarBehavior.FLOATING,
      margin = flet.margin.only(left=20, right=20, bottom=40),
      bgcolor="#14171A",
      content= flet.Row(
          controls=[
              flet.Icon(name=flet.icons.SAVE_ALT_OUTLINED,color="blue"),
              flet.Text("Page saved successfully!")]
      ),
    )

    col = flet.Column(
        width= page.width,
        height= page.height,
        alignment= flet.MainAxisAlignment.START,
        horizontal_alignment= flet.CrossAxisAlignment.CENTER,
        controls= [
           flet.Image(src="C:\\Users\\image.jpg", height= 350, width= page.width, fit=flet.ImageFit.FILL),
           button,
           snackbar
         ]
    )

    page.add(col)
    page.update()

flet.app(target = main)
```

My App
Snackbar
UPDATE
55%
Save Page
Menu
Gift
Calendar
Exit

My App
Snackbar
UPDATE
55%
Page saved successfully!
close
Save Page
Menu
Gift
Calendar
Exit

Page Summary

Snackbar control displays brief messages at the bottom of the screen in a Flet app, providing feedback or alerts to users.

Keywords

behavior
dismiss_direction
duration
action_color
close_icon_color
margin
padding

Discussion

1. How do you customize the appearance and behavior of a Snackbar, such as adding action buttons, custom styling, or duration?
2. What are some best practices for using Snackbar to provide context-aware feedback or error messages to users?
3. Can you discuss the accessibility considerations when using Snackbar control, such as ensuring that messages are clear and understandable for users with disabilities?

AlertDialog

An **AlertDialog** is a popup floating panel that contains a message requiring the user's acknowledgment. AlertDialogs require user interaction through the use of buttons. Some AlertDialog messages are critical and need more acknowledgment, while others may simply report on application operations that are less significant. AlertDialog displays messages on warnings, confirmation, information, errors etc.

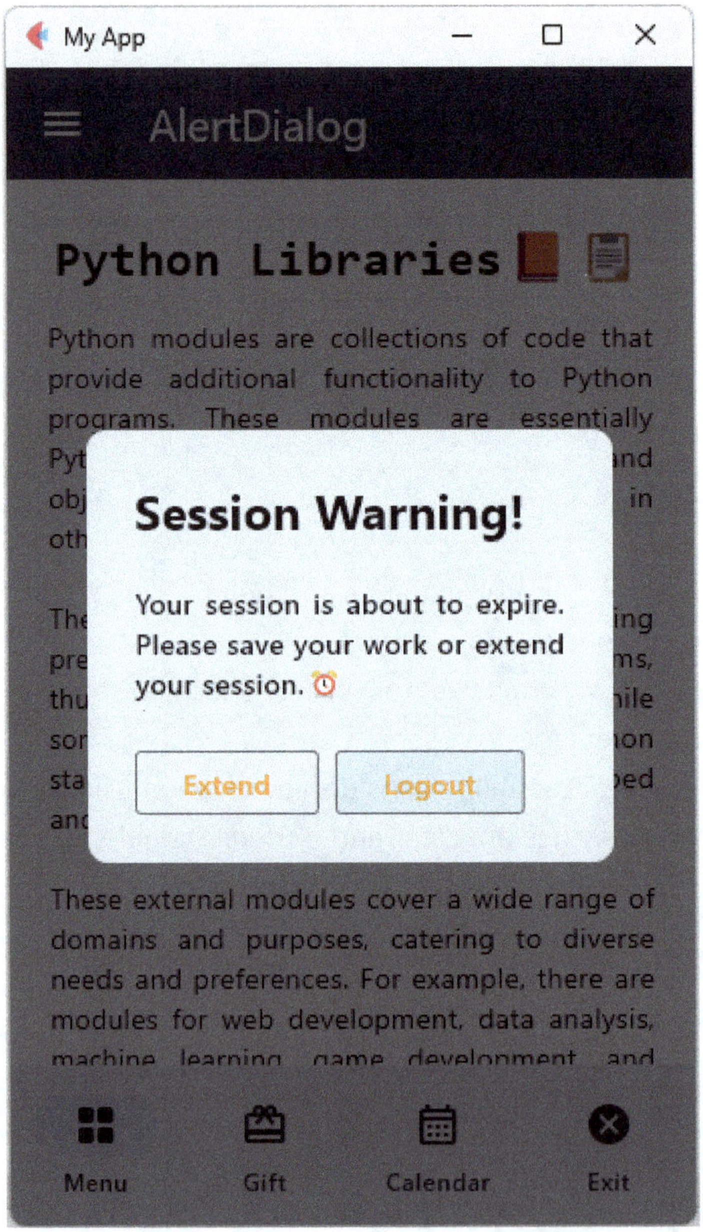

Available Methods

Property	Value	Property	Value
content	Control	shape	OutlinedBorder
open	bool	title_padding	PaddingValue
modal	bool	content_padding	PaddingValue
title	Control	actions_padding	PaddingValue
actions	List[Control]	actions_alignmnet	MainAxisAlignment
elevation	float	inset_padding	PaddingValue
icon	Control	semantic_label	string
bgcolor	string	disabled	bool
adaptive	bool	visible	bool

open = bool

When **open** is set to True, the AlertDialog is displayed. When False, it is closed.

```
dialog = flet.AlertDialog(
  open= True,
)
```

title = Control

This property sets the header of the message, providing a clear indication of the dialog's purpose.

```
dialog = flet.AlertDialog(
  open= True,
  title= flet.Text("Settings Saved", weight=flet.FontWeight.BOLD),
)
```

content = Control
This is the main message of the AlertDialog. It can take any form of control, but Text controls are typically used for straightforward messages.

```
    dialog = flet.AlertDialog(
      open= True,
      title= flet.Text("Settings Saved", weight=flet.FontWeight.BOLD),
      content= flet.Text("Your settings have been saved successfully.",
                         weight=flet.FontWeight.W_500)
      )
```

actions = List[*Controls]
This defines a list of controls, mostly buttons, that allow the user to carry out actions in response to the dialog.

```
    dialog = flet.AlertDialog(
       actions= [
         flet.OutlinedButton(text="OK",style=flet.ButtonStyle(color="green")),
         flet.OutlinedButton(text="Undo",style=flet.ButtonStyle(color="green")),
      ])
```

icon = Control

The **icon** provides visual description to the control. Typically, icons are placed above the title.

```
dialog = flet.AlertDialog(
  icon= flet.Icon(name= flet.icons.SAVE_OUTLINED, color= "#00334c"),
  )
```

elevation = float

This property indicates the depth of the AlertDialog, creating a visual effect of raised shadow to distinguish it from the background.

```
dialog = flet.AlertDialog(
  elevation= 10,
)
```

bgcolor = string

The **bgcolor** property specifies the background color of the AlertDialog.

```
dialog = flet.AlertDialog(
  bgcolor= "#14171A",
  title= flet.Text("Settings Saved", weight=flet.FontWeight.BOLD,color="white"),
  content= flet.Text("Your settings have been saved successfully.",color="white"),
    )
```

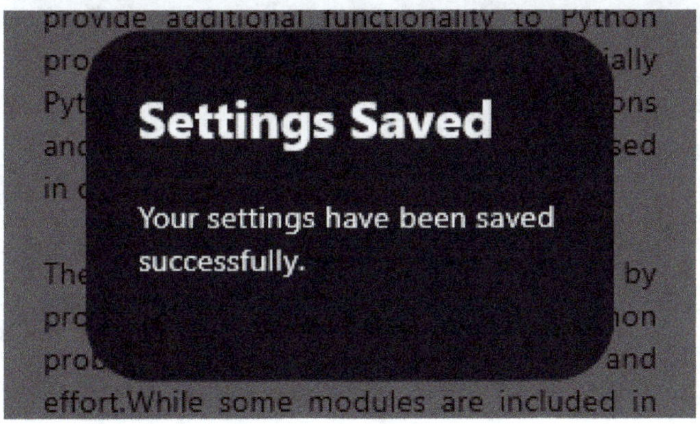

modal = bool
This indicates whether the AlertDialog is **modal**. When set to True, it means the dialog must be acknowledged before the user can interact with the rest of the application. This is typically used for critical messages that require immediate attention.

```
dialog = flet.AlertDialog(
  modal= True,
  )
```

semantic_label = string
This provides a semantic label for the AlertDialog, which can be used by screen readers to improve accessibility by describing the purpose or content of the dialog.

```
dialog = flet.AlertDialog(
  semantics_label= "settings status",
  )
```

title_padding = float, flet.padding.all, flet.padding.only
This property defines the padding around the title, affecting the space between the title text and the edges of the dialog.

content_padding = float, flet.padding.all, flet.padding.only
This sets the space between the content of the AlertDialog and its edges.

action_padding = float, flet.padding.all, flet.padding.only
The **action_padding** specifies the space around the action buttons.

```
dialog = flet.AlertDialog(
  title_padding= 25,
  content_padding= flet.padding.all(10),
  actions_padding = flet.padding.only(left=100),
  title= flet.Text("Settings Saved", weight=flet.FontWeight.BOLD),
  content= flet.Text("Your settings have been saved successfully."),
  actions= [
      flet.OutlinedButton(text="Ok",),
      flet.OutlinedButton(text="Undo",),
  ]
)
```

inset_padding = float, flet.padding.all, flet.padding.only
This defines the padding between the dialog and the edges of the screen, ensuring the dialog is properly inset within the viewable area.

```
dialog = flet.AlertDialog(
  open= True,
  bgcolor= "#14171A",
  inset_padding= 0,
  title= flet.Text("Settings Saved", weight=flet.FontWeight.BOLD,color="white"),
  content= flet.Text("Your settings have been saved successfully.",color="white"),
  actions= [
      flet.OutlinedButton(text="Ok",),
      flet.OutlinedButton(text="Undo",),
  ]
  )
```

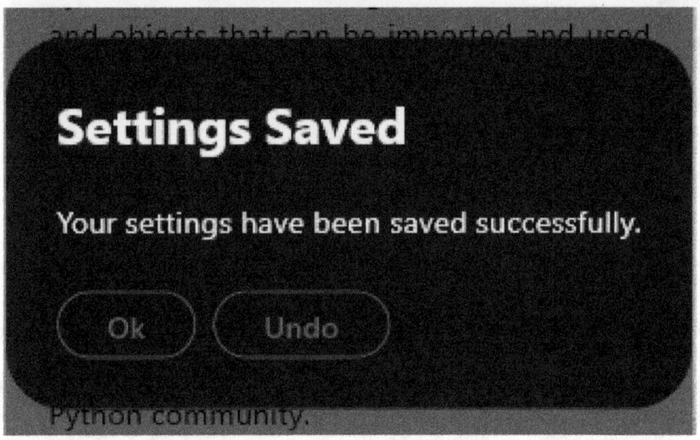

shape = OutlinedBorder
The **shape** defines the appearance of the AlertDialog, by specifying the shape. The available shapes include

- flet.RoundedRectangleBorder(type: str, radius: int)
- flet.StadiumBorder(type: str)
- flet.CircleBorder(type: str)
- flet.BeveledRectangleBorder(type: str, radius: int)
- flet.OutlinedBorder(type: str)
- flet.ContinousRectangleBorder(type: str, radius: int)


```
dialog = flet.AlertDialog(
  shape= flet.RoundedRectangleBorder(radius=10),
  )
```

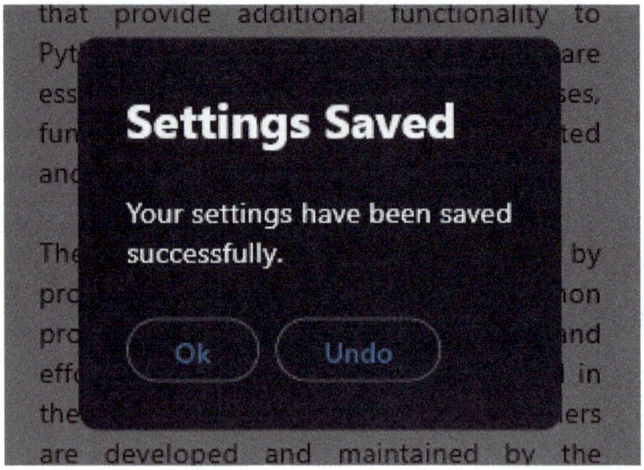

actions_alignment = MainAxisAlignemnt

Determines the alignment of the action buttons within the dialog. Common alignments include START, END, CENTER, SPACE_BETWEEN, SPACE_EVENLY and None.

```
dialog = flet.AlertDialog(
  actions_alignment= flet.MainAxisAlignment.SPACE_BETWEEN,

  title= flet.Text("Settings Saved", weight=flet.FontWeight.BOLD,),
  content= flet.Text("Your settings have been saved successfully."),
  actions= [
      flet.OutlinedButton(text="Ok",),
      flet.OutlinedButton(text="Undo",),
  ]
  )
```

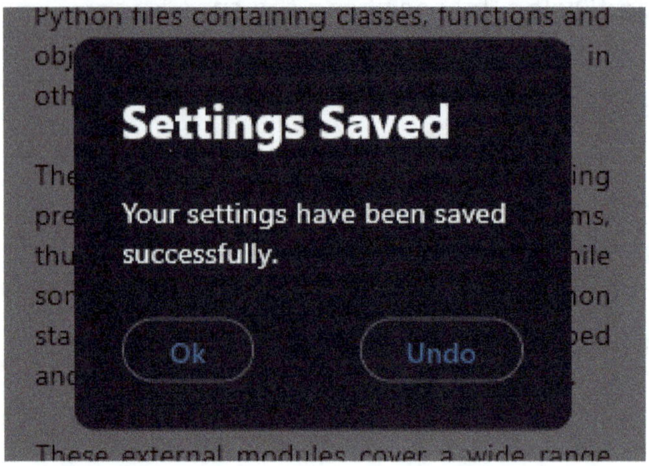

Python **Code 3.3.0**

```python
import flet

def main(page: flet.Page):
    page.title = "My App"
    page.bgcolor = 'white'
    page.padding = flet.padding.only(top=5, left=10, right=5)

    page.appbar = flet.AppBar(
      color= flet.colors.WHITE,
      title= flet.Text("Maths Geeks"),
      bgcolor="#00334c",
    )
    page.drawer = flet.NavigationDrawer()

    nav = flet.NavigationBar(
        destinations= [
           flet.NavigationDestination(
                 label="Menu",
                 icon=flet.icons.GRID_VIEW_ROUNDED
            ),
            flet.NavigationDestination(
                label="Gift",
                icon=flet.icons.WALLET_GIFTCARD_OUTLINED
             ),
             flet.NavigationDestination(
                label="Calendar",
                icon=flet.icons.CALENDAR_MONTH_OUTLINED
             ),
            flet.NavigationDestination(
                label="Exit",
                icon=flet.icons.CANCEL
            )
        ]
    )
    page.navigation_bar = nav

    def confirmDelete(e):
        confirm = e.control.key
        course = page.get_clipboard()

        if confirm == "cancel":
           dialog.open = False
        else:
            if course == "course1":
                page.remove(course1)
            if course == "course2":
                page.remove(course2)
            if course == "course3":
                page.remove(course3)

            dialog.open = False
        page.update()

    def delete(e):
        course = e.control.key
        dialog.open = True
        page.set_clipboard(course)
        page.update()

    dialog = flet.AlertDialog(
      bgcolor= "#14171A",
      modal=True,
      shape= flet.RoundedRectangleBorder(radius=10),
      actions_alignment= flet.MainAxisAlignment.END,
      title= flet.Text("Delete Conformation", weight=flet.FontWeight.BOLD,color="white"),
      content= flet.Text("Are you sure you want to delete this item?.",color="white"),
      actions= [
          flet.OutlinedButton(key = "delete", text="Delete", on_click=confirmDelete),
          flet.OutlinedButton(key = "cancel", text="Cancel", on_click=confirmDelete),
      ]
    )
    course1 = flet.ListTile(
        leading= flet.Image(src="C:\\Users\\Asiedu\\Desktop\\orela\\education.png", height=50, width=50, fit=flet.ImageFit.FILL),
        title= flet.Text('Linear Equation', size= 20,color="white"),
        trailing= flet.IconButton(key= "course1", icon=flet.icons.DELETE_OUTLINE, icon_color="white", highlight_color="red", on_click= delete),
        bgcolor= "#00334c"
    )
    course2 = flet.ListTile(
        leading= flet.Image(src="C:\\Users\\Asiedu\\Desktop\\orela\\education.png", height=50, width=50, fit=flet.ImageFit.FILL),
        title= flet.Text('Circle Theorem', size= 20,color="white"),
        trailing= flet.IconButton(key= "course2", icon=flet.icons.DELETE_OUTLINE, icon_color="white", highlight_color="red", on_click= delete),
        bgcolor= "#00334c"
    )
    course3 = flet.ListTile(
        leading= flet.Image(src="C:\\Users\\Asiedu\\Desktop\\orela\\education.png", height=50, width=50, fit=flet.ImageFit.FILL),
        title= flet.Text('Integration', size= 20,color="white"),
        trailing= flet.IconButton(key= "course3", icon=flet.icons.DELETE_OUTLINE, icon_color="white", highlight_color="red", on_click= delete),
        bgcolor= "#00334c"
    )

    col = flet.Column(
        width= page.width,
        alignment= flet.MainAxisAlignment.START,
        horizontal_alignment= flet.CrossAxisAlignment.CENTER,
        controls= [
          flet.Image(src="C:\\backimage.jpg", height=200, width=page.width, fit=flet.ImageFit.FILL),
          flet.Text("Course Overview", size=30, font_family="Georgia", width= flet.FontWeight.BOLD),
        ]
    )

    page.add(col)
    page.add(course1)
    page.add(course2)
    page.add(course3)
    page.add(dialog)
    page.update()

flet.app(target = main)
```

My App
Maths Geeks
Course Overview
Linear Equation
Circle Theorem
Integration
Menu
Gift
Calendar
Exit

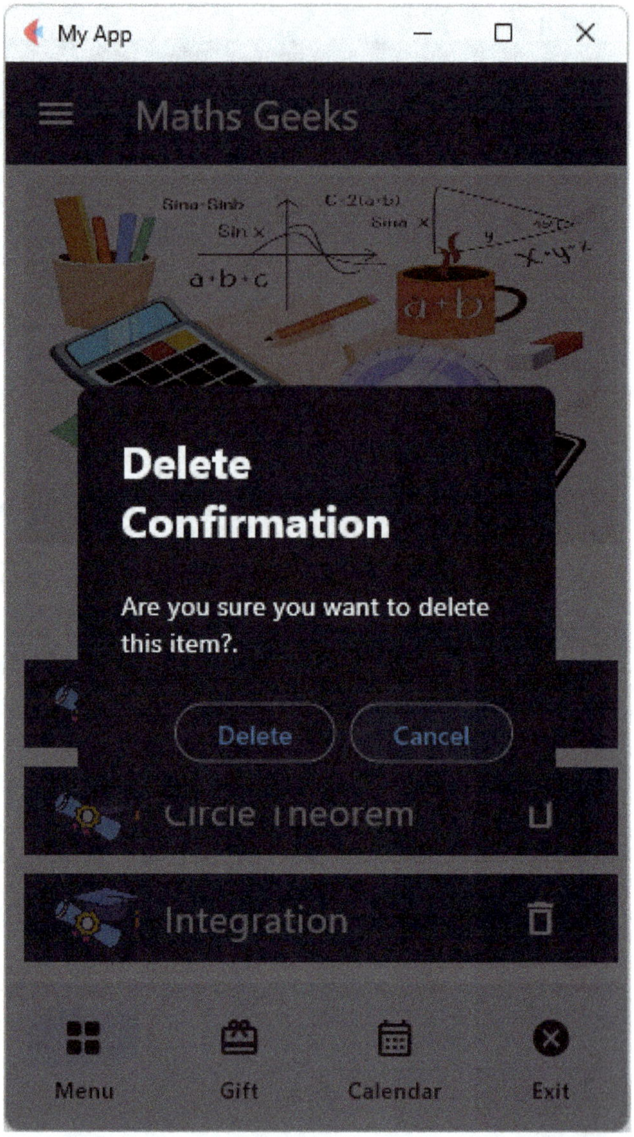
My App
Maths Geeks
Delete Confirmation
Are you sure you want to delete this item?.
Delete
Cancel
Integration
Menu
Gift
Calendar
Exit

Page Summary

AlertDialog control displays a modal dialog window in a Flet app, prompting users for input or confirmation.

Keywords

shape
modal
actions
title_padding
inset_padding
actions_padding
semantic_label
actions_alignment

Discussion

1. How can you customize the appearance and behavior of an AlertDialog, such as adding custom buttons, title, or content?
2. What are some techniques for handling user interactions with an AlertDialog, such as reacting to button presses or dismissing the dialog?
3. Can you discuss the user experience implications of using AlertDialogs, such as avoiding interruptive or overly frequent dialogs?

TextField

The **TextField** is a user interface control used for text input. It allows users to enter and edit text in a form field. Text fields are commonly used in forms, search bars, and anywhere text input is required.

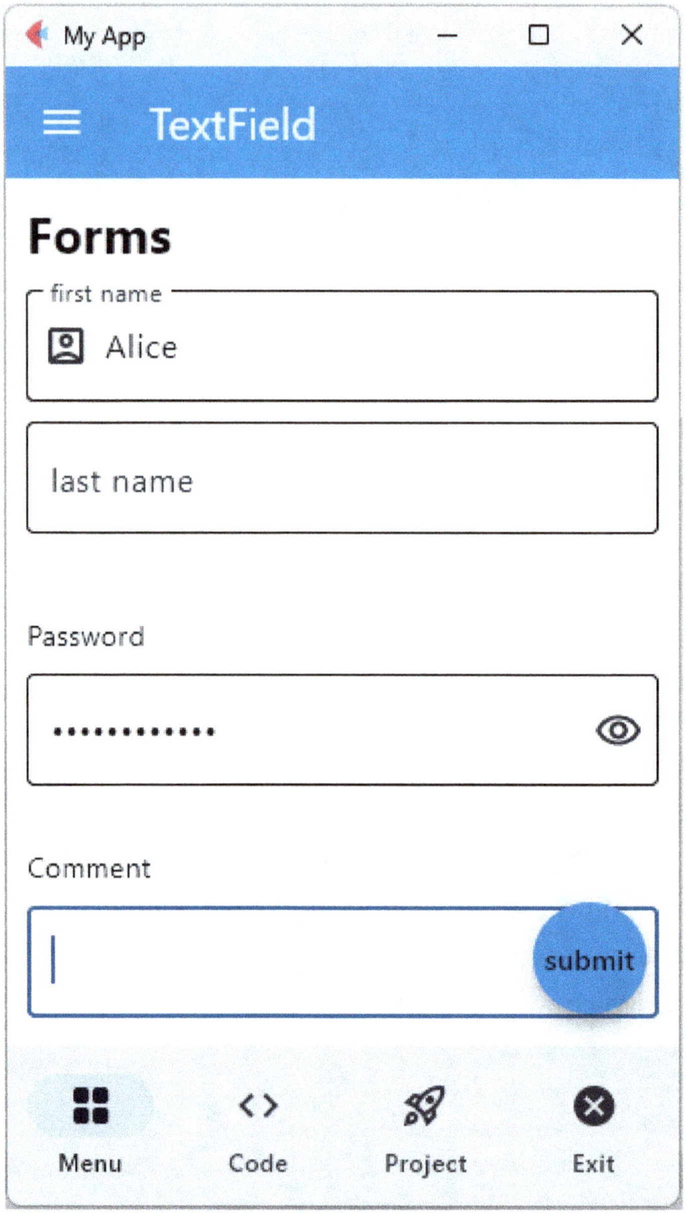

Available Methods

Property	Value	Property	Value
value	string	cursor_color	string
keyboard_Type	KeyboardType	cursor_width	float
multiline	bool	cursor_height	float
max_lines	int	cursor_radius	float
min_lines	int	selection_color	string
max_length	int	input_filter	InputFilter
password	bool	on_change	function
can_reveal_password	bool	on_submit	function
read_only	bool	on_focus	function
shift_enter	bool	on_blur	function
text_align	TextAlign	text_size	float
autofocus	bool	text_style	TextStyle
capitalization	TextCapitalization	label	string
autocorrect	bool	label_style	TextStyle
enable_suggestions	bool	icon	string
smart_dashes_type	bool	border	InputBorder
smart_quotes_type	bool	color	string
show_cursor	bool	bgcolor	string
filled	bool	border_radius	BorderRadiusValue
hint_text	string	border_width	float
hint_style	TextStyle	border_color	string
helper_text	string	focused_color	string
helper_text_style	TextStyle	focused_bgcolor	string
counter_text	string	focused_border_width	float
counter_text_style	TextStyle	focused_border_color	string
error_text	string	content_padding	PaddingValue
error_text_style	TextStyle	dense	bool
prefix	Control	suffix	Control
prefix_icons	string	suffix_icons	string
prefix_text	string	suffix_text	string
prefix_style	TextStyle	suffix_style	TextStyle

on_change = function (Events)

An event that fires whenever the text in the TextField is changed or edited.

```
def textFunc(e):
    value = e.control.value
    page.update()

textfield = flet.TextField(
    on_change = textFunc,
)
```

on_submit = function (Event)

An event that fires when the user submits the text, usually by pressing the Enter key.

```
def submitFunc(e):
    print('form submitted')
    page.update()

textfield = flet.TextField(
    on_submit= submitFunc,
)
```

on_focus = function (Event)

An event that fires when the TextField gains focus. This is achieved by clicking the field.

```
def focusFunc(e):
    print('field focused')
    page.update()

textfield = flet.TextField(
    on_focus = focusFunc,
)
```

value = string (get)

The **value** defines the current input text in the TextField. Value can be set and retrieved.

```
def focusFunc(e):
    value = e.control.value
    print(value)
    page.update()

textfield = flet.TextField(
    on_change= textFunc,
)
```


value = string (set)
Setting the **value** in the TextField:

```
textfield = flet.TextField(
        value= "Alice Konadu"
    )
```

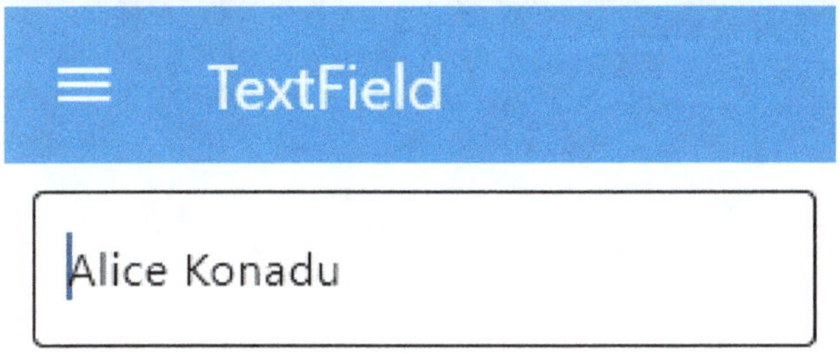

multiline = bool
When this property is set to True, the TextField can extend beyond a single line, accommodating larger text inputs such as messages or comments.

```
textfield = flet.TextField(
        multiline= True
    )
```

min_lines = int
This property specifies the minimum number of lines the TextField should display.

max_lines = int
The **max_lines** also specifies the maximum number of lines the TextField should display.

max_length = int
This property defines the maximum number of characters allowed in the TextField.

```
textfield = flet.TextField(
        min_lines= 2,
        max_lines= 5,
        max_length= 50)
```


password = bool

When **password** is set to True, the input text is obscured with characters such as dots or hashes for password entry.

```
    textfield = flet.TextField(
        password= True
    )
```

can_reveal_password = bool

When **can_reveal_password** is True, the TextField allows the user to toggle the visibility of the password. This property adds a suffix icon (eye and eye_slash) to toggle between visibility.

```
    textfield = flet.TextField(
        password= True,
        can_reveal_password= True
    )
```

text_align = flet.TextAlign

This defines the text alignment within the TextField. Possible values could be LEFT, RIGHT, CENTER and JUSTIFY.

```
    textfield = flet.TextField(
        text_align= flet.TextAlign.RIGHT
    )
```

read_only = bool
When set to True, prevents the user from modifying the text in the TextField.

```
textfield = flet.TextField(
    read_only= True
)
```

shift_enter = bool
This property defines the behavior of the Shift + Enter key combination. Typically used for adding new lines in a multiline TextField.

```
textfield = flet.TextField(
    shift_enter= True
)
```

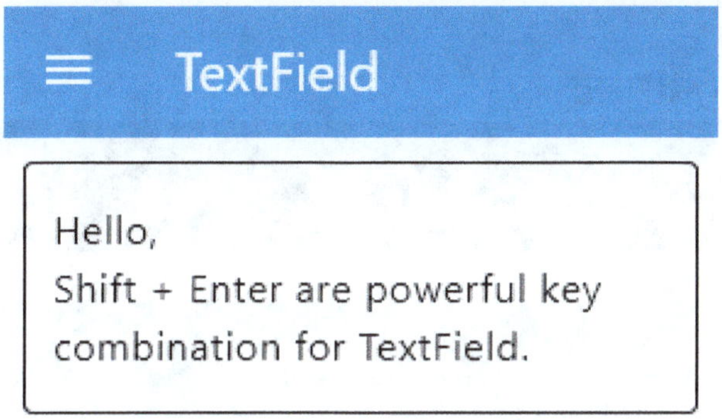

capitalization = flet.TextCapitalization
This method defines the text capitalization behavior, such as None, WORD, SENTENCES or CHARACTERS.

```
textfield = flet.TextField(
    capitalization=flet.TextCapitalization.WORDS,
)
```

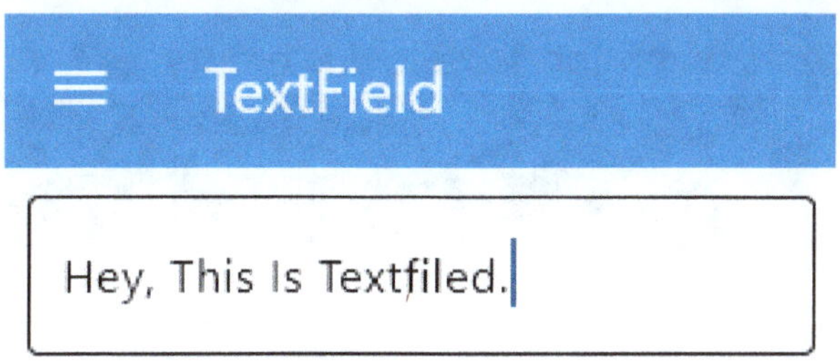

autocorrect = bool
When set to True, enables automatic correction of input text.

```
textfield = flet.TextField(
    autocorrect= True
)
```


keyboard_type = flet.KeyboardType

The **keyboard_type** specifies the type of keyboard to be displayed, such as NUMBER, NAME, EMAIL, PHONE, DATETIME, STREET_ADDRESS, TEXT, URL, MULTILINE and None

```
textfield = flet.TextField(
    keyboard_type= flet.KeyboardType.NUMBER
)
```

enable_suggestions = bool

When this property is set to True, it enables text suggestions while typing.

```
textfield = flet.TextField(
    enable_suggestions = True
)
```

show_cursor = bool

When set to False, the cursor is invisible in the TextField.

```
textfield = flet.TextField(
    show_cursor= False
)
```

hint_text = string

This provides a hint or placeholder text that appears when the TextField is empty.

```
textfield = flet.TextField(
    hint_text= "first name"
)
```

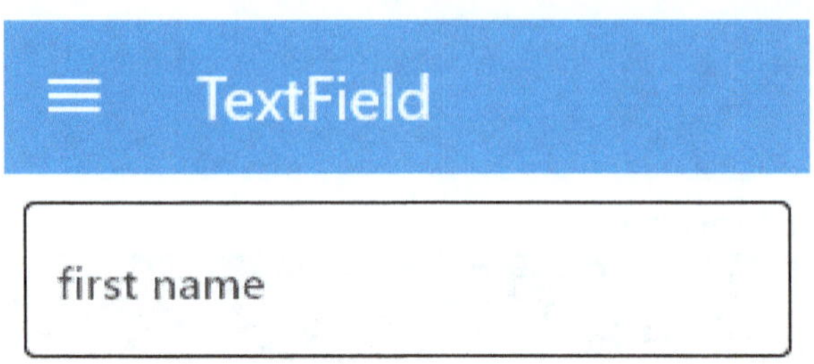

 |

hint_style = flet.TextStyle#

This property is used to format the hint_text using the TextStyle#.

```
textfield = flet.TextField(
    hint_text= "first name",
    hint_style= flet.TextStyle()
)
```

helper_text = string

This displays additional text below the TextField to assist the user.

```
textfield = flet.TextField(
    helper_text = "type username",
)
```

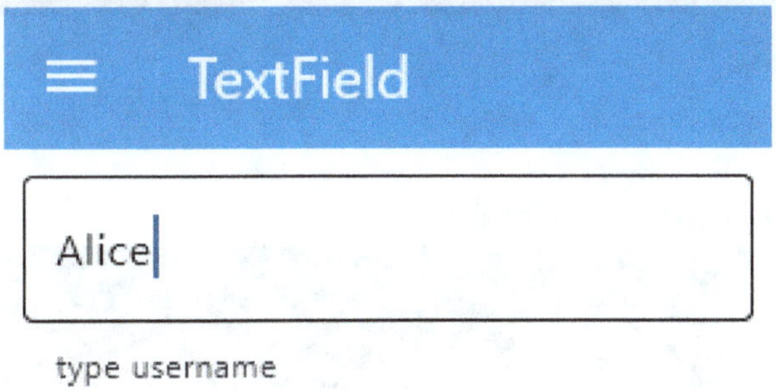

helper_text_style = TextStyle#

This property is used to format the **helper_text** using the TextStyle#.

```
textfield = flet.TextField(
    helper_text= "username",
    helper_text_style= flet.TextStyle()
)
```

counter_text = string

This displays a character counter below the TextField.

```
def textFunc(e):
    counter = len(e.control.value)
    e.control.counter_text = counter
    page.update()

textfield = flet.TextField(
    on_change= textFunc,
)
```


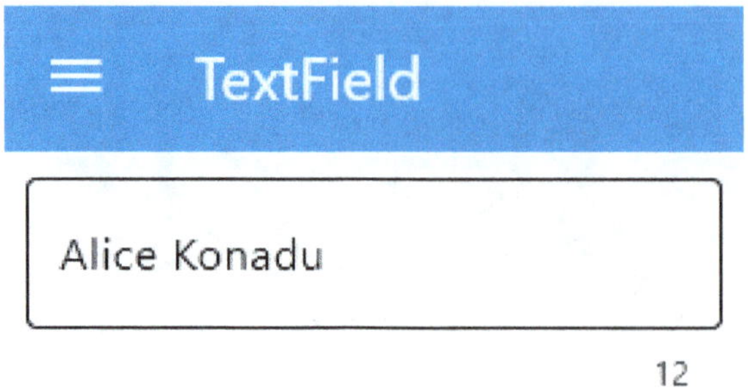

counter_text_style = TextStyle#
This property is used to format the **counter_text** using the TextStyle#.

```
textfield = flet.TextField(
    counter_text= "10",
    counter_text_style= flet.TextStyle()
)
```

text_size = float
The **text_size** property defines the size of the text in the **TextField**.

```
textfield = flet.TextField(
    text_size= 20
)
```

TextStyle

text_style = flet.TextStyle
The **text_style** property can be used to format the input text in the **TextField**. The Flet TextStyle provides several methods for formatting text.

- size
- height
- italic
- weight
- decoration
- decoration_color
- decoration_tickness
- decoration_style
- font_family
- bgcolor
- color
- shadow
- letter_spacing
- foreground
- font_family

size = float

The size property defines the size of the text

```
textfield = flet.TextField(
    text_tyle = flet.TextStyle(
        size= 20
    )
)
```

italic = bool

This property determines whether the text should be slanted or not.

```
textfield = flet.TextField(
    text_style = flet.TextStyle(
        italic= True
    )
)
```

color = string

The **color** specifies the color of the text in the TextField.

```
textfield = flet.TextField(
    text_style = flet.TextStyle(
        color = "red",
    )
)
```

font_family = string

The **font_family** specifies the kind of front style to use.

```
    textfield = flet.TextField(
        text_style = flet.TextStyle(
            font_family= "Georgia"
        )
    )
```

bgcolor = string

This property defines the background color of the text.

```
    textfield = flet.TextField(
        text_style = flet.TextStyle(
            bgcolor= "green"
        )
    )
```

decoration = flet.TextDecoration

This property decorates text with lines. Decoration values include UNDERLINE, OVERLINE, LINE_THROUGH and NONE.

```
    textfield = flet.TextField(
        text_style = flet.TextStyle(
            decoration= flet.TextDecoration.UNDERLINE
        )
    )
```

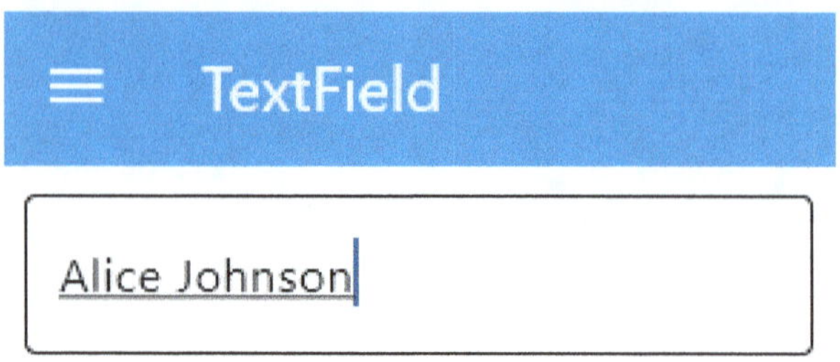

decoration_style = flet.TextDecorationStyle

After applying decoration to text, **decoration_style** let you choose line styles to apply to the text. This includes WAVY, DASHED, DOTTED, DOUBLE and SOLID.

```
    textfield = flet.TextField(
        text_style = flet.TextStyle(
            decoration= flet.TextDecoration.UNDERLINE,
            decoration_style= flet.TextDecorationStyle.DASHED
        )
    )
```

letter_spacing = float

This specifies the spaces between the characters in the text of the TextField.

```
    textfield = flet.TextField(
        text_style = flet.TextStyle(
            letter_spacing= 5
        )
    )
```

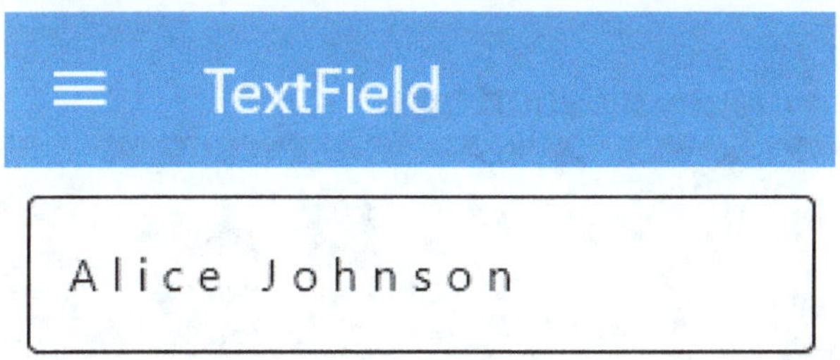

weight = flet.FontWeight

The weight property determines the thickness of the text in the TextField.

```
    textfield = flet.TextField(
        text_style = flet.TextStyle(weight= flet.FontWeight.BOLD )
    )
```

label = string

This property defines the label, which describes the TextField.

```
textfield = flet.TextField(
    label= "Username"
)
```

label_style = flet.TextStyle#

This provides the mechanism to format the label using the TextSyle#

```
textfield = flet.TextField(
    label_style= flet.TextStyle()
)
```

error_text = string

This displays error text below the TextField when input validation fails.

```
def textFunc(e):
    value = str(e.control.value)
    if not value.isalpha():
        e.control.error_text = "Input must not contain numbers"
    page.update()

textfield = flet.TextField( on_change= textFunc )
```

 |

icon = string

The **icon** specifies the icon control, which is typically placed before the TextField.

```
textfield = flet.TextField(
    icon= flet.icons.ACCOUNT_BOX,
)
```

prefix = Control

The **prefix** property adds a leading control within the TextField. The control can be anything including image.

```
textfield = flet.TextField(
    prefix= flet.Image(src="C:\\elderly1.png", height=40, width=40, )
)
```

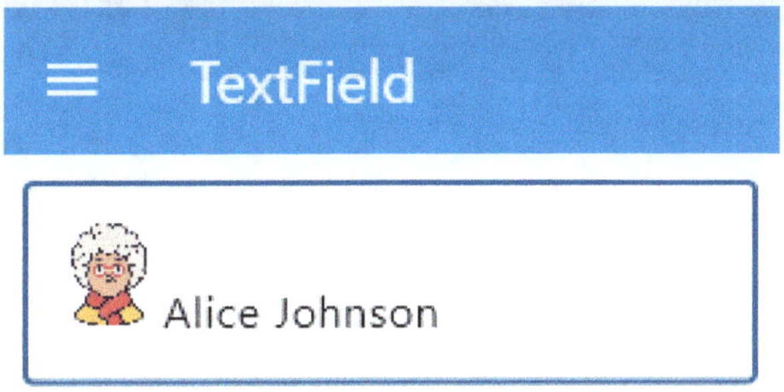

prefix_icon = string

This method specifies the leading icon within the TextField.

```
textfield = flet.TextField( prefix_icon= flet.icons.ACCOUNT_BOX_OUTLINED)
```

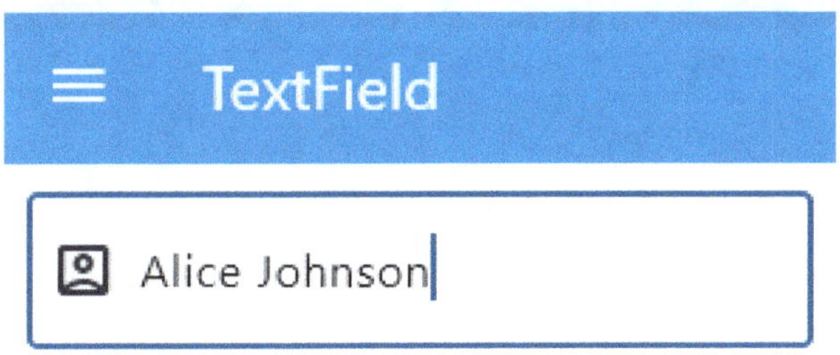

prefix_text = string

This property specifies the leading text within the TextField.

```
textfield = flet.TextField(
    prefix_text = "Mr."
)
```

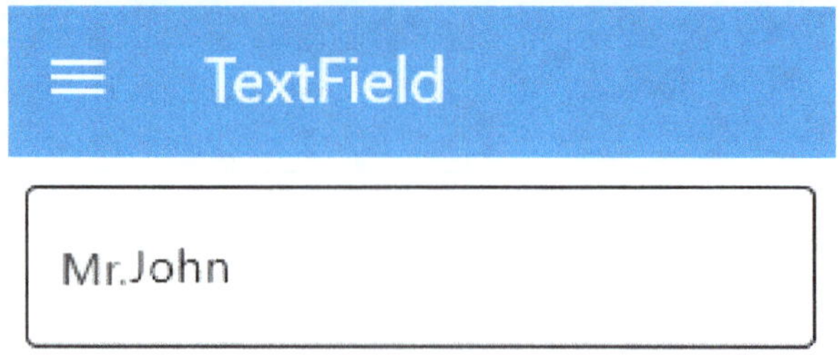

suffix = Control

The **suffix** specifies the control, which is placed at the end of the TextField.

```
textfield = flet.TextField(
    suffix= flet.Image("C:\\search.png", width=40, height=40)
)
```

suffix_icon = string

This is the icon, placed at the right end of the TextField.

```
textfield = flet.TextField(
    suffix_icon= flet.icons.REMOVE_RED_EYE
)
```

suffix_text = string

This property specifies the trailing text within the TextField.

```
textfield = flet.TextField(
    suffix_text = "@gmail.com"
)
```

color = string

The **color** property defines the color for the text in the TextField.

```
textfield = flet.TextField(
    color= "orange"
)
```

bgcolor = string

This property specifies the background color of the TextField.

```
textfield = flet.TextField(
    bgcolor = "grey"
)
```

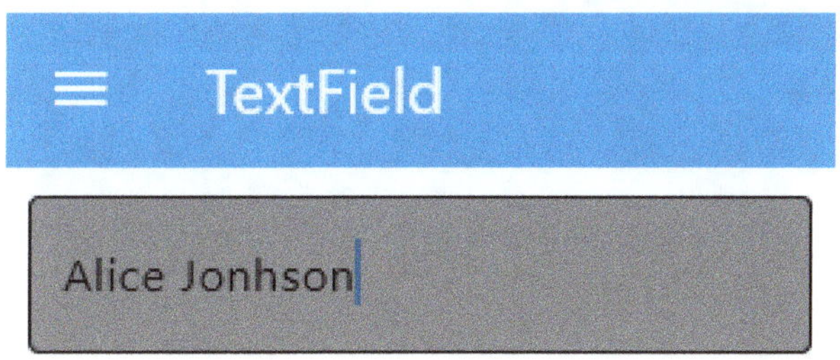

input_filter = flet.InputFilter
This specifies the type of input allowed, such as numeric, alphabetic or custom filters.

```
    textfield = flet.TextField(
        input_filter= flet.TextOnlyInputFilter() #flet.NumbersOnlyInputFilter()
    )
```

cursor_width = float
This defines the thickness of the cursor in the TextField.

cursor_height = float
This is the height of the cursor within the TextField.

cursor_color = string
The cursor_color defines the color of the cursor.

cursor_radius = float
This defines the degree of curvature of the cursor.

```
    textfield = flet.TextField(
        cursor_color= "red",
        cursor_width= 10,
        cursor_height= 30
    )
```

selection_color = string
This specifies the color used to highlight selected text.

```
    textfield = flet.TextField(
        selection_color= "green"
    )
```

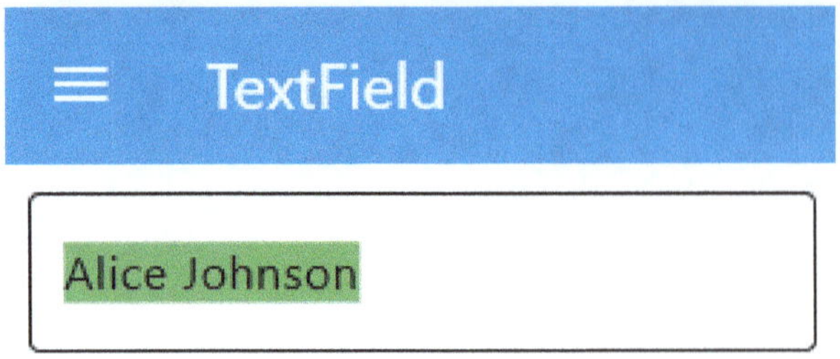

border_color = string

This property defines the color of the TextField outer edges.

```
    textfield = flet.TextField(
        border_color= "orange"
    )
```

border_radius = float, flet.border_radius.all, flet.border_radius.only

This property defines the degree of curvature of the TextField box.

```
    textfield = flet.TextField(
        border_color= "orange",
        border_radius= flet.border_radius.only(top_left=10, bottom_right=10)
    )
```

border_width = float

The **border_width** specifies the thickness of the TextField's border.

```
    textfield = flet.TextField(
        border_color= "orange",
        border_width= 6
    )
```

border = flet.InputBorder

This property defines the style of the TextField border, such as UNDERLINE, OUTLINE or None.

```
textfield = flet.TextField(
    border= flet.InputBorder.UNDERLINE
)
```

content_padding = float, flet.padding.all, flet.padding.only

The **content_padding** specifies the space between the input text and the TextField edges.

```
textfield = flet.TextField(
    content_padding= flet.padding.only(left=150)
)
```

focus_border_color = string

The border color when the TextField gains focus.

```
textfield = flet.TextField(
    focused_border_color= flet.colors.with_opacity(0.6, "red")
)
```

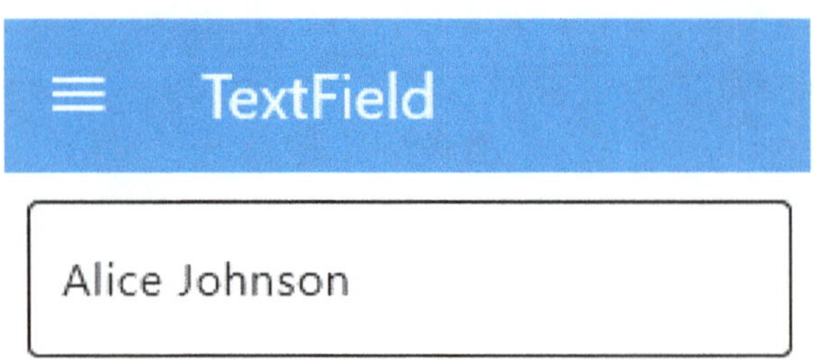

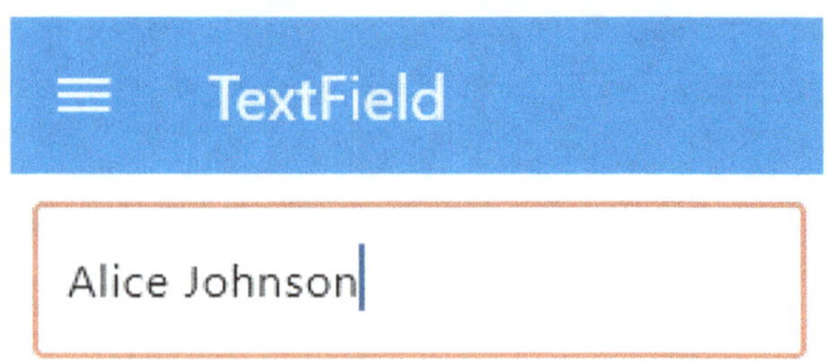

Python **Code 3.4.0**

```python
import flet

def main(page: flet.Page):
    page.title = "My App"
    page.bgcolor = 'white'
    page.padding = flet.padding.only(left=20, right=20)

    profiles = {"alice":'Alice', "bob":'Bob'}

    def formValidate(e):
        user = username.value
        pas = password.value

        length = len(profiles)
        usernameData = list(profiles.values())
        passwordData = list(profiles.keys())

        for i in range(length):
            if user == usernameData[i] and pas == passwordData[i]:
                logdisplay.value = "Login successful"
                page.update()
                break
            else:
                username.error_text = 'Username or password is wrong',
                username.value = ""
                logdisplay.value = "Login unsuccessful"
                page.update()


    username = flet.TextField(
        label= "Username",
        prefix_icon= flet.icons.ACCOUNT_BOX_OUTLINED,
    )

    password = flet.TextField(
        label= "Password",
        password= True,
        can_reveal_password= True,
    )

    logdisplay = flet.Text()

    loginButton = flet.ElevatedButton(
        text= "submit",
        bgcolor="#14171A",
        color= "white" ,
        on_click= formValidate
    )

    backgroundImage = flet.Image(src="C:\\bgimage.jpg", width=page.width, height=page.height, fit=flet.ImageFit.FILL,opacity=0.1)

    loginImage = flet.Image(src="C:\\logimage.png", width=100, height=100, fit=flet.ImageFit.FILL)

    stack = flet.Stack(
        width= page.width,
        height= page.height,
        controls=[
           backgroundImage,
           flet.Column(
               width= page.width,
               height= page.height,
               alignment= flet.MainAxisAlignment.CENTER,
               horizontal_alignment=flet.CrossAxisAlignment.CENTER,
               controls=[
                 logdisplay,
                 loginImage,
                 flet.Text("Granny", size= 50, color="#14171A", weight=flet.FontWeight.BOLD, font_family="Georgia"),
                 flet.Text('login'),
                 username,
                 password,
                 loginButton

               ]
           )
        ]
    )

    page.add(stack)
    page.update()

flet.app(target = main)
```

My App
Login successfully
Granny
login
Username
Alice
Password
alice
submit

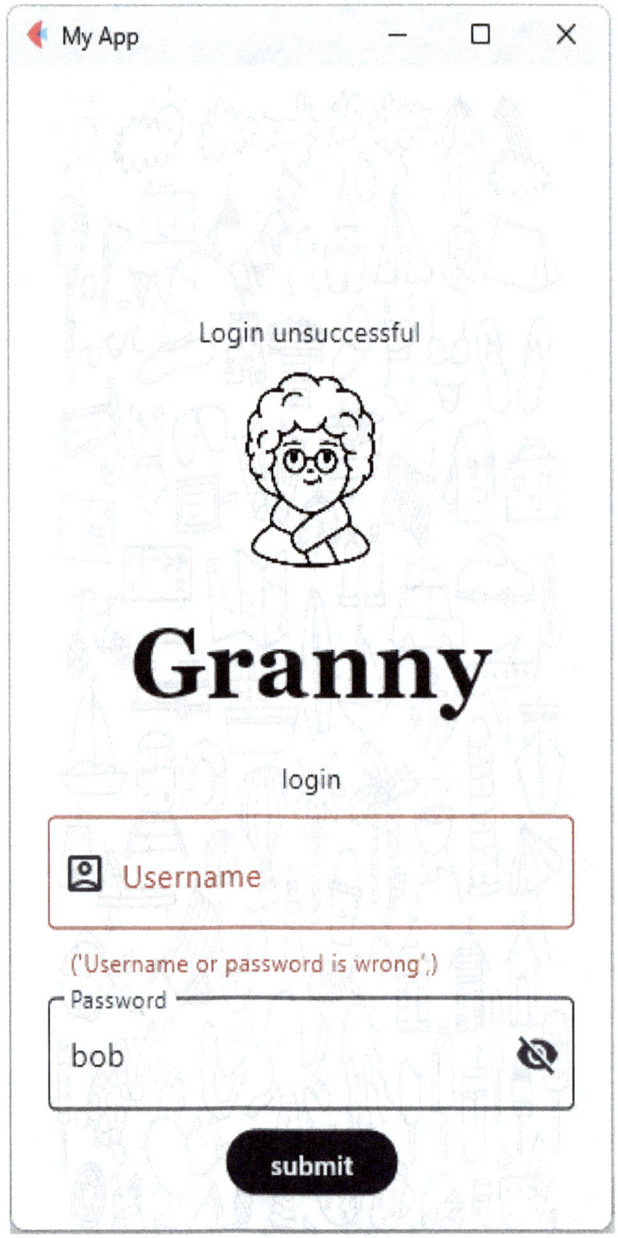
My App
Login unsuccessful
Granny
login
Username
('Username or password is wrong',)
Password
bob
submit

Page Summary

TextField control allows users to input text in a Flet app, with options for customization and validation.

Keywords

password
multiline
filled
read_only
value
autocorrect
capitalization
prefix
suffix
error_text

Discussion

1. How can you customize the appearance and behavior of a TextField, such as adding placeholder text, input validation, or input masking?
2. What are some techniques for handling user interactions with a TextField, such as reacting to text changes or keyboard events?
3. Can you discuss the accessibility considerations when using TextField controls, such as providing clear labels and hints for input fields?

Dropdown

The **Dropdown** control is a versatile UI element that allows users to select an option from a list of choices. It is commonly used in forms and settings where users need to choose from a predefined set of options.

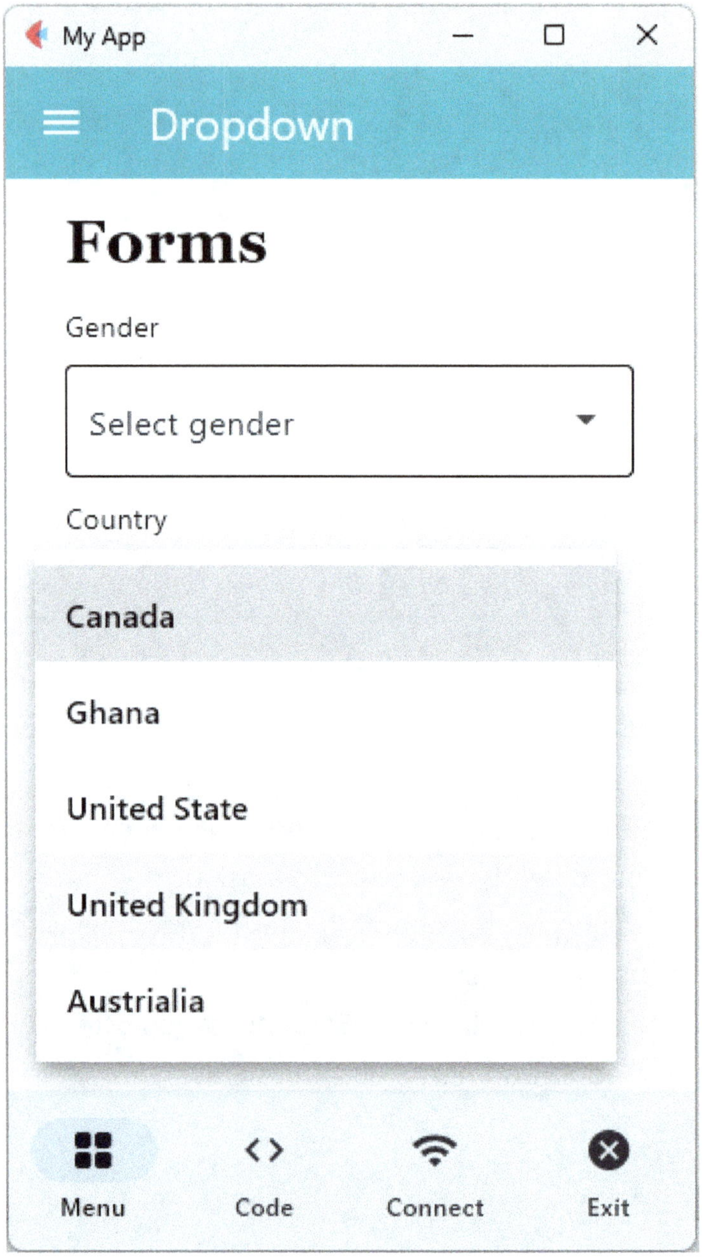

 |

Available Methods

Property	Value	Property	Value
value	string	focused_border_width	float
options	List[Options]	focused_border_color	string
alignment	Alignment	content_padding	float
on_change	Function	dense	bool
on_focus	Function	hint_text	string
on_blur	Function	hint_style	TextStyle
text_size	float	helper_text	string
text_style	TextStyle	helper_style	TextStyle
label	string	counter_text	string
label_style	TextStyle	counter_style	TextStyle
icon	string	error_text	string
autofocus	bool	error_style	TextStyle
border	InputBorder	prefix	Control
color	string	prefix_icon	string
bgcolor	string	prefix_text	string
border_radius	BorderRadiusValue	prefix_style	TextStyle
border_width	float	suffix	Control
border_color	string	suffix_icon	string
filled	bool	suffix_text	string
focused_color	string	suffix_style	TextStyle
focused_bgcolor	string	ref	Ref

on_change = function

This property assigns a function that is triggered whenever an option is selected.

```
def userSelection(e):
    pass

dropdown = flet.Dropdown(
    on_change = userSelection
    )
```


on_focus = function

This fires an event whenever the Dropdown gains focus.

```
def focused(e):
    pass

dropdown = flet.Dropdown(
    on_focus = focused
    )
```

value = string

The **value** property holds the currently selected value of the Dropdown. This can be retrieved from user's selection or set programmatically.

```
def userSelection(e):
    value = e.control.value
    print(value)

dropdown = flet.Dropdown(
    on_change = userSelection
    )
```

label = string

The **label** defines what the Dropdown is about. It indicates the purpose or context of the Dropdown to the user.

```
dropdown = flet.Dropdown(
    label= "select your city"
    )
```

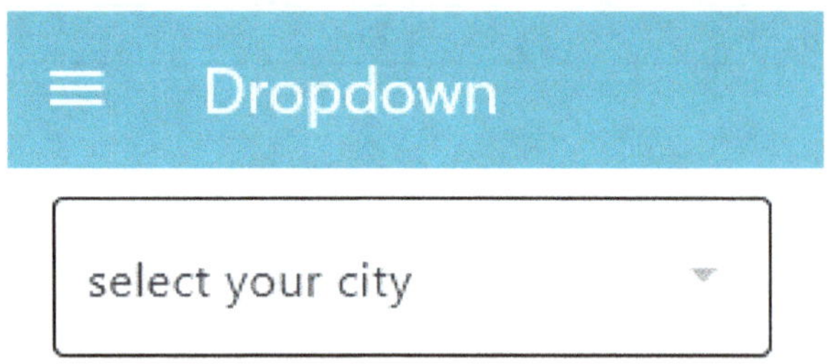

filled = bool

When set to True, this property activates **bgcolor** (background color) and **focus_bgcolor** (focused background color) property.

```
dropdown = flet.Dropdown(
    filled= True
    )
```


TextStyle

label_style = flet.TextStyle

The **label_style** property can be used to format the label in the **Dropdown**. The Flet TextStyle provides several methods for formatting the label.

- size
- height
- italic
- weight
- decoration
- decoration_color
- decoration_tickness
- decoration_style
- font_family
- bgcolor
- color
- shadow
- letter_spacing
- foreground
- font_family

size = float

The **size** property defines the size of the label.

```
dropdown = flet.Dropdown(
    label="select your city",
    label_style= flet.TextStyle(size=10)
    )
```

italic = bool

This property determines whether the text should be slanted or not.

```
dropdown = flet.Dropdown(
    label="select your city",
    label_style= flet.TextStyle(italic= True)
    )
```

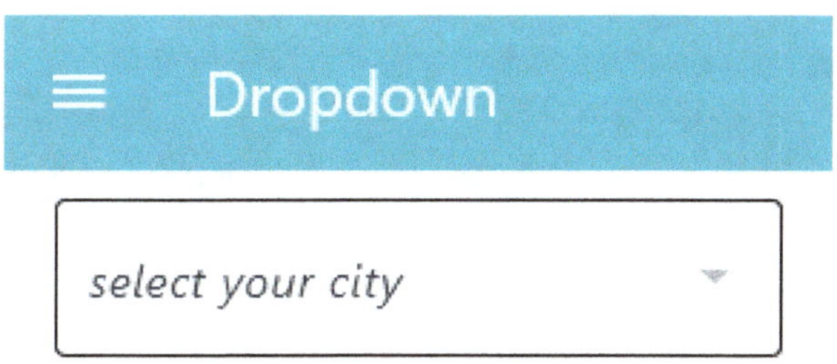

color = string

The **color** specifies the color of the label in the Dropdown.

```
dropdown = flet.Dropdown(
    label="select your city",
    label_style= flet.TextStyle(color="green")
    )
```

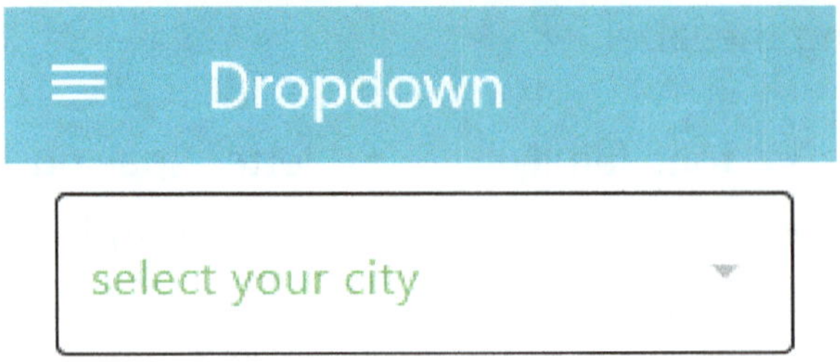

font_family = string

The **font_family** specifies the kind of front style to use.

```
dropdown = flet.Dropdown(
    label="select your city",
    label_style= flet.TextStyle(font_family="Consolas")
    )
```

bgcolor = string

This property defines the background color of the label.

```
dropdown = flet.Dropdown(
    label="select your city",
    label_style= flet.TextStyle(bgcolor="green")
    )
```

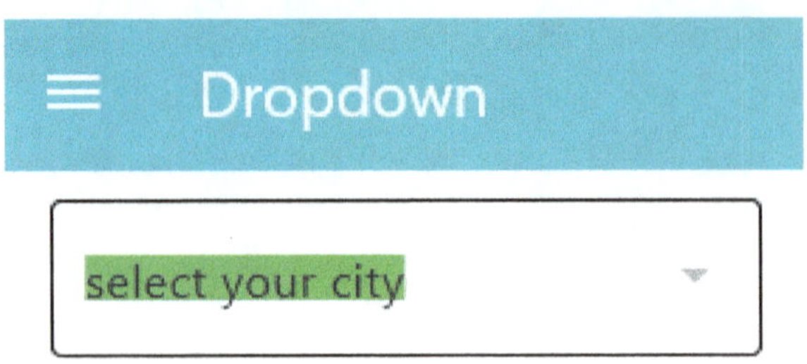

decoration = flet.TextDecoration

This property decorates the label with lines. Decoration values include UNDERLINE, OVERLINE, LINE_THROUGH and NONE.

```
    dropdown = flet.Dropdown(
        label="select your city",
        label_style= flet.TextStyle(decoration=flet.TextDecoration.OVERLINE)
        )
```

decoration_style = flet.TextDecorationStyle

After applying decoration to text, **decoration_style** let you choose line styles to apply to the label. This includes WAVY, DASHED, DOTTED, DOUBLE and SOLID.

```
     dropdown = flet.Dropdown(

        label="select your city",
        label_style= flet.TextStyle(
            decoration= flet.TextDecoration.UNDERLINE,
            decoration_style= flet.TextDecorationStyle.DOUBLE,
            decoration_thickness= 1.5, decoration_color= "orange"
            )
        )
```

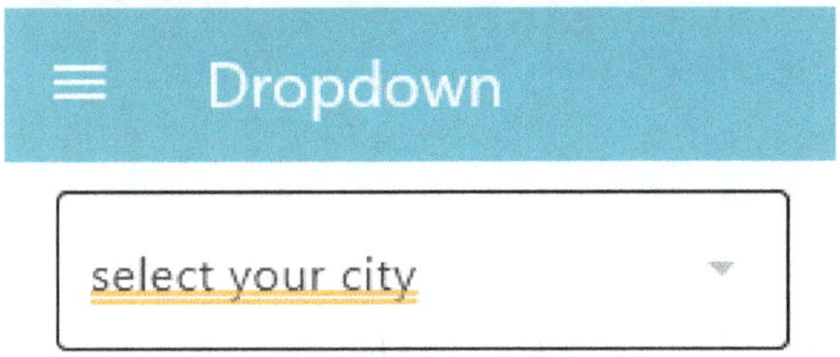

letter_spacing = float

This specifies the spaces between the characters in the text of the Dropdown box.

```
    dropdown = flet.Dropdown(
        label="select your city",
        label_style= flet.TextStyle(letter_spacing= 5 )
        )
```

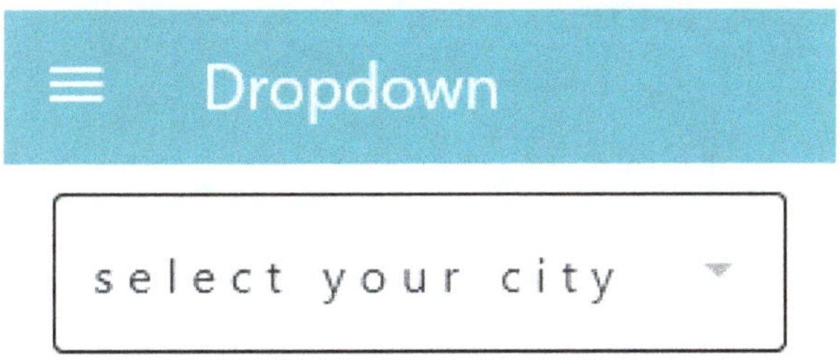

options = List[*flet.dropdown.Option]

This is a list of items that users can select from, in the Dropdown.

```
    dropdown = flet.Dropdown(
        label="select your city",
        options= [
            flet.dropdown.Option("New York"),
            flet.dropdown.Option("Chicago"),
            flet.dropdown.Option("Houston"),
        ]
        )
```

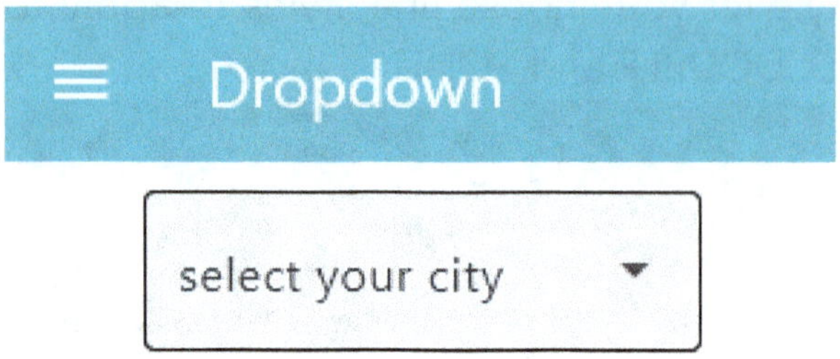

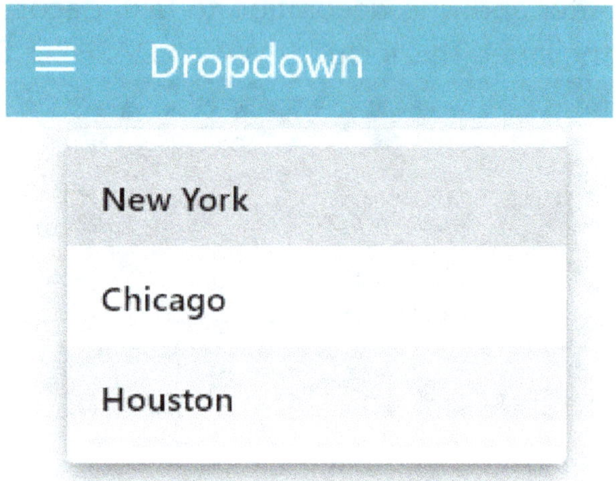

icon = string

The **icon** property specifies the icon, typically placed before the Dropdown box.

```
    dropdown = flet.Dropdown(
        icon= flet.icons.LANGUAGE_OUTLINED,
        label="Choose a language",
        )
```

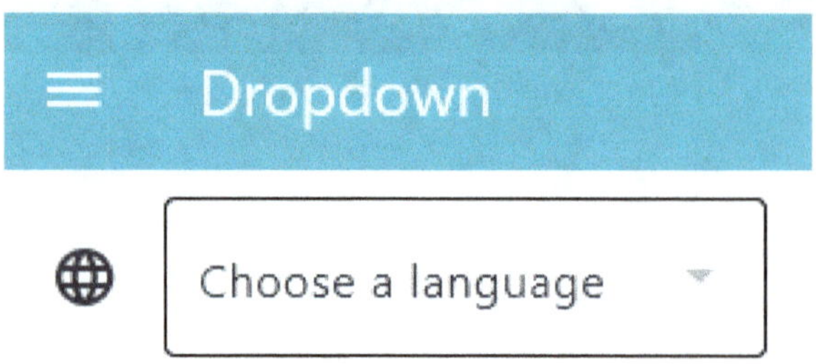

helper_text = string

This property provides additional information or guidance about the Dropdown to help users understand its purpose or how to use it.

```
dropdown = flet.Dropdown(
    label="Select your gender",
    helper_text="Your sex",
    )
```

hint_text = string

This property displays a hint or placeholder inside the Dropdown when no option is selected. It helps indicate what kind of selection is expected from the user.

```
dropdown = flet.Dropdown(
    hint_text="Your sex",
    options=[
        flet.dropdown.Option("Male"),
        flet.dropdown.Option("Female"),
    ]
    )
```

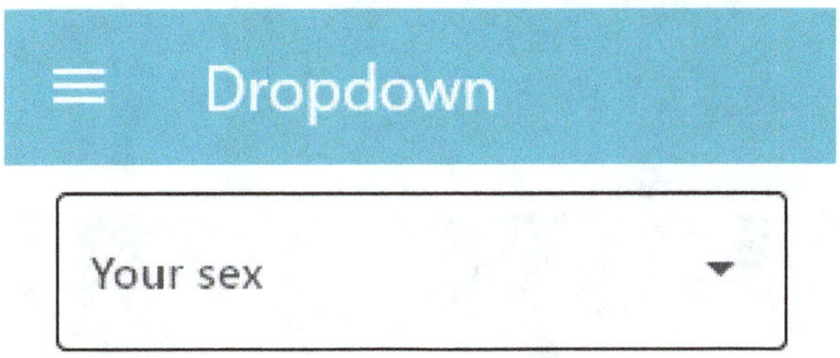

hint_style = TextStyle#

This allows you to format **hint_text** using the TextStyle method.

```
dropdown = flet.Dropdown(
    hint_style= flet.TextStyle(),
    )
```


error_text = string

This property displays an error message below the Dropdown when there is a validation error or some issue that the user needs to be aware of. It helps inform the user about what went wrong and how to correct it.

```
def userSelection(e):
    value = e.control.value
    if value =="Houston":
        e.control.error_text = "Houston can not be selected at this time"
    page.update()

dropdown = flet.Dropdown(
    on_change= userSelection,
    label= "Select a city",
    options=[
        flet.dropdown.Option("New York"),
        flet.dropdown.Option("Califonia"),
        flet.dropdown.Option("Houston"),
    ]
    )
```

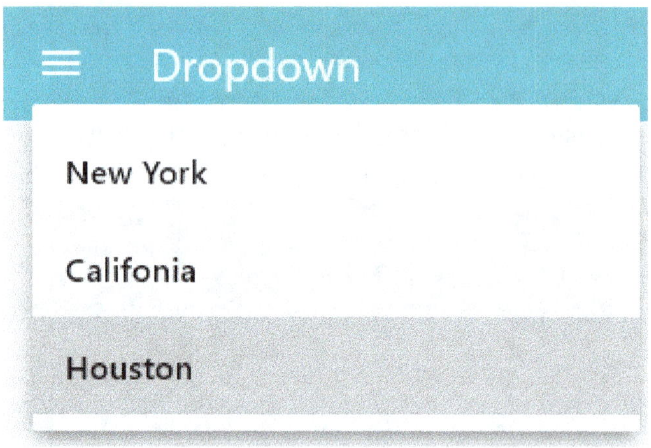

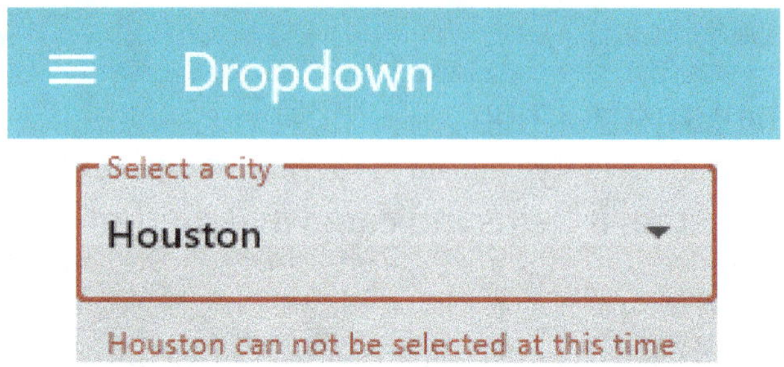

text_size = float

This property defines the text size of the Dropdown items.

```
dropdown = flet.Dropdown(
    text_size= 20,
    text_style = flet.TextStyle(weight= flet.FontWeight.BOLD),
    options=[flet.dropdown.Option('1 New York'),flet.dropdown.Option('2. London'),]
    )
```

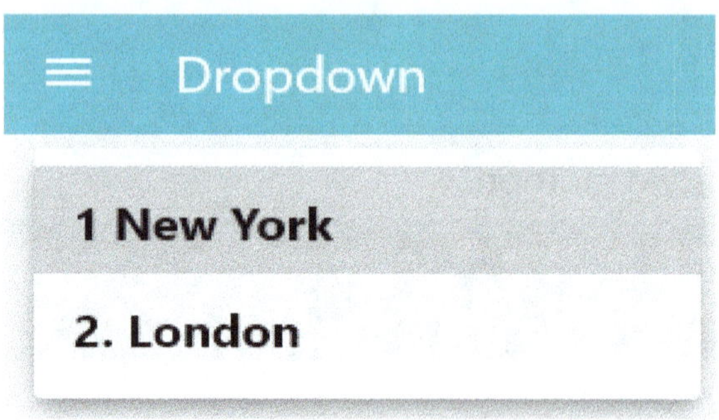

counter_text = string

This property displays the number of characters within the selected item.

```
def userSelection(e):
    length = len(e.control.value)
    e.control.counter_text = length
    page.update()

dropdown = flet.Dropdown(
    on_change= userSelection,
    label= "Choose your country",
    options=[
        flet.dropdown.Option("United State"),
        flet.dropdown.Option("Ghana"),
    ]
    )
```

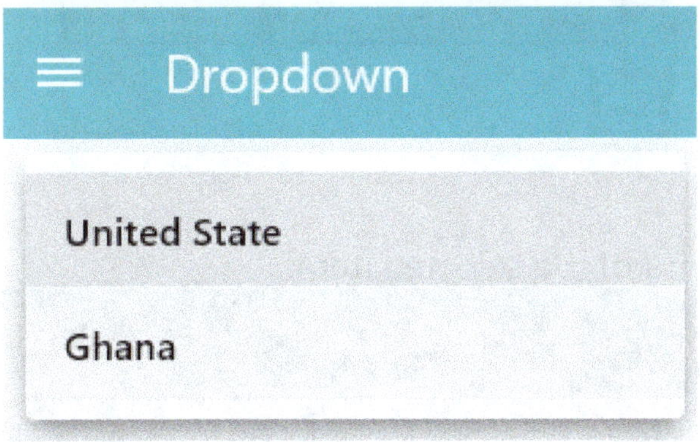

prefix = control

This property allows you to add a control before the Dropdown content.

```
dropdown = flet.Dropdown(
    prefix= flet.Text('I love '),
    label= "Select your best city",
    options=[
        flet.dropdown.Option('New York'),
        flet.dropdown.Option('London')
    ]
    )
```

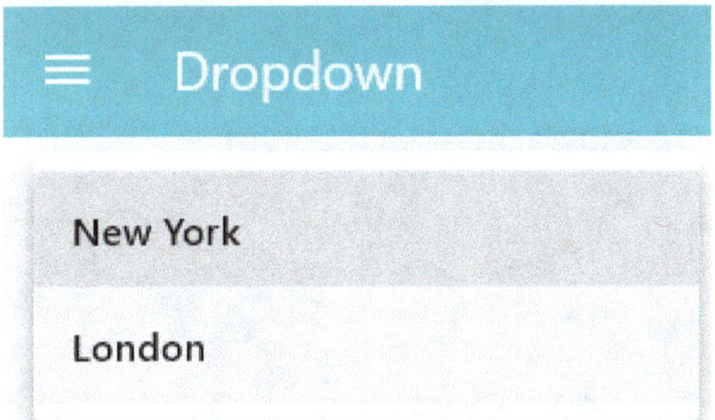

prefix_icon = string

This property specifies the icon to be placed before the selected Dropdown item.

```
dropdown = flet.Dropdown(
    prefix_icon= flet.icons.ABC_OUTLINED,
    options=[
        flet.dropdown.Option('English'),
        flet.dropdown.Option('French'),]
    )
```

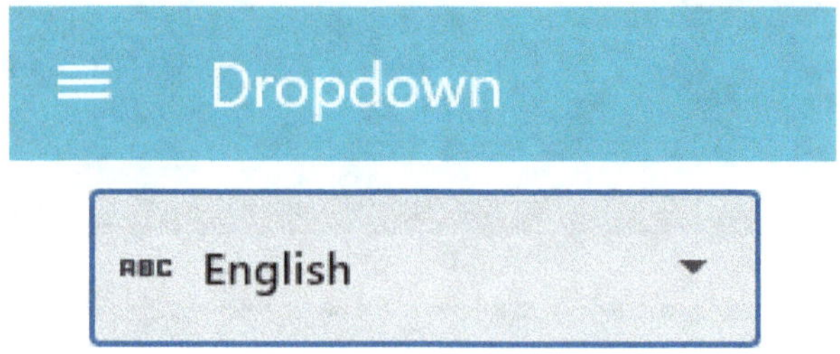

suffix = control

This is the property, that adds a content at the end of the selected item.

```
dropdown = flet.Dropdown(
    suffix= flet.Text("@ United State"),
    options=[
        flet.dropdown.Option('Georgia State University'),
        flet.dropdown.Option('University of South Carolina'),]
    )
```

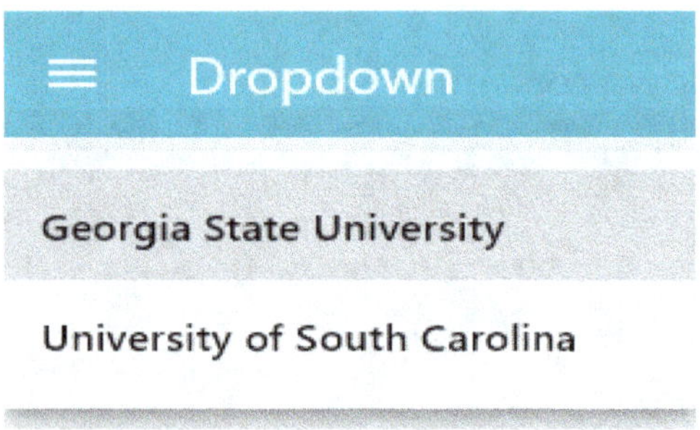

suffix_icon = string

This property specifies the icon to be placed at the end of the selected item.

```
dropdown = flet.Dropdown(
    suffix_icon= flet.icons.ABC_OUTLINED,
    options=[
        flet.dropdown.Option('English'),
        flet.dropdown.Option('French'),]
    )
```


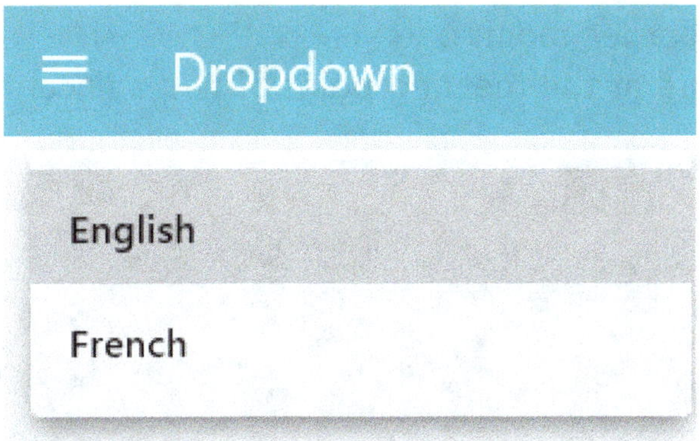

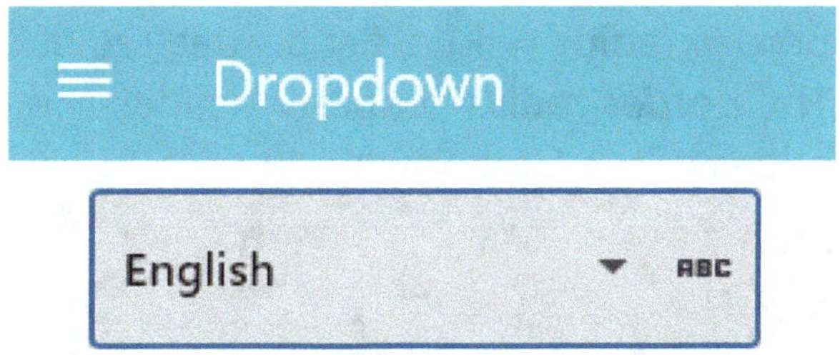

border = InputBorder
This property defines the style of the Dropdown border, such as UNDERLINE, OUTLINE or None.

```
dropdown = flet.Dropdown(
    border= flet.InputBorder.UNDERLINE,
    label="Choose your language",
    options=[
        flet.dropdown.Option('English'),
        flet.dropdown.Option('French'),]
    )
```

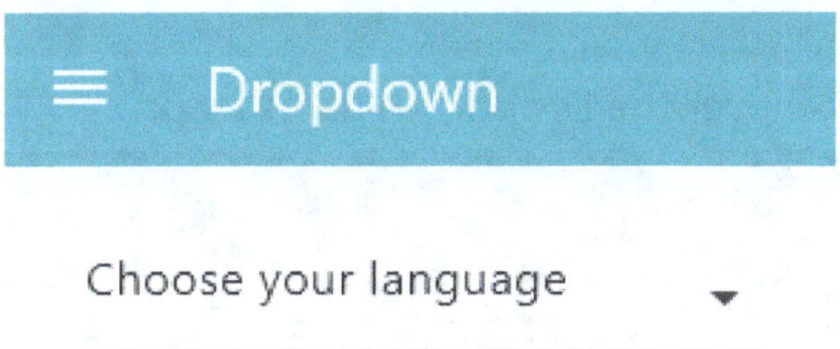

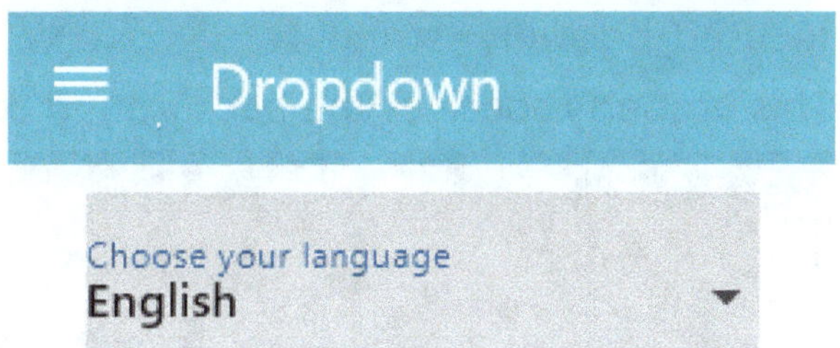

bgcolor = string
The **bgcolor** property defines the background color of the Dropdown.

```
dropdown = flet.Dropdown(
    bgcolor= "green",
    filled= True,
    label="Choose your language",
    )
```

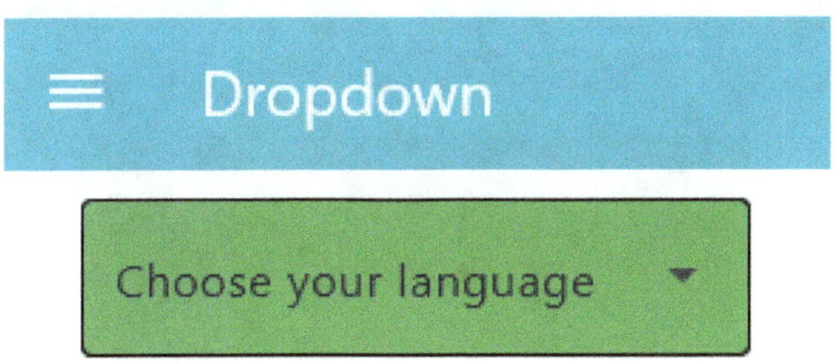

border_radius = float, flet.border_radius.all, flet.border_radius.only

The **border_radius** property defines the curvature at the meeting point of two adjacent edges of the Dropdown.

```
dropdown = flet.Dropdown(
    border_radius= flet.border_radius.only(
            top_left=0, top_right=0,
            bottom_left=10, bottom_right=10),
    border_color= "orange",
    border_width= 3,
    label="Choose your language",
    )
```

focused_bgcolor = string

This property specifies the background color whenever the Dropdown gains focus.

```
dropdown = flet.Dropdown(
    focused_bgcolor= 'orange',
    focused_border_color= 'green',
    focused_color= "black",
    focused_border_width= 2,
    filled= True,
    label = "Select a language",
    options=[
        flet.dropdown.Option('English'),
        flet.dropdown.Option('French'),]
    )
```

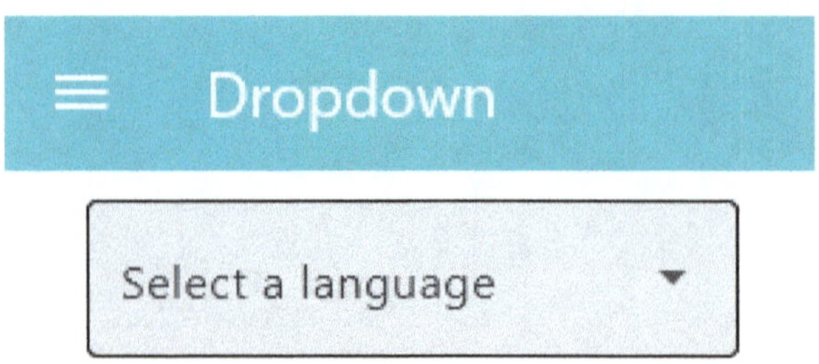

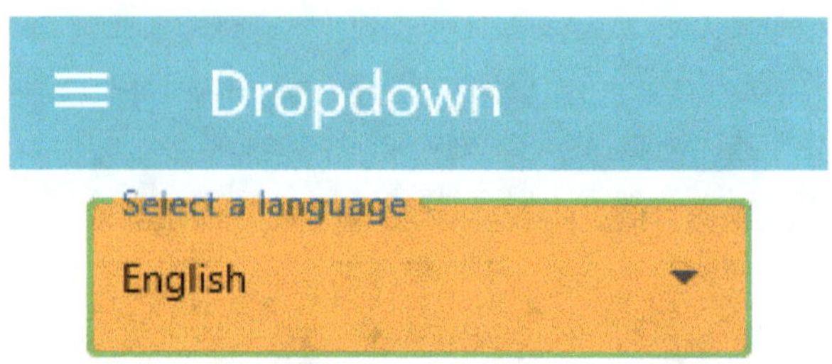

Python **Code 3.5.0**

```
import flet

def main(page: flet.Page):
    page.title = "My App"
    page.bgcolor = 'white'
    page.padding = flet.padding.all(5)

    page.appbar = flet.AppBar(
      color= flet.colors.WHITE,
      title= flet.Text("Pizza Hub"),
      bgcolor=("#14171A"),
      actions=[flet.IconButton(icon=flet.icons.FOOD_BANK_OUTLINED)]
    )
    page.drawer = flet.NavigationDrawer()

    nav = flet.NavigationBar(
        bgcolor=("#14171A"),
        destinations= [
           flet.NavigationDestination(
                 label="Menu",
                 icon=flet.icons.GRID_VIEW_ROUNDED
            ),

            flet.NavigationDestination(
                label="Order",
                icon=flet.icons.WALLET_GIFTCARD_OUTLINED
             ),

             flet.NavigationDestination(
                label="Food",
                icon=flet.icons.DINING_OUTLINED
             ),

            flet.NavigationDestination(
                label="Exit",
                icon=flet.icons.CANCEL
            )
        ]
    )
    page.navigation_bar = nav

    def selectedPizza(e):
        value = e.control.value
        print(value)

    def selectedCocktail(e):
        value = e.control.value
        print(value)

    pizzaDropdown = flet.Dropdown(
        border_radius= flet.border_radius.only(top_left=0, top_right=0, bottom_left=20, bottom_right=20),
        border_width= 2,
        label="Choose Pizza",
        on_change= selectedPizza,
        width= 250,
        options=[
            flet.dropdown.Option("\U0001F355 Pepperoni"),
            flet.dropdown.Option("\U0001F355 Hawaiian"),
            flet.dropdown.Option("\U0001F355 White Pizza"),
            flet.dropdown.Option("\U0001F355 Chicago Deep-Dish"),
            ]
        )

    cocktailDropdown = flet.Dropdown(
        border_radius= flet.border_radius.only(top_left=0, top_right=0, bottom_left=20, bottom_right=20),
        border_width= 2,
        label="Choose Cocktail",
        on_change= selectedCocktail,
        width= 250,
        options=[
            flet.dropdown.Option("\U0001F379 Margarita"),
            flet.dropdown.Option("\U0001F379 Mojito"),
            flet.dropdown.Option("\U0001F379 Negroni"),
            flet.dropdown.Option("\U0001F379 Whiskey Sour"),
            ]
        )

    pizza = flet.Row(
        alignment = flet.MainAxisAlignment.SPACE_EVENLY,
        controls=[
            flet.Image(src="C:\\Users\\Asiedu\\Desktop\\orela\\pizza.png", height=50,  width=50, fit=flet.ImageFit.FILL),
            pizzaDropdown
        ]
    )

    cocktail = flet.Row(
        alignment = flet.MainAxisAlignment.SPACE_EVENLY,
        controls=[
            flet.Image(src="C:\\Users\\Asiedu\\Desktop\\orela\\cocktail.png", height=50,  width=50, fit=flet.ImageFit.FILL),
            cocktailDropdown
        ]
    )

    col = flet.Column(
        width= page.width,
        height= page.height,
        alignment= flet.MainAxisAlignment.START,
        horizontal_alignment= flet.CrossAxisAlignment.CENTER,
        controls= [
                flet.Image(src="C:\\Users\\Asiedu\\Downloads\\Premium Vector _ Pizza slides.jpg", height=150, width=150, fit=flet.ImageFit.FILL),
                flet.Text("Order Your Favorite Pizza", size= 30, font_family="Georgia", text_align=flet.TextAlign.CENTER),
                cocktail,
                pizza,
        ]
    )

    page.add(col)
    page.update()

flet.app(target = main)
```


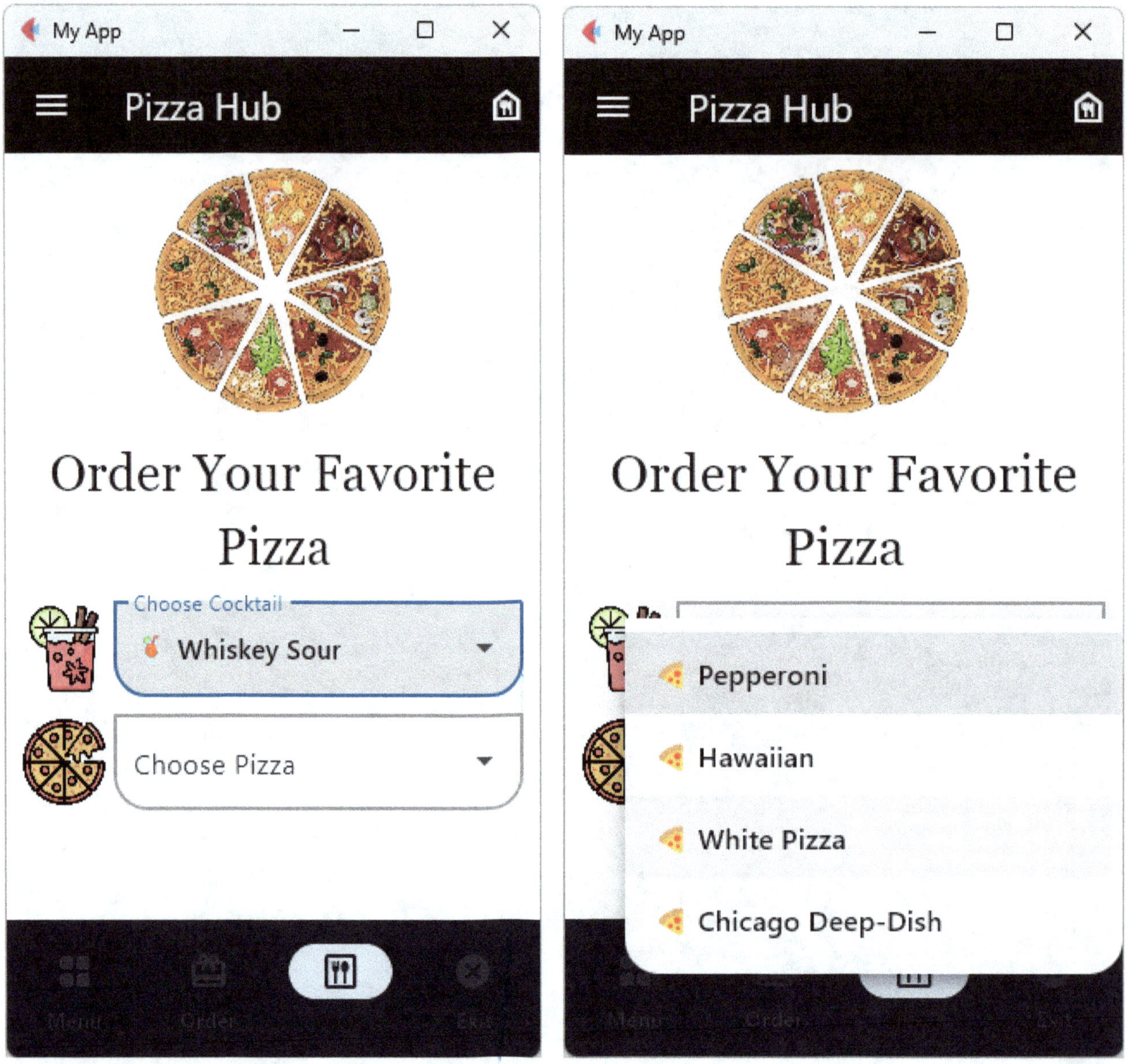
My App
Pizza Hub
Order Your Favorite Pizza
Choose Cocktail
Whiskey Sour
Choose Pizza
My App
Pizza Hub
Order Your Favorite Pizza
Pepperoni
Hawaiian
White Pizza
Chicago Deep-Dish

Page Summary

DropDown control creates a dropdown menu in a Flet app, allowing users to select options from a list.

Keywords

value
label
filled
options
alignment

Discussion

1. How can you customize the appearance and behavior of a DropDown, such as adding placeholder text, input validation, or dropdown item styling?
2. What are some techniques for handling user interactions with a DropDown, such as reacting to selection changes or displaying additional options based on user input?
3. Can you discuss the accessibility considerations when using DropDown controls, such as ensuring that it is navigable and usable for users with disabilities?

Page Views

Navigation and Routing

Navigation and routing are crucial in application development, particularly for managing complexity and organizing content effectively. Applications, especially mobile apps, cannot accommodate all content on a single page. Instead, content must be distributed across multiple pages, accessible through a well-defined routing system.

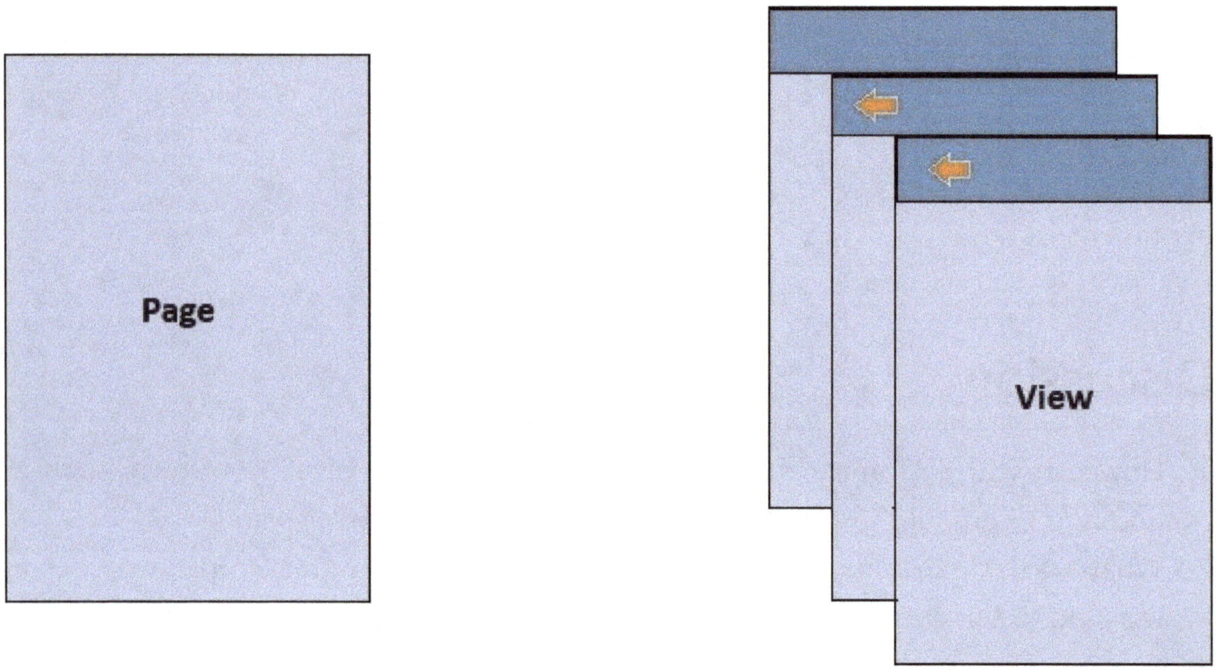

Flet's Approach to Navigation

In Flet, pages are referred to as Views and are managed by the Flet.Page component. Here's how Flet handles navigation:

- **View Stacking**: Views in Flet are layered on top of each other, forming a stack. The view at the top of this stack is the currently displayed view.
- **Navigating Back**: To return to the previous view, you remove (pop) the top view from the stack. This action reveals the next view in line, effectively navigating back to the previous page.

Managing Views with Flet.Page

- **Page Views Property**: The page.views property holds a collection of all views in the stack, representing the navigation history.
- **Current View**: The last view in the page.views list is the one currently displayed. This list must always contain at least one view, known as the root view.
- **Simulating Transitions**: To navigate to a new view, you change the page.route and append a new view to the end of the page.views list. To go back, you pop the last view from the list and update the route accordingly in the page.on_view_pop event.

Building Reliable Navigation

For a consistent and reliable navigation system, it's important to centralize the logic that constructs views based on the current route. This ensures that the navigation history stack is always correctly built from the route, maintaining a coherent and intuitive user experience.

By organizing navigation and routing in this way, Flet allows developers to create applications that are both efficient and user-friendly, handling complex content distribution seamlessly across multiple views.

View

Property	Value	Property	Value
route	string	end_drawer	NavigationDrawer
controls	List[controls]	vertical_alignment	MainAxisAlignment
appbar	AppBar	horizontal_alignment	CrossAxisAlignment
bottom_appbar	BottomAppBar	spacing	float
floating_action_button	FloatingActionButton	padding	float
floating_action_button_location	OffsetValue	bgcolor	string
navigation_bar	NavigationBar	scroll	scrollMode
drawer	NavigationDrawer	auto_scroll	bool
on_scroll	function	fullscreen_dialog	bool
adaptive	bool	on_scroll_interval	float

The **View** control functions similarly to a Container, adding controls linearly in a vertical order. It also exhibits the main Page by including elements like an AppBar#, FloatingActionButton#, NavigationDrawers# and NavigationBars#. A View creates a page that is stacked or appended to the views list using page.views.append(view).

The page.views Methods

Methods	Function
page.views.append(view)	For adding a view to the view list.
page.views.remove(view)	For removing a particular view.
page.views.copy()	For copying the whole list of views.
page.views.clear()	For deleting the entire list of views.
page.views.count()	For counting the views.
page.views.extend()	For appending a list of views to the view list.
page.views.insert(index, view)	For inserting a view at a particular index.
page.views.sort()	For sorting the view list.
page.views.index(view)	For accessing the index of a particular view.
page.views.reverse()	For arranging the views in a reverse order.
page.views.pop()	For removing the last view from the view list.

The *page.views.pop()* method is particularly significant as it removes the currently opened view or page from the View list, enabling navigation to the previous view or page.

Most View properties have been studied in the previous chapters. Refer to the section on AppBar, NavigationDrawers, FloatingActionButton, NavigationBar, space, padding and others for more details.

route = string

The **route** property is a string that defines the address for a view to be navigated to.

```
view = flet.View(
        route="view1",
        )
page.views.append(view)
```

controls = List[*Controls]

The **controls** property is a list that adds various UI elements (controls) to the View.

```
view = flet.View(
          controls= [
              flet.Text('Text1'),
              flet.Text('Text2'),
          ]
        )
```

appbar = AppBar#

The **appbar** property allows adding a top bar to the view. This typically include elements like the title, navigation icons, and action items.

```
view = flet.View(
        appbar= flet.AppBar()
      )
```

floating_action_button = FloatingActionButton#

The **floating_acction_button** property adds a floating action button to the view.

```
view = flet.View(
        floating_action_button = flet.FloatingActionButton()
  )
```

on_scroll = function

The on_scroll event is triggered when the view is scrolled.

```
def viewScroll(e):
    pass

view = flet.View(
        "view1",
        on_scroll= viewScroll
  )
```


spacing = float

The **spacing** property defines the space between the controls within the view.

```
view = flet.View(
        "view1",
        spacing= 10
    )
```

vertical_alignment = MainAxisAlignment#

The **vertical_alignment** method controls the alignment of child Controls along the main axis of a layout. There are several options available: CENTER, END, NONE, SPACE_AROUND, START, SPACE_EVENLY and SPACE_BETWEEN.

```
view = flet.View(
    vertical_alignment= flet.MainAxisAlignment.CENTER
)
```

horizontal_alignment = CrossAxisAlignment#

The **horizontal_alignment** method controls the alignment of child Controls along the cross axis of a layout. There are several options available: CENTER, END, NONE, BASELINE, START and STRETCH.

```
view = flet.View(
    horizontal_alignment= flet.CrossAxisAlignment.START
)
```

bgcolor = string

The **bgcolor** specifies the background color of the view.

```
view = flet.View(
    bgcolor= "white"
)
```

auto_scroll = True

The **page.auto_scroll** property is a Boolean method. When set to True, it automatically moves the scrollbar position to the end when children are updated.

```
view = flet.View(
    auto_scroll= True
)
```


Steps to Create Views and Navigate Through Them

① Creating the homepage View

Python **Code 3.6.0**

```
import flet

def main(page: flet.Page):
    page.title = "My App"
    page.bgcolor = 'white'
    page.padding = flet.padding.only(top= 50, left=10, right=10)

    drawer = flet.NavigationDrawer()

    navbar = flet.NavigationBar(
        destinations= [
           flet.NavigationDestination(
                 label="Menu",
                 icon=flet.icons.GRID_VIEW_ROUNDED
             ),
            flet.NavigationDestination(
                label="Code",
                icon=flet.icons.CODE
             ),
             flet.NavigationDestination(
                label="Project",
                icon=flet.icons.ROCKET_LAUNCH_OUTLINED
             ),
            flet.NavigationDestination(
                label="Exit",
                icon=flet.icons.CANCEL
            )
        ]
    )

    cakeButton = flet.OutlinedButton(
        height=100,
        width= 100,
        content= flet.Container(padding=5, content=flet.Column(controls=[flet.Image(src="C:\\cake.png"), flet.Text('Cake',size= 12)])),
        style= flet.ButtonStyle(shape=flet.RoundedRectangleBorder(radius=10)),
        on_click= lambda _:page.go("cakepage")
    )

    iceButton = flet.OutlinedButton(
        height=100,
        width= 100,
        content= flet.Container(padding=5, content=flet.Column(controls=[flet.Image(src="C:\\ice-cream.png"), flet.Text('Ice')])),
        style= flet.ButtonStyle(shape=flet.RoundedRectangleBorder(radius=10)),
        on_click= lambda _:page.go("icepage")
    )

    friedButton = flet.OutlinedButton(
        height=100,
        width= 100,
        content= flet.Container(padding=5, content=flet.Column(controls=[flet.Image(src="C:\\fried-rice.png"), flet.Text('Fried')])),
        style= flet.ButtonStyle(shape=flet.RoundedRectangleBorder(radius=10)),
        on_click= lambda _:page.go("friedpage")
    )

    buttonGroup = flet.Row(
        width= page.width,
        alignment= flet.MainAxisAlignment.SPACE_EVENLY,
        controls=[
          cakeButton,
          iceButton,
          friedButton
        ]
    )

    homepage = flet.View(
        appbar= flet.AppBar(bgcolor="#1da1f2", color= "white", title=flet.Text("HomePage")),
        navigation_bar= navbar,
        drawer= drawer,
        horizontal_alignment= flet.CrossAxisAlignment.CENTER,
        controls=[
            flet.Image(src="C:\\homeimage.jpg", width=page.width,height= 200, fit=flet.ImageFit.FILL),
            flet.Text('Great Chef', size=30, font_family="Georgia", weight=flet.FontWeight.BOLD),
            buttonGroup
        ]
    )

    page.views.append(homepage)
    page.update()

flet.app(target = main)
```

There are three buttons in the homepage. Each button will route or navigate to a particular page or view.

- Cake button will route to the Cake page.
- Ice button will route to the Ice cream page.
- Fried button will route to the Fried page

In the next step, we will create our three views without routing functions. The functions would be implemented later.

② Creating Views

Python **Code 3.6.1**

```python
import flet

def main(page: flet.Page):
    page.title = "My App"
    page.bgcolor = 'white'
    page.padding = flet.padding.only(top= 50, left=10, right=10)

    drawer = flet.NavigationDrawer()

    navbar = flet.NavigationBar(
        destinations= [
           flet.NavigationDestination(
                label="Menu",
                icon=flet.icons.GRID_VIEW_ROUNDED
            ),
            flet.NavigationDestination(
               label="Code",
               icon=flet.icons.CODE
            ),
             flet.NavigationDestination(
               label="Project",
               icon=flet.icons.ROCKET_LAUNCH_OUTLINED
            ),
            flet.NavigationDestination(
               label="Exit",
               icon=flet.icons.CANCEL
            )
        ]
    )

    cakeButton = flet.OutlinedButton(
        height=100,
        width= 100,
        content= flet.Container(padding=5, content=flet.Column(controls=[flet.Image(src="C:\\cake.png"), flet.Text('Cake',size= 12)])),
        style= flet.ButtonStyle(shape=flet.RoundedRectangleBorder(radius=10)),
        on_click= lambda _:page.go("cakepage")
    )

    iceButton = flet.OutlinedButton(
        height=100,
        width= 100,
        content= flet.Container(padding=5, content=flet.Column(controls=[flet.Image(src="C:\\ice-cream.png"), flet.Text('Ice')])),
        style= flet.ButtonStyle(shape=flet.RoundedRectangleBorder(radius=10)),
        on_click= lambda _:page.go("icepage")
    )

    friedButton = flet.OutlinedButton(
        height=100,
        width= 100,
        content= flet.Container(padding=5, content=flet.Column(controls=[flet.Image(src="C:\\fried-rice.png"), flet.Text('Fried')])),
        style= flet.ButtonStyle(shape=flet.RoundedRectangleBorder(radius=10)),
        on_click= lambda _:page.go("friedpage")
    )

    homeButton = flet.OutlinedButton(
        height=100,
        width= 100,
        content= flet.Container(padding=5, content=flet.Column(controls=[flet.Image(src="C:\\house.png"), flet.Text('Home')])),
        style= flet.ButtonStyle(shape=flet.RoundedRectangleBorder(radius=10)),
        on_click= lambda _:page.go("home")
    )

    buttonGroup = flet.Row(
        width= page.width,
        alignment= flet.MainAxisAlignment.SPACE_EVENLY,
        controls=[
          cakeButton,
          iceButton,
          friedButton
        ]
    )

    cakeButtonGroup = flet.Row(
        width= page.width,
        alignment= flet.MainAxisAlignment.SPACE_EVENLY,
        controls=[
          homeButton,
          iceButton,
          friedButton
        ]
    )

    iceButtonGroup = flet.Row(
        width= page.width,
        alignment= flet.MainAxisAlignment.SPACE_EVENLY,
        controls=[
          homeButton,
          cakeButton,
          friedButton
        ]
    )
    friedButtonGroup = flet.Row(
        width= page.width,
        alignment= flet.MainAxisAlignment.SPACE_EVENLY,
        controls=[
          homeButton,
          cakeButton,
          iceButton,
        ]
    )



    homepage = flet.View(
        appbar= flet.AppBar(bgcolor="#1da1f2", color= "white", title=flet.Text("HomePage")),
        navigation_bar= navbar,
        drawer= drawer,
        horizontal_alignment= flet.CrossAxisAlignment.CENTER,
        controls=[
            flet.Image(src="C:\\homeimage.jpg", width=page.width,height= 200, fit=flet.ImageFit.FILL),
            flet.Text('Great Chef', size=30, font_family="Georgia", weight=flet.FontWeight.BOLD),
            buttonGroup
        ]
    )

    cakepage = flet.View(
        route="cakepage",
        appbar= flet.AppBar(title=flet.Text("Cake Page"),),
        navigation_bar= navbar,
        horizontal_alignment= flet.CrossAxisAlignment.CENTER,
        controls=[
            flet.Image(src="C:\\cake.jpg", width=page.width,height= 200, fit=flet.ImageFit.FILL),
            flet.Text('Ouch!, Awesome Cake', size =30, font_family="Georgia"),
            cakeButtonGroup
        ]
    )

    icepage = flet.View(
        route="icepage",
        appbar= flet.AppBar(title=flet.Text("Ice cream Page"),),
        navigation_bar= navbar,
        horizontal_alignment= flet.CrossAxisAlignment.CENTER,
        controls=[
            flet.Image(src="C:\\icecream.jpg", width=page.width,height= 200, fit=flet.ImageFit.FILL),
            flet.Text('Oh wow!, A chilled Ice cream?', size =30, font_family="Georgia"),
            iceButtonGroup
        ]
    )

    friedpage = flet.View(
        route="friedpage",
        appbar= flet.AppBar(title=flet.Text("Fried Page"),),
        navigation_bar= navbar,
        horizontal_alignment= flet.CrossAxisAlignment.CENTER,
        controls=[
            flet.Image(src="C:\\fried.jpg", width=page.width,height= 200, fit=flet.ImageFit.FILL),
            flet.Text('Yummy!, Spicy Rolls', size =30, font_family="Georgia"),
            friedButtonGroup
        ]
    )

    page.views.append(cakepage)
    page.update()

flet.app(target = main)
```


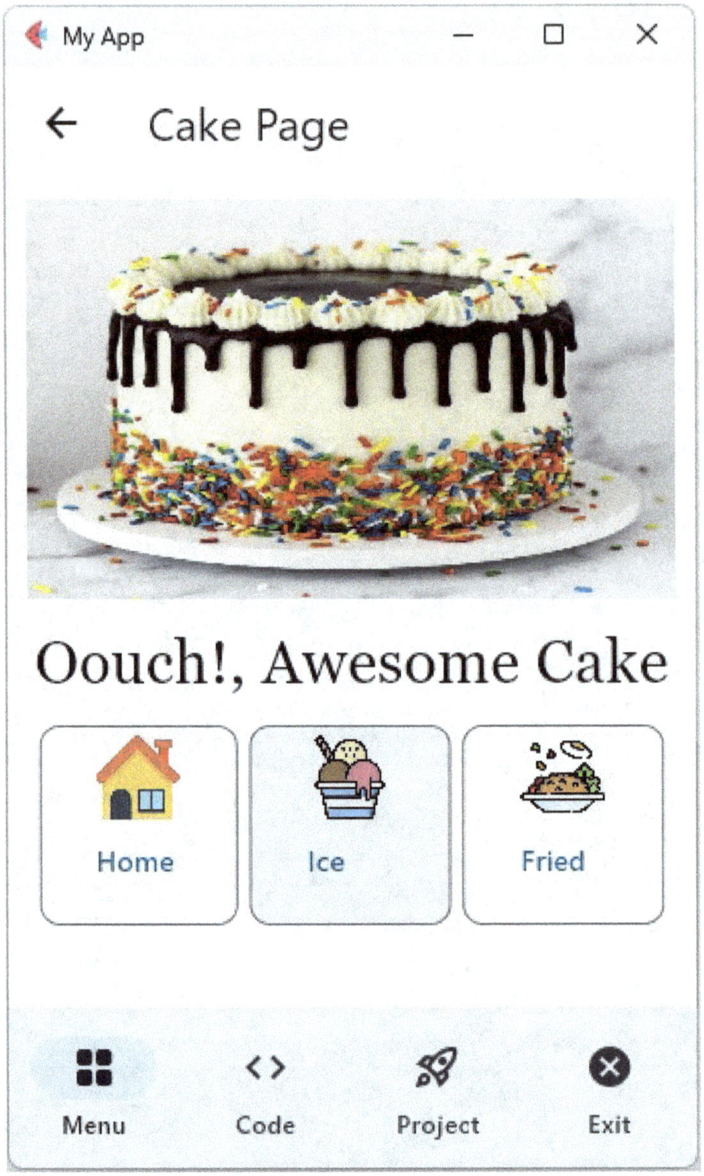

In the above code, we only implemented adding views (the cake page) to the page, but not routing yet. It is evident that the cake view or page has replaced the homepage upon appending a view.

To implement routing techniques, we need to define two functions to handle appending and removing views.

③ Assigning functions

Python **Code 3.6.2**

```python
import flet

def main(page: flet.Page):
    page.title = "My App"
    page.bgcolor = 'white'
    page.padding = flet.padding.only(top= 50, left=10, right=10)

    drawer = flet.NavigationDrawer()

    navbar = flet.NavigationBar(
        destinations= [
            flet.NavigationDestination(
                label="Menu",
                icon=flet.icons.GRID_VIEW_ROUNDED
            ),
            flet.NavigationDestination(
                label="Code",
                icon=flet.icons.CODE
            ),
            flet.NavigationDestination(
                label="Project",
                icon=flet.icons.ROCKET_LAUNCH_OUTLINED
            ),
            flet.NavigationDestination(
                label="Exit",
                icon=flet.icons.CANCEL
            )
        ]
    )

    def appendView(route):
        page.views.clear()
        page.views.append(homepage),

        if page.route == "cakepage":
            page.views.append(cakepage)

        elif page.route == 'icepage':
            page.views.append(icepage)

        elif page.route == 'friedpage':
            page.views.append(friedpage)

        else:
            page.views.append(homepage)

        page.update()


    def removeView(view):
        page.views.pop()
        current_view = page.views[-1]
        page.go(current_view.route)


    cakeButton = flet.OutlinedButton(
        height=100,
        width= 100,
        content= flet.Container(padding=5, content=flet.Column(controls=[flet.Image(src="C:\\cake.png"), flet.Text('Cake',size= 13)])),
        style= flet.ButtonStyle(shape=flet.RoundedRectangleBorder(radius=10)),
        on_click= lambda _:page.go("cakepage")
    )

    iceButton = flet.OutlinedButton(
        height=100,
        width= 100,
        content= flet.Container(padding=5, content=flet.Column(controls=[flet.Image(src="C:\\ice-cream.png"), flet.Text('Ice')])),
        style= flet.ButtonStyle(shape=flet.RoundedRectangleBorder(radius=10)),
        on_click= lambda _:page.go("icepage")
    )

    friedButton = flet.OutlinedButton(
        height=100,
        width= 100,
        content= flet.Container(padding=5, content=flet.Column(controls=[flet.Image(src="C:\\fried-rice.png"), flet.Text('Fried')])),
        style= flet.ButtonStyle(shape=flet.RoundedRectangleBorder(radius=10)),
        on_click= lambda _:page.go("friedpage")
    )

    homeButton = flet.OutlinedButton(
        height=100,
        width= 100,
        content= flet.Container(padding=5, content=flet.Column(controls=[flet.Image(src="C:\\house.png"), flet.Text('Home')])),
        style= flet.ButtonStyle(shape=flet.RoundedRectangleBorder(radius=10)),
        on_click= lambda _:page.go("homepage")
    )

    buttonGroup = flet.Row(
        width= page.width,
        alignment= flet.MainAxisAlignment.SPACE_EVENLY,
        controls=[
          cakeButton,
          iceButton,
          friedButton
        ]
    )

    cakeButtonGroup = flet.Row(
        width= page.width,
        alignment= flet.MainAxisAlignment.SPACE_EVENLY,
        controls=[
          homeButton,
          iceButton,
          friedButton
        ]
    )

    iceButtonGroup = flet.Row(
        width= page.width,
        alignment= flet.MainAxisAlignment.SPACE_EVENLY,
        controls=[
          homeButton,
          cakeButton,
          friedButton
        ]
    )
    friedButtonGroup = flet.Row(
        width= page.width,
        alignment= flet.MainAxisAlignment.SPACE_EVENLY,
        controls=[
          homeButton,
          cakeButton,
          iceButton,
        ]
    )



    homepage = flet.View(
        appbar= flet.AppBar(bgcolor="#1da1f2", color= "white", title=flet.Text('HomePage')),
        navigation_bar= navbar,
        drawer= drawer,
        horizontal_alignment= flet.CrossAxisAlignment.CENTER,
        controls=[
            flet.Image(src="C:\\homeimage.jpg", width=page.width,height= 200, fit=flet.ImageFit.FILL),
            flet.Text('Great Chef', size=30, font_family="Georgia", weight=flet.FontWeight.BOLD),
            buttonGroup
        ]
    )

    cakepage = flet.View(
        route="cakepage",
        appbar= flet.AppBar(title=flet.Text('Cake Page'), leading=flet.IconButton(icon=flet.icons.ARROW_BACK, on_click=removeView)),
        navigation_bar= navbar,
        horizontal_alignment= flet.CrossAxisAlignment.CENTER,
        controls=[
            flet.Image(src="C:\\case.jpg", width=page.width,height= 200, fit=flet.ImageFit.FILL),
            flet.Text('Ooochi, Awesome Cake', size =30, font_family="Georgia"),
            cakeButtonGroup
        ]
    )

    icepage = flet.View(
        route="icepage",
        appbar= flet.AppBar(title=flet.Text('Ice cream Page'), color= "white", bgcolor="cyan", leading=flet.IconButton(icon=flet.icons.ARROW_BACK, on_click=removeView)),
        navigation_bar= navbar,
        horizontal_alignment= flet.CrossAxisAlignment.CENTER,
        controls=[
            flet.Image(src="C:\\icecream.jpg", width=page.width,height= 200, fit=flet.ImageFit.FILL),
            flet.Text('Oh wow!, A chilled Ice cream!', size =30, font_family="Georgia"),
            iceButtonGroup
        ]
    )

    friedpage = flet.View(
        route="friedpage",
        appbar= flet.AppBar(title=flet.Text('Fried Page'), color= "white", bgcolor="teal", leading=flet.IconButton(icon=flet.icons.ARROW_BACK, on_click=removeView)),
        navigation_bar= navbar,
        horizontal_alignment= flet.CrossAxisAlignment.CENTER,
        controls=[
            flet.Image(src="C:\\fried.jpg", width=page.width,height= 200, fit=flet.ImageFit.FILL),
            flet.Text('Yummy!, Spicy Rolls', size =30, font_family="Georgia"),
            friedButtonGroup
        ]
    )

    page.on_route_change = appendView
    page.on_view_pop = removeView,
    page.go(page.route)
    page.update()

flet.app(target = main)
```

 |

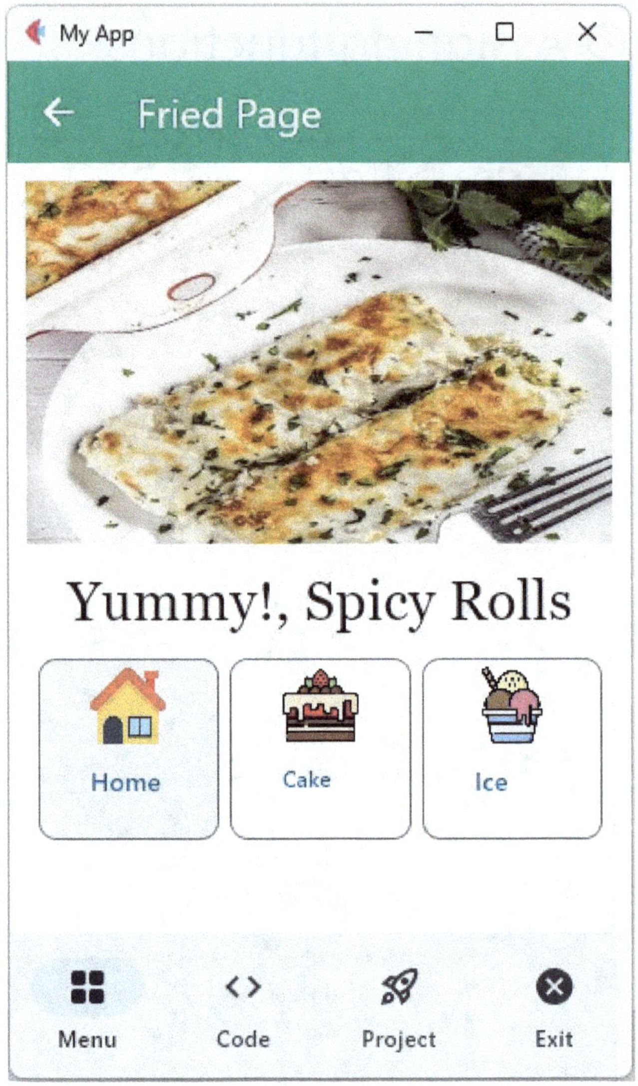

The above code provides complete navigation using page.go(route) method. The route is a string that refers to a particular page. The cakeButton, iceButton and friedButton each trigger an event when pressed using **page.go(route**) to open the corresponding page or view.

The page.go(route) method is managed by our defined function appendView which appends the view each time a button is pressed. Flet recognizes this function by registering it to the page using **page.on_route_change**.

The page.on_view_pop also registers the removeView function, which handles popping views, enabling navigation to the previous page.

Page Summary

Page View control creates a scrollable view with multiple pages in a Flet app, allowing users to swipe between different content views.

Keywords

route
spacing
padding
appbar
controls
end_drawer

Discussion

1. How do you implement a Page View with custom page transitions or animations to enhance the user experience?
2. What are some strategies for managing state and content synchronization between different pages in a Page View?
3. Can you discuss the performance implications of using Page View controls, especially when rendering a large number of pages or complex content within each page?

MenuBar

A **MenuBar** is a control element that typically appears at the top of the application window or screen. It provides a set of menus that contain options and commands for user to interact with the application. Menus are commonly found in desktop and web applications, but they are less common in mobile applications.

Each menu in the **MenuBar** may include a set of **SubmenuButton**'s to organize menu items using **MenuItemButton**'s. This structure helps to group related commands and options, making the application more organized and user-friendly.

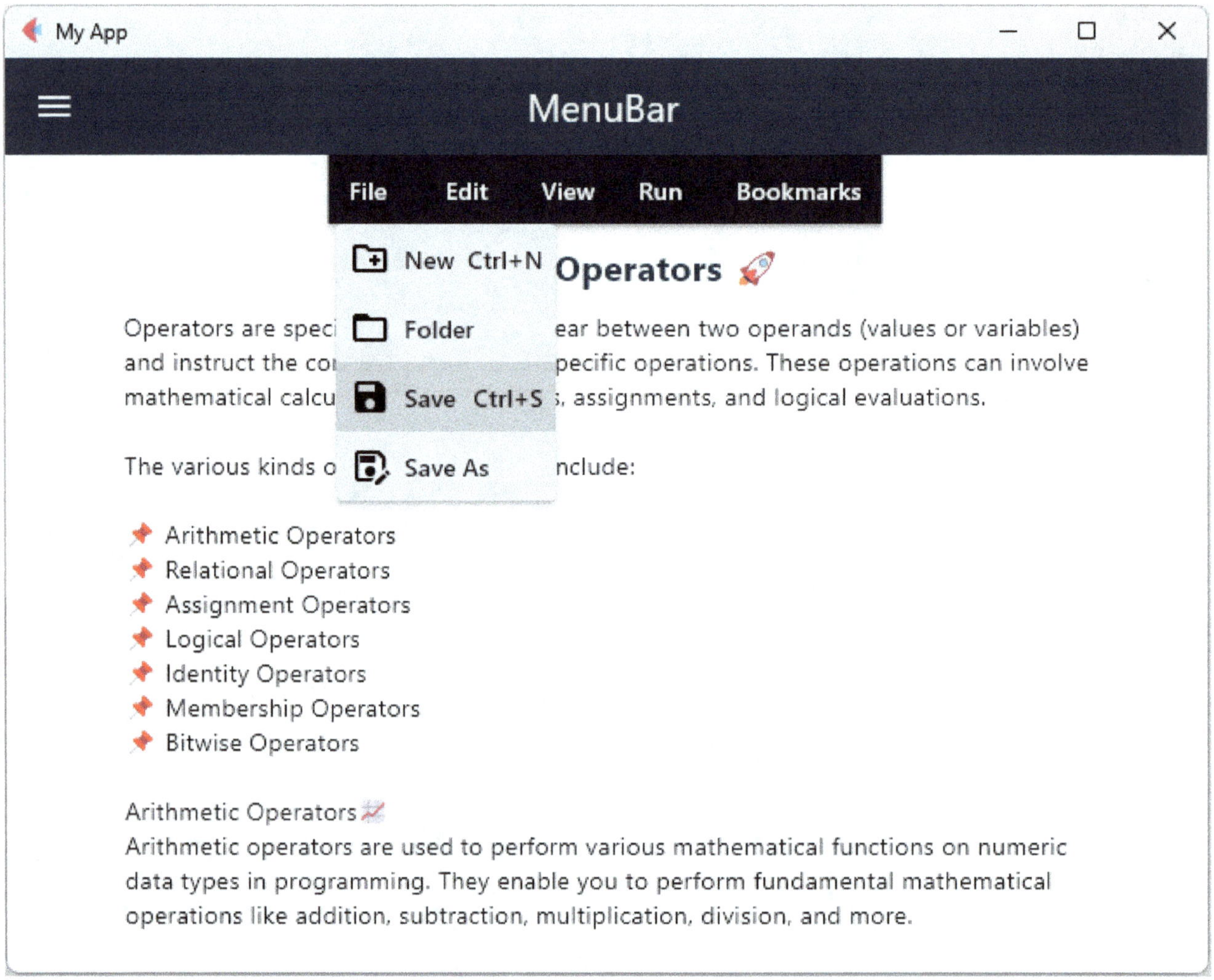

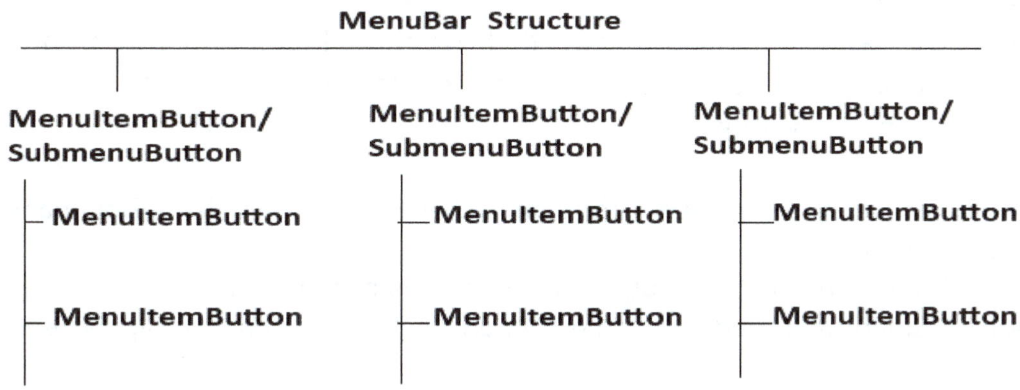

Available Methods

Property	Value	Property	Value
controls	List[Controls]	expand	bool
clip_behavior	ClipBehavior	style	MenuStyle

controls = List[*Controls]

The **controls** property defines a list of menu items (Controls) typically **SubMenuButton**.

```
menubar = flet.MenuBar(
        controls= [
            flet.SubmenuButton(content=flet.Text('File')),
            flet.SubmenuButton(content=flet.Text('Edit')),
            flet.MenuItemButton(content=flet.Text('View'))
        ]
    )
```

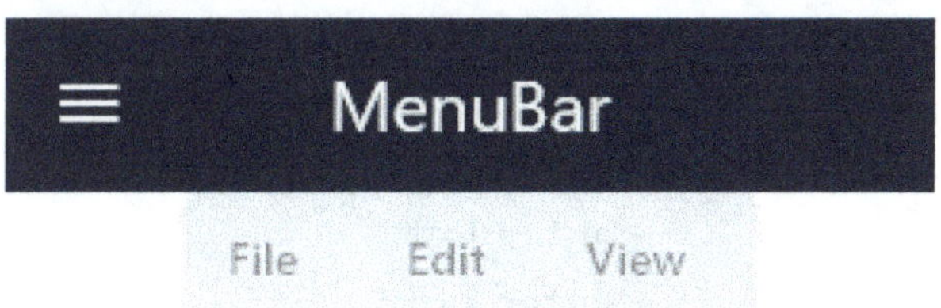

clip_behavior = ClipBehavior
This property defines how the menu items that overflows the boundaries of the MenuBar is handled. That is, if the overflow menu items should be clipped (cut off) or displayed. The available methods include:

NONE: No clipping is applied. Menu items that overflow the menubar's boundaries will be rendered outside of it.
HARD_EDGE : Overflow menu items outside menubar are not displayed.
ANTI_ALIAS : It smooths the edges of the clipped content making the clipped edge appear smoother.
ANTI_ALIAS_WITH_SAVE_LAYER : It provides even smoother edges.

```
menubar = flet.MenuBar(
    clip_behavior=flet.ClipBehavior.HARD_EDGE,
)
```

MenuStyle

The **MenuStyle** property of the **MenuBar** provides methods to style or decorate the menubar. This can be done by using the style property. The available methods include:

Property	Value	Property	Value
alignment	Alignment	padding	PaddingValue
bgcolor	string	side	BorderSide
shadow_color	string	shape	OutlinedBorder
surface_tint_color	string	mouse_cursor	MouseCursor
elevation	float		

alignment = flet.alignment
The alignment is used to apply alignment or aligns the menubar within the page. The available methods include:

top_left
top_right
top_center
bottom_left
bottom_right
bottom_center
center_left
center_right
center


```
menubar = flet.MenuBar(
    style= flet.MenuStyle(
       alignment= flet.alignment.center_left,
    )
)
```

bgcolor = string

The **bgcolor** determines the background color of the menubar.

```
menubar = flet.MenuBar(
    controls= [
        flet.SubmenuButton(content=flet.Text('File', color="white")),
        flet.SubmenuButton(content=flet.Text('Edit', color="white")),
        flet.SubmenuButton(content=flet.Text('View', color="white"))
    ],
    style= flet.MenuStyle(bgcolor= "black",)
)
```

elevation = float

The **elevation** is the degree of shadow effect of the MenuBar.

```
menubar = flet.MenuBar(
    style= flet.MenuStyle(elevation= 20)
)
```

 |

shadow_color = string
The **shadow_color** defines the shadow effect color for the MenuBar.

```
menubar = flet.MenuBar(
    style= flet.MenuStyle(shadow_color="green")
)
```

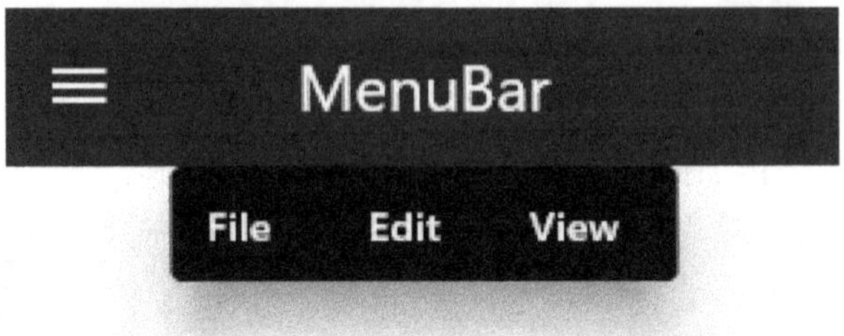

surface_tint_color = string
The **surface_tint_color** defines a faded background color for the MenuBar.

```
menubar = flet.MenuBar(
    style= flet.MenuStyle(surface_tint_color="orange")
)
```

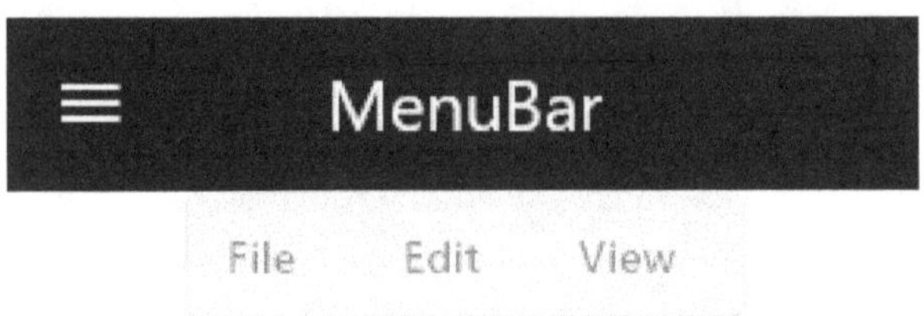

padding = float, flet.padding.all, flet.padding.only
The padding property defines the space around the menu items and the edges of the MenuBar.

```
menubar = flet.MenuBar(
    style= flet.MenuStyle(padding= 20)
)
```

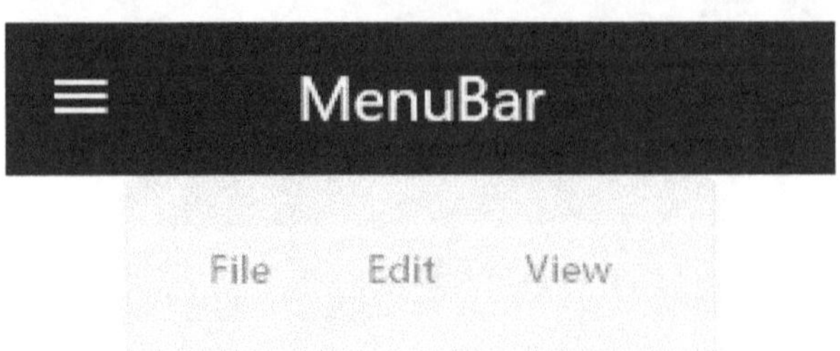

mouse_cursor = MouseCursor
This defines the appearance of the mouse cursor when it hovers over the MenuBar or its menu items. The available methods include:

RESIZE_LEFT	CONTEXT_MENU	HELP	RESIZE_COLUMN	RESIZE_ROW
ALIAS	COPY	MOVE	RESIZE_DOWN	RESIZE_UP
ALL_SCROLL	DISAPPEARING	NO_DROP	RESIZE_DOWN_LEFT	TEXT
BASIC	FORBIDDEN	NONE	RESIZE_DOWN_RIGHT	VERTICAL_TEXT
CELL	GRAB	PRECISE	RESIZE_LEFT_RIGHT	WAIT
CLICK	GRABBING	PROGRESS	RESIZE_RIGHT	ZOOM_IN
RESIZE_UP_RIGHT	RESIZE_UP_LEFT	RESIZE_UP_DOWN	ZOOM_OUT	

```
menubar = flet.MenuBar(
    style= flet.MenuStyle(mouse_cursor= flet.MouseCursor.CLICK)
)
```

side = BorderSide
The **side** property determines the width and color of the edges of the MenuBar.

```
menubar = flet.MenuBar(
    style= flet.MenuStyle(side= flet.BorderSide(width=2, color="red"))
)
```

shape = flet.OutlinedBorder
The **shape** defines the appearance of the MenuBar by specifying the shape. The available shapes include

- flet.RoundedRectangleBorder(type: str, radius: int)
- flet.StadiumBorder(type: str)
- flet.CircleBorder(type: str)
- flet.BeveledRectangleBorder(type: str, radius: int)
- flet.OutlinedBorder(type: str)
- flet.ContinousRectangleBorder(type: str, radius: int)


```
    menubar = flet.MenuBar(
        style= flet.MenuStyle(shape= flet.RoundedRectangleBorder(radius=20))
    )
```

SubmenuButton

A **SubmenuButton** is a user interface component that functions as a part of a menu, typically found within a MenuBar, that opens a secondary menu when clicked. This secondary menu is known as a submenu.

Property	Value	Property	Value
content	Control	on_open	function
controls	List[Control]	on_close	function
leading	Control	on_hover	function
trailing	Control	on_focus	function
clip_behavior	ClipBehavior	on_blur	function
style	ButtonStyle	offset	OffsetValue
alignment_offset	OffsetValue	key	string

content = Control
The **content** property represents the label of the menu item. This can be any control but the Text is typically used.

```
menubar = flet.MenuBar(
    controls= [
        flet.SubmenuButton(content=flet.Text('File', color="white")),
        flet.SubmenuButton(content=flet.Text('Edit', color="white")),
        flet.SubmenuButton(content=flet.Text('View', color="white")),
        flet.SubmenuButton(content=flet.Text('Form', color="white")),
    ],
)
```

controls = List[*Control]
This property defines the list of controls typically MenuItemButton in the submenu.

```
flet.SubmenuButton(
    controls= [
       flet.MenuItemButton(content=flet.Text("New File", color="black")),
       flet.MenuItemButton(content=flet.Text("Open Folder", color="black")),
       flet.MenuItemButton(content=flet.Text("Save", color="black")),
            ],
    content=flet.Text('File', color="white")
    ),
```

leading = control
The **leading** specifies the leftmost control, displayed next to the **content** (label), which can help in identifying the purpose of the item.

```
flet.SubmenuButton(
    leading = flet.Icon(name= flet.icons.FOLDER, color="orange"),
    content=flet.Text('File', color="white")
),
```

trailing = control
The **trailing** defines the rightmost control next to the content or label.

```
flet.SubmenuButton(
    trailing = flet.Icon(name= flet.icons.FOLDER, color="Green"),
    content=flet.Text('File', color="white")
),
```

clip_behavior = ClipBehavior
This property defines how the submenu items outside boundaries behave. The available methods include: NONE, HARD_EDGE, ANTI_ALIAS and ANTI_ALIAS_WITH_SAVE_LAYER.

```
flet.SubmenuButton(
    clip_behavior= flet.ClipBehavior.HARD_EDGE,
    content=flet.Text('File', color="white")
),
```


ButtonStyle

The **ButtonStyle** is used to style or decorate the **SubmenuButton** and **MenuItemButton** by using the **style** property.

color	shadow_color	surface_tint_color	elevation
bgcolor	animation_duration	padding	side
overlay_color	shape		

color = string
The **color** determines the color of the content or label.

```
flet.SubmenuButton(
    style = flet.ButtonStyle(color="blue"),
    content=flet.Text('File')
),
```

bgcolor = string
This color determines the background color of the content or label.

```
flet.SubmenuButton(
    style = flet.ButtonStyle(bgcolor="green"),
    content=flet.Text('File')
),
```

surface_tint_color = string
This applies a faded background color to the item.

```
flet.SubmenuButton(
    style = flet.ButtonStyle(surface_tint_color="red"),
    content=flet.Text('File')
),
```

overlay_color = string
This applies a background color to the item, whenever it gains focus.

```
flet.SubmenuButton(
    style = flet.ButtonStyle(overlay_color= "Orange"),
    content=flet.Text('File')
),
```

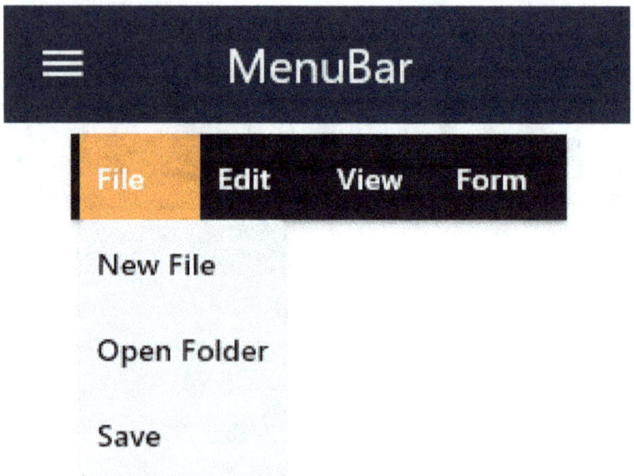

padding = float, flet.padding.all, flet.padding.only
This determines the space around the item and the edges of the MenuBar.

```
flet.SubmenuButton(
    style = flet.ButtonStyle(padding= 30),
    content=flet.Text('File', color="white")
),
```

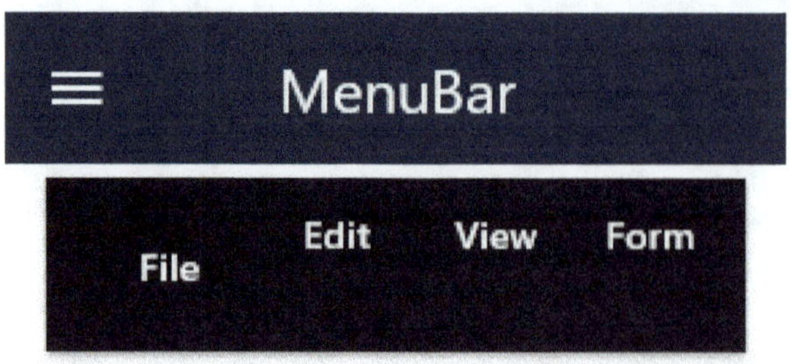

alignment_offset = flet.Offset
The alignment_offset method defines the spatial positioning of the item with the Menubar.

```
flet.SubmenuButton(
    alignment_offset= flet.Offset(x = 20, y = 50),
    content=flet.Text('File', color="white")
),
```

on_open = function
An event that fires when the submenu is opened.

on_close = function
This property fires event upon closing the item's submenu.

on_hover = function (Desktop)
This assigns an event when the mouse button passes over the item.

on_focus = function
An event that fires whenever the item gains focus.

on_blur = function
This is a function to get executed when the menu item loses focus.

```
flet.SubmenuButton(
    on_open = lambda _: print("File is Opened"),
    on_close = lambda _: print("File is Closed"),
    on_hover = lambda _: print("Hovered"),
    on_focus = lambda _: print("File has gained Focus"),
    on_blur = lambda _: print("File loses focus"),
    content=flet.Text('File', color="white")
),
```


MenuItemButton

A **MenuItemButton** is a user interface component typically found within a submenu or context menu, which contains a list of items that a user can select from. These items can represent actions, commands, or options related to the application.

Property	Value	Property	Value
content	Control	on_click	function
leading	Control	on_hover	function
trailing	Control	on_focus	function
clip_behavior	ClipBehavior	on_blur	function
style	ButtonStyle	key	string

content = Control

The **content** property defines the clickable submenu item. This item can be any kind of control but text is used in most cases.

```
menubar = flet.MenuBar(
  controls= [
     flet.SubmenuButton(
       content=flet.Text('File', color="white"),
       controls= [
           flet.MenuItemButton(content=flet.Text("New File" , color="black")),
           flet.MenuItemButton(content=flet.Text("Save As", color="black")),
               ],
           ),
    )
```

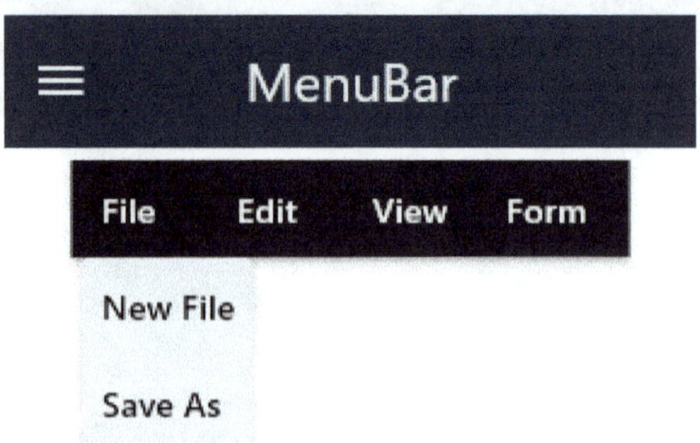

 |

leading = Control
This is the left control, next to the content purposely for giving more description to the item.

```
flet.MenuItemButton(
    content=flet.Text("New File" , color="black"),
    leading=flet.Icon(name=flet.icons.CREATE_NEW_FOLDER_OUTLINED,color="blue")
    ),

flet.MenuItemButton(
    content=flet.Text("Save As" , color="black"),
    leading=flet.Icon(name= flet.icons.SAVE_AS_OUTLINED, color="blue")
    ),
```

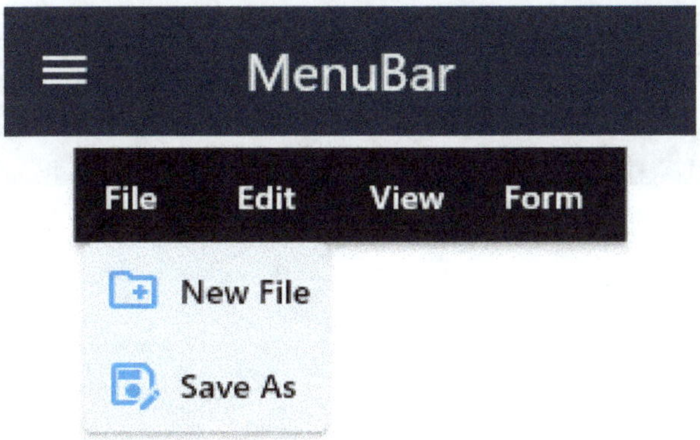

trailing = Control
The **trailing** property sets a control at the right side of the item.

```
flet.MenuItemButton(
    content=flet.Text("New File" , color="black"),
    trailing= flet.Text("Ctrl+N")
  ),
flet.MenuItemButton(
    content=flet.Text("Save As" , color="black"),
    trailing= flet.Text("Ctrl+S")
  ),
```

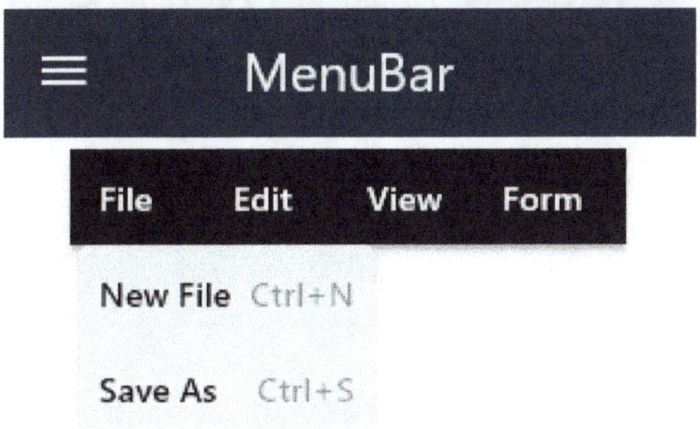

style = ButtonStyle
The **style** property allows you to use the ButtonStyle control to style or decorate the item. The available options include:

color	shadow_color	surface_tint_color	elevation
bgcolor	animation_duration	padding	side
overlay_color	shape		

color = string
The **color** defines the text color of the submenu items.

```
flet.MenuItemButton(
      content=flet.Text("New File"),
      style= flet.ButtonStyle(color="Blue")
),
```

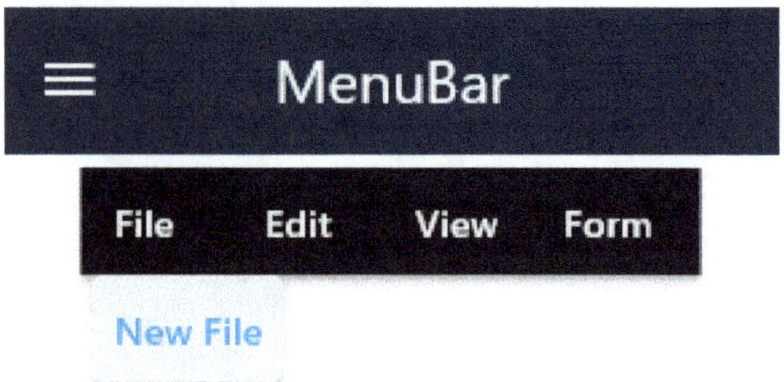

bgcolor = string
This defines the background color of the submenu item.

```
flet.MenuItemButton(
      style= flet.ButtonStyle(bgcolor= "teal"),
      content=flet.Text("Undo",color="white"),
),
```

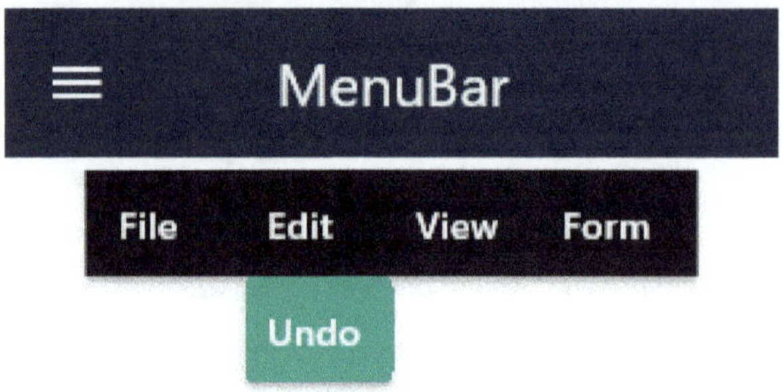

on_click = function
This property fires an event or execute a callback function when the submenu item is clicked.

```
def newFile(e):
    print('new File')

def saveAs(e):
    print('save As')


item1 = flet.MenuItemButton(
        content=flet.Text("New File"),
        on_click = newFile
        )

Item2 = flet.MenuItemButton(
        content=flet.Text("Save As"),
        on_click = saveAs
        )
```

on_focus = function
A function to be executed, when the submenu item gains focus.

on_blur = function
An event to fire when submenu item loses focus.

on_hover = function
This defines a function to be executed whenever the mouse passes over the item.

```
flet.MenuItemButton(
     content = flet.Text("New File"),
     on_hover = lambda _: print('Hovered'),
     on_blur = lambda _: print('lost Focus'),
     on_focus = lambda _: print('gained Focus'),
),
```


Python **Code 3.7.0**

```
import flet

def main(page: flet.Page):
    page.title = "My App"
    page.bgcolor = 'white'
    page.padding = flet.padding.only(top=5, left=5, right=5)

    page.appbar = flet.AppBar(
      color= flet.colors.WHITE,
      title= flet.Text("Word Counter"),
      bgcolor="#00334c",
      center_title= True
    )
    page.drawer = flet.NavigationDrawer()

    nav = flet.NavigationBar(
        destinations= [
          flet.NavigationDestination(
                label="Menu",
                icon=flet.icons.GRID_VIEW_ROUNDED
           ),
           flet.NavigationDestination(
               label="Gift",
               icon=flet.icons.WALLET_GIFTCARD_OUTLINED
            ),
            flet.NavigationDestination(
               label="Calendar",
               icon=flet.icons.CALENDAR_MONTH_OUTLINED
            ),
           flet.NavigationDestination(
               label="Exit",
               icon=flet.icons.CANCEL
           )
    ])

    page.navigation_bar = nav

    def counter(e):
        counterbox.value = len(textbox.value)
        page.update()

    def cleaner(e):
        textbox.value = ""
        counterbox.value = ""
        page.update()

    def capitalize(e):
        textbox.value = textbox.value.capitalize()
        page.update()

    def uppercase(e):
        textbox.value = textbox.value.upper()
        page.update()


    textbox = flet.TextField(multiline= True,height = 150, width= page.width )
    counterbox = flet.TextField(height = 50, width = 50  )

    countMenu = flet.MenuItemButton(content=flet.Text("Count", color="black"), on_click= counter )

    capitalizeSubMenu = flet.MenuItemButton(content=flet.Text("Capitalize"), on_click= capitalize)
    uppercaseSubMenu = flet.MenuItemButton(content=flet.Text("Uppercase"), on_click= uppercase )
    cleanSubMenu = flet.MenuItemButton(content=flet.Text("Clean"), on_click= cleaner )

    editMenu = flet.SubmenuButton(content=flet.Text("Edit", color="black"), controls=[capitalizeSubMenu, uppercaseSubMenu])
    formatMenu = flet.SubmenuButton(content=flet.Text("Format", color="black"), controls=[cleanSubMenu])
    windowMenu = flet.SubmenuButton(content=flet.Text("window", color="black"))

    menubar = flet.MenuBar(style= flet.MenuStyle(bgcolor="#1da1f2",shape=flet.RoundedRectangleBorder(radius=0), ),
                           controls=[countMenu,editMenu,formatMenu,windowMenu]
                           )

    col = flet.Column(
        width= page.width,
        alignment= flet.MainAxisAlignment.START,
        horizontal_alignment= flet.CrossAxisAlignment.CENTER,
        controls= [ menubar,flet.Container(height=20),textbox,counterbox,]
    )

    page.add(col)
    page.update()

flet.app(target = main)
```


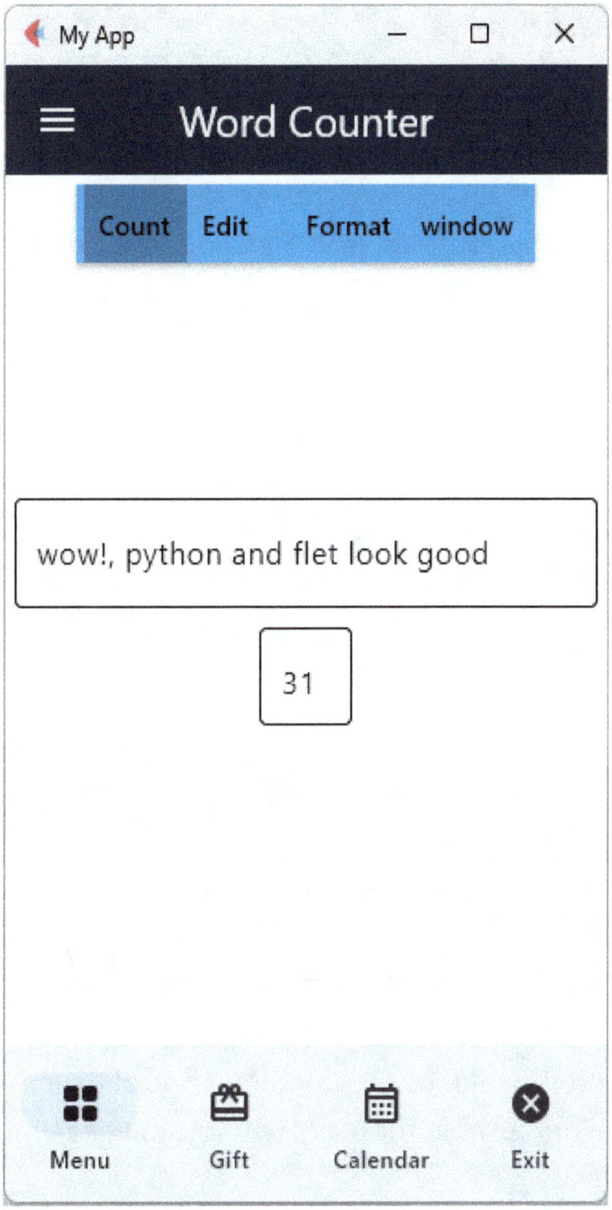
My App
Word Counter
Count
Edit
Format
window
wow!, python and flet look good
31
Menu
Gift
Calendar
Exit

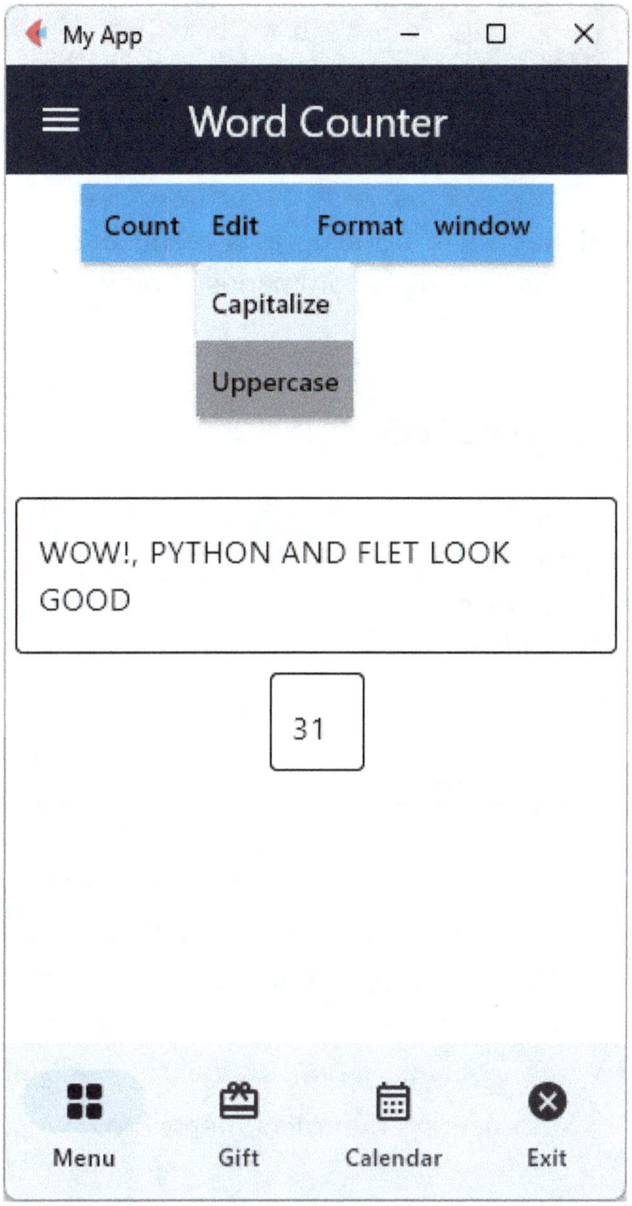
My App
Word Counter
Count
Edit
Format
window
Capitalize
Uppercase
WOW!, PYTHON AND FLET LOOK GOOD
31
Menu
Gift
Calendar
Exit

Page Summary

MenuBar control creates a menu bar with multiple options in a Flet app, providing access to various commands or actions.

Keywords

controls
clip_behavior
MenuStyle
expand

Discussion

1. How do you implement a MenuBar with custom menu items, icons, or shortcuts to match the app's design language and theme?
2. What are some strategies for managing state and content synchronization between different menu items in a MenuBar?
3. Can you discuss the accessibility considerations when using MenuBar controls, such as ensuring that menu items are navigable and usable for users with disabilities?

ProgressBar

The **ProgressBar** is a material design linear progress indicator. It visually represents the continuous execution of a process through a function connected by a control.

Determinate ProgressBar:
These progress indicators have a specific value at each point in time. The value should increase monotonically from **0.0** to **1.0** at which the indicator is complete.
Indeterminate ProgressBar:
These progress indicators do not have a specific value at each point in time. They indicate that, progress is being made without showing how much progress remains.

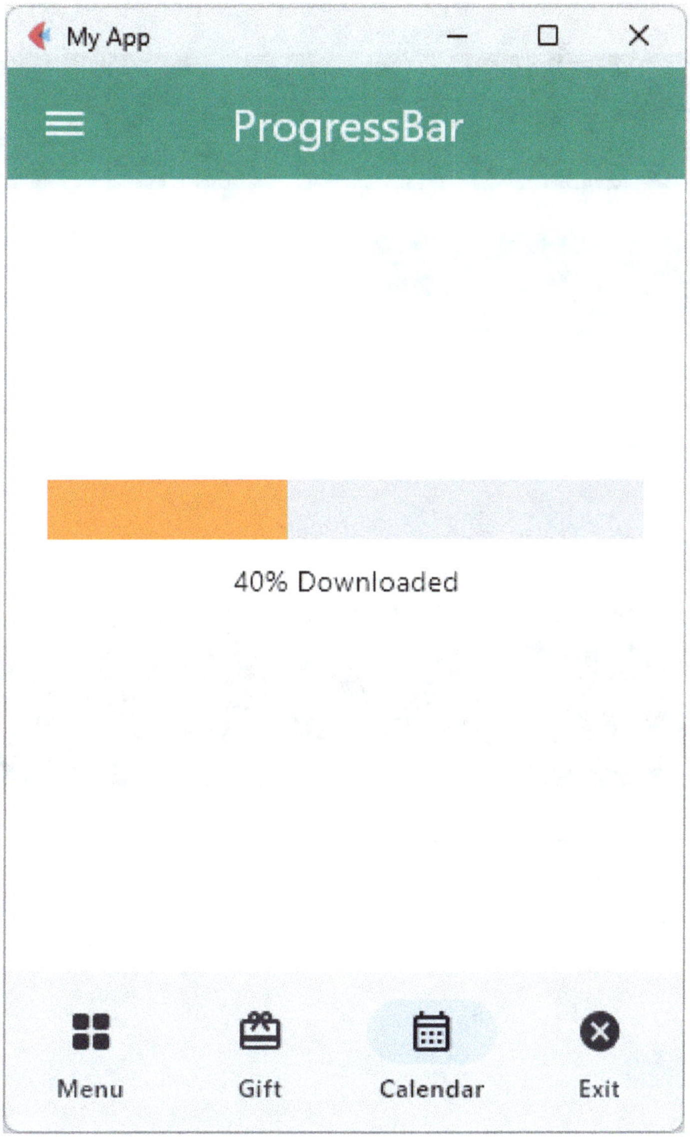

Available Methods

Property	Value	Property	Value
value	float	color	string
bar_height	float	bgcolor	string

value = float

This property sets the current progress value of the ProgressBar. For determinate progress, it should be a number between **0.0** and **1.0**. For indeterminate progress, the value should be null.

```
    progress = flet.ProgressBar(

        value= 0.6
    )
```

bar_height = float

The **bar_height** defines the overall height of the ProgressBar.

```
    progress = flet.ProgressBar(
        bar_height= 20,
        value= 0.6
    )
```

color = string

This property sets the color of the progress indicator.

```
progress = flet.ProgressBar(
    color= "orange",
    value= 0.6
)
```

bgcolor = string

The **bgcolor** property sets the background color of the ProgressBar.

```
progress = flet.ProgressBar(
    bgcolor= "Green",
    color= "Orange",
    value= 0.6
)
```

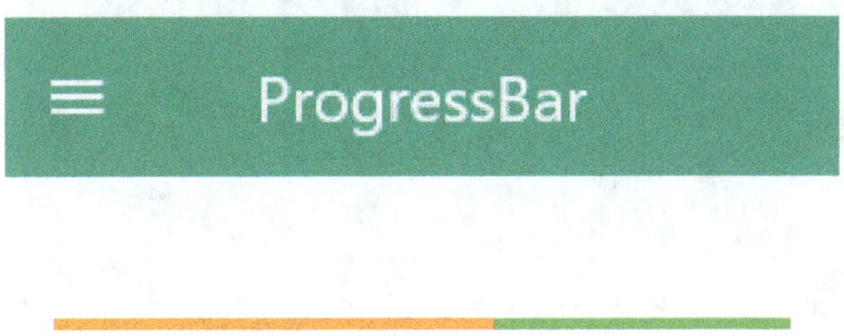

Python Code 3.8.0

```python
import flet
import time

def main(page: flet.Page):
    page.title = "My App"
    page.bgcolor = 'white'
    page.padding = flet.padding.only(top=50, left=20, right=20)

    page.appbar = flet.AppBar(
      color= flet.colors.WHITE,
      title= flet.Text("ProgressBar"),
      bgcolor="teal",
      center_title= True
    )
    page.drawer = flet.NavigationDrawer()

    nav = flet.NavigationBar(
        destinations= [
           flet.NavigationDestination(
                 label="Menu",
                 icon=flet.icons.GRID_VIEW_ROUNDED
            ),
            flet.NavigationDestination(
                label="Gift",
                icon=flet.icons.WALLET_GIFTCARD_OUTLINED
             ),
             flet.NavigationDestination(
                label="Calendar",
                icon=flet.icons.CALENDAR_MONTH_OUTLINED
             ),
            flet.NavigationDestination(
                label="Exit",
                icon=flet.icons.CANCEL
            )
    ])

    page.navigation_bar = nav

    def loader(e):
        i = 1
        while i <=10:
            progress.value = i/10
            readings.value = f"{i*10}% Downloaded"
            time.sleep(2)
            i = i+1
            page.update()


    progress = flet.ProgressBar(
        color= "Green",
        value = 0.0,
        height=10
    )

    readings = flet.Text(size=20)

    start = flet.OutlinedButton(text="Start", on_click = loader)

    col = flet.Column(
        width= page.width,
        alignment= flet.MainAxisAlignment.CENTER,
        horizontal_alignment= flet.CrossAxisAlignment.CENTER,

        controls=[progress, readings, flet.Container(height=20),start]
    )

    page.add(col)
    page.update()

flet.app(target = main)
```


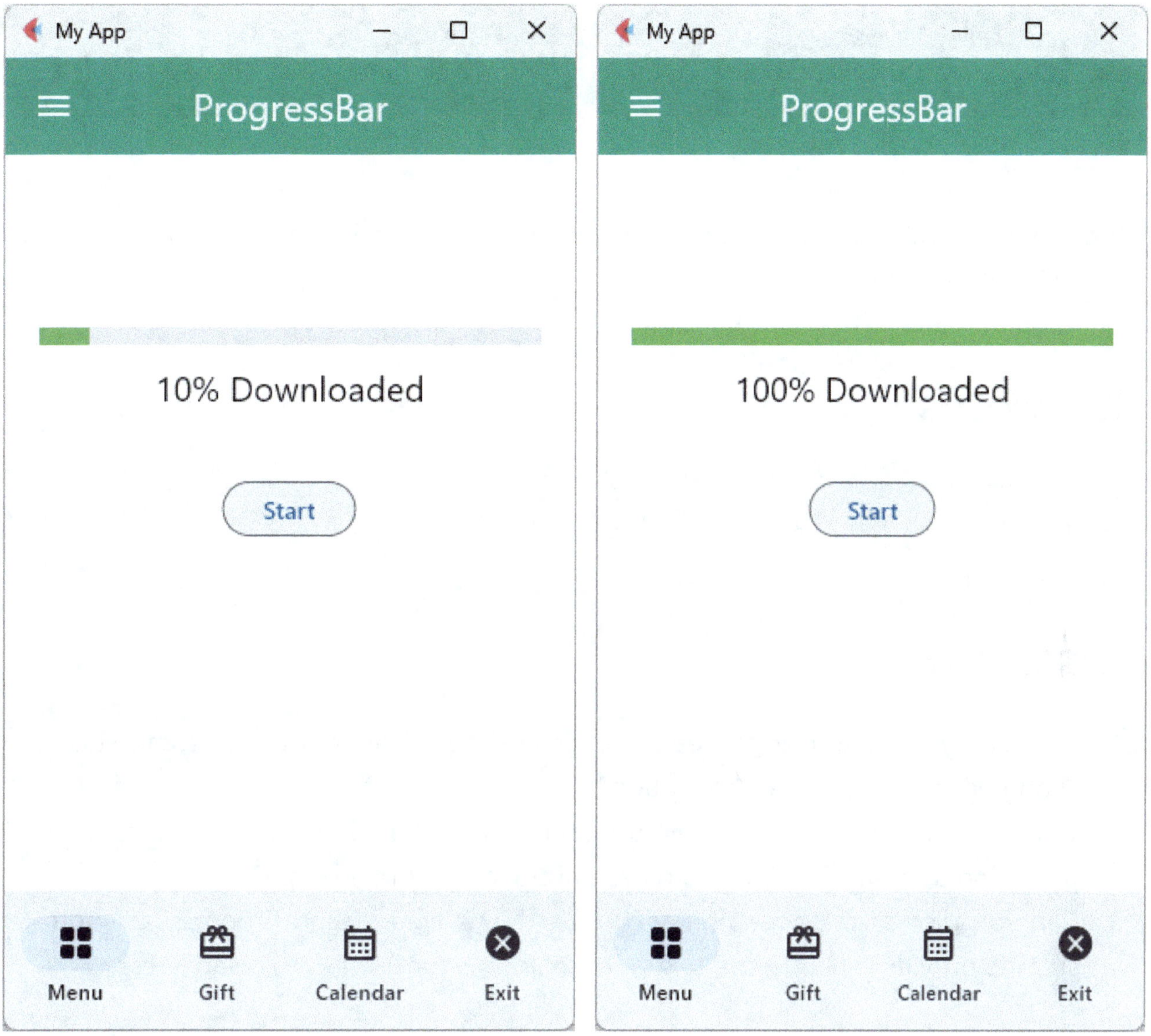
My App
ProgressBar
10% Downloaded
Start
Menu
Gift
Calendar
Exit
My App
ProgressBar
100% Downloaded
Start
Menu
Gift
Calendar
Exit

Page Summary

ProgressBar control displays the progress of a task or operation in a Flet app, providing visual feedback to users.

Keywords

bar_height
value

Discussion

1. How can you customize the appearance and behavior of a ProgressBar, such as changing its color, size, or animation?
2. What are some techniques for updating the progress value dynamically and providing accurate feedback to users during long-running tasks?
3. Can you discuss the accessibility considerations when using ProgressBar control, such as providing alternative text or descriptions for users with disabilities?

FilePicker

The **FilePicker** is a user interface component that allows users to select or save files from their local filesystem. It provides an intuitive way for users to upload files, open files, or select files for various operations within an application. The FilePicker can be used in web, desktop, and mobile applications.

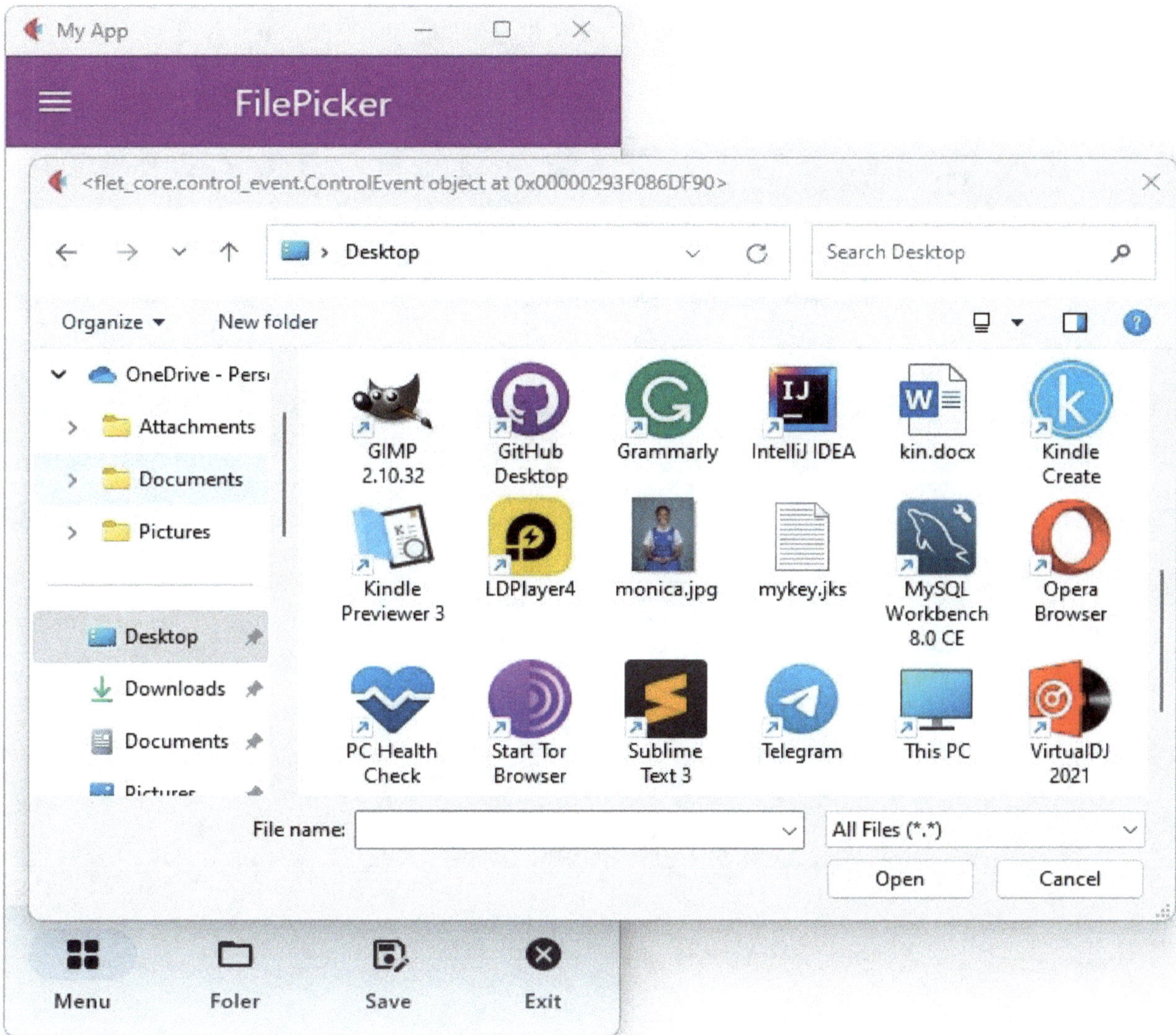

Desktop

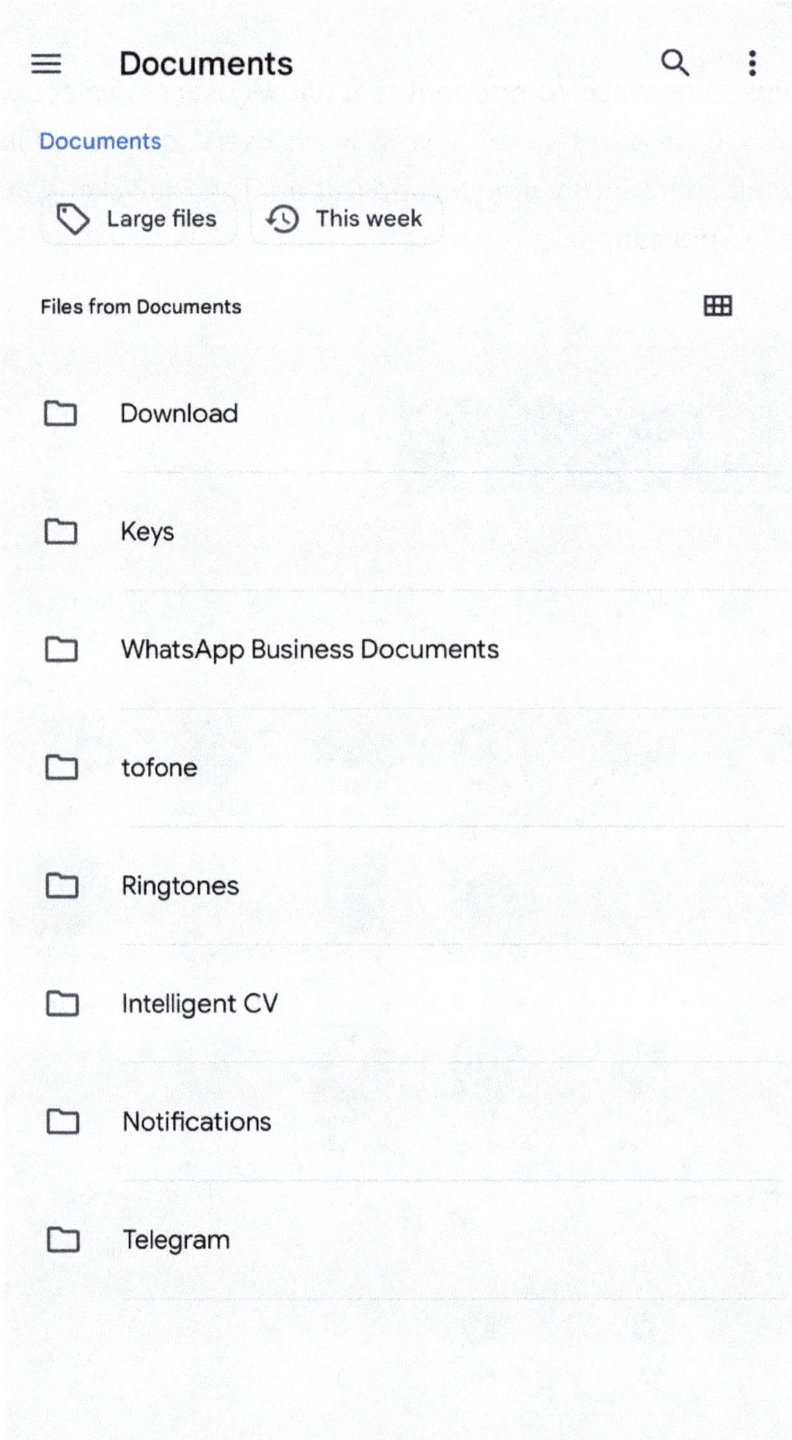
Documents
Documents
Large files
This week
Files from Documents
Download
Keys
WhatsApp Business Documents
tofone
Ringtones
Intelligent CV
Notifications
Telegram

Mobile

Available Methods

Property	Value	Property	Value
on_result	function	ref	Ref
on_upload	function	visible	bool

on_result = function
An event handler that is triggered when the file dialog is closed.

```
filepicker = flet.FilePicker(
    on_result= lambda _: print("File Dialog is closed")
)
```

on_upload = function
This fires when the file upload progress is updated.

```
filepicker = flet.FilePicker(
    on_upload= lambda _: print("File has been uploaded")
)
```

Available Functional Methods

Set Methods		Get Methods	
pick_files	upload	result	initial_directory
save_file	allow_extension	dialog_title	event_handlers
get_directory_path	allow_multiple	file_name	file_type

pick_files()

This property opens a file dialog to allow file selection and upload. It provides several methods for configuring the dialog.

dialog_title	file_type	allow_multiple
initial_directory	allowed_extention	

dialog_title: Sets the title of the file dialog window, giving context to the user about the purpose of the file selection.

initial_directory: Specifies the target directory to open the file.

file_type: Defines the type of files that are allowed for uploading, ensuring that only the specified file types can be selected. Available file types include:

ANY	AUDIO	IMAGE
CUSTOME	VIDEO	MEDIA

allowed_extension: Specifies the kind of file extensions required for the files to be uploaded, adding an extra layer of filtering based on file extension.

allow_multiple: Permits selecting more than one file if set to True. This is useful for bulk uploads or multi-file operations.

```
def openDialog(e):
    filepicker.pick_files(
     dialog_title="Choose Image",
     file_type= flet.FilePickerFileType.IMAGE,
     allowed_extensions= ["png", "jpg"],
     allow_multiple=True
    )

filepicker = flet.FilePicker(
    on_result = lambda _:print("File Dialog is Opened"),
    )

button = flet.OutlinedButton(
    text="upload",
    on_click = openDialog
    )
```


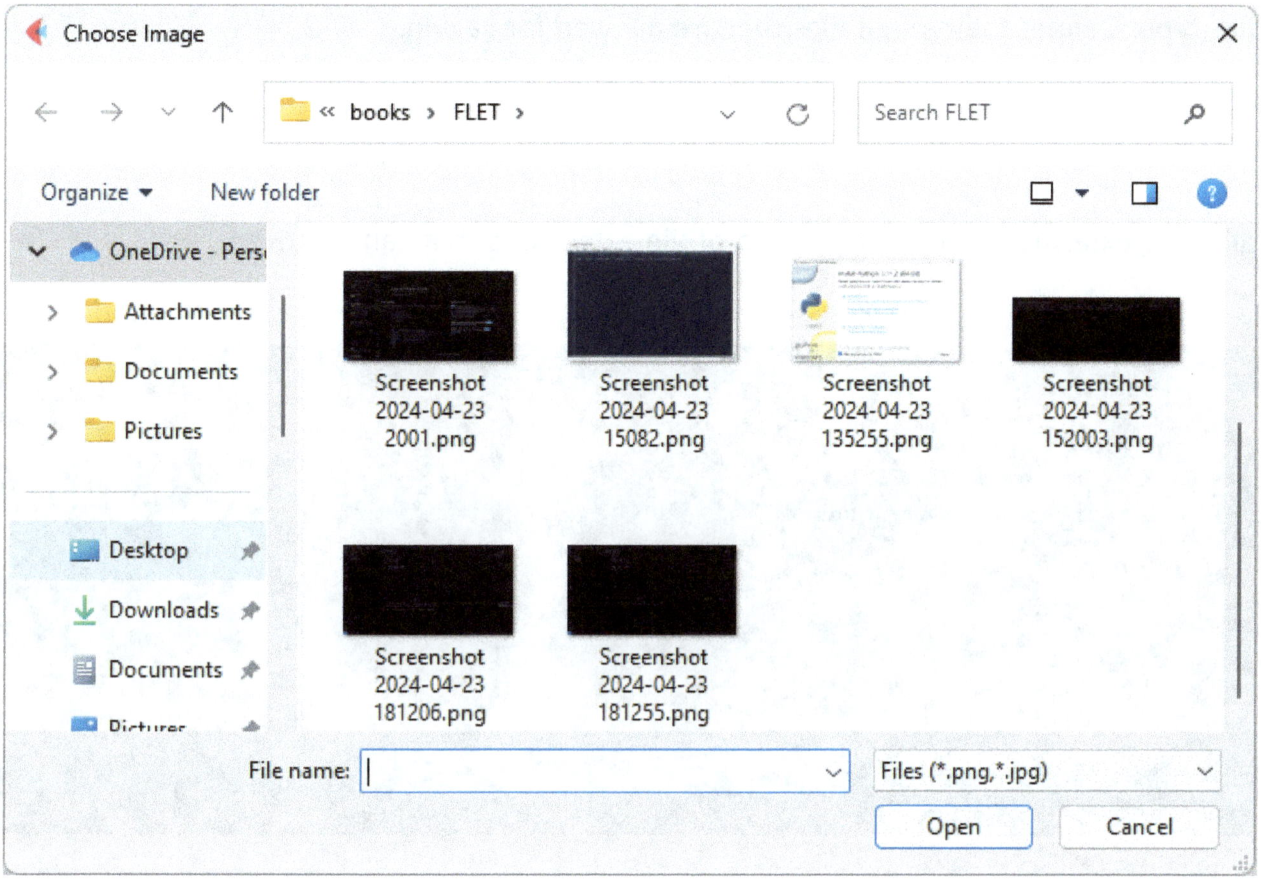

save_file()

This opens a file dialog to allow file saving. This method facilitates saving files from the application to the user's filesystem.

dialog_title	file_type	file_name
initial_directory	allowed_extention	

file_name: This property sets the name of the file to be saved.

dialog_title: Sets the title of the file dialog window, giving context to the user about the purpose of the file saving.

initial_directory: Specifies the target directory to open the file.

file_type: Defines the type of files that are allowed for saving.

ANY	AUDIO	IMAGE
CUSTOME	VIDEO	MEDIA

allowed_extension: Specifies the kind of file extensions that can be saved.

```
def saveDialog(e):
    filepicker.save_file(
     file_name= "myvideo.mp4",
     dialog_title="Save File",
     allowed_extensions=['mp4', 'mvi']
    )

filepicker = flet.FilePicker(
    on_result = lambda _:print("File Dialog is Saved"),
)

button = flet.OutlinedButton(
    text="save",
    on_click = saveDialog
)
```

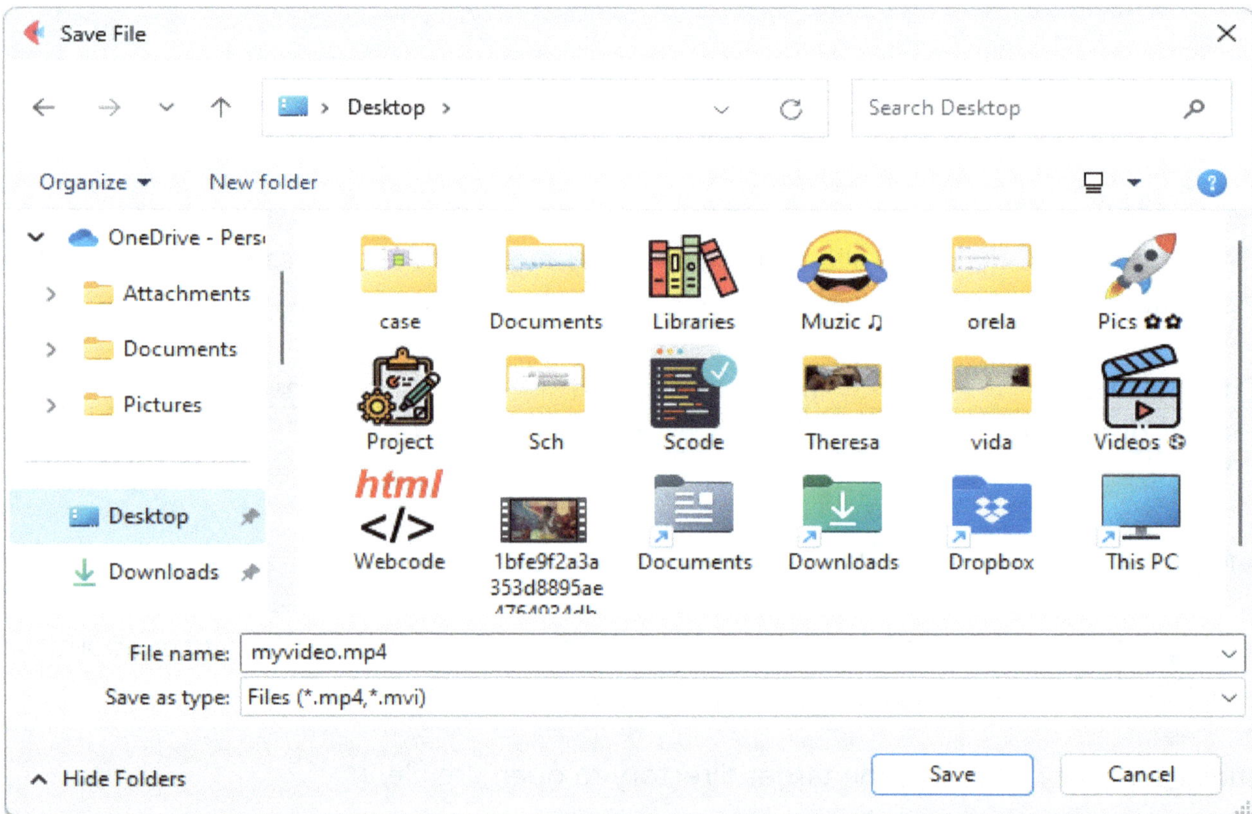

result

The **result** provides several methods to get the file metadata, such as files, name, size, path and type, which can be used for further processing within the application.

files
name
path
target
data
page
control

result.files	It returns a list of the selected files.
result.path	It returns the path of the selected file.
result.name	This returns the name of the selected file.
result.target	This returns the path of the specified initial folder.
result.control	This references the parent control.

Getting Names and Paths of Selected Files

```
def openFile(e):
    name_List = []              #Creating name list
    path_List = []              #Creating path list
    value = filepicker.result.files

    for i in value:
        name_List.append(i.name)  #Adding names to list
        path_List.append(i.path)  #Adding paths to list

    print(name_List)
    print(path_List)

filepicker = flet.FilePicker(on_result = openFile )

button = flet.OutlinedButton(      #Button to open filepicker
    text="upload",
    on_click = lambda _: filepicker.pick_files(allow_multiple=True)
 )
```


Python Code 3.9.0

```
import flet

def main(page: flet.Page):
    page.title = "My App"
    page.bgcolor = 'white'
    page.padding = flet.padding.only(top=10, left=20, right=20)

    page.appbar = flet.AppBar(
      color= flet.colors.WHITE,
      title= flet.Text("FilePicker"),
      bgcolor="Purple",
      center_title= True
    )
    page.drawer = flet.NavigationDrawer()

    nav = flet.NavigationBar(
        destinations= [
            flet.NavigationDestination(
                 label="Menu",
                 icon=flet.icons.GRID_VIEW_ROUNDED
            ),
            flet.NavigationDestination(
                label="Foler",
                icon=flet.icons.FOLDER_OPEN_OUTLINED
             ),
             flet.NavigationDestination(
                label="Save",
                icon=flet.icons.SAVE_AS_OUTLINED
             ),
            flet.NavigationDestination(
                label="Exit",
                icon=flet.icons.CANCEL
            )
    ])

    page.navigation_bar = nav

    def openFile(e):
        listNames = ""
        value = filepicker.result.files
        if filepicker.result != None and filepicker.result.files != None:
           for i in value:
               listNames = listNames +"\n"+i.name

           showPickFiles.value = listNames
           showPickFiles.visible = True

        else:
            showPickFiles.value = ""
            showPickFiles.visible = False

        page.update()

    filepicker = flet.FilePicker(on_result = openFile )

    button = flet.OutlinedButton( text="upload", on_click = lambda _: filepicker.pick_files(allow_multiple=True))

    showPickFiles = flet.TextField(multiline= True, visible= False, border_width=0,text_align=flet.TextAlign.CENTER)

    col = flet.Column(
        width= page.width,
        alignment= flet.MainAxisAlignment.START,
        horizontal_alignment= flet.CrossAxisAlignment.CENTER,
        controls=[
               flet.Text('Book Drive', size= 50 ,weight= flet.FontWeight.BOLD, font_family="Georgia"),
               flet.Image(src="C:\\image1.jpg", width=page.width, height=150, fit = flet.ImageFit.FILL),
               flet.Row(alignment= flet.MainAxisAlignment.CENTER, vertical_alignment= flet.CrossAxisAlignment.CENTER,
                        controls=[flet.Image(src="C:\\fileup.png", width=50, height=50, fit = flet.ImageFit.FILL),
                                  flet.Text('Upload a Book', size=30)]),
               button, showPickFiles, filepicker,
        ]
    )
    page.add(col)
    page.update()

flet.app(target = main)
```

My App
FilePicker
Book Drive
Upload a Book
upload
Menu
Foler
Save
Exit

My App
FilePicker
Book Drive
Upload a Book
upload
beeware.pdf
briefcase.pdf
Menu
Foler
Save
Exit

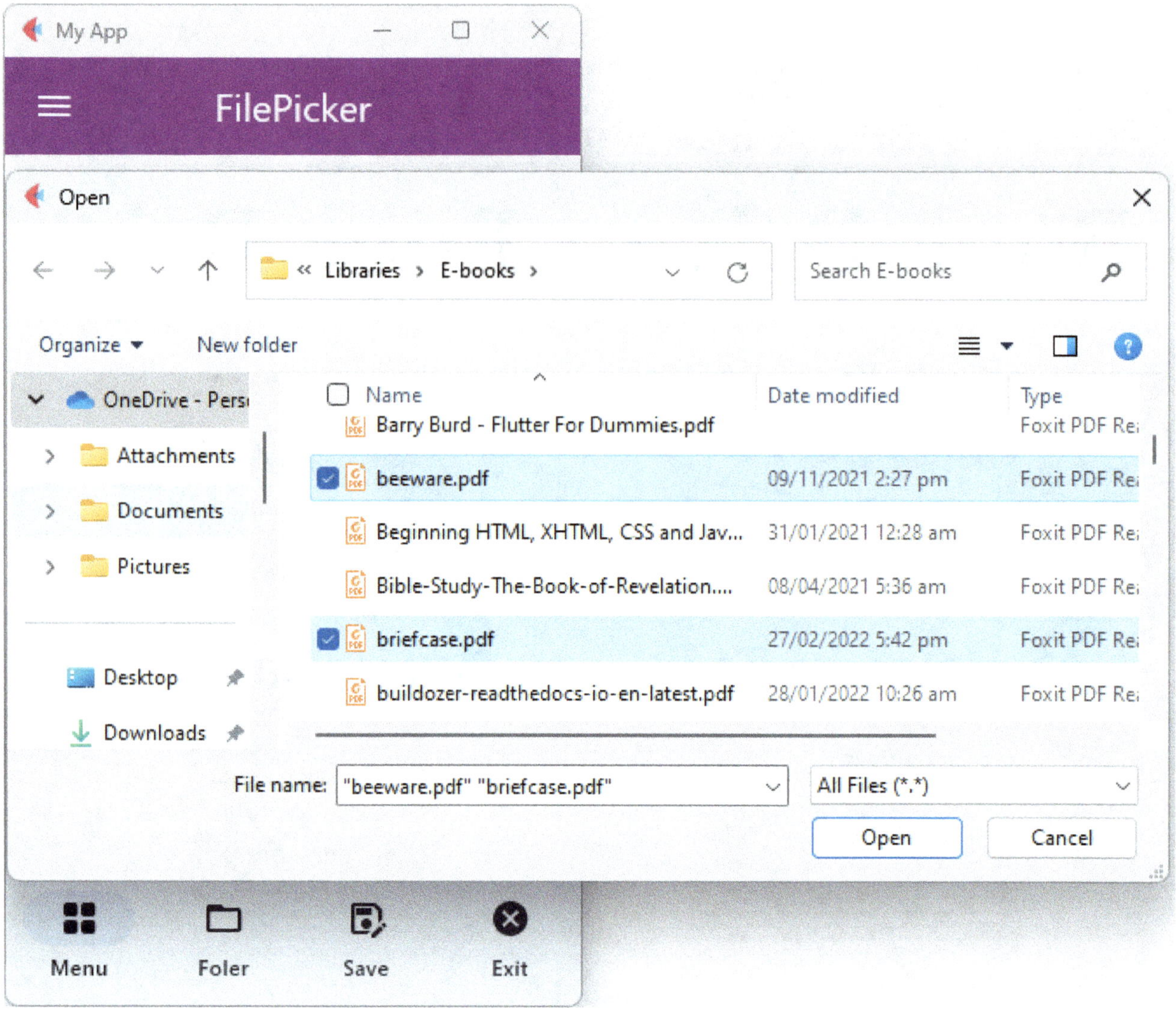
My App
FilePicker
Open
Libraries › E-books ›
Search E-books
Organize
New folder
OneDrive - Pers
Attachments
Documents
Pictures
Desktop
Downloads
Name
Date modified
Type
Barry Burd - Flutter For Dummies.pdf
Foxit PDF Re
beeware.pdf
09/11/2021 2:27 pm
Foxit PDF Re
Beginning HTML, XHTML, CSS and Jav...
31/01/2021 12:28 am
Foxit PDF Re
Bible-Study-The-Book-of-Revelation....
08/04/2021 5:36 am
Foxit PDF Re
briefcase.pdf
27/02/2022 5:42 pm
Foxit PDF Re
buildozer-readthedocs-io-en-latest.pdf
28/01/2022 10:26 am
Foxit PDF Re
File name:
"beeware.pdf" "briefcase.pdf"
All Files (*.*)
Open
Cancel
Menu
Foler
Save
Exit

Page Summary

FilePicker control allows users to select files from the device's file system in a Flet app, with options for filtering and validation.

Keywords

upload
result
save_file
pick_files
on_result
on_upload

Discussion

1. How do you implement a FilePicker with custom file filters, such as limiting the selection to specific file types or sizes?
2. What are some strategies for handling user interactions with a FilePicker, such as reacting to file selection changes or errors?
3. Can you discuss the security implications of using FilePicker control, such as protecting against malicious file uploads or downloads?

Audio

The **Audio** is a control that allows you to play multiple audio files simultaneously. It is non-visual control and should be added to the **page.overlay** list.

Lighten

PACKAGING

To build your Flet app that uses the Audio control, add **- - include-packages** flet_audio to the flet build command. For example:

flet build apk - -include-packages flet_audio

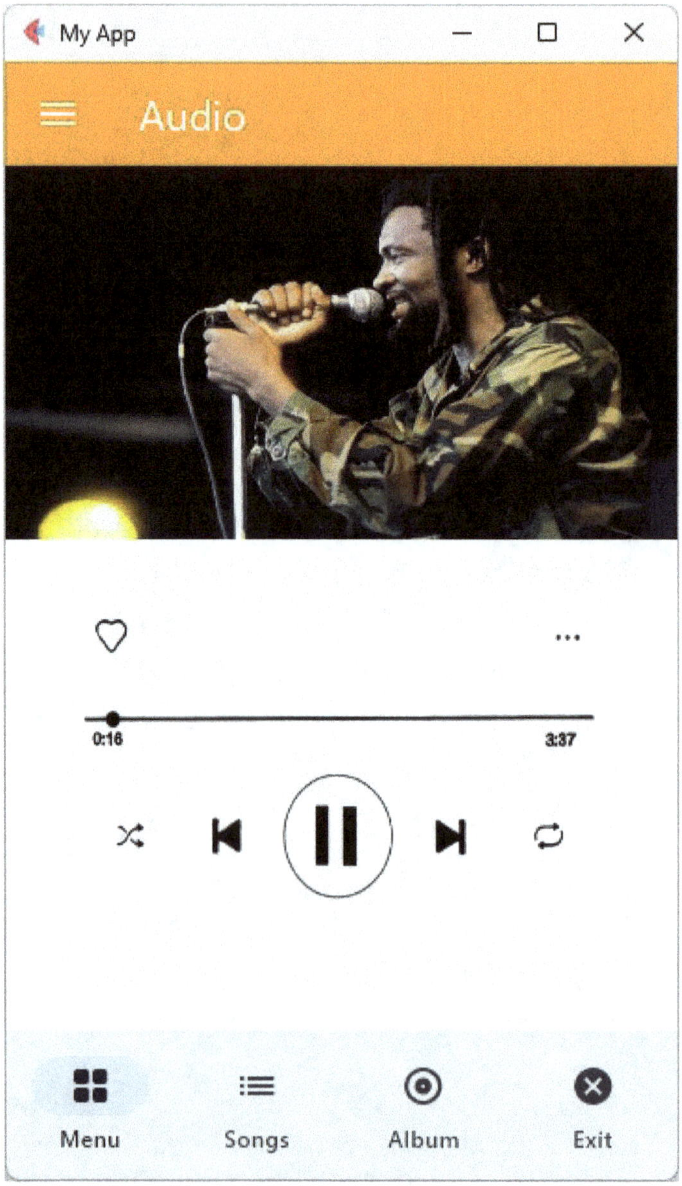

Available Methods

Property	Value	Property	Value
src	str	release_mode	ReleaseMode
src_base64	str	on_loaded	function
autoplay	bool	on_duration_changed	function
volume	float	on_state_changed	function
balance	float	on_position_changed	function
playback_rate	float	on_seek_complete	function

src = string
This defines the source of the audio file.

```
    audio = flet.Audio(
            src="C:\\Muzic ♬\\regae ♬\\Bob Marley - Redemption Song.mp3",
    )
```

autoplay = bool
When this property is set to True, audio is played automatically when it is loaded or when the application is opened.

```
    audio = flet.Audio(
            autoplay= True,
    )
```

volume = float
This sets the intensity of the sound.

```
    audio = flet.Audio(
            src="C:\\Muzic ♬\\regae ♬\\Bob Marley - Redemption Song.mp3",
            volume = 25,
    )
```


balance = float
The balance property sets the stereo balance.
-1: The left channel is a full volume; the right channel is silent.
1: The right channel is at full volume; the left channel is silent.
0: Both channels are at the same volume.

> **# Note**
>
> Setting balance is supported on Windows and Linux only.

playback_rate = float
This sets the speed rate at which the audio plays back.

```
audio = flet.Audio(
        playback_rate= 10,
)
```

release_mode = flet.audio.ReleaseMode
This property determines what the control should do after playing the audio. There are three options:

- **release**: Releases all the resources used by the control.
- **stop**: Stops the audio immediately after playing but keep all resources intact for replay.
- **loop**: Plays the audio again repeatedly.

```
audio = flet.Audio(
        release_mode= flet.audio.ReleaseMode.LOOP
)
```

on_loaded: Fires when the audio is loaded by the control.

on_duration_changed: Fires when the duration of the audio changes.

on_state_change: Fires when the state of the audio changes. The available states are

- **stopped**
- **playing**
- **paused**
- **completed**
- **disposed.**

on_position_changed: Fires when the audio cursor position changes.

on_seek_complete: Fires when the user seeks to a new position, either forward or backward.

```
audio = flet.Audio(
        on_loaded= lambda _:print("Music is loaded"),
        on_duration_changed= lambda _:print("Music Duration has Changed"),
        on_state_changed= lambda _:print('State has changed'),
        on_position_changed= lambda _:print('Positioned has changed'),
        on_seek_complete = lambda _:print('New position seeked')
)
```

Available Functional Methods

get_current_position	pause	resume
get_duration	play	seek
release		

get_current_position()

Retrieves the current position for the audio control in milliseconds.

```
audio = flet.Audio(
        src="C:\\Muzic ♬\\regae ♬\\Bob Marley - Redemption Son.mp3",
        on_position_changed= lambda _:print(audio.get_current_position())
)
```


get_duration()

Returns the total duration of the audio in milliseconds.

```
audio = flet.Audio(
        src="C:\\Muzic ♬\\regae ♬\\Bob Marley - Redemption.mp3",
        on_loaded= lambda _:print(audio.get_duration())
)
```

pause()

Suspends playing the audio.

```
def isPause(e):
    audio.pause()

audio = flet.Audio(
        src="C:\\Muzic ♬\\regae ♬\\Bob Marley - Redemption Song.mp3",
  )
pause = flet.IconButton(icon= flet.icons.PAUSE, on_click= isPause)
```

play()

This plays the audio from the beginning.

```
audio = flet.Audio( src="C:\\Muzic ♬\\cool ♬\\celien.mp3",)

play = flet.IconButton(icon= flet.icons.PAUSE, on_click= lambda _:audio.play())
```

resume()

This resumes the audio from the current position after it has been paused.

```
audio = flet.Audio(src="C:Muzic ♬\\cool ♬\\celine.mp3",)

resume = flet.IconButton(icon= flet.icons.PAUSE, on_click= lambda _:audio.resume())
```

seek(position_milliseconds: int)

Moves the cursor to a new position in the audio.

```
audio = flet.Audio(src="C:\\Muzic ♬\\cool ♬\\celine.mp3",)

seek = flet.IconButton(icon= flet.icons.FORWARD, on_click= lambda _:audio.seek(10))
```


Python *Code 4.0.0*

```python
import flet

def main(page: flet.Page):
    page.title = "My App"
    page.bgcolor = 'white'
    page.padding = flet.padding.all(0)

    page.appbar = flet.AppBar(
      color= flet.colors.WHITE,
      title= flet.Text("Music Player"),
      bgcolor= "#00334c"
    )
    page.drawer = flet.NavigationDrawer()

    nav = flet.NavigationBar(
        destinations= [
            flet.NavigationDestination(
                 label="Menu",
                 icon=flet.icons.GRID_VIEW_ROUNDED
            ),
            flet.NavigationDestination(
                label="Songs",
                icon=flet.icons.LIST
             ),
             flet.NavigationDestination(
                label="Album",
                icon=flet.icons.ALBUM_OUTLINED
             ),
            flet.NavigationDestination(
                label="Exit",
                icon=flet.icons.CANCEL
            )
    ])

    page.navigation_bar = nav

    def onLoaded(e):
        duration.value = round((audio.get_duration()/60000), 2)
        remaining.value = 0
        play_pause.content = play
        page.update()

    def onPosition(e):
        audio_duration = audio.get_duration()/60000 #in minute
        audio_position = audio.get_current_position()/60000  #in minute
        remaining.value = round(audio_position, 2)
        reading_scale.value = round(audio_position/audio_duration,2)
        page.update()

    def onPlay(e):
        audio.play()
        play_pause.content = pause
        page.update()

    def onPause(e):
        audio.pause()
        play_pause.content = resume
        page.update()

    def onResume(e):
        audio.resume()
        play_pause.content = pause
        page.update()

    def onPlayback(e):
        audio.release_mode = flet.audio.ReleaseMode.LOOP
        playback_stop.content = stop
        page.update()

    def onStop(e):
        audio.release_mode = flet.audio.ReleaseMode.STOP
        playback_stop.content = playback
        page.update()

    def onSeekForward(e):
        posit = int(audio.get_current_position()) +6000
        audio.seek(position_milliseconds=posit)

    def onSeekBackward(e):
        posit = int(audio.get_current_position()) -6000
        audio.seek(position_milliseconds=posit)

    audio = flet.Audio(
            src="C:\\Users\\Asiedu\\Desktop\\Muzic ♬\\regae ♬\\Bob Marley - Redemption Song (from the legend album, with).mp3",
            on_loaded= onLoaded,
            on_position_changed= onPosition,
    )



    remaining = flet.Text()
    duration = flet.Text()
    reading_scale = flet.ProgressBar(color="#00334c", value=0, expand=True)

    reading = flet.Container(padding=10,
        content=flet.Row(alignment= flet.CrossAxisAlignment.CENTER,vertical_alignment= flet.MainAxisAlignment.CENTER,
        controls=[remaining, reading_scale, duration])
    )

    play_pause = flet.Container()
    play = flet.IconButton(icon= flet.icons.PLAY_CIRCLE,icon_size=25, on_click= onPlay)
    pause = flet.IconButton(icon= flet.icons.PAUSE_CIRCLE,icon_size=25, on_click= onPause)
    resume = flet.IconButton(icon= flet.icons.PLAY_CIRCLE,icon_size=25, on_click= onResume)

    seek_forward = flet.IconButton(icon= flet.icons.ARROW_CIRCLE_RIGHT_OUTLINED , icon_size=25, on_click= onSeekForward)
    seek_backward = flet.IconButton(icon= flet.icons.ARROW_CIRCLE_LEFT_OUTLINED,icon_size=25, on_click= onSeekBackward)

    playback = flet.IconButton(icon= flet.icons.REPEAT_OUTLINED, bgcolor="orange", on_click = onPlayback)
    stop = flet.IconButton(icon= flet.icons.REPEAT_OUTLINED, on_click= onStop)
    playback_stop = flet.Container(content=stop)

    button_controls = flet.Container(padding=10,
        content=flet.Row(alignment= flet.MainAxisAlignment.CENTER,vertical_alignment= flet.CrossAxisAlignment.CENTER,
        controls=[seek_backward, play_pause,seek_forward, playback_stop])
    )

    col = flet.Column(
        width= page.width,
        height= page.height,
        alignment= flet.MainAxisAlignment.START,
        horizontal_alignment= flet.CrossAxisAlignment.CENTER,
        controls=[
                flet.Image(src="C:\\Users\\Asiedu\\Desktop\\orela\\music_label.jpg", width=page.width, height=250, fit = flet.ImageFit.FILL),
                reading,button_controls,audio
            ]
    )
    page.add(col)
    page.update()

flet.app(target = main)
```

My App
Music Player
1.08
3.82
Menu
Songs
Album
Exit

Page Summary

Audio control plays audio files or streams in a Flet app, with options for playback control and customization.

Keywords

autoplay
volume
balance
playback_rate
release_mode

Discussion

1. How can you customize the appearance and behavior of an Audio control, such as adding playback controls, visualizations, or equalizers?
2. What are some techniques for handling user interactions with an Audio control, such as reacting to playback events or errors?
3. Can you discuss the performance implications of using Audio controls, especially when streaming or playing large audio files?

Video

The Video control is a UI component that allows users to play video files within a Flet application.

Note

PREREQUISTES

On Linux, the limpy package must be installed. On Ubuntu/Debian you can install it with **sudo apt install libmpv-dev mpv**

PACKAGING

To build your Flet app that uses Video control, add --include-package flet_video to flet build command, for example:

flet build apk --include-packages flet_video

Available Methods

Property	Value	Property	Value
playlist	List[VideoMedia]	playlist_mode	PlaylistMode
title	string	shuffle_playlist	bool
autoplay	bool	height	float
volume	float	alignment	Alignment
fit	ImageFit	filter_quality	FilterQuality
playback_rate	float	aspect_ratio	float
fill_color	string	subtitle_configuaration	VideoSubtitleConfiguration
wakelock	bool	on_loaded	function
pitch	float	on_error	function
show_controls	bool	on_enter_fullscreen	function
muted	bool	on_exit_fullscreen	function

title = string

This sets the title of the video. It is visible inside the window's volume mixer.

```
video = flet.Video(

  title="my video",
)
```


playlist = List[*VideoMedia]

The **playlist** property defines the list of VideoMedia objects containing the sources of video files.

```
video = flet.Video(
  playlist= [
      flet.VideoMedia(resource = "C:\\myvideo1.mp4"),
      flet.VideoMedia(resource = "C:\\myvideo2.mp4"),
  ],
)
```

autoplay = bool

It automatically plays the video when set to True.

```
video = flet.Video(
  autoplay= True,
)
```

volume = float

This sets the intensity of the video sound.

```
video = flet.Video(
  volume= 23,
)
```

fit = ImageFit

The **fit** property determines how the video fits within the viewport. The available options include: CONTAIN, COVER, FILL, FIT_HEIGHT, FIT_WIDTH, NONE and SCALE_DOWN.

```
video = flet.Video(
  fit= flet.ImageFit.FILL
)
```

playback_rate = float

Determines the rate at which a video should start playing again after finishing. The default value is 1.0

```
video = flet.Video(
  playback_rate= 2.0
)
```


fill_color = string
This defines the background color or color of the video frame.

```
video = flet.Video(
  playlist= [
      flet.VideoMedia(resource = "C:\\myvideo1.mp4"),
  ],

  fill_color= "teal",
  height= 200,
  width= page.width
)
```

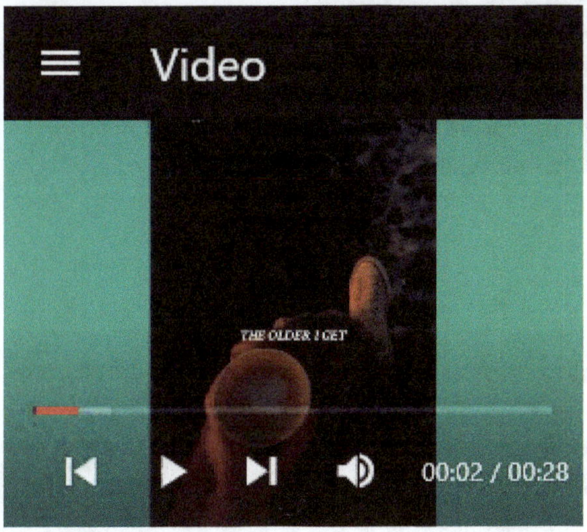

pitch = float
The **pitch** sets the pitch of the audio track in the video. It has default value of 1.0

```
video = flet.Video(
    pitch= 1.3
)
```

muted = bool
This property plays the video without sound when set to True. It is False by default.

```
video = flet.Video(
    muted= True
)
```


show_control = bool

This property shows the video controls (such as play, pause, etc.) when set to True. It is True by default.

```
    video = flet.Video(
      show_controls= True,

      playlist= [flet.VideoMedia(resource = "C:\\myvideo1.mp4"),]
      height= 200,
      width= page.width
    )
```

playlist_mode = PlaylistMode

Determines the mode in which videos should play. Available options are LOOP, NONE and SINGLE.

```
    video = flet.Video(
      playlist_mode= flet.PlaylistMode.LOOP
    )
```

shuffle_playlist = bool

Plays videos randomly from the playlist when set to True. It is False by default.

```
    video = flet.Video(
      shuffle_playlist= True
    )
```

alignment = Alignment

Determine the alignment of the video viewport. The available options include center, center_left, center_right, top_center, top_left, top_right, bottom_center, bottom_left and bottom_right.

```
    video = flet.Video(
      alignment= flet.alignment.bottom_left,
    )
```


aspect_ratio = float

This sets the aspect ratio of the video player.

```
video = flet.Video(
  aspect_ratio= 3.5,
)
```

filter_quality = FilterQuality

This property sets the quality of the video filter. The available methods are HIGH, LOW, MEDIUM and NONE.

```
video = flet.Video(
  filter_quality= flet.FilterQuality.HIGH,
)
```

subtitle_configuration = VideoSubtitleConfiguration

This property defines the subtitle configuration for the video player. The value is of type **VideoSubtitleConfiguration** which has the following properties:

src: The source of the subtitles (URL or local asset file).
title: The title of the subtitles.
language: The language of the subtitles.
text_style: The style of the subtitle text.
text_scale_factor: The scale factor of the subtitles.
text_align: The alignment of the subtitles.
padding: The padding around the subtitles.
visible: Whether or not the subtitles should be visible.

```
video = flet.Video(

  subtitle_configuration= flet.VideoSubtitleConfiguration(
      src= "https://www.lightmovies.com/tomjerry/subtitle",
      title= "Tom and Jerry subtitle",
      language= "English",
      text_scale_factor= 2,
      text_align= flet.TextAlign.CENTER,
      padding= flet.padding.all(20),
      visible= True
  ))
```


wakelock = bool

This determines whether to acquire wake lock while playing the video. The device's display will not go to standby or sleep whiles playing the video when wakelock is set to True.

```
video = flet.Video(
      wakelock= True,
    )
```

on_loaded = function

Fires when the video is loaded.

on_enter_fullscreen= function

Fires when the video enters fullscreen mode.

on_exit_fullscreen = function

Fires when the video exits fullscreen mode.

on_error = function

Fires when an error occurs during video playback.

```
    video = flet.Video(

      on_loaded= lambda _:print("video has started playing"),
      on_enter_fullscreen= lambda _:print("video switched to fullscreen"),
      on_exit_fullscreen= lambda _:print("video has exited from fullscreen"),
      on_error=lambda _:print("Error has occur")
    )
```

pause_upon_entering_background_mode = bool

This pauses the video when the application enters the background mode.

```
video = flet.Video(
      pause_upon_entering_background_mode= True,
    )
```

resume_upon_entering_foreground_mode = bool

This resumes the video when the application enters the foreground mode.

```
video = flet.Video(
      resume_upon_entering_foreground_mode= True,
    )
```


Available Functional Methods

next	get_duration	previous
play	playlist_add	seek
play_or_pause	playlist_remove	stop
pause	is_completed	jump_to
get_current_position	is_playing	playlist

play()
This plays the video.

```
video = flet.Video(
  playlist= [
            flet.VideoMedia(resource = "C:\\video1.mp4"),
            flet.VideoMedia(resource = "C:\\video2.mp4"),
             ],
  height= 300,
  fit= flet.ImageFit.FILL
  )

playButton = flet.TextButton(text="next", on_click= lambda _: video.play())
```

next()
This is used to play the next video in the VideoMedia of the playlist.

```
video = flet.Video(
  playlist= [
            flet.VideoMedia(resource = "C:\\video1.mp4"),
            flet.VideoMedia(resource = "C:\\video2.mp4"),
             ],
  height= 300,
  fit= flet.ImageFit.FILL
  )

nextButton = flet.TextButton(text="next", on_click= lambda _: video.next())
```


previous()

This method plays the previous video in the VideoMedia of the playlist.

```
playlist =  [
          flet.VideoMedia(resource = "C:\\video1.mp4"),
          flet.VideoMedia(resource = "C:\\video2.mp4"),
      ],
video = flet.Video(
      playlist= playlist,
      height= 300,
    )
previous = flet.TextButton(text="next", on_click= lambda _:video.previous())
```

play_or_pause()

This plays the video if paused or pauses the video if it is playing.

```
playlist =  [
          flet.VideoMedia(resource = "C:\\video1.mp4"),
          flet.VideoMedia(resource = "C:\\video2.mp4"),
      ],
video = flet.Video(
      playlist= playlist,
      height= 300,
    )
playPause = flet.TextButton(text="next", on_click= lambda _:video.play_or_pause())
```

is_playing()

This property returns True if the video player is currently playing, False otherwise.

```
    def videoStat(e):
        value =  video.is_playing()
        print(value)

    playlist =  [
          flet.VideoMedia(resource = "C:\\video1.mp4"),
          flet.VideoMedia(resource = "C:\\video2.mp4"),
      ],
    video = flet.Video(
      playlist= playlist,
      height= 300,
    )
```


is_completed()
This method returns True if the video player has reached the end of the currently playing VideoMedia in the playlist, False otherwise.

```
def videoStat(e):
    value =  video.is_completed()
    print(value)

playlist =  [
      flet.VideoMedia(resource = "C:\\video1.mp4"),
      flet.VideoMedia(resource = "C:\\video2.mp4"),
  ],
video = flet.Video(playlist= playlist, height= 300,)
```

playlist_add(VideoMedia)
The **playlist_add()** appends VideoMedia to the playlist.

```
def videoStat(e):
    video.playlist_add(video3)

playlist =  [
      flet.VideoMedia(resource = "C:\\video1.mp4"),
      flet.VideoMedia(resource = "C:\\video2.mp4"),
  ],

video3 = flet.VideoMedia(resource = "C:\\video3.mp4"),

video = flet.Video(playlist= playlist, height= 300,)
```

playlist_remove(index)
This removes the VideoMedia at the specified index from the playlist.

```
def videoStat(e):
    video.playlist_remove(1)

playlist =  [
      flet.VideoMedia(resource = "C:\\video1.mp4"),
      flet.VideoMedia(resource = "C:\\video2.mp4"),
  ],

video = flet.Video(playlist= playlist, height= 300,)
```


Python **Case 4.1.0**

```
import flet

def main(page: flet.Page):
    page.title = "My App"
    page.bgcolor = 'white'
    page.padding = flet.padding.all(0)

    page.appbar = flet.AppBar(
      color= flet.colors.WHITE,
      title= flet.Text("Video Player"),
      bgcolor= "#00334c"
    )
    page.drawer = flet.NavigationDrawer()

    nav = flet.NavigationBar(
        destinations= [
            flet.NavigationDestination(
                 label="Menu",
                 icon=flet.icons.GRID_VIEW_ROUNDED
            ),
            flet.NavigationDestination(
                label="Videos",
                icon=flet.icons.LIST
             ),
             flet.NavigationDestination(
                label="Playlist",
                icon=flet.icons.PLAYLIST_PLAY_OUTLINED
             ),
            flet.NavigationDestination(
                label="Exit",
                icon=flet.icons.CANCEL
            )
    ])

    page.navigation_bar = nav

    def playBack(e):
        video.playlist_mode = flet.PlaylistMode.LOOP
        page.update()

    def autoPlay(e):
        video.autoplay = True
        page.update()

    playlist =  [
          flet.VideoMedia(resource = "C:\\Users\\Asiedu\\video1.mp4"),
          flet.VideoMedia(resource = "C:\\Users\\Asiedu\\video2.mp4")
      ]

    video = flet.Video(playlist= playlist, height= 300,)

    stop = flet.IconButton(icon= flet.icons.STOP_CIRCLE_OUTLINED, on_click=lambda _:video.stop())
    playback = flet.IconButton(icon= flet.icons.REPEAT, on_click = playBack)
    autoplay = flet.IconButton(icon= flet.icons.PLAYLIST_PLAY, on_click = autoPlay)

    buttonRow = flet.Row(alignment= flet.MainAxisAlignment.CENTER,
                         vertical_alignment=flet.CrossAxisAlignment.CENTER,
                         controls=[autoplay, stop, playback])

    col = flet.Column(
        width= page.width,
        height= page.height,
        alignment= flet.MainAxisAlignment.START,
        horizontal_alignment= flet.CrossAxisAlignment.CENTER,
        controls=[video,buttonRow]
    )

    page.add(col)
    page.update()

flet.app(target = main)
```


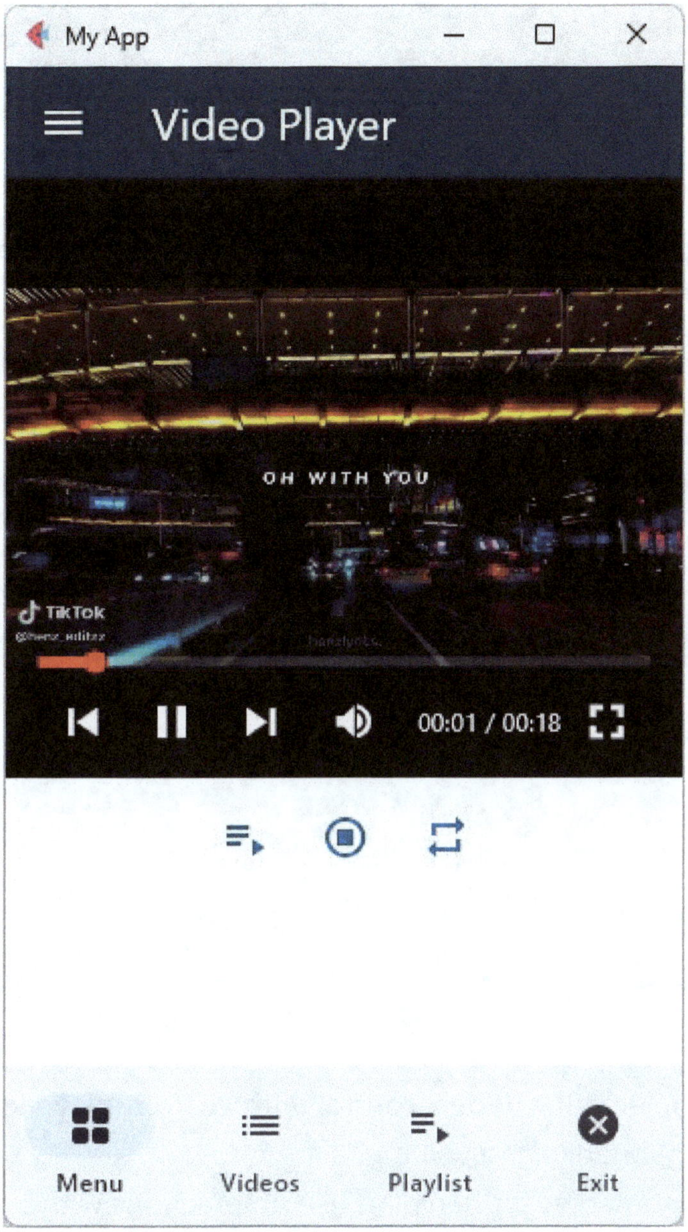
My App
Video Player
OH WITH YOU
TikTok
00:01 / 00:18
Menu
Videos
Playlist
Exit

Page Summary

Video control plays video files or streams in a Flet app, with options for playback control and customization.

Keywords

autoplay
volume
balance
play
pause
stop
resume
playback_rate
release_mode

Discussion

1. How do you implement a Video control with custom playback controls, such as seeking, pausing, or adjusting volume?
2. What are some strategies for handling user interactions with a Video control, such as reacting to playback events or errors?
3. Can you discuss the accessibility considerations when using Video controls, such as providing alternative text or descriptions for users with disabilities?

GestureDetector

The **GestureDetector** is a control that allows its content (child) to detect and respond to various user interactions, such as taps, double taps, long presses and swipes. It provides a way to handle complex touch gestures and customize the behavior of UI elements based on these interactions.

Example 1, using the Tap property to listen to gesture by a Container.
A tap detection responds to a single tap interaction.

Python — Code 4.3.0

```python
import flet

def main(page: flet.Page):
    page.title = "My App"
    page.bgcolor = 'white'
    page.padding = flet.padding.all(20)

    page.appbar = flet.AppBar(
      color= flet.colors.WHITE,
      title= flet.Text("GestureDetector"),
      bgcolor= "blue"
    )
    page.drawer = flet.NavigationDrawer()

    def changeColor(e):
        mycontainer.bgcolor = "Green"
        page.update()

    mycontainer = flet.Container(
     width=page.width, height=200, bgcolor= "Orange", border_radius=10)

    gesture = flet.GestureDetector(
       on_tap= changeColor,
       content= mycontainer
    )


    page.add(gesture)
    page.update()

flet.app(target = main)
```


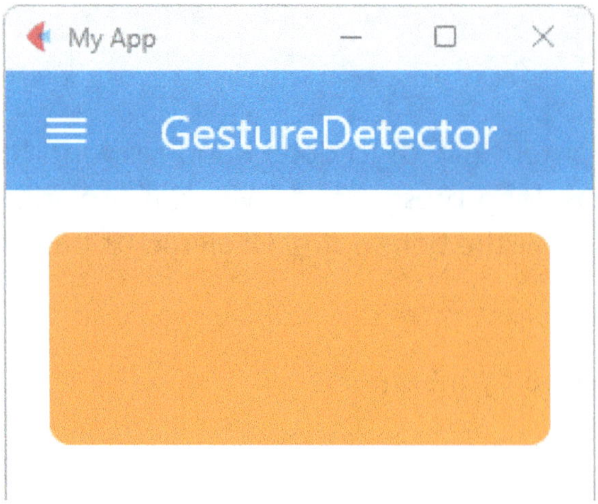

initial state

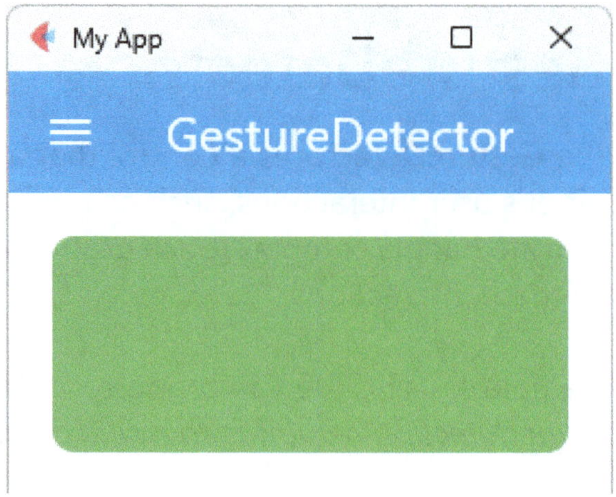

final state

Example 2: Using the **on_double_tap** to count the number of taps

```
    def countTab(e):
        initial_value = int(counter.value)
        current_value = initial_value + 1
        counter.value = str(current_value)
        page.update()

    mycontainer = flet.Container(width=page.width, height=100, bgcolor= "teal")
    gesture = flet.GestureDetector(on_double_tap = countTab, content= mycontainer)

    counter = flet.Text("0")

    col = flet.Column( width= page.width,height= page.height,
        alignment= flet.MainAxisAlignment.START,
        horizontal_alignment= flet.CrossAxisAlignment.CENTER,
        controls=[gesture, counter]
    )
```

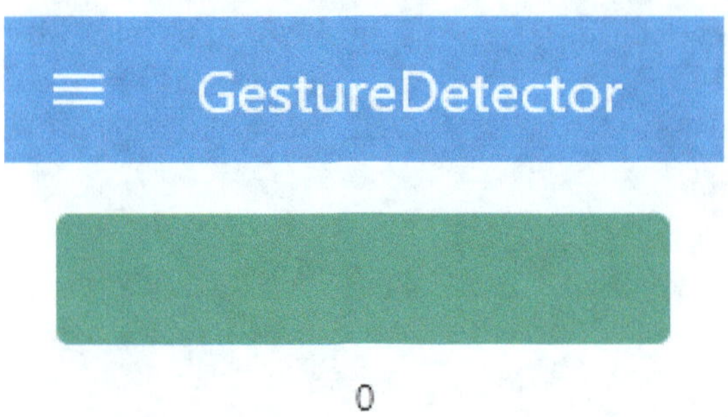

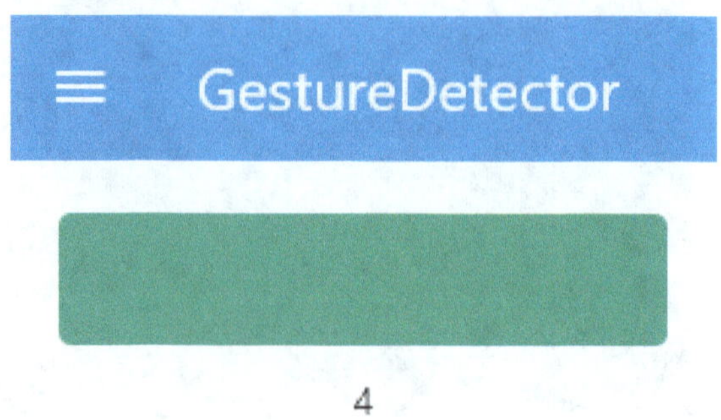

Other Methods

Methods	Function
on_tap	A callback function that is triggered when the user taps on the control.
on_tap_down	Fires when a tap gesture begins (touch down).
on_tap_up	Fires when a tap gesture ends (touch up).
on_multi_tap	Fires when a multi-tap gesture is detected.
on_multi_down	Fires when multiple touch points are detected (multi-touch down).
on_multi_tap_touches	Specifies the number of taps needed for a multi-tap gesture.
on_multi_long_press	Fires when a multi-touch long press is detected.
on_double_tap	A callback function that is fired when the user double-taps on the control.
on_double_tap_down	A callback function that is called when a double tap has contacted the screen at a particular location.
on_long_press_start	A callback function that is invoked when the user performs a long press on the control.
on_long_press_end	Fires when a long press gesture ends.
on_secondary_tap	Fires when a secondary (e.g., right mouse button) tap is detected.
on_secondary_tap_down	Fires when a secondary tap gesture begins.
on_secondary_tap_up	Fires when a secondary tap gesture ends.
on_pan_start	A callback function that is triggered during pan gesture (a drag that can move in any direction).
on_pan_update	Fires when a pan gesture is updated.
on_pan_end	Fires when a pan gesture ends.
on_scale_start	A callback function that handles pinch-to-zoom or other scaling gestures.
on_scale_update	Fires when a scale gesture is updated.

on_scale_end	Fires when a scale gesture ends.
on_enter	A callback function that is invoked when the mouse pointer enters the control.
on_exit	A callback function that is called when the mouse pointer leaves the control.
on_hover	A callback function that is called when the mouse pointer passes over the control.
on_horizontal_drag_start	Fires when a horizontal drag gesture begins.
on_horizontal_drag_update	Fires when a horizontal drag gesture is updated.
on_horizontal_drag_end	Fires when a horizontal drag gesture ends.
on_vertical_drag_start	Fires when a vertical drag gesture begins.
on_vertical_drag_update	Fires when a vertical drag gesture is updated.
on_vertical_drag_end	Fires when a vertical drag gesture ends.

Page Summary

GestureDetector control detects various gestures such as taps, drags, and swipes in a Flet app, allowing for custom touch interactions.

Keywords

taps
double tap
long press
swipes

Discussion

1. How can you customize the behavior of a GestureDetector to detect specific gestures or combinations of gestures?
2. What are some techniques for handling gesture callbacks and providing feedback to users based on their interactions?
3. Can you discuss the performance implications

Remarks

First and foremost, I thank the Almighty God for a successful journey so far and for being the master behind this brain. His guidance and blessings have been instrumental in every step of my personal and professional life. Without His support, none of this would have been possible.

I would also like to extend my heartfelt thanks to you, the reader, for choosing to read this book. Your interest and time are deeply appreciated. Writing this book has been a labor of love, and it is my hope that it serves as a valuable resource on your journey to becoming a developer. The path of a developer is both challenging and rewarding, and I believe that the insights and knowledge shared in these pages will equip you with the tools and inspiration you need to succeed.

As you immerse yourself in the world of software development and cyber security, remember that continuous learning and perseverance are key. The tech industry is ever-evolving, and staying curious and committed will help you navigate its dynamic landscape. I encourage you to experiment, innovate, and always strive for excellence.

In addition to the technical aspects, I hope this book also instills in you a sense of responsibility. Technology has the power to transform lives and communities, and as developers, we hold the potential to make a positive impact. Use your skills not only to build great products but also to contribute to the greater good. Whether it's through creating accessible software, improving security, or engaging in social interventions, your work can make a difference.

I genuinely appreciate your feedback and contributions. Engaging with readers like you helps me grow as a writer and a professional. If you have any questions, thoughts, or suggestions, please do not hesitate to reach out. Your input is invaluable, and I look forward to hearing from you.

Once again, thank you for your time and interest in this book. I wish you the best of luck on your journey as a developer. May you find success, fulfillment, and joy in your endeavors.

If there is anything you want to ask or discuss, please reach out to me at ouereila@gmail.com.

About the Author

Williams Asiedu is a seasoned software engineer, writer, and philanthropist, holding a Master's degree in Computer Science. With a robust career in software development and a keen interest in cyber security, Williams has become a prominent figure in the tech industry. His expertise spans various facets of software engineering, and his innovative solutions have significantly contributed to advancements in the field.

Beyond his technical prowess, Williams is deeply committed to social causes. He actively participates in social interventions aimed at improving the lives of marginalized communities. His philanthropic efforts focus on bridging the digital divide, ensuring that technology and its benefits are accessible to all, regardless of their socio-economic background.

As a writer, Williams Asiedu shares his extensive knowledge through his books and articles, offering insights into the ever-evolving world of software and cyber security. His writing is not only informative but also inspiring, encouraging readers to explore and embrace the potential of technology in making positive societal changes.

Williams's dedication to his field and his compassionate approach to philanthropy make him a respected and influential figure. His contributions continue to inspire and drive progress, both in technology and in creating a more equitable world.

Acknowledgements

I would like to extend my heartfelt thanks to everyone who contributed to the success of this project. Your support and encouragement have been invaluable.
First and foremost, I express my deepest gratitude to the Almighty God for granting me the strength, wisdom, and perseverance to complete this book. His guidance has been my constant companion throughout this journey.

A special thank you goes to my dear **Anokyewaa Theresa**. Your unwavering support, inspiration, and encouragement have been the bedrock upon which this project was built. Your belief in me, even during the most challenging times, has kept me motivated and focused. God bless you abundantly for being such a vital part of my life and work.

I also wish to acknowledge the contributions of my colleagues and friends who provided insights, feedback, and moral support. Your input has helped shape this book and improve its quality. To my mentors and educators, thank you for imparting your knowledge and guiding me throughout my academic and professional journey.

To my readers, thank you for your interest in this book. Your willingness to explore the world of software development and cyber security inspires me to continue writing and sharing knowledge. I hope this book serves as a valuable resource and motivates you to achieve your goals.

Finally, to everyone who believed in this project and supported it in any way, thank you. Your encouragement and faith have made a significant impact. This book is a testament to the power of collaboration, support, and unwavering dedication.

May God bless you all 👏.

Author's Note

Dear Readers,

I am delighted to present this book as a culmination of my passion for programming and dedication to sharing knowledge. As an author, software engineer, and philanthropist, I've always believed in the transformative power of technology and education. Through these pages, I aim to demystify the world of programming, making it accessible to everyone, regardless of background or experience.

I extend my heartfelt gratitude to the Almighty for guiding me on this journey and to you, the reader, for investing your time and trust in exploring this book. It is my sincere hope that the insights shared within these pages will inspire you to embark on your own journey in the world of development.

I welcome your contributions, questions, and feedback. Please feel free to reach out to me at email@gmail.com or forms with any inquiries or thoughts you may have.
Thank you for joining me on this adventure.

Warm regards,
Williams Asiedu

www.ingramcontent.com/pod-product-compliance
Lightning Source LLC
LaVergne TN
LVHW080005210926
848481LV00011B/2949